Organization Theory
CASES AND APPLICATIONS

The West Series in Management

Don Hellriegel   *Texas A & M University*
John W. Slocum, Jr.   *Southern Methodist University*
CONSULTING EDITORS

Organization Theory
CASES AND APPLICATIONS

Richard L. Daft

TEXAS A&M

Kristen M. Dahlen

TEXAS A&M

West Publishing Company
ST. PAUL   NEW YORK   LOS ANGELES   SAN FRANCISCO

Library of Congress Cataloging in Publication Data

Daft, Richard L.
    Organization theory.

    1. Organization—Case studies. 2. Management—
Case studies. I. Dahlen, Kristen M. II. Title.
HD31.D136   1984   658.4   83-23258
ISBN 0-314-77876-4

Contents

II   Design and Structure 43

III   Internal Organization Processes 115

IV   Organization Dynamics 183

V View From the Top 255

Preface

Why a book of case problems in organization theory? The answer is clear to those who teach organization theory at undergraduate and M.B.A. levels. Textbooks and readings typically come across to students as too academic, too theoretical, and too abstract. Students are exposed to theories of organization, but not to applications. They learn the concepts, but without an opportunity to practice applying these concepts to deepen their understanding of organizations.

Organization theory is an exciting field of study. It has evolved rapidly in the last few years. Organization theory concepts can be a source of valuable ideas for managers and students. Organization theory is relevant to everyday problem-solving and decision-making in organizations. One challenge of organization theory coursework is to teach theoretical concepts and to show how to translate those concepts into practical applications. When the ideas and theory are interesting and practical, students become more competent and informed about organizations.

The purpose of this book is to help translate organization theory concepts into practical application. This book is designed to be used with textbooks or readings that provide students with a theoretical background in organization theory. The case problems included here help illuminate those theories, and provide opportunities for students to use concepts when they solve problems in organizations. From what colleagues tell us, and based on our own teaching of organization theory, the absence of interesting, challenging case problems is often the difference between a good organization theory course and a great one. No current book has been available as a supplementary text devoted to case problems in organizations, so this book was designed to fill that need.

SPECIAL FEATURES

The first challenge in assembling a book of case problems was to identify and read the hundreds of cases available on each topic. The second and more important challenge was to select a final set of cases that were highly relevant to organization theory and of special interest to students. The cases in this book have several unique and helpful features.

1. The cases reflect a wide variety of organizational settings. They cover organizations as diverse as the Girl Scouts, the Department of Defense, Sears Roebuck, and Club

Med. The cases represent both large and small organizations, are located in Canada and other countries as well as the United States, and include not-for-profit hospitals and schools along with business organizations. Some cases are short and to the point, others are longer and more complex. At least one exercise is included on each major topic to provide an auxiliary vehicle to illustrate concepts to students and help them understand the usefulness and application of the principles involved.

2. The cases were selected because of their high interest level. They represent real people in real organizations. They are not made up, and are not written from secondary material. A major criterion for selection was that they be well written and enjoyable to read. Most of the cases have been classroom tested on students.

3. The cases cover the breadth of organization theory topics. They pertain to traditional organization topics such as environment, bureaucracy, effectiveness, size, technology, and structure. Cases have also been included to reflect emerging areas of organization theory, such as decision-making processes, power and politics, information processing and control. The total package provides broad representation of issues and problems that are in the domain of organization theory.

4. The cases are organized into a topic matrix. Organizational problems are sufficiently complex that more than one issue is typically involved. Thus the matrix gives both primary and secondary topic applications for the case. Some cases can be used with multiple topics. Referring back to the same case often provides continuity for students and helps them tie together diverse concepts. Checking a specific topic in the matrix will indicate which cases are appropriate. Once a case is identified, additional topics are designated. The topic headings make the case book compatible with virtually any organization theory textbook.

5. Additional resources for classroom use are provided. Instructors who use this book will be provided with additional material in the Instructor's Resource Manual. The Manual provides handout materials to be used with some cases and role-play exercises. The Manual suggests ideas for classroom discussion and analysis. Discussion questions are also provided. An integral part of the case book is the Instructor's Resource Manual, and we have devoted great effort to providing a valuable supplement.

ACKNOWLEDGEMENTS

This book, like most books, reflects the ideas and hard work of a number of people. First and foremost, we would like to thank the case authors. They studied organizations, wrote the cases, and gave us permission to use their work. Some of the authors are organization theorists, some are not, but they have all contributed enormously to this project. We would also like to thank the publishers who gave permission to use their publications.

We also extend appreciation to our administrators and colleagues here at Texas A&M University. Lyle Schoenfeldt, Management Department Head, and Bill Mobley, Dean of the College of Business, have created an excellent climate for academic projects of all types, and have provided the resources to accomplish this one. A number of colleagues have provided assistance and intellectual stimulation along the way. These colleagues include Bob Albanese, Jody Fry, Ricky Griffin, Don Hellriegel, Irene Hoadley, Gareth Jones, Lee Lyon, Don Parks, George Rice, Jim Skivington, David Van Fleet, and Dick Woodman, and we thank each of them for the positive contribution made to this book.

For assistance with typing, permissions, and a thousand other details, we thank Argie Butler, Nila Reece, and Phyllis Washburn.

Finally, we thank the editors at West. Dick Fenton and Esther Craig did their usual excellent work. Despite a number of problems along the way, they always supported the project and helped us solve problems so the book could be completed.

The activities of these people have produced a book that, when used with a current textbook in organization theory, makes an exciting package. The package contains both theory and application. In one sense, the ultimate goal of any scientific discipline is to make concepts and discoveries available to lay people and practitioners through the teaching process. We hope this book facilitates the teaching process in organization theory by providing students with opportunities for realistic application.

R.L.D.
K.M.D.

Organization Theory
Topic Matrix

Case Title	Setting	Environment	Systems Approach	Bureaucracy	Technology	Structure	Goals & Effectiveness	Control & Information	Decision-Making	Change	Conflict	Power & Politics	Strategy	Internal Culture
Part I: Open Systems														
1. They Sang the Low Down, Loss of Market Share Blues	Brewery	1											2	
2. Pine Mountain State University	University	1		2		2	2							
3. The Truth About Girl Scouts	Club	1				2	2	2						2
4. Rondell Data Corporation	Engineering	1					2			2	2			
5. Artisan Industries	Small Manufacturer	2	1				2						2	
6. Organizations You Have Known	Exercise	2	1	2										
Part II: Design and Structure														
7. The Cold Equations	Future-Space			1	2			2						
8. Outdoor Outfitters, Ltd.	Retail			1			2	2						
9. How Sears Became a High-Cost Operator	Retail			1		2							2	
10. Premium Fasteners, Inc.	Manufacturing				1					2				
11. Olson Locker Plant	Meat Processor				1									
12. Creative Sentence Corp.	Exercise			1	1	2	2		2					
13. Aeronautical Systems Corp.	Electrical			2		1								
14. Atlas Electronics Corporation (A)	Electrical					1						2		
15. Atlas Electronics Corporation (B)	Electrical					1						2		
16. Calgary Police Dept.	Police	2			2	1		2						

1 = primary topic
2 = secondary topic

Case Title	Setting	Environment	Systems Approach	Bureaucracy	Technology	Structure	Goals & Effectiveness	Control & Information	Decision-Making	Change	Conflict	Power & Politics	Strategy	Internal Culture
17. Club Méditerranée	Leisure-Recreational	2		2		1								
18. Organizational Coordination	Exercise					1								
Part III: Internal Organization Processes														
19. The Welfare Dept.	Government				2		1			2				
20. The University Art Museum	University					2	1							
21. Measuring Organizational Effectiveness	Exercise						1							
22. Identifying Organizational Goals	Exercise						1							
23. Layoff at Old College	University			2			1		2	2	2			
24. Denver Department Stores	Retail							1						
25. The Fat Boy Program	Armed Forces							1						
26. A New Division	Mining					2		1		2				
27. Making of a Bad Cop	Police						2	1				2		2
28. Chicago Police Force	Police							1						
29. University Control Graph	Exercise							1						
30. The Bogged-Down Bus Business	Transportation	2							1		2			
31. Queen Elizabeth Hospital	Hospital	2							1	2				
32. Memorial Hospital	Hospital						2		1	2	2			
33. Infinite Processes, Inc.	R & D								1		2			
Part IV: Organization Dynamics														
34. Canco Incorporated	Service								2	1				
35. School of Education: Case of a Contracting Organization	University	2		2		2	2			1		2		
36. A Crisis Change Program	City Department					2				1				
37. Mail Route Improvement vs. The Manana Principle	U.S. Post Office			2		2				1	2			
38. Municipal Light	Utility							2		1	2		2	
39. Atlantic Store Furniture	Manufacturing				2					1				
40. Space Support Systems, Incorporated	R & D					2				1				
41. The Old Stack Problem	Exercise								2	1				
42. Missouri Campus Bitterly Divided	University	2		2					2	2	2	1		
43. The Air Force A-7D Brake Problem	Manufacturing									2	1			2
44. The Plane the Pentagon Couldn't Stop	Government			2						1		1		
45. The Education of David Stockman	Government	2		2					1			1		
46. Political Processes in Organizations	Exercise										1			
Part V: View From the Top														
47. The Man Who Killed Braniff	Transportation	2							2				1	2
48. Palace Products	Manufacturing	2				1			2	2		2	1	
49. Panalba	Pharmaceutical	2					2		2			2	1	
50. Recreation Products, Inc.	Sports Equipment			2	2	1							1	

1 = primary topic
2 = secondary topic

Guide To Case Analysis

Students of biology, chemistry, and the physical sciences learn their fields through practicing and experimenting with theories and materials in the laboratory. As a student of organization theory, your laboratory will exist in the case problems and experiential exercises presented in this book. The cases and exercises provide the opportunity to experiment with real organizations in the classroom setting.

Organization theory, like any field, can be learned at three different levels: memorization, understanding, and application. Memorization is the lowest level of learning and involves the simple recitation of facts and simple concepts. Understanding involves deeper learning. It includes the ability to deal with relationships among concepts and to deal with concepts in different contexts. Application is the highest level of learning. Concepts have to be very well understood to apply them to the real world. Mastery of concepts sufficient to solve problems or to diagnose real organizational situations is a significant accomplishment. Learning to understand and apply organization theory concepts can be effectively and pleasantly accomplished through case study.

Cases and exercises do not replace the textbook and lectures. The organization the-ory textbook, readings, and/or lectures provide a theoretical background. The material in this casebook is a supplement; it extends the learning process to the real world. The goal of studying organization theory with cases is to enable you to apply what is taught from a textbook to a real situation, a reconciliation of theory with life. Managers use theories and models in their day-to-day management of organizations. Often these models are intuitive and implicit. Sometimes they are explicit, just as in an organization theory textbook. Whatever the nature of the theory or model they use, managers must react to situations relying on past experience and acquired skills to analyze and assess the issues and arrive at a solution. Case study develops your skill in analyzing problems and generating solutions based on your understanding of the theories and models of organization processes and behavior.

This book contains a variety of case materials and experiential exercises. The cases can be categorized by the educational objective of the instructor and the role of you, the student. The two educational objectives and the associated learning processes are summarized in Exhibit A. The first type of case learning is theory application/illustration. In this type of case the problem or issue outlined in the situation has usually been solved, and it is your responsibility to analyze the outcome and its consequences. Cases selected for this type of analysis may not emphasize any problem, but present real-life situations that can be used to explain and illustrate theories and models of organization theory. The facts in the case may be focused toward specific theories, but seemingly irrelevant material will also be included. Sometimes you will be asked to evaluate the solution in the case and to propose an alternative solution if necessary. The second type of case educational objective is problem analysis. Cases used for this objective may be relatively complex. Your role will be to analyze and interpret the situation. You will have to sort out the facts of the case, determine cause-and-effect relationships, and design a solution and plan for implementation. The primary goal is to solve the problem. The illustration of theories and models is not the primary goal of the case, but theories and models will be used to help identify alternatives and justify your solution.

Another approach to learning organization theory is through experiential exercises. Experiential exercises engage you directly in the material. Cases require intellectual analysis of an external situation. By contrast, you become an ongoing participant in the organizational situation when you are involved in an exercise. Experiential exercises require intellectual involvement and critical thinking, but are designed to also engage your real-life experience in the analy-

sis. You are required to become involved in an organizational situation, either in terms of an assigned role or as a participant observer. After the exercise is completed, the skills you will use to interpret your experiences are similar to those used with other case studies: problem analysis skills help you separate cause from effect and arrive at timely solutions, and theory application skills require you to recognize concepts and relationships in the context of the organizational situation. A few of the exercises require role-playing in which individuals will be assigned specific identities within an organization situation. You will have the opportunity to test your analytical and conceptual skills in responding to your role and in discussing your interpretation of the unfolding drama.

As you develop your analytical and conceptual skills through cases and exercises, you will be able to master the understanding and use of organization theory. Many of the cases combine more than one objective. A specific case might be used to practice the application of theory, or to engage you in the identification and solution of the problem. Exercises can also be approached through problems to be solved or the application of theories and models. For any of these materials to enrich your learning experience requires your involvement. An integral part of the learning process is your commitment to preparing the analysis or application and becoming involved in class discussion. Remember, the cases serve a dual purpose: to

EXHIBIT A   THE EDUCATIONAL OBJECTIVE AND LEARNING PROCESSES ASSOCIATED WITH CASE ANALYSIS

	Theory Application/Illustration	Problem Analysis
Learning Focus	1. Understand concepts. 2. Develop skill in use of concepts.	1. Develop skill in identifying and analyzing problems. 2. Develop skill in designing solutions and plans for implementation.
Learning Procedure	1. Identify examples of theories through relationships in case. 2. Determine inconsistencies with theory. Use concepts to evaluate behavior and predict outcomes.	1. Gather and interpret relevant facts, diagnose critical problems. 2. Use concepts to develop and support a solution and plan of action.

develop your skills in problem solution and to increase your ability to apply theory to real situations. To assist you in achieving these learning objectives, we suggest the following steps as a guide to get you started.

THEORY APPLICATION/ILLUSTRATION

This casebook is intended to be used in conjunction with a textbook or a collection of readings that defines and outlines theories and models of organization. In studying the theories of organization, the cases enable you to see examples of the dimensions and relationships within the theories to be used when solving real problems. Applying theory to the case gives you a deeper understanding of how the theory works in the real world. Theory application enables you to relate the facts of the organizational situation to theoretical predictions about organizational processes. The cases and exercises provide you with practice in testing theories from your textbook or readings against the real world.

The application of theories and models to cases is an art that has to be developed through practice and creativity. The framework presented in Exhibit B illustrates the three steps required to move you through the process of theory application. The basic elements are identification, relationships, and inconsistencies.

1. Identification. What is the major emphasis of the case in terms of organization theory? The primary conceptual topic will be identified by the section heading under which the case appears. However, few cases are limited to one concept. Within the general topic area, what set of variables, ideas, and topics from the textbook are illustrated within the case? You must be familiar with the relevant theories and descriptions of organizational frameworks. Then you should review the processes described within the case, the interactions of the participants, and additional facts that may relate to the theories and models. Try to find as many illustrations of the theory as you can within the case.

2. Relationships. After identifying the specific concepts relevant to the case situation, describe the relationships among variables. Try to determine whether the predictions made by a theory are illustrated in the case. For example, do the number of rules and procedures reflect the organization's size and stage of development? Is the observed decision-making process what you would predict based on the level of uncertainty confronting managers? Is the organization's structure appropriate for the rate of change in the environment? Does internal organization culture reflect the values symbolized by top management? One test of an organizational theory is whether predicted relationships occur within organizations. By examining theoretic relationships you can understand cause-and-effect relationships and test whether the theory helps you understand the situation. If so, knowledge of one variable will enable you predict and have knowledge of other variables. Understanding relationships is necessary for determining the impact of contextual factors on the organization under discussion.

EXHIBIT B   STEPS IN USING CASES FOR THEORY APPLICATION/ILLUSTRATION

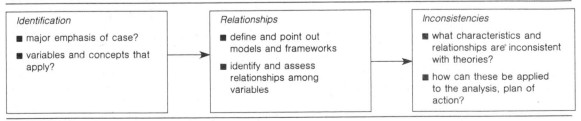

Identification	Relationships	Inconsistencies
■ major emphasis of case? ■ variables and concepts that apply?	■ define and point out models and frameworks ■ identify and assess relationships among variables	■ what characteristics and relationships are inconsistent with theories? ■ how can these be applied to the analysis, plan of action?

3. Inconsistencies. When discussing relationships among variables, are there instances in which the relationships in the case are inconsistent with theoretical predictions? Perhaps formalization is not consistent with the organization size, or structure is not consistent with the environment. Situations in real life will not identically mirror theory from the textbook, although situations will be similar enough to theory to be useful in understanding the theory. Inconsistencies are an opportunity to challenge and refine your understanding of a theory. Perhaps a model only applies in certain situations. Perhaps other variables are at work that are overwhelming a specific relationship. Identifying inconsistencies and then digging into why they exist is an excellent way to both test and increase your understanding of the organizational theories and models. Occasionally there will be a case that defies theory, possibly presenting familiar variables with inconsistent results or outcomes. In your analysis, bring out these anomalies.

PROBLEM ANALYSIS

Problem analysis frequently requires greater involvement in the case than does theory application. Problem analysis includes and goes beyond the application of theory. Theory application can be accomplished without identifying and solving problems in the case. Problem analysis goes beyond theory by asking students to analyze the situation and propose a solution, as illustrated in Exhibit C.

An important lesson in identifying and solving problems in a case is to realize that one reading of the case is not sufficient for fully understanding the issues presented. You should allocate your time so that at least two readings will be possible. The first time through, read to get an overall sense of the setting, situation. You may initially assess all the variables involved, and the relative importance of each, and the nature and scope of the situation. After you interpret the facts of the organization, you will be able to move on to the following steps.

1. Data collection and interpretation. After carefully reading the case, make note of the data that will be useful in determining the state of the situation and the issues to be dealt with. The purposes of this step is to sort out irrelevant from relevant data and to develop a diagnosis of the current situation. You may initially assess all the variables involved, and the relative importance of each, and the nature and scope of the situation. After you interpret the facts of the organization, you will be able to move on to the following steps.

2. Critical issues. After diagnosing and analyzing the facts of the situation, you will need to isolate the critical issues or problems to be solved. One way to think about problems is to look for factors that threaten the survival, goals, or performance of the organization or its major departments. Without identifying the real problem, any suggestion for solution will be inappropriate. Isolating the main problem can be quite frustrating, and you may never be absolutely certain you are correct. With careful attention, constant questioning, and practice, your skill at identifying critical issues will improve.

EXHIBIT C   STEPS IN USING CASES FOR PROBLEM ANALYSIS

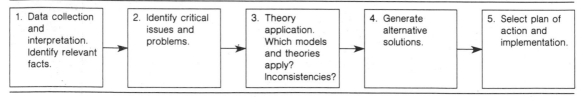

| 1. Data collection and interpretation. Identify relevant facts. | 2. Identify critical issues and problems. | 3. Theory application. Which models and theories apply? Inconsistencies? | 4. Generate alternative solutions. | 5. Select plan of action and implementation. |

To begin with, think in terms of cause and effect; do not confuse the symptoms with the problem. Dig beneath the surface and determine if something more basic is generating the problem you have identified. For example, you may observe such things as intergroup conflict, a seemingly inappropriate organization structure, poor control, or lack of communication. But to conclude the problem is intergroup conflict or poor control is ignoring the roots or causes of these issues, and thus reduces your chances of finding a successful solution. After identifying the problem or issue, write it in a one-sentence statement that concisely conveys the main concern. By reducing your thoughts to one sentence, you force yourself to focus on a primary issue.

3. Theory application.
Having identified the critical issue, consider your analysis in light of the work you may have previously done with the theories and models that related to the case. Can the theories be used to understand the problem? Are the relationships clearer when viewed in light of the models? If the situation appears to be inconsistent with the theory, is this part of the problem? How can knowledge of the theory assist you in generating possible solutions?

4. Generating solutions.
Based on the issue or problem you have identified and the theories and models you have studied, brainstorm a list of possible solutions. In brainstorming you should write down every possibility. Do not evaluate the feasibility or rationality of each; just write them down. You should not limit yourself to the strict amount of information provided in the case, i.e., be creative in dealing with the situation.

Having generated a list of wide-ranging possibilities, review your problem statement and identify those alternatives that have a direct link with solving the problem. Combine similar suggestions and begin eliminating alternatives based on your earlier analysis of the situation: constraints of the organization, theoretical concepts, goals and objectives, interacting variables.

5. Selection of course of action and plan for implementation.
Using your narrowed list of alternatives, begin a detailed analysis of each. Determine the criteria you will use in evaluating each solution. What requirements must a course of action meet? Are there cost constraints? What about timeliness? Resource availability? Are there constituents to consider? Future shock waves? List the pros and cons of each course of action in terms of the criteria you have specified. It may be necessary to make inferences and judgments based on the data provided in the case; this is encouraged as long as you also develop sound and logical arguments to support your interpretations.

The next step of the analysis is to select the best course of action based on the pros and cons and logical assessment of each alternative. You should state the specific steps you recommend and why. You should be sensitive to the arguments against your decision and should be prepared to refute any challenges to your reasoning. Be willing to take risks that can be supported by your analysis of the situation. Indeed, a bonus to solving problems in cases, compared with solving "real world" problems, is that you can take risks without having to answer for the consequences. Be creative and imaginative in developing your answers, but be aware that you will have to logically defend your solution.

Your recommendation should also include a plan for implementation. Consider personnel, time frames, and the sequence of events. In designing the implementation plan you will again be forced to consider your problem definition and analysis. Will your plan address the problem? What are the ramifications of implementing this plan? How will you address them? Many solutions die because no one considered how to introduce the solution or did not consider the possible roadblocks.

CONCLUSION

An observation you will make all too quickly when studying the cases in this book: there is never enough information to make the right decision. You can't be certain you have identified the best answer. Other students may have developed different solutions and may present effective arguments for them. There is no perfect answer to a case problem. Each solution may be effective to some extent, but none will be 100% accurate. Moreover, no one ever has all the information that would be useful or desirable when analyzing a problem or making a decision. You will just have to make do with what you have, draw logical inferences and assumptions from the available data, and support your arguments with evidence found in the case and theory. Remember, you are being asked to deal with "reality," and there is a lack of information in the real world too.

As you progress through your organization theory course and the casebook, relate the material, concepts, and theory to your life beyond the classroom. Continue to develop and refine your analytical skills when viewing situations in which you live and participate every day. Look for examples of the theories and models in your own environment. In the classroom, be prepared for discussion, be involved, offer your insights, make constructive criticism, and expect to receive the same from your peers. The case method of learning is most effective when everyone is involved in the analysis and discussion and is willing to experiment with the application of theoretical concepts to the real world. Our intent in designing this casebook has been to challenge, stimulate, and facilitate your learning of organization theory. We also hope that you find this collection of case materials and exercises interesting, and that you find the learning process enjoyable. Case problems provide a laboratory setting for your experimentation, and the laboratory is often the most exciting part of the learning process.

Organization Theory
CASES AND APPLICATIONS

I

Open Systems

1

They Sang the Low Down, Loss of Market Share Blues

Ten years ago it was a solid, profitable small business, locally and privately owned, in its third generation of family management. Its single consumer product, which enjoyed steady and effortless sales, was number one in its market, its share an enviable 29%.

Five years ago that good fortune had been turned to bad by competition from a national giant. The firm was still profitable, but it had fallen to number two on a market share that had dwindled to 14%.

Three years ago the situation had grown still worse, thanks to persistent competition and a catastrophic product quality problem. Market share was down to 6%. The company had to make a comeback—or go out of business.

Today, market share is up to 10%, and it's expected to hit 13% for 1980.

The company is Dixie Brewing Co. of New Orleans. The product is Dixie Beer. The fight to bring it back is a lesson in imaginative marketing—a demonstration that one industry's routine procedures may be revolutionary strategies in another. The managers of Dixie Brewing have looked beyond their industry, beyond the company's successful past, for new and creative ideas.

The Dixie Brewing Co. was founded in 1907 by Valentine Merz, who took on 10 competing local breweries in the New Orleans market. By 1970, only three local breweries were still doing business, and Dixie was the best-selling beer in New Orleans. Sure, there were dozens of domestic and foreign imports sold there. But Dixie had a price advantage, and in those days the price of a beer was more important than brand. Dixie, though, had a brand advantage as well: It had the image of *the* local beer in the Jefferson and Orleans parishes (metropolitan New Orleans), which accounted for 75% of sales.

The company appeared to have few problems. The presidency had passed to the founder's grandson, Cyril Mainergra. Ownership was closely held within the Mainergra family, a compatible group. Dixie Beer practically sold itself. A Dixie salesman would simply walk into a tavern and buy everyone a Dixie. At a supermarket the salesman simply

Written by John R. Halbrooks. Reprinted with the permission of *INC.* Magazine, September, 1980. Copyright © 1980 by INC. Publishing Company, 38 Commercial Wharf, Boston, MA 02110.

asked the manager how much beer he needed that week.

But in 1970 all that began to change. Philip Morris acquired the Miller Brewing Co., nationally number seven (although barely a factor in New Orleans), and threw all its marketing expertise toward making Miller High Life number one in the nation. No longer would Miller compete on price; they began to sell image. By 1975 Miller was number four among all brewers and number one in New Orleans, its share of the market 17%.

While Miller was aggressively marketing its beer nationwide, Dixie continued to do business as usual, selling its beer as casually as though it were just a distributor. By 1975, Dixie's share of its market had dropped from 29% to 17.5%. Dixie, however, was still *the* local beer. Sales slipped only slightly during the Miller onslaught. The market was growing, and Dixie still produced 220,000 barrels annually.

Then in July, 1975, Dixie laid a new floor in its brewhouse. Some phenol, an acidic compound in the flooring, leaked into open cooling vats in the cellars below, contaminating make-up water. That contaminated water was pumped upstairs and brewed into beer. Although the bad beer did not prove toxic, its terrible medicinal taste made it impossible to drink.

That medicinal-tasting beer, unfortunately, went out to taverns and stores around New Orleans over the Fourth of July, traditionally the biggest week of the year for beer sales, bigger even than Mardi Gras. And to compound the error, Dixie was slow to trace the source of contamination. For three weeks, bad beer was replaced with more bad beer.

The results were catastrophic. Over a six-week period, Dixie's sales fell by 55%. The image of the local beer was shattered, and Dixie settled into a slow, steady sales decline.

As soon as the contamination problem had been solved, president Cyril Mainergra set to work resuscitating Dixie. In December 1975 Mainergra hired Dan Hooten, an aggressive young district field sales manager at Lever Bros., as sales manager. A month later, Mainergra hired Robert Oertling as Dixie's brewmaster. He told Hooten and Oertling that they had his blessing to do whatever needed to be done to save Dixie Brewing Co.

Together, Hooten and Oertling began a much-needed plant modernization that consumed $500,000 in 1976 alone. At the same time, they instituted a cost-cutting program that eliminated truck routes and streamlined the bottling and garage operations.

Hooten's efforts to stop the erosion in sales were hampered by Dixie's poor image. "I remember calling on one tavern," Hooten says. "The manager threw me out, said he'd never serve Dixie, that we were a schlock operation. Well, I'm like anyone else. You tell me often enough that I'm not going to make it and I get stubborn. Dammit, we are going to make it."

By the fall of 1977, though, it was clear that stubbornness alone wouldn't save Dixie. Market share was down to 6%, and traditional sales methods had done nothing to slow the decline. Hooten was desperate to get Dixie back into the hands of New Orleans beer drinkers. If conventional methods didn't work, they would try unconventional methods.

Hooten's first inspiration was a sample giveaway—unheard of in the beer industry, but common in supermarket merchandising. One weekend, he handed out 60,000 six-packs of Dixie in residential neighborhoods around the city. The flood of free beer did what it was meant to do—it prevented Dixie's sales from sinking further.

The giveaway's success showed Hooten that what was routine procedure in one industry might be revolutionary in another. He decided that to survive Dixie would have to acquire an eye for the unorthodox, an ability to look beyond its own industry and its past successes for new creative ideas.

Hooten didn't know what those ideas would be. Surprised by the success of the giveaway, he hadn't planned any followup. Now he began to search for another marketing coup that would feed the momentum of Dixie's turnaround.

At this point, in December 1977, Cyril Mainergra died of a heart attack. The Mainergra family asked Dan Hooten to become president of the company.

Half a year later, Hooten found the marketing technique he was looking for. Like the beer sampling, the idea came from grocery marketing. Hooten decided to try using coupons—on a grand scale.

In June 1978, Hooten took out a full-page ad in New Orleans's morning newspaper, the *Times-Picayune*. The ad described the brewery's quality control improvements and invited everyone to try some Dixie beer for free. At the bottom of the ad was a "Dixie Bill" that could be mailed to the brewery for a coupon worth $1.80 toward the purchase of a six-pack of Dixie Beer.

It was hard to believe anything so prosaic as coupons could generate such excitement. "I don't think anything like this had ever been tried before in the beer industry," says Hooten. The reaction was explosive. An AP photo of Hooten holding a six-pack of Dixie and a copy of the ad was picked up by newspapers all over the country. Papers in Canada, England, and Australia also ran the photo.

With the morning circulation of over 200,000, the *Times-Picayune* had printed nearly half a million dollars' worth of Dixie Bills. "If they'd all been redeemed," Robert Oertling admits, "it would have bankrupted us." Hooten budgeted for 10 times the average coupon redemption, or about 125,000 returns, and held his breath. When the totals were tabulated, 94,000 bills had been redeemed.

"After our beer sampling," says Hooten, "we'd failed to follow up with effective advertising. This time we were ready." Television testimonials by delighted new Dixie fans began to work their magic. In 1978, Dixie's sales increased by 9% over 1977 to 127,000 barrels.

With Dixie's sales climbing at last, Hooten began to do something that had never been done before at the Dixie Brewing Co. He began to *sell* beer. Dixie had always operated on the assumption that beer sold itself. In fact, nearly all breweries worked on that assumption. In the 1950s and 1960s, beer companies were primarily production-oriented; beer was differentiated less by brand than by price. But in the 1970s, Miller's marketing onslaught changed the rules of the game. Miller rocked the industry by leaping from seventh to second position among all brewers in only seven years.

Hooten's response to the marketing challenge was not to mimic Miller, but to examine the very basis of sales in the beer industry. What he found was that beer was sold with a single sales force and a single sales pitch.

"I had found it very difficult," Hooten says, "to sell to a tavern manager, who looks at profit by the unit, and then switch to a supermarket, where the manager is concerned about volume and profit per linear foot."

Hooten's unorthodox solution to this dicotomy was to split his sales force. It was his twist on a practice common in the grocery industry, where sales is divided into product groups. Hooten had only one product, but he had two quite dissimilar sales outlets.

So Hooten hired a sales manager, Ron Sprinkle, like himself a Lever Bros. veteran. In early 1979, Hooten and Sprinkle set about breaking Dixie's sales force into an on-premise group (restaurants and taverns) and an off-premise group (groceries and convenience stores).

In on-premise sales, Dixie continues to emphasize the rebuilding of Dixie's representation in taverns and restaurants around New Orleans. Tom Murry, Dixie's on-premise sales manager, has pushed aggressive service and a more professional sales approach (stressing profitability and return on investment) that attempts to give the manager "a reason to buy." These efforts have won Dixie 40 new accounts in the first quarter of 1980.

But clearly, it is off-premise sales that offer Dixie its greatest immediate potential for growth. Off-premise sales account for two-thirds of Dixie's total barrelage. "We began to do more and more that was not all that new in the grocery industry," says Ron Sprinkle, "but was new in the beer industry. The beer companies lag about 10 to 15 years behind other consumer product companies."

Dixie sales supervisors had worked in relative autonomy before Ron Sprinkle conducted a sales analysis of 90 stores and drew up coverage plans for sales calls. Sales supervisors began to call on better accounts more frequently. And Sprinkle had supervisors begin to lavish attention on the headquarters of food store chains, which in the past had received mailings but had rarely been called on. Sprinkle saw that although stores often operated as individual profit centers, it was headquarters that set policy. By selling headquarters, Dixie could make gains in a dozen stores at once.

The manager of the off-premise sales division, Tom Voelkel, compiled data on market brand and package ranking from state tax figures to provide his sales supervisors with support in their sales presentations. But, as Ron Sprinkle says, "It's not so much the figures as the way you use them that's important."

Voelkel massages data and statistics so well he seems to find a way to use any figure to his advantage. When he enters a grocery, Voelkel knows immediately what sales tack he will take. If he is pushing Dixie's bread-and-butter 12-ounce one-way (nonreturnable) package, he may suggest increasing Dixie's shelf space at the expense of Miller. When the store manager refuses, saying that Miller is his best-selling beer, Voelkel is ready with a market breakdown that shows Dixie's 12-ounce package outsells Miller's 16-ounce package. "Why not give us some of that 16-ounce space?" he will ask.

Perhaps the most unusual tactic Dixie has employed involves its private-label beer. Dixie had been producing its beer under special labels for certain grocery chains, but it had never exploited the natural marketing advantage a private label gave it —the foot in the door for Dixie sales supervisors.

Sprinkle and Voelkel conducted a study of private-label beer sales at Schwegmann Giant Super Markets, whose 10 stores do about 30% of the grocery business in the city. They then made a slide presentation before Schwegmann's buying committee.

In every store that was surveyed, Schwegmann's Beer was positioned down among the economy brands. Miller and Anheuser-Busch, the market leaders, held prime space—at eye level as the consumer turned the corner.

Dixie's presentation to Schwegmann's was an appeal to logic and reason. Why position Schwegmann's Beer down among the economy brands? Taking Schwegmann's Beer—and Dixie, of course—and putting them next to the premium brands dramatizes the price differential. An attractive price and good shelf position is bound to increase sales of Schwegmann's Beer, which will draw customers to Schwegmann's stores. And the higher the sales of both Schwegmann's and Dixie, the greater Dixie's barrelage and the lower its costs.

So, Dixie suggested, why not let us work with your managers to set your stores? Unfolding diagrams to show Schwegmann's exactly how Dixie would display and stock beer at each outlet, Dixie won store-setting privileges for all Schwegmann stores.

Dixie is confident that in the 60 stores it helps set today—a figure Hooten is sure Dixie can double—its beer is well positioned, all its packages are available, and it won't get caught out of stock.

Hooten also broke with tradition by budgeting generous amounts for advertising Dixie. Convincing beer drinkers that "local is better" is critical to Dixie's success, he and Sprinkle believe. They spend $2 a barrel on advertising (a figure even national brewers did not exceed until recently) to let local beer drinkers know that Dixie is fresher and that the brewery represents a tradition in New Orleans that should not die out. "Dixie is as much a part of New Orleans," Sprinkle says, "as red beans and rice, as the French Quarter itself."

So far Hooten's search for unorthodox solutions to Dixie's problems has paid off. By the end of 1979, Dixie had passed a faltering Schlitz for third position on New Orleans beer charts with about 10% of the market. By year-end, Hooten wants a 13% market share and a shot at Anheuser-Busch. Miller's astonishing 47% market share looks unassailable in the near future.

The hopes for the boost that will push Dixie up over the top and back into profits ride on another unlikely hero, the "long neck," the 12-ounce returnable bottle that has suffered at the hands of the convenient throw-aways. The long neck offers almost double the profit margin of the non-returnable because it can simply be refilled and sent back out.

Miller and Anheuser-Busch, which ship from Fort Worth and Houston respectively, downplay the long neck because of high freight costs. Many merchants also look down on the long neck because they don't like to bother with returnable bottles.

Yet, despite recalcitrant merchants and the lack of enthusiasm by the national breweries, the long neck made an imperceptible advance in 1979 after a decade of falling sales. And Dixie's long neck was up 9% in the first quarter of 1980 over the same period a year before.

In a marketing test last year, Dixie introduced the long neck in several stores. The results showed that the long neck did not cannibalize Dixie's other packages, but ate into competitors' sales. Dixie's total sales volume in those stores increased by between 24% and 60%.

Hooten has high hopes for the long neck. It is symbolic, as is Dixie, of everything the major brewers are not. And it represents Dixie's new marketing strategy: to look to the past or the future, in your own backyard or outside the industry, for new ideas. Dan Hooten has made the unorthodox orthodox at the Dixie Brewing Co.

2

Pine Mountain State University

BACKGROUND

Pine Mountain is a university of 22,000 students located in the southeastern United States. It offers a full range of programs at both the undergraduate and graduate levels, including the doctorate in 17 areas. The college was founded in 1873 as a small private liberal arts college. It became a state teachers college in 1927 and a full-fledged state university in 1946. During the last 30 years enrollment has increased by 10,000 students from 12,000 to 22,000.

The school is one of two major universities in the state. It is located in a town of about 50,000 residents situated in a rural area. The closest large city (population 250,000) is about 90 miles away.

There are five other state-supported colleges in the state. Only one of these is a major university; the others are teacher colleges. The other major state university is located in a major metropolitan area with a population of about one million. Its enrollment is about 17,000 students, most of whom are enrolled in the night program. This other university offers doctorates only in business and in education. Its enrollment has increased greatly in the past 15 years from 3,000 to its present level.

The state in which both universities are located has been severely affected by a national recession. Unemployment in the state has averaged 10.5% over the past 18 months. Inflation has averaged about 8% for each of the last two years. The state legislative allocation for higher education has not increased during the past two years. During the 1960s, the allocation increased an average of 10% each year.

THE SITUATION

Pine Mountain State recently completed a reorganization in order to better deal with what its top administration believed to be the contingencies in the environment. As they saw it, the university was faced with several key problems listed below:

1. how to cope with increasing enrollments in the face of a decline in real dollar allocations (adjusted for inflation) from

From B. J. Hodge and William P. Anthony, *Organization Theory: An Environmental Approach.* Copyright © 1979 by Allyn & Bacon, Inc. Reprinted with permission.

the legislature,

2. how to cope with increasing calls for accountability and financial responsibility continually being made by various legislators and the state board of trustees,
3. how to manage the internal operations of the university to better cope with the increase in enrollments, faculty, and staff that occurred during the late 1960s and early 1970s,
4. what posture it should take in relation to its sister university in the urban area, and
5. how to develop other sources of funds from alumni, foundations, corporations, and the federal government to supplement legislative appropriations.

After extensive study, the top administrative staff of Pine Mountain State developed a comprehensive reorganization plan that established several new units of the university and consolidated others. The role of most of the units was redefined. The intent of the reorganization was to keep the university in better tune with its environment so that it could more easily assess environmental opportunities and constraints in order to react more quickly with an appropriate response. Exhibits 2-1 and 2-2 show both the old and the new formal organizational structures of the university.

The new structure has been in operation for about 18 months. The top administrators believe the structure is enabling the university to better respond to its environment. However, they realize continuing adjustments need to be made, so an organizational development committee was established to

EXHIBIT 2-1 PINE MOUNTAIN STATE UNIVERSITY'S OLD ORGANIZATION CHART

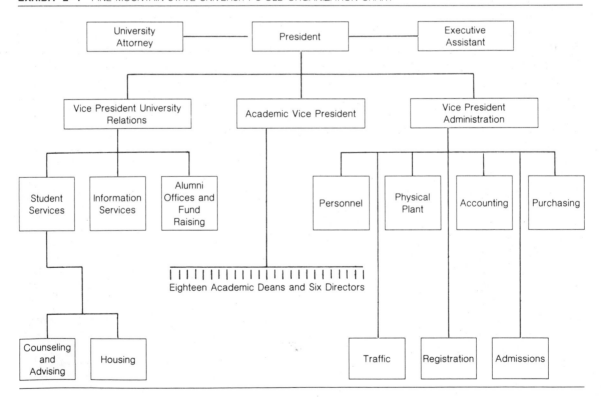

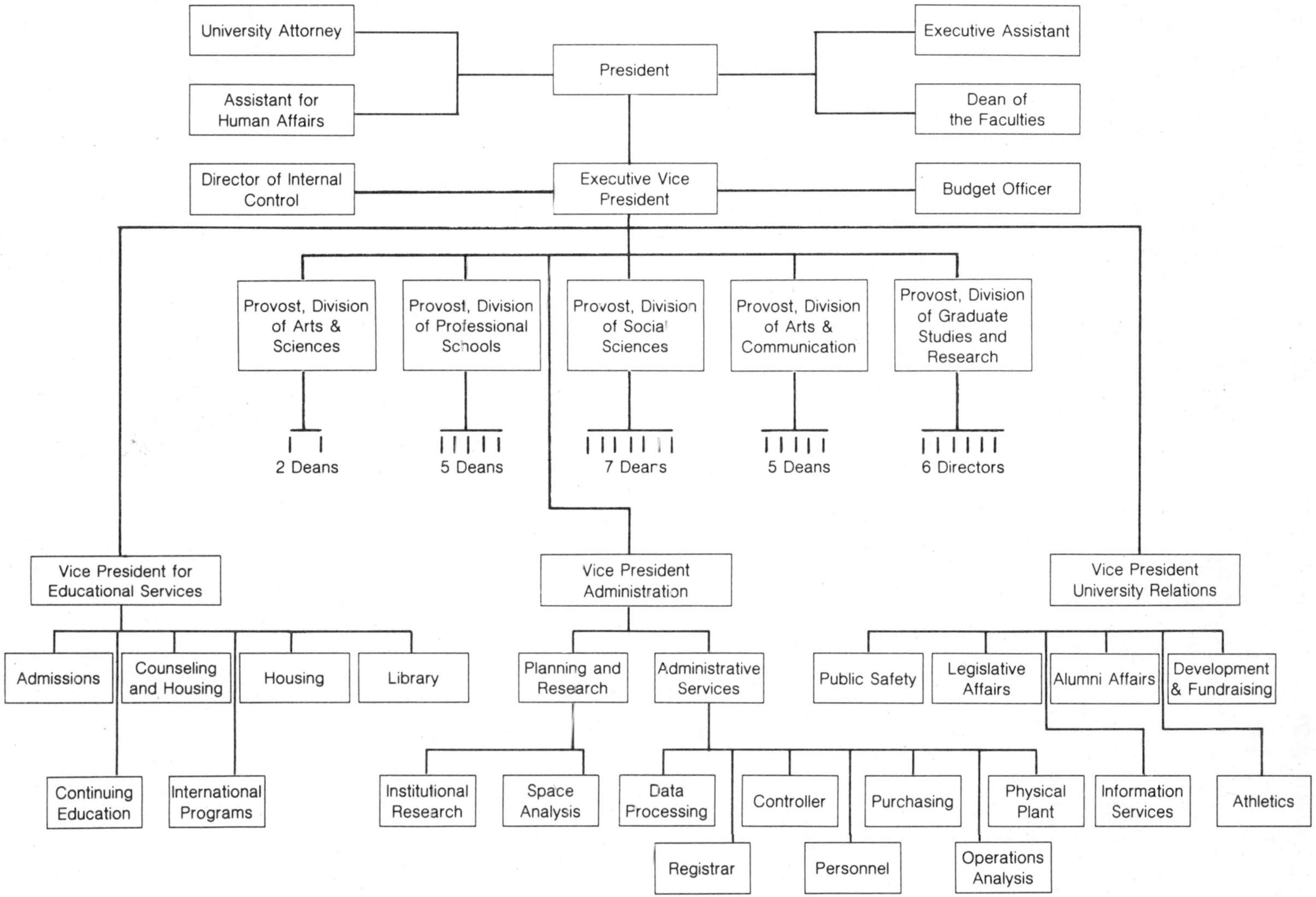

EXHIBIT 2-2 PINE MOUNTAIN STATE UNIVERSITY'S NEW ORGANIZATION CHART

monitor and receive inputs on the implementation of the new structure. The committee is to evaluate the inputs and to pass them on to the top administrators. The committee was formed at the time of reorganization but has only met three times since reorganization.

THE ISSUES

Since the reorganization, the following criticisms have been raised by the faculty, students, legislature, board of trustees, alumni, and federal government.

Legislature.

The university seems top heavy with administrators. At a time of financial austerity it does not seem appropriate to create so many new, highly-paid positions.

Trustees.

Pine Mountain State spends for administration twice the amount spent by the other major state university and four times the amount spent by a teachers college. Even worse is the fact that the budgeting and accounting system is less accurate now than it was before.

Students.

The registration process is worse than ever. The lines are longer and it is more difficult to get the classes desired. Classes are overcrowded; professors are never around for counseling and advising. Parking is terrible—there is never a place to park now. The top administration is isolated and is not responsive to the needs of the students. The president is unwilling to meet with students to discuss their problems.

Faculty.

The president is impossible to contact. There are too many levels of administration; everything is too centralized. An individual college cannot do its own fundraising, alumni relations, purchasing, or publicity without first going through the appropriate university office. There is no money for new faculty positions or for raises since the administration has taken all new positions and money. The internal allocation of resources is unfair. Arts and Sciences receives too many resources compared to its enrollment, while the professional colleges that have experienced tremendous student growth do not get enough.

Alumni.

The university seems to be more coordinated now than in the past. Instead of being contacted by four or five different people for financial contributions, only one contact is made by the development office. The alumni affairs office seems to have good current addresses on all alumni.

Federal government.

The accounting and management of federally sponsored research seems to be better coordinated. The university now has one main office concerned with this effort.

Since the reorganization, financial gifts from alumni have increased from $40,000 annually to about $500,000 annually. Gifts from corporations and foundations have increased from $15,000 to $100,000 annually. Federal government grants have decreased from $12,000,000 annually to $9,500,000 annually. Legislative appropriations have remained constant at $48,000,000 annually. Tuition for a 14-hour load has increased from $210 per quarter to $260 per quarter.

3

The Truth About
Girl Scouts

On March 11, 1982, 52 Girl Scouts assembled at the United Nations to present a "Gift of Water" to the world. It was a lovely ceremony. Water donated to the scouts from each of the states and from Puerto Rico and the District of Columbia was ceremoniously poured into a common vessel, the contents of which were to be spilled, a few months later, at the ceremonial planting of a tree at a new scout conference center. Certificates explaining the waters' origins and importance were on display at the U.N., which has declared the 1980s the International Drinking Water and Sanitation Decade. Mrs. Gouletas-Carey appeared on behalf of her husband, the governor of New York, to proclaim Girl Scout Week in the state.

The occasion was the seventieth anniversary of the Girl Scouts of the United States of America, and the ceremony epitomized the organization it celebrated. Like Girl Scouting, it was pretty. It was feminine. It was pregnant with symbolism. It expressed the virtues of charity and service, with overtones of national and international harmony. And most of all, it was uncontroversial—nobody, but nobody, could quarrel with water. ("I think water is *so* important," explains Frances Hesselbein, national executive director of GSUSA, "because without it, there's no life.") The ceremony, in short, was the ideal Girl Scout Event.

It was an auspicious moment for a successful event. At that point, the 1980s were looking good. Hopes were high, for the first time in about 12 distressing years. The 1970s had been terrible, and scouting wasn't used to terrible. Never during its first 50 years had GSUSA seen a single year of falling enrollment. In 1950, in recognition of its solid and worthy position in the national life, Congress had even conferred upon it a congressional charter, that it might "continue to inspire the rising generation with the highest ideals of character, patriotism, conduct, and attainment." In 1969, the peak year of its enrollment, it had claimed a membership of 3,921,000, which made it the largest girls' organization in the world. The thing had looked impregnable. And then in 1971 the numbers had just started falling...A few years later, GSUSA had lost fully a million girls.

Action was called for, and was undertaken. The 1970s were a time of change—big change—and apparently to good effect, for in 1979 the decline seemed finally to have been arrested.

So it was with well-earned pride and confidence that GSUSA undertook this grand new endeavor for the 1980s. It was announced that day at the U.N. that scouts all over the nation planned a variety of water projects to last for the next 10 years. Some scouts would "conserve, clean, and care about" water; some would cook seafood dishes; others would "help people cope" with hurricanes. For scouts all over the land, the 1980s were declared to be the Decade of Water. Water could not have been a more appropriate symbol, for in its frantic attempts to anticipate and accommodate the needs of a changing world, the organization threw out much of what had been best in it and offered girls who wanted to be scouts something very like water—colorless, tasteless, and liquid...

Early Girl Scouts camped outdoors and studied tracking, the Morse code, knot-tying ("A knowledge of knots is useful in every trade or calling," claims the first handbook), shooting ("It is one of the best ways to 'Be Prepared' "), and archery ("excellent practice for the eye, and good exercise for the muscles. It makes no noise, does not disturb game or warn the enemy"). They also Cultivated the Faculty of Remembering Time, Observed Details of People ("It is very instructive to note the different people we meet and try to form estimates of their character and disposition by their look and clothes"), and dealt "with small natural bits of information likely to escape any but specially trained eyes and senses." All this was seasoned with the "true life" examples of Girl Scout heroines who triumphed over adversity and danger by following the Law— "Brave girls whose pluck we admire."

And she wasn't kidding about wanting Girl

Scouting to be for all girls;...Mrs. Low (founder of the Girl Scouts) had set up a three-tiered national structure to deliver her program. All Girl Scout troops were to be members of regional councils, and all councils were to be chartered by a single national office (GSUSA). GSUSA itself was to operate no troops. Rather, its full-time job was to provide the basic idea and program materials—it was to be, so to speak, the R&D of scouting.

Councils sprang up everywhere. Growth was explosive. There were eight American Girl Scouts in 1912; in 1915 their numbers had risen to 5,000, and by 1920, to something like 42,000. This growth continued unabated. For if there was one fact about scouting that was true from day one, it was this: *girls like it.* They took to it like ducks to water.

It was inevitable that Girl Scouting should eventually feel the effects of the upheavals of the 1960s. Major changes had, of course, already been made since the days of Mrs. Low.

The organization adopted a "managerial idea," installing a "corporate planning system," which operated on the notion—as explained by Mrs. Hesselbein, who has published on the subject in *Philanthropy Monthly*—that management and planning are synonymous, and that planning has to be based on "hard data, demographic research, and local council experiences" about the "expressed preferences" of girls and leaders.

In line with its new principle, GSUSA began asking its constituency what it preferred. It began seeking statistics. It held discussion groups. It sent around surveys. It started offering "try-its"—"new ways of applying the basic principles." By 1977 the results—the "hard data"—were in. It remained only to take the "action steps," i.e., to revise.

The revisions were complete in 1980, and GSUSA enthusiastically presented its redesigned program, which consists of seven new books for girls and leaders, including new handbooks, to the councils at a series of national program conferences.

In a way, scouting has been "feminist" from the start. Seventy years ago, Mrs. Low enjoined her girls, "Be womanly. None of us like women who ape men. An imitation diamond is not as good as a real diamond." And her program made clear that this statement was positive as well as negative. Being "womanly" was different from being a man, but it was no less studied and energetic a pursuit, and she intended her scouts to do it proudly and well.

Scouts of the 1980s, though, practice the feminism of the 1980s, which is a completely different—and much more defensive—kettle of fish. The handbook for girls aged six to eleven, for example, includes a game in which scouts clip from magazines pictures representing "men's work," "women's work," and "both"—or a least, the handbook corrects itself, "what some photographer or artist showed as these kinds of work. What do you think—are they right? Ask yourselves, 'Who says so?' "

In line with the new Girl Scout feminism, the badge book, too, has been changed. A badge is still the same sort of thing it was when I was a scout in the mid-'60s—an award received upon completion of an exploratory project on a specified subject. The badges are listed in a special book, each with its eight to ten requirements underneath it. I had the cooking badge, for example, which required me, among other things, to learn the four food groups, prepare a breakfast, and bake a cake; when I had done all this I received an embroidered cloth patch to sew on my uniform.

The cooking badge, in fact, is a good example—it was popular in my troop but girls today can't earn it, because it's been excised from the book. Nowadays a scout can still earn such old favorites as "Hobbies and Pets" and "Books," but if she's interested in her kitchen, she has to shoot for either a badge called "Exploring Foods" (which requires her to prepare a meatless meal and some foods from other cultures) or another called "Healthy Eating" (which includes both try-

ing new foods and keeping "a record of the texture, taste, look, and smell of each one," and some lessons in consumer skepticism: "In what way do commercials teach good or poor eating habits?").

But no more sexist cooking. And no more sexist sewing, either—today's girls can study, instead, for their badges in "Textiles and Fibers" or "Art to Wear."

Girl Scouts now read just about every activity in vocational terms. Motherhood is considered a "career" choice—listed in the new Girl Scout book *Careers to Explore,* right along with Gas Station Attendant and President of the United States. And with such options, of course, it makes sense that a scout should get started young; in the same book, six- to eleven-year-olds are invited to diagram their career potential: listing a favorite toy, for example, as well as who uses it and what job it helps you prepare for.

Even leaders who are enthusiastic about the career program agree that it has to be sold with a song and a dance; girls tend not to warm to it as is. "It's better," one says, "when you don't say 'careers'—the more we work them into just plain troop fun, the more they respond." For example, she says her girls really like the role-playing suggested in the career book. "We did the one that asked, 'What would you do if your boss was a man who insisted you get his cup of coffee?' There were a couple of girls who were quite insistent about 'Gee, well, let him get his own coffee,' and a couple who said, 'What if he fires me?' It was a lot of fun."

Browsing further through the book, one wonders how much fun her scouts would have with the following outstandingly ungirlish problem:

Imagine you are in your mid-twenties. You are married and have a two-year-old child. After two years at home, you're ready to return to full-time work. You find a job with hours from 9:00 to 5:00, five days a week, paying $11,111 a year. Now you will need to combine your roles as homemaker and parent with your full-time paying job.

In small groups, determine the daily household chores and activities that must be done by you and your husband on a typical working day. . . . Decide who will do each chore. . . . Does one person have more time than the other?. . . Or is the work evenly divided?. . . How much time is there for the child?. . . Ask a group of males in your age range to do this exercise. How do your results compare?

It would hardly be surprising if such remote lessons failed, on a personal level, to register. Sure enough, when every now and again the program does ask girls to "define their own career interests," the plight of the working mother is forgotten, and the old familiar song emerges straight from their own hearts and lives. These girls almost invariably want to "explore" modeling or the stage. "Fashions, Fitness, and Makeup," for example, was the career-exploration choice of the girls who enacted the secretary's coffee dilemma.

No matter what they choose to explore, they explore in the preferred Girl Scout mode, which is heavily documental. Girl Scouting has embraced social science. The scouts are fanatic chart-makers, graph-drawers, listers, and calculators, and this business of reduce-and-quantify is not limited to careers.

For example, girls are asked to fill out a "Me and Others Profile." This is a chart that lists on its vertical axis a lot of interpersonal skills ("I am able to: trust; consider the feelings of; give assistance when problems physical, mental, or emotional seem difficult for," etc.), and on its horizontal axis, a lot of people ("Older females," "people from racial, ethnic, religious groups not my own," etc.). This allows a girl to, say, give herself a "2" in "asking for the help of" a "close friend." "Girls like this 'Know yourself' stuff," one leader explains casually. "This is easy."

When not contemplating herself, today's Girl Scout is supposed to be expressing herself. "Letting your feelings show can help make you feel better," a handbook claims. "Here are some ways to let feelings out

that won't hurt you or anyone else." The list includes "Cry if you want to" ("A Scout is Cheerful"?) and "Draw a really ugly picture."

In the past, Girl Scouts were supposed to learn about themselves by losing themselves in activity. Where the self was concerned, they preferred industry to analysis. The original handbook, for example, enjoins: "Too soft a bed tends to make people dream, which is unhealthy and weakening. Don't lay abed in the morning thinking how awful it is to have to get up. Rouse out at once and take a smart turn of some quick exercise." And then it proceeds directly to the mundane. "Learn to breathe through your nose. Breathing through the mouth makes you thirsty. So does chewing gum."

There is one subject on which the Girl Scout program has gotten less rigorous and analytical, and that is nature. Instead of the detailed instruction in outdoor skills and the study of plant and animal life that characterized Low's program, today's handbook emphasizes "contemplation" —sitting in a circle and reciting Edna St. Vincent Millay. Nature is pictured as a playground for a girl's fancy. "The next time your troop is anywhere where there are a lot of flowers, pretend that all of you are bees and butterflies. Zigzag from one flower to another. Look at blossoms from the insect point of view. . . . Make friends with an earthworm," it enthuses. "Stop and say 'thank you' to a tree."

This change is important, because the case can be made that nature—or more specifically, camping—*is* Girl Scouting. "Girls are scouts for lots of reasons, most of which are camping," the leader of a New Jersey troop told me. "Camping is the glue that holds scouting together."

It is certainly true that time and again girls say that camping is what they love most about the program—but not, it seems, for its inspirational aspects. What they really love is playing messy games with their friends ("shaving cream fights!") and learning outdoor skills.

Things may have gotten a bit soft in the Girl Scout program, but at GSUSA headquarters they most definitely have not. In particular, GSUSA is not soft about public relations. It has cultivated a genius for gesture. In 1979, for example, it lent its endorsement to the United Nations Year of the Child—children; how nice. Ever mindful of its image, GSUSA has also been aware during the past decade of the need to recruit minorities—and, of course, to make sure everyone knew of it. Conferences were staged on "Girl Scouting for Black Girls" and on "Girl Scouting—Mexican-American Style." GSUSA printed special literature to speak to minorities in their own idioms. For its grand project in 1981 it ran a survey, conducted by the National Urban League, to assess the impact of minority participation on Girl Scouting and also the extent of "Girl Scout and public awareness of minority participation in Girl Scouting." Most people, it turned out, thought it was all a real good idea.

At the same time, GSUSA began to realize it was losing a still more valuable minority—volunteers. There are 572,000 adults in scouting, and about 1% are paid staff. By 1979 there were 141 troops nationwide without leaders, and even more girls who wanted to be scouts for whom there were no troops at all. Women had begun returning to the work force, and it was suddenly necessary for GSUSA to motivate them to volunteer.

GSUSA's strategy was canny. It added a new perk to volunteering; now leading a troop was handy not just to a woman's soul but to her career. (Today a Girl Scout troop leader, tomorrow. . . .) Put simply, the Girl Scouts entered adult education.

Of course, GSUSA had always offered various sorts of training to its volunteer leaders: in the skills of the outdoors, for example, in the Girl Scout philosophy, and even in the simple management of a group. Today, however, GSUSA offers courses ranging from "the arts to computer technology," from "camping to financial management." In 1980, GSUSA secured accreditation by the Council for Noncollegiate Continuing Education, a United States agency, to grant units of credit toward academic degrees to participants in these courses.

These units of credit, explains Mrs. Hesselbein, "are a kind of recognition, whether you are working toward a degree or whether you are a homemaker, of the importance of your contribution." Such recognition is not, however, awarded for the simple contribution of leading a troop; it is only awarded for the taking of classes. And what a volunteer learns in those classes need not have any effect on what she does with her scouts, but it may well help her to complete a degree or secure a paid position later. Apparently, volunteerism has yielded to careerism.

Nowhere is this change better exemplified than in the development of the Edith Macy Conference Center. "Camp Edith Macy," a training center for Girl Scout leaders, was established in Westchester County, New York, in 1926. Its donor dreamed that it would become "a university in the woods." In its early days, students "really roughed it" there, sleeping in tents and cooking out.

In 1980, however, GSUSA began construction of an $8 million, 200-person conference center on the Macy property. The center, now unfortunately called a "miniversity in the woods," features technologically up-to-the-minute conference facilities (video-complete, touch-of-a-button automatic, color-coded), rooms that would do a decent hotel proud, and complete food service in a luxury dining room. Still, it continues to claim "woodsiness" because, as its glossy-printed descriptive literature explains, the building's "wood and stone construction materials are in harmony with those found in the region."

Camp Edith Macy is not a bad metaphor for today's characterless scouting, which, in its urge to modernize, has lost its clear identity—the raison d'être and sense of mission that was uniquely its own and served generations of contented girls very well.

Girl Scouting's structure has something to do with this turn of events. The structure of the organization may have been what did it in. Right from the start, scouting has offered its local councils tremendous autonomy. This means that the organization is flexible beyond the ordinary, a quality that is both its strength and, currently, its weakness.

Girl Scout councils are separately incorporated and set up their own structures for instituting and negotiating with their troops. And although they must adhere to certain standards in order to use the Scout name, it is possible for councils to be permanently chartered. This has the happy effect of allowing them to adjust to regional preferences—potentially a source of great strength. But regional preferences are subject to considerable fluctuation because local Girl Scouting is almost completely run by volunteers, and, as with any all-volunteer organization, no one has much control over the staff. Councils, therefore, are rather vulnerable to the fads or fashions that prevail in their communities. This vulnerability may explain the "hard data" that arrived in the 1970s—the data that led GSUSA to conclude, wrongly, that the assumptions on which the old program was based were obsolete.

In forming this conclusion, the organization bent to pressure from its councils but managed to overlook a substantial and persuasive argument for keeping things as they were—namely, the nature of the girls. Girls are not interested in making friends with an earthworm or making a "Me and Others Profile." Confronted with the new program, they plump determinedly for its most reassuringly traditional aspects.

Ask the members of any troop, anywhere, what badges they have and the answers are always the same: Camping, Child Care, First Aid, Books. They'll tell you, with sincere faces, that they enjoy the serious aspects of scouting, too—but what they mean is the old, volunteer-service sort of thing. A gum-chewing blonde named Heidi clasps her hands together—glittery-blue nail polish gleaming—when she talks about Christmas caroling at an old-folks home. "They smile at you and stuff," she says. A 13-year-old scout from

the Bronx summed it all up beautifully. "The best part," she said, "is working with all of our friends and helping people out."

The message is clear: one generation does not a transformation make. Girls wandered away from scouting in the 1970s because of unusual times, not because they were unusual creatures. And their return to scouting in 1979 probably had more to do with societal changes than it did with the trendy new program—which may be why, in 1980, after their exploratory blip upward, those numbers headed right back down again. In 1979, enrollment reached 2,961,000, but thereafter it declined and by 1982 had slid to 2,819,000. Tales of professional success have not, apparently, instilled staying power in today's Girl Scouts.

The example of the Boy Scouts seems to confirm this failure. Faced with a similarly declining enrollment, BSA, after some initial waffling, held fast to its traditional program, to the point at which the program looked positively quaint. But this quaintness, as it turns out, did not deter boys from becoming Scouts. Again, structure has a lot to do with it. There is relatively little regional variation in Boy Scouting: central control is strong and, as a result, the organization is stable and sturdy.

The cornerstone of Scouting's stability, however, is its doctrine. Of course BSA made some superficial changes to keep in step with the times. But its stated purpose remains in the words of Ralph Derian, Scout Executive for the Greater New York Councils, "to help young people grow to responsible adulthood. We feel," he continues, "that whether it hurts or not, it is our responsibility to train kids to be better kids, and we have to stick to those principles."

This attitude is echoed in the 1979 edition of BSA's handbook, which still claims, with a straight face, to be second only to the Bible in offering "answers to the questions a boy wonders about." "Yes," it claims, "it's fun to be a Boy Scout!"

Despite its revisions, the handbook's language dates from the 1940s: "Camp! There's a word that's filled with fun and adventure for every real boy!" And the graphics and typeface are out of the early '60s—except that some of the scout faces are blackened in. On the frontispiece is a photo of the author: "William 'Green Bar Bill' Hillcourt, Author, Naturalist, and World Scouter," an old man pictured in a Boy Scout uniform, complete with short pants, knee socks, and neckerchief. The frontispiece also declares the Boy Scouts to be "four million strong for America." (The Girl Scout handbook's frontispiece is a misty pastel drawing of butterflies and flowers; it's a lot less alarming but it doesn't pack a fraction of the punch.)

It sounds like a joke, but they come in droves to read this book. In the three years since it has been out (data on 1982 are not yet available), BSA has not only reversed its decline, but has brought its numbers steadily back up each year, to a total of 3,246,000. Where careers have failed, the romance of old-style Baden-Powellism has succeeded. Tales of heroism and duty have sold a lot of kids on scouting in the past couple of years.

As far as numbers are concerned, there can't be much question about which of the two scoutings took the right programmatic direction.

But the numbers aren't all—or even the most important part—of what's disappointing in the new Girl Scouting. A far more significant disappointment is the character of the changes. For although GSUSA clearly had to modernize (every organization needs to catch up, occasionally, with changing times), it modernized wrongly, and so suffered what might be called a loss of spirit. Some may say that today's Boy Scouting has its objectionable aspects, but everyone will agree that it is firmly, recognizably Boy Scouting. The new Girl Scouting, on the other hand, mirrors the conventional wisdom, and so looks just like everything else. To begin to look like everything else is to lose one's own spirit. At one point, the late Mrs. Low expressed the hope that "We will make scouting so much a part of the American life that people will recognize the spirit and say, 'Why of course. She is a Girl Scout.'" Sorry, Mrs. Low.

4

Rondell Data Corporation

"God damn it, he's done it again!"

Frank Forbus threw the stack of prints and specifications down on his desk in disgust. The Model 802 wide-band modulator, released for production the previous Thursday, had just come back to Frank's Engineering Services Department with a caustic note that began, "This one can't be produced, either..." It was the fourth time Production had kicked the design back.

Frank Forbus, director of engineering for Rondell Data Corp., was normally a quiet man. But the Model 802 was stretching his patience; it was beginning to look just like other new products that had hit delays and problems in the transition from design to production during the eight months Frank had worked for Rondell. These problems were nothing new at the sprawling old Rondell factory; Frank's predecessor in the engineering job had run afoul of them too, and had finally been fired for protesting too vehemently about the other departments. But the Model 802 should have been different. Frank had met two months before (July 3, 1978) with the firm's president, Bill Hunt, and with fact-ory superintendent Dave Schwab to smooth the way for the new modulator design. He thought back to the meeting...

"Now we all know there's a tight deadline on the 802," Bill Hunt said, "and Frank's done well to ask us to talk about its introduction. I'm counting on both of you to find any snags in the system, and to work together to get that first production run out by October second. Can you do it?"

"We can do it in Production if we get a clean design two weeks from now, as scheduled," answered Dave Schwab, the grizzled factory superintendent. "Frank and I have already talked about that, of course. I'm setting aside time in the card room and the machine shop, and we'll be ready. If the design goes over schedule, though, I'll have to fill in with other runs, and it will cost us a bundle to break in for the 802. How does it look in Engineering, Frank?"

"I've just reviewed the design for the second time," Frank replied. "If Ron Porter can keep the salesmen out of our hair, and avoid any more last minute changes, we've got a shot.

I've pulled the draftsmen off three other overdue jobs to get this one out. But, Dave, that means we can't spring engineers loose to confer with your production people on manufacturing problems."

"Well, Frank, most of those problems are caused by the engineers, and we need them to resolve the difficulties. We've all agreed that production bugs come from both of us bowing to sales pressure, and putting equipment into production before the designs are really ready. That's just what we're trying to avoid on the 802. But I can't have 500 people sitting on their hands waiting for an answer from your people. We'll have to have *some* engineering support."

Bill Hunt broke in, "So long as you two can talk calmly about the problem I'm confident you can resolve it. What a relief it is, Frank, to hear the way you're approaching this. With Kilmann (the previous director of engineering) this conversation would have been a shouting match. Right, Dave?" Dave nodded and smiled.

"Now there's one other thing you should both be aware of," Hunt continued. "Doc Reeves and I talked last night about a new filtering technique, one that might improve the signal-to-noise ratio of the 802 by a factor of two. There's a chance Doc can come up with it before the 802 reaches production, and if it's possible, I'd like to use the new filters. That would give us a real jump on the competition."

Four days after that meeting, Frank found that two of his key people on the 802 design had been called to Production for emergency consultation on a bug found in final assembly: two halves of a new data transmission interface wouldn't fit together because recent changes in the front end required a different chassis design for the back end.

Another week later, Doc Reeves walked into Frank's office, proud as a new parent, with the new filter design. "This won't affect the other modules of the 802 much," Doc had said. "Look, it takes three new cards, a few connectors, some changes in the wiring harness, and some new shielding, and that's all."

Frank had tried to resist the last-minute design changes, but Bill Hunt had stood firm. With a lot of overtime by the engineers and draftsmen, Engineering Services should still be able to finish the prints in time.

Two engineers and three draftsmen went onto 12-hour days to get the 802 ready, but the prints were still five days late reaching Dave Schwab. Two days later, the prints came back to Frank, heavily annotated in red. Schwab had worked all day Saturday to review the job, and had found more than a dozen discrepancies in the prints—most of them caused by the new filter design and insufficient checking time before release. Correction of those design faults had brought on a new generation of discrepancies; Schwab's cover note on the second return of the prints indicated he'd had to release the machine capacity he'd been holding for the 802. On the third iteration, Schwab committed his photo and plating capacity to another rush job. The 802 would be at least one month late getting into production. Ron Porter, Vice President for Sales, was furious. His customer needed 100 units *NOW,* he said. Rondell was the customer's only late supplier.

"Here we go again," thought Frank Forbus.

COMPANY HISTORY

Rondell Data Corp. traced its lineage through several generations of electronics technology. Its original founder, Bob Rondell, had set the firm up in 1920 as "Rondell Equipment Co." to manufacture several electrical testing devices he had invented as an engineering faculty member at a large university. The firm branched into radio broadcasting equipment in 1947, and into data transmission equipment in the early 1960s. A well-established corps of direct sales people, mostly engineers, called on industrial, scientific and government accounts, but concentrated heavily on original equipment manufacturers. In this market, Rondell had a long-standing reputation as a source of high-quality, innovative designs. The firm's sales-people fed a continual stream of challenging problems into the Engineering Department, where the creative genius of Ed "Doc" Reeves and several dozen other engineers "converted problems to solutions" (as the sales brochure bragged). Product design formed the spearhead of Rondell's growth.

By 1978, Rondell offered a wide range of products in its two major lines. Broadcast equipment sales had benefitted from the growth of UHF TV and FM radio; it now accounted for 35% of company sales. Data transmission had blossomed, and in this field an increasing number of orders called for unique specifications, ranging from special-ized display panels to entirely untried designs.

The company had grown from 100 employ-ees in 1947 to over 800 in 1978. (Exhibit 4-1 shows the current organization chart of key employees.) Bill Hunt, who had been a stu-dent of the company's founder, had presided over most of that growth, and took great pride in preserving the "family spirit" of the old organization. Informal relationships between Rondell's veteran employees formed the backbone of the firm's day-to-day operations; all the managers relied on personal contact, and Hunt often insisted that the absence of bureaucratic red tape was a key factor in recruiting outstanding engineering talent. The personal management approach extended throughout the factory. All exempt employees were paid on a straight salary plus a share of the profits. Rondell boasted an extremely loyal group of senior employees, and very low turnover in nearly all areas of the company.

The highest turnover job in the firm was Frank Forbus's. Frank had joined Rondell in January of 1978, replacing Jim Kilmann, who had been director of engineering for only 10 months. Kilmann, in turn, had replaced Tom MacLeod, a talented engineer who had made a promising start, but had taken to drink after a year in the job. MacLeod's predecessor had been a genial old timer who retired at 70 after

30 years in charge of engineering. (Doc Reeves had refused the directorship in each of the recent changes, saying, "Hell, that's no promotion for a bench man like me. I'm no administrator.")

For several years, the firm had experienced a steadily increasing number of disputes between research, engineering, sales, and production people—disputes generally cen-tered on the problem of new product intro-duction. Quarrels between departments became more numerous under MacLeod, Kilmann, and Forbus. Some managers associ-ated those disputes with the company's recent decline in profitability—a decline that, in spite of higher sales and gross reve-nues, was beginning to bother people in 1977. President Bill Hunt commented:

Better cooperation, I'm sure, could increase our output by 5-10%. I'd hoped Kilmann could solve the problems, but pretty obviously he was too young, too arrogant. People like him—that conflict type of personality—bother me. I don't like strife, and with him it seemed I spent all my time smoothing out arguments. Kilmann tried to tell everyone else how to run their departments, without having his own house in order. That approach just wouldn't work, here at Rondell. Frank Forbus, now, seems much more in tune with our style of organization. I'm really hopeful now.

Still, we have just as many problems now as we did last year. Maybe even more. I hope Frank can get a handle on Engineering Services soon···

THE ENGINEERING DEPARTMENT: RESEARCH

According to the organization chart (see Exhibit 4-1), Frank Forbus was in charge of both research (really the product develop-ment function) and engineering services (which provided engineering support). To Forbus, however, the relationship with research was not so clear-cut:

Doc Reeves is one of the world's unique people, and none of us would have it any other way. He's a creative genius. Sure, the chart says he

21

EXHIBIT 4–1   RONDELL DATA CORPORATION   1978 ORGANIZATION CHART

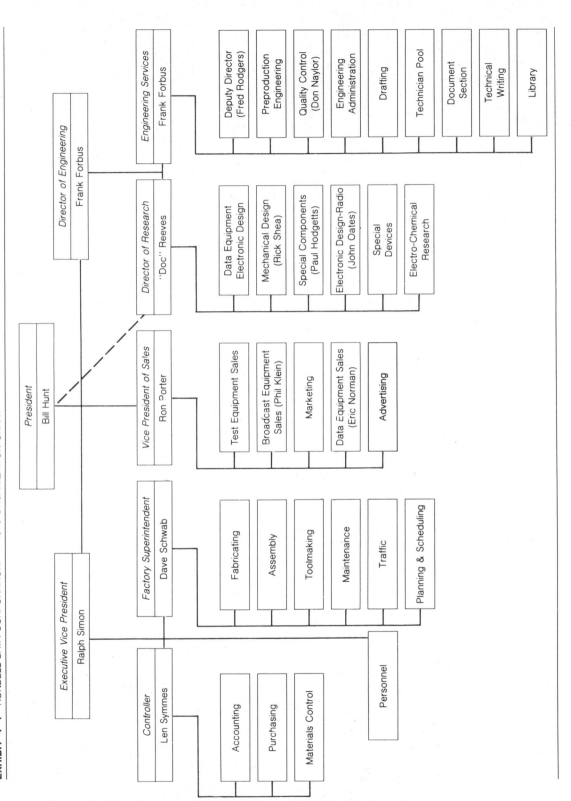

works for me, but we all know Doc does his own thing. He's not the least bit interested in management routines, and I can't count on him to take any responsibility in scheduling projects, or checking budgets, or what-have-you. But as long as Doc is director of research, you can bet this company will keep on leading the field. He has more ideas per hour than most people have per year, and he keeps the whole engineering staff fired up. Everybody loves Doc —and you can count me in on that, too. In a way, he works for me, sure. But that's not what's important.

"Doc" Reeves—unhurried, contemplative, casual, and candid—tipped his stool back against the wall of his research cubicle and talked about what *was* important:

Development engineering. That's where the company's future rests. Either we have it there, or we don't have it.

There's no kidding ourselves that we're anything but a bunch of Rube Goldbergs here. But that's where the biggest kicks come from— from solving development problems, and dreaming up new ways of doing things. That's why I so look forward to the special contracts we get involved in. We accept them not for the revenue they represent, but because they subsidize the basic development work which goes into all our basic products.

This is a fantastic place to work. I have a great crew and they can really deliver when the chips are down. Why, Bill Hunt and I (he gestured toward the neighboring cubicle, where the president's name hung over the door) are likely to find as many people here at work at ten p.m. as at three in the afternoon. The important thing here is the relationships between people; they're based on mutual respect, not on policies and procedures. Administrative red tape is a pain. It takes away from development time.

Problems? Sure, there are problems now and then. There are power interests in production, where they sometimes resist change. But I'm not a fighting man, you know. I suppose if I were, I might go in there and push my weight around a little. But I'm an engineer, and can do more for Rondell sitting right here, or working with

my own people. That's what brings results.

Other members of the Research Department echoed Doc's views and added some additional sources of satisfaction with their work. They were proud of the personal contacts they built up with customers' technical staffs—contacts that increasingly involved travel to the customers' factories to serve as expert advisors in preparation of overall system design specifications. The engineers were also delighted with the department's encouragement of their personal development, continuing education, and independence on the job.

But there were problems, too. Rick Shea, of the mechanical design section, noted,

In the old days I really enjoyed the work—and the people I worked with. But now there's a lot of irritation. I don't like someone breathing down my neck. You can be hurried into jeopardizing the design.

John Oates, head of the radio electronic design section, was another designer with definite views:

Production engineering is almost nonexistent in this company. Very little is done by the preproduction section in engineering services. Frank Forbus has been trying to get preproduction into the picture, but he won't succeed because you can't start from such an ambiguous position. There have been three directors of engineering in three years. Frank can't hold his own against the others in the company. Kilmann was too aggressive. Perhaps no amount of tact would have succeeded.

Paul Hodgetts was head of special components in the R & D department. Like the rest of the department he valued bench work. But he complained of engineering services.

The services don't do things we want them to do. Instead, they tell us what they're going to do. I should probably go to Frank, but I don't get any decisions there. I know I should go through Frank, but this holds things up, so I often go direct.

THE ENGINEERING DEPARTMENT: ENGINEERING SERVICES

The Engineering Services Department provided ancillary services to R & D, and served as liaison between engineering and the other Rondell departments. Among its main functions were drafting; management of the central technicians' pool; scheduling and expediting engineering products; documentation and publication of parts lists and engineering orders; preproduction engineering (consisting of the final integration of individual design components into mechanically compatible packages); and quality control (which included inspection of incoming parts and materials, and final inspection of subassemblies and finished equipment). Top management's description of the department included the line, "ESD is responsible for maintaining cooperation with other departments, providing services to the development engineers, and freeing more valuable people in R & D from essential activities which are diversions from and beneath their main competence."

Many of Frank Forbus's 75 employees were located in other departments. Quality control people were scattered through the manufacturing and receiving areas, and technicians worked primarily in the research area or the prototype fabrication room. The remaining ESD personnel were assigned to leftover nooks and crannies near production or engineering sections.

Frank Forbus described his position:

My biggest problem is getting acceptance from the people I work with. I've moved slowly rather than risk antagonism. I saw what happened to Kilmann, and I want to avoid that. But although his precipitate action had won over a few of the younger R & D people, he certainly didn't have the department's backing. Of course it was the resentment of other departments which eventually caused his discharge. People have been slow accepting me here. There's nothing really overt, but I get a negative reaction to my ideas.

My role in the company has never been well defined, really. It's complicated by Doc's unique position, of course, and also by the fact that ESD sort of grew by itself over the years, as the design engineers concentrated more and more on the creative parts of product development. I wish I could be more involved in the technical side. That's been my training, and it's a lot of fun. But in our setup, the technical side is the least necessary for me to be involved in.

Schwab (production head) is hard to get along with. Before I came and after Kilmann left, there were six months intervening when no one was really doing any scheduling. No work loads were figured, and unrealistic promises were made about releases. This puts us in an awkward position. We've been scheduling way beyond our capacity to manufacture or engineer.

Certain people within R & D, for instance John Oates, head of the radio electronic design section, understand scheduling well and meet project deadlines, but this is not generally true of the rest of the R & D department, especially the mechanical engineers who won't commit themselves. Most of the complaints come from sales and production department heads because items—like the 802—are going to production before they are fully developed, under pressure from sales to get out the unit, and this snags the whole process. Somehow, engineering services should be able to intervene and resolve these complaints, but I haven't made much headway so far.

I should be able to go to Hunt for help, but he's too busy most of the time, and his major interest is the design side of engineering, where he got his own start. Sometimes he talks as though he's the engineering director as well as president. I have to put my foot down; there are problems here that the front office just doesn't understand.

Sales people were often observed taking their problems directly to designers, while production frequently threw designs back at R & D, claiming they could not be produced and demanding the prompt attention of particular design engineers. The latter were frequently observed in conference with production supervisors on the assembly floor. Frank went on:

The designers seem to feel they're losing something when one of us tries to help. They feel it's a reflection on them to have someone take over what they've been doing. They seem to want to carry a project right through to the final stages, particularly the mechanical people. Consequently, engineering services people are used below their capacity to contribute and our department is denied functions it should be performing. There's not as much use made of engineering services as there should be.

Frank Forbus's technician supervisor added his comments:

Production picks out the engineer who'll be the "bum of the month." They pick on every little detail instead of using their heads and making the minor changes that have to be made. The fifteen-to-twenty-year people shouldn't have to prove their ability any more, but they spend four hours defending themselves and four hours getting the job done. I have no one to go to when I need help. Frank Forbus is afraid. I'm trying to help him but he can't help me at this time. I'm responsible for fifty people and I've got to support them.

Fred Rodgers, who Frank had brought with him to the company as an assistant, gave another view of the situation:

I try to get our people in preproduction to take responsibility but they're not used to it and people in other departments don't usually see them as best qualified to solve the problem. There's a real barrier for a newcomer here. Gaining people's confidence is hard. More and more, I'm wondering whether there really is a job for me here.

(Rodgers left Rondell a month later.) Another of Forbus's subordinates gave his view:

If Doc gets a new product idea you can't argue. But he's too optimistic. He judges that others can do what he does—but there's only one Doc

Reeves. We've had 900 production change orders this year—they changed 2,500 drawings. If I were in Frank's shoes I'd put my foot down on all this new development. I'd look at the reworking we're doing and get production set up they way I wanted it. Kilmann was fired when he was doing a good job. He was getting some system in the company's operations. Of course, it hurt some people. There is no denying that Doc is the most important person in the company. What gets overlooked is that Hunt is a close second, not just politically but in terms of what he contributes technically and in customer relations.

This subordinate explained that he sometimes went out into the production department but that Schwab, the production head, resented this. Personnel in production said that Kilmann had failed to show respect for oldtimers and was always meddling in other departments' business. This was why he had been fired, they contended.

Don Taylor was in charge of quality control. He commented:

I am now much more concerned with administration and less with work. It is one of the evils you get into. There is tremendous detail in this job. I listen to everyone's opinion. Everybody is important. There shouldn't be distinctions—distinctions between people. I'm not sure whether Frank has to be a fireball like Kilmann. I think the real question is whether Frank is getting the job done. I know my job is essential. I want to supply service to the more talented people and give them information so they can do their jobs better.

THE SALES DEPARTMENT

Ron Porter was angry. His job was supposed to be selling, he said, but instead it had turned into settling disputes inside the plant and making excuses to waiting customers. He jabbed a finger toward his desk:

You see that telephone? I'm actually afraid nowadays to hear it ring. Three times out of five, it will be a customer who's hurting because we've failed to deliver on schedule. The other two calls will be from production or ESD, telling me some schedule has slipped again.

The Model 802 is typical. Absolutely typical. We padded the delivery date by six weeks, to allow for contingencies. Within two months the slack had evaporated. Now it looks like we'll be lucky to ship it before Christmas. (It was now November 28.) We're ruining our reputation in the market. Why, just last week one of our best customers—people we've worked with for 15 years—tried to hang a penalty clause on their latest order.

We shouldn't have to be after the engineers all the time. They should be able to see what problems they create without our telling them.

Phil Klein, head of broadcast sales under Porter, noted that many sales decisions were made by top management. Sales was under-staffed, he thought, and had never really been able to get on top of the job.

We have grown further and further away from engineering. The director of engineering does not pass on the information that we give him. We need better relationships there. It is very difficult for us to talk to customers about development problems without technical help. We need each other. The whole of engineering is now too isolated from the outside world. The morale of ESD is very low. They're in a bad spot —they're not well organized.

People don't take much to outsiders here. Much of this is because the expectation is built up by top management that jobs will be filled from the bottom. So it's really tough when an outsider like Frank comes in.

Eric Norman, order and pricing coordinator for data equipment, talked about his own relationships with the production department:

Actually, I get along with them fairly well. Oh, things could be better, of course, if they were more cooperative generally. They always seem to say, "It's my bat and my ball, and we're playing by my rules." People are afraid to make production mad; there's a lot of power in there.

But you've got to understand that production has its own set of problems. And nobody in Rondell is working any harder than Dave Schwab to try to straighten things out.

THE PRODUCTION DEPARTMENT

Dave Schwab had joined Rondell just after the Korean War, in which he had seen combat duty (at the Yalu River) and intelligence duty at Pyong Yang. Both experiences had been useful in his first year of civilian employment at Rondell's: the wartime factory superintendent and several middle managers had been, apparently, indulging in highly questionable side deals with Rondell's suppliers. Dave Schwab had gathered evidence, revealed the situation to Bill Hunt, and had stood by the president in the ensuing unsavory situation. Seven months after joining the company, Dave was named Factory Superintendent.

His first move had been to replace the fallen managers with a new team from outside. This group did not share the traditional Rondell emphasis on informality and friendly personal relationships, and had worked long and hard to install systematic manufacturing methods and procedures. Before the reorganization, production had controlled purchasing, stock control, and final quality control (where final assembly of products in cabinets was accomplished). Because of the wartime events, management decided on a check-and-balance system of organization and removed these three departments from production jurisdiction. The new production managers felt they had been unjustly penalized by this reorganization, particularly since they had uncovered the behavior that was detrimental to the company in the first place.

By 1978, the production department had grown to 500 employees, of whom 60% worked in the assembly area—an unusually pleasant environment that had been commended by *Factory* magazine for its colorful decoration, cleanliness, and low noise level. An additional 30% of the work force, mostly skilled machinists, staffed the finishing and fabrication department. About 60 others performed scheduling, supervisory, and maintenance duties. Production workers were nonunion, hourly-paid, and participated in both the liberal profit-sharing program and the stock purchase plan. Morale in production was traditionally high, and turnover was extremely low.

Dave Schwab commented:

To be efficient, production has to be a self-contained department. We have to control what comes into the department and what goes out. That's why purchasing, inventory control, and quality ought to run out of this office. We'd eliminate a lot of problems with better control there. Why, even Don Naylor in QC, would rather work for me than for ESD; he's said so himself. We understand his problems better.

The other departments should be self-contained, too. That's why I always avoid the underlings, and go straight to the department heads with any questions. I always go down the line.

I have to protect my people from outside disturbances. Look what would happen if I let unfinished, half-baked designs in here—there'd be chaos. The bugs have to be found before the drawings go into the shop, and it seems I'm the one who has to find them. Look at the 802, for example. (Dave had spent most of Thanksgiving Day [it was now November 28] red-pencilling the latest set of prints.) ESD should have found every one of those discrepancies. They just don't check drawings properly. They change most of the things I flag, but then they fail to trace through the impact of those changes on the rest of the design. I shouldn't have to do that.

And those engineers are tolerance crazy. They want everything to a millionth of an inch. I'm the only one in the company who's had any experience with actually machining things to a millionth of an inch. We make sure that the things that engineers say on their drawings actually have to be that way and whether they're obtainable from the kind of raw material we buy.

That shouldn't be production's responsibility, but I have to do it. Accepting bad prints

wouldn't let us ship the order any quicker. We'd only make a lot of junk that had to be reworked. And that would take even longer.

This way, I get to be known as the bad guy, but I guess that's just part of the job. (He paused with a wry smile.) Of course, what really gets them is that I don't even have a degree.

Dave had fewer bones to pick with the sales department because, he said, they trusted him.

When we give Ron Porter a shipping date, he knows the equipment will be shipped then.

You've got to recognize, though, that all of our new product problems stem from sales making absurd commitments on equipment that hasn't been fully developed. That always means trouble. Unfortunately, Hunt always backs sales up, even when they're wrong. He always favors them over us.

Ralph Simon, age 65, executive vice president of the company, had direct responsibility for Rondell's production department. He said:

There shouldn't really be a dividing of departments among top management in the company. The president should be czar over all. The production people ask me to do something for them, and I really can't do it. It creates bad feelings between engineering and production, this special attention that they [R & D] get from Bill. But then Hunt likes to dabble in design. Schwab feels that production is treated like a poor relation.

THE EXECUTIVE COMMITTEE

At the executive committee meeting of December 6, it was duly recorded that Dave Schwab had accepted the prints and specifications for the Model 802 modulator, and had set Friday, December 29, as the shipping date for the first 10 pieces. Bill Hunt, in the chairperson's role, shook his head and changed the subject quickly when Frank tried to open the agenda to a discussion of interdepartmental coordination.

The executive committee itself was a brainchild of Rondell's controller, Len Symmes, who was well aware of the disputes that plagued the company. Symmes had convinced Bill Hunt and Ralph Simon to meet every two weeks with their department heads, and the meetings were formalized with Hunt, Simon, Ron Porter, Dave Schwab, Frank Forbus, Doc Reeves, Symmes, and the personnel director attending. Symmes explained his intent and the results:

Doing things collectively and informally just doesn't work as well as it used to. Things have been gradually getting worse for at least two years now. We had to start thinking in terms of formal organization relationships. I did the first organization chart, and the executive committee was my idea too—but neither idea is contributing much help, I'm afraid. It takes top management to make an organization click. The rest of us can't act much differently until the top people see the need for us to change.

I had hoped the committee especially would help get the department managers into a constructive planning process. It hasn't worked out that way because Mr. Hunt really doesn't see the need for it. He uses the meetings as a place to pass on routine information.

MERRY CHRISTMAS

"Frank, I didn't know whether to tell you now, or after the holiday." It was Friday, December 22, and Frank Forbus was standing awkwardly in front of Bill Hunt's desk.

"But, I figured you'd work right through Christmas Day if we didn't have this talk, and that just wouldn't have been fair to you. I can't understand why we have such poor luck in the engineering director's job lately. And I don't think it's entirely your fault. But. . ."

Frank only heard half of Hunt's words, and said nothing in response. He'd be paid through February 28. . .He should use the time for searching. . .Hunt would help all he could. . .Jim Kilmann was supposed to be doing well at his own new job, and might need more help. . .

Frank cleaned out his desk, and numbly started home. The electronic carillon near his house was playing a Christmas carol. Frank thought again of Hunt's rationale: conflict still plagued Rondell—and Frank had not made it go away. Maybe somebody else could do it.

"And what did Santa Claus bring you, Frankie?" he asked himself.

"The sack. Only the empty sack."

5

Artisan Industries

Artisan Industries was a nine-million-dollar-a-year, family-run manufacturer of wooden decorative products.

They were approaching their first fall sales season since last year's successful turnaround under the direction of the new 29-year-old President, Bill Meister. Last fall had begun with a year-to-date loss of $125,000 and, through Meister's actions, had ended with a $390,000 profit. This had been the first profit in several years and capped a challenging eight months for the new president.

Meister had hired his first man while his father was still president, bringing in 27-year-old Bob Atwood from the local office of a "Big Eight" firm to begin modernizing the accounting system. On June 10th, 1977, Bob was in Bill's office for further and, he hoped, final discussion of plans for this fall season. Artisan's sales were quite seasonal and on June 10th there were about two more months during which production would exceed sales. Atwood, concerned with the company's limited capital, proposed a production plan to hold the inventory build-up to $1,600,000, or about twice the level shown on the last full computer listing.

The president, based on his feel for conditions after the successful 1976 season and viewing sales in the first weeks of 1977, believed total sales for this year would really beat Bob's estimate of the same as last year's and reach $9,000,000. But he would like to have stronger support for his opinions; a lot rested on this estimate. If sales were much beyond their plans he could expect to lose most of them and create difficulties with his customers. New customers might even be lost to the competition. Bill was also concerned with developing contingency plans for dealing effectively with the potential oversold condition. Besides getting more production from the plants at the last minute, there might be good ideas that involved the customers and salespeople. For example, if all orders couldn't be filled, should some be fully shipped and others dropped, or should all be shipped 75-95% complete? Overall in 1976 orders had been shipped 75% complete and during the peak months this had fallen to 50%. Partial shipments might be a way to keep everyone happy. If orders are canceled

Reprinted by permission of Frank C. Barnes, Associate Professor,
University of North Carolina at Charlotte.

should they be the ones from the small "mom and pop" stores or the large department stores? The small stores are more dependable customers, but on the other hand large department stores systematically evaluate suppliers on their order completion history. Also the department store buyers must commit funds when they place an order, thus their resources are idle until the order is filled. There are potential benefits from good communications, for if you inform the buyer of any delay quickly he can cancel that order and order something he can get. Such sensitivity to the customer's needs could win the company many friends and aid Meister in building a desirable reputation. On the other hand, poor communication could cause the opposite. Meister wondered if there was some way to usefully involve the salespeople, many of whom had left a sales representative organization six months earlier to work solely for Artisan.

After about mid-August total annual sales were limited to what had been built up in inventory beforehand and production through mid-November. Thus holding back now put a lid on total sales for the season.

If, on the other hand, the sales plan was not reached there could also be serious consequences. Last year after the fall sales period the inventory loan had been paid off for the first time since the 1960s. This had made a very favorable impression on the lending institutions and brought a reduction in the high interest rates (from 12% to 10¼%). They considered Bill a "super-star," with his youth, professional appearance, and modern ideas, and their fears for the Artisan loan were diminishing. Trouble at this time might erase all this and suggest last year was just a fluke.

If sales didn't materialize, inventories could be held down by cutting back on production. But Bill believed the plants operate inefficiently during any cutbacks and such moves very likely saved nothing. He held a similar opinion of temporary second shifts. In many past years over-production early in the year had resulted in big layoffs in December and January and in the financial drain of carrying over large inventories. Meister was highly interested in building an effective work environment for people at Artisan, where attitudes were historically poor. The employees—workers and supervisors—had little exposure to "professional" managers and had much to learn. The long process had been begun, but a layoff now could undermine all his efforts and, he felt, lose him what little confidence and support he had been able to encourage.

The strategy for this fall was of critical importance to Bill and his hopes for Artisan and his future.

ARTISAN'S HISTORY

Artisan Industries is the product of a classical entrepreneur—W.A. (Buddy) Meister. After a variety of attempts at self-employment, such as running a dry-cleaning shop, a food shop, and an appliance store, he began to have some success making wooden toys. One try in 1950 with his father and brothers failed, leaving Buddy with an old tin building and some worn-out equipment.

During the next few years Buddy put his efforts into making a collection of 10 to 15 toys, sold via direct mail, house-to-house, on television, and on the roadside, all without a sales representative. One day a visiting gummed-tape salesman offered to take on the line and a pattern of using outside sales reps was established.

The first attempt at a trade show was a last-minute entry into the regional gift show 40 miles away. Out of sympathy for Buddy, Artisan was allowed to pay the $25-a-week rent after the show. Buddy brought home $3,000 in sales but lacked the money to produce them until a friend offered a loan. The orders were produced in a dirt-floor barn. In the following months, Buddy and his wife drove off to other markets, showing the goods in their motel room.

In 1953 sales reached $15,000, then climbed to $30,000 in 1954, $60,000 in 1955, and $120,000 in 1956. Then in April the plant, or barn, burned down destroying everything.

With hardly a delay Buddy jumped into rebuilding and sales continued to double. In 1958, success allowed Artisan to move into a 30,000-square-foot building and continue using its two old buildings for finishing and shipping. Then in March of 1960 these two burned down. Again Buddy fought back and sales doubled into 1961. The rate of growth slowed to 50% in 1962.

The third and most disastrous fire occurred in February of 1963. The entire main plant was burned to the ground with the exception of the new office, which stood under one foot of water and was damaged by smoke and water. The company was in the middle of manufacturing its show orders and the only thing saved was the inventory in the paint shop. All the jigs were burned and before work could begin new jigs and patterns had to be made. "Only the plant in Spencer, built only a year before, saved us. The entire operation, with the exception of the office, was moved to Spencer, and working three shifts, we were able to keep most of the 200 employees. Many employees worked night and day for approximately six months to help us get on our feet again." Before Christmas of 1963 the company was back in full operation in the main plant.

Sales reached $4 million in 1967 and $8 million in 1972. During that six-year span Buddy's five children reached ages to begin full-time jobs in the company. The youngest, Bill, was last to join. Typical of the youngest, he had it best, having all the "toys" his father could provide. He attended Vanderbilt, where he majored in Business Administration and the "good life." But his good time was at last interrupted by graduation and retirement to Artisan.

Bill wanted no major role in the company but over the next three years found himself getting more involved. Buddy had developed no modern management systems; accounting was ineffective, sales was in the control of outside reps, manufacturing was outdated and unprofessional. The lack of order fit Buddy's style—close personal control and manipulation. As the company problems increased, family conflict intensified. Bill's older brother lost the support of his father and the support of the other side and left. Bill moved up to the role of spokesman for a change.

In early 1975, though sales were booming, the financial situation at Artisan was "tight." A second shift was in operation, though production was generally inefficient. By October sales had slackened and in November, to hold inventories down, layoffs began. Accounts receivable were worsening and the worried bankers were forcing the company to pay off some of its $2,500,000 loan. The inventory was reduced some and accounts payable were allowed to increase. In December the plant was closed for three weeks and $100,000 in cash was raised through a warehouse sale. But in the end, 1975 closed with a loss of over a million dollars.

As 1976 began the sales picture looked bad. Even with the large inventory there was difficulty shipping because it contained the wrong things. Since it tied up capital, production of salable items was limited. There were more layoffs and shutdowns in January. Some old suppliers cut off the company's credit. In February, under the threat of the local bank calling the loan, Bill and Bob negotiated a new loan with a New York firm. This was composed of an inventory loan with a ceiling of $500,000, an accounts receivable loan of up to $1 million, and a long-term loan on the warehouse and real estate of approximately $350,000. "The package was finalized and the funds transferred about one week prior to payment deadline with the Bank. Had we not completed the deal with the other group, there was no way we could have made the $25,000 payment," according to Bill.

As the troubles deepened in the spring, Buddy had few solutions and, worse, blocked Bill's actions. The atmosphere in the company became grim. As Bill put it: "It became a fight between who was going to make decisions about what. Through the spring the conflict between us continued at a heightened pace. The effect was that most people became very nervous because no one understood who was really in control. With the company in the financial condition it was then, the last thing it needed was a power struggle over who should be in charge. So in April I went to Buddy and explained the situation that the company needed one person who was clearly in authority and in control, that one person would be better than two, and that I felt that he should leave or I should leave. He suggested that since he had gotten there first, I should leave." Bill went to the mountains for good.

But two weeks later, under pressure from the lenders, Buddy stepped aside and Bill became the chief executive.

In May 1976 when Bill Meister became president, Artisan was in critical condition. Sales had fallen off dramatically, there had been little profit for three years, the number of employees had fallen from 600 to 370, modern management systems existed in no area of the company, and there were few qualified managers. "When I took over, sales were running 50% off and we could not get a line of credit through our suppliers, we were on a cash basis only, inventory was still relatively high, accounts receivable were running over 120 days, manufacturing was without anyone in charge, and the company was sustaining a loss of approximately $10,000 a week. The general situation looked pretty hopeless."

BILL MEISTER'S FIRST YEAR AS PRESIDENT

When Bill became president in May changes began. Although Bill controlled many of the changes, others were the result of actions by his managers or outside forces. By mid-summer of 1976 he had reestablished contact with a business professor he particularly respected at his alma mater and was in regular contact with a management professor at a local school. The small number of trained managers, their lack of experience, and the absence of cooperation among them was a serious handicap to his rebuilding effort. He hoped interaction with the professors would make up for the lack of inside managers to interact with.

Exhibit 5-1 shows the organization chart in June 1977. Buddy moved up to Chairman, but remained around the office. Bill's sister Edith and Uncle Sam helped in the sales area. Another sister, Sally, worked for Bob Atwood in accounting. A new man, Will Shire, was over production, mainly Plant One. Two long-term men, Charles Scott and Jack Lander, headed the plants. Two other long-term employees were in management: Cal Robb over the computer and Richard Bare over purchasing. A young man, Richard Barnes, had been hired recently for plant engineering. Paul Morgan had been with Artisan about two years in design.

Marketing.

The company was one of four making up the wooden decorative products industry. Sales were seasonal, peaking with the Christmas period. Artisan's customers were some 13,000 retail shops that were serviced by outside sales representatives. Regional market shows were an important part of the marketing activity. The product line consisted of over 1,400 items and included almost anything for the customer. The largest item was a tea-cart and the smallest a clothes-pin type desk paper clip. New products were continually coming up; about 100 a year were added to the line. Practically no items were ever dropped. The top 100 products averaged 5,000 units a year. The first 25 items had doubled the sales units of the next group. Two hundred and fifty sold over 1,000 units. The average wholesale price was $3.75. The top item sold 31,000 units last year for about $75,000 in sales. The 200th had sales over $10,000.

Marketing was the function where Bill wanted to spend most of his time. His father had left this mainly with outsiders, but Bill was determined to put the company in charge of its own marketing. He attended all shows and found out firsthand what was going on. He felt the outside sales reps had let Artisan slide into making anything they could sell easily, regardless of costs and profits.

Bill hired a local young man with good design talent, but little experience, to set up a design department. They soon came up with a new "theme" line of items that became the talk of the industry, and Bill planned to try others. He engaged a New York advertising agency for a professional program of advertising in the trade journals and publicity in the newspapers. He produced an artistic catalog with color photographs rather than the dull listing used before.

There had been no price increases in quite a while, and with the recent inflation Atwood estimated the current sales prices would not yield a profit. In mid-October an immediate price increase appeared imperative if 1976 was to end with a profit. But there was great concern about the advisability of such action in the middle of the major sales season. Also, waiting on new price lists to institute the increase in an ordinary manner would not accomplish a 1976 profit; orders already acknowledged or in-house, but not yet acknowledged, exceeded what could be shipped. In fact, as Bill, his sister Edith from sales, Bob Atwood, the computer manager, Cal Robb, and the university professor met to decide what to do, a 30-page order from one store chain for $221,000 at the old prices sat in front of them. Bob and Cal took the position that no further orders should be acknowledged until the customer had been written that prices were increased and asked to mail a reconfirmaton if they still wanted the goods. Edith felt the price increase was very risky and would be very difficult to implement at this time, if even possible. But she had difficulty explaining her views and Bob, with Cal, out-talked her. Bill listened to their arguments as little was accomplished. Only when the consultant added his weight to Edith's views and pointed out the manipu-

EXHIBIT 5-1　ORGANIZATION CHART—ARITSAN INDUSTRIES—JUNE 1977

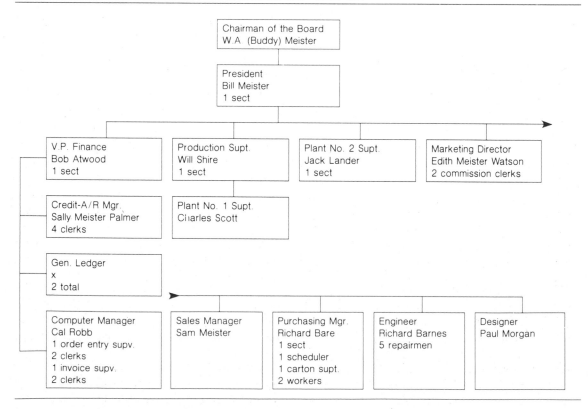

lation and lack of good problem-solving did any practical ideas develop.

A 16% price increase was instituted immediately. The orders awaiting acknowledgment were examined that afternoon and on a priority basis the salespeople were called and informed of the necessity of the increase and asked to contact their customers for immediate approval. When possible, and with moderation, orders at the new prices were given priority over those at the old prices. Within a few days the new prices were contributing to profits.

Bill's most aggressive move was to cancel, in November 1976, the company's long agreement with E. Fudd Associates, a sales representative firm. Accounting for 60% of their sales, Fudd, with 50 salespeople, had handled Artisan's business in about 20 states for many years, and had even lent the company money during the previous December. But Fudd was an old-style "character" much like Buddy—and Bill had been unable to systematically discuss market strategies or improvement ideas with him. Bill felt the 15% commission Fudd was setting could be better used as 10% directly to the salespeople and 5% in a company-controlled advertising budget.

Bill had planned to deal with E. Fudd Associates after the first of the year. It would take careful action to break with Fudd and assist any reps wishing to go independent on Artisan's line. But an accidental leak forced Bill's hand in the middle of the critical sales season. Bill did not back off but broke with Fudd immediately. Fudd countered with suits against Artisan, threats of displacing Artisan's goods with others, claims of tossing Artisan out of major regional market shows, and even withholding back, unpaid commissions on salespeople going with Artisan. Fudd spread rumors of Artisan's impending bankruptcy and sued any sales reps leaving him. Though there were bad moments, Bill held firm and in a few weeks it was over. Bill had gotten all the sales personnel he wanted, was lined up for his own space in the critical

shows, and the rumors were going against Fudd.

Accounting.

With the hiring of Bob Atwood in the fall of 1975, improvement in the accounting systems began, though slowly. By the spring of 1977 the outside service bureau had been replaced by a small in-house computer to handle order-entry and invoicing, including an inventory listing.

The small computer system was delivered in January of 1977. Prior to that $85,000 to $100,000 a year had been spent for assistance from the service bureau. This assistance had been primarily invoicing. After orders were manually checked for accuracy and credit, they went to the service bureau where a warehouse picking ticket was prepared. Then after shipment a form went back to initiate the invoice. Besides invoicing, they produced a monthly statement of bookings and shippings that summarized activity by item, customer, and state. The bureau was not involved with accounts receivable; aging was a manual process that took 30 days and was possibly only accurate to within $25,000. In 1975 checks had been posted, taking about three hours per day, and then forwarded directly to the lender. This had added three to four days of work for Atwood.

The computer had caused a small management crisis for Bill. Cal Robb and Bob Atwood, neither of whom had any special knowledge or experience with computers, had selected the system they wanted with no help beyond that of computer salespeople. With only verbal agreements and several contract notebooks from the supplier, they pressured Bill for his approval. When he failed to act they saw him as foot-dragging and lacking respect for their opinions. With the counsel of the university consultant, Bill took the unpopular step of sending them back to prepare a proper proposal and timetable. In work with the vendor, several serious omissions were found and corrected, and all agreed the further documentation had been worthwhile. Bill approved the project.

The new system consisted of a 48K "small" computer with a 450-line-per-minute printer —two disc drives with two million bytes each, and seven CRTs. Monthly rental amounted to about $4,000. The software was developed in-house by Robb using basic systems supplied by the vendor at no charge. Robb was the only staff for the computer. He was 36, with a business administration degree with some concentration in accounting from a good state university. Prior to Atwood's hiring he had been controller.

By May, inventory accounting was on the computer. The inventory listings computing EOQs were available but inaccurate. Atwood believed a couple of months of debugging was necessary before computer inventory control would be possible. The data needed for the EOQ model were all old and inaccurate; lead times, prepared by a consultant years ago, were considered by all to be way off. They and the standards hadn't been studied in five to six years. For now Atwood felt these listings would be of some help in operating the existing production scheduling system. (EOQ stands for the Economic Order Quantity inventory model.)

By June, invoicing was fully on the computer and the lender had stopped requiring the direct mailing of checks. About 3,000 invoices were prepared each month. The A/R systems, including statements and weekly aging of delinquent accounts, were operational, and about 2,500 statements were being prepared monthly. The controller felt both systems were running well and providing for good control. The computer supplier felt they had been lucky to get the system operational as quickly as they did. (A/R means accounts receivable, A/P means accounts payable.)

Cal expects inventory control will be on the computer by February. In another month he will add A/P payroll and general ledger. Production control must wait on others' work and input.

Monthly preparation of financial state-ments had begun in January. Production costing for the statements had been based on historical indices, but Bob reported little resulting error. The statements were out, in typed form, 30 days after the close of the period.

Production.

There were two plants, roughly identical and five miles apart, each with about 60,000 square feet. Kiln dry lumber, mainly high-quality Ponderosa Pine, was inventoried in truck trailers and covered sheds at the rear of the plant. The lumber width, totally random, depended on the tree, and the length was from 8-16 feet, in multiples of two. The thickness started at the lumber mill at 4, 5, or 6 "quarter" ("quarter" meaning ¼ inch, therefore 4 quarters is 1"). By the time it reached the plant it was about ⅛" less.

The rough mill foreman reviewed the batch of production orders he was given about every week and decided on the "panels" the plant would need. A panel is a sheet of wood milled to a desired thickness and with length and width at the desired dimension or some multiple. Clear panels, ones with no knots, can be made from lower grade lumber by cutting out the defects and then gluing these smaller pieces into standard panels. Artisan did no such gluing but cut high-quality, clear lumber directly to the desired length and width. The necessary panels would be made up in the rough mill from lumber or from purchased glued panels. Artisan spent about as much on purchased panels as it did on raw lumber, paying about twice as much for a square foot of panel as for a square foot of lumber. Surfacers brought the wood to the desired thickness, the finished dimension plus some excess for later sanding. Rip saws cut the lumber to needed width and cut-off saws took care of the length. About 30 people worked in this area, which had about 12% of the labor cost.

The plant superintendent worked with the machine room foreman to decide on the sequence in which orders would be processed. Scheduled due-dates for each department were placed on the orders in production control but they followed up on the actual flow of orders only if a crisis developed. In the machine room 22 workers (17% of the labor cost) shaped panels to the final form. The tools included shapers, molders, routers, and borers. Patterns and jigs lowered the skill requirements, still the highest in the plant. This part of the plant was noisiest and dustiest.

In the third department, sanding, the parts were sanded by women working mainly at individual stations. There were 24 people here. The sanded components were moved to a nearby temporary storage area on the carts, which originated at machining. It was estimated there were 6-8 wooden parts in an average item. In addition there were purchased parts such as turnings and glass or metal parts. Sanding added about 19% of the direct labor to the products.

The assembly foreman kept an eye on the arrival of all parts for an order. Assembly began when all parts were available. Eighteen people assembled the items using glue, screws, nail guns, or hammer and nails. Jigs assisted the work where possible and usually only one person worked on an order. Fourteen percent of direct labor derived from this step. Little skill was needed and dust and noise weren't a problem.

The assembled items were moved promptly to the separate finishing area. Here they were dipped by hand into stains and sprayed with several clear coats. After oven-drying they proceeded to packing. Most were packed individually into cartons made in the company's small plant. Finishing and packing employed about 50 people and accounted for 34% of direct labor costs. The new 60,000 square foot finished goods warehouse was two miles away.

The labor rates ranged from $2.65 to $5.60 per hour. The average was probably $3.00, with about a dozen people making over $4.00. Factory overhead was about 60% of direct labor. Labor costs as a percent of the wholesale selling price ran about 20%; direct material, 35%. Variable costs totaled about 75%, with about another $1,800,000 in total company fixed costs. There was a three percentage point difference between the plants in labor costs. The capacity of the plant with 150 people working was estimated to be less than $110,000 a week. Indirect labor amounted to about 12% of plant overhead.

Most jobs did not require high skill levels. The average jobs in the rough mill and machine room, where the skilled jobs were, required no more than five weeks to master because the person would usually already have advanced skills. Elsewhere a week was adequate. Everyone but the supervisors and workers considered the work pace quite slow.

Production Scheduling.

The production control department began the scheduling process. Exhibit 5-2 outlines the production scheduling system. About every week, sometimes longer, the clerk prepared a batch of production orders for each plant. Several factors determined when a batch of orders was prepared: whether the plants said they needed more work, how sales were doing, what the situation was in the warehouse, etc. The clerk examined the "Weekly Inventory Listing" for items that appeared low and the file of "Progress Control Charts" to see if the items were already on a production order. He converted the information to an available supply in weeks and selected any with less than eight weeks. If the total of orders gotten this way did not add up to an aggregate amount he had in mind, such as $60,000 to $100,000, he went back through the lists for more things to run.

"Production Sheets," or shop orders, were prepared for each item. These contained a drawing and a list of materials and process steps. The data was already prepared and came from consultant studies several years old. The order contained a date the part was due through each department based on standard lead times, for example, one week in the rough mill, three days in machining, etc. The actual work in the plant at the time did not alter lead-times. At the same time a "Progress Control Chart" was prepared for each order. These remained in production control to trace the flow of orders.

The batch of orders was then handed to the plant superintendent who decided exactly how the items would be run. Daily each department gave production control a "Parts Completion Report," listing production from that department—order number, part number, and number produced. The production control clerk posted this information to the "Progress Control Charts." This reporting cycle used to be every two hours. The clerk

reported these charts were not actually used to control production progress; they aided in locating an order if a question arose, but one still had to go out on the floor to be sure.

A brief look at the inventory listing for December showed the first 20 items were 23% of the inventory value. The 10th group of 20 items was 2% of inventory; the cumulative value to this point was 82%. The fortieth item had $1,800 in inventory and the two-hundredth $625.

Turning through the notebook for Plant One "Process Control Charts" on one day showed almost 300 open orders, perhaps 30-50% past the due date. Several items had two or even three different production orders two weeks or so apart. The order size appeared to

EXHIBIT 5–2   PRODUCTION SCHEDULING SYSTEM

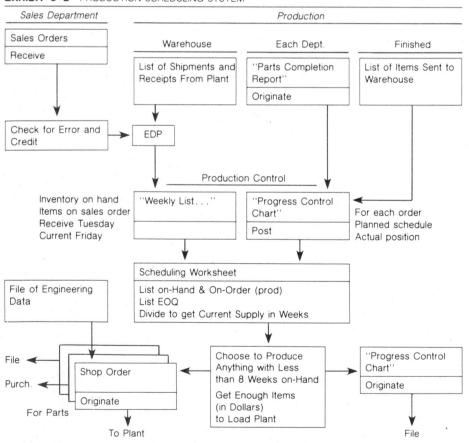

average 200 at most. One in 10 was for more than 250 pieces. Only a couple were for 500 or more; the maximum was 1,000 pieces. The typical items appeared to contain about six parts and each took three to five processing steps.

The engineer was trying to estimate standards for new items as they were priced. A quick look at eight of them showed a total of 1,800 minutes of set-up time for the eight and a total of 6,400 minutes per 100 units of run-time. The set-up times ranged from 100 to 250 minutes for the products, but several of the parts required no set-up in some departments and where there was set-up it amounted to 25% to 50% of the run time for 100. Many parts required less than 30 minutes of processing in a department. The lot size on these ranged from 100 to 200 units; seven were priced around $4.00 and one at $25.00.

Production Problems.

Bill feels production efficiency is a major problem. In talks with machinery salespeople and other visitors to the plant over recent years, Bill has come to feel the machinery is generally appropriate. But based on guesses about his competitors he feels his labor costs must be reduced. Earlier attempts to work with the plant superintendents and the various supervisors to systematically improve output met with no success. The supervisors had been unable to identify the needs for change in the plant or to develop the programs for bringing about improvement. To help the supervisors begin to improve their operations, a weekly production meeting was begun in June 1976. At the meeting the supervisors were to examine the total dollar output and total labor cost for each plant for the past week, compare it to the labor percent goal, 16%, set by Bill, and think about what could be done to improve operations for the coming week. Data on department performance was not available. During the first several meetings, the visiting consultant had to provide direction and ideas; the plant superintendent and his

supervisors volunteered no ideas about what specifically limited last week's output. Bill reported some discussion of problems began three or four months later. It was Bill's opinion that this kind of thinking and planning was not required under his father's management. The supervisors in general felt nothing was wrong in the plant and really seemed puzzled at the thought of doing anything except continuing what they had always done.

In March of 1977, after a good deal of thought and search Bill hired two young men for the production system. One man, Will Shire, aged 28, was hired to be general superintendent over everyone in production, and the other, Richard Barnes, aged 27, was to be manufacturing engineer. It appeared the plant simply needed good management rather than any single big change that could be brought from the outside. Both of these men were young, college trained, and experienced in a wood industry.

Significant resistance from the old superintendent and most of the supervisors seemed probable. Consequently, the new men were briefed on this problem. As expected, things did not advance smoothly. Even as the new men gained familiarity with the operation no significant changes were observed. The expected complaints and rumors were heavy, and Bill ignored them as best he could. However after three months on the job the complaints still persisted and, more importantly, the new superintendent did not appear to have command of the situation. He had not developed his appraisal of what needed to be done and had no comprehensive plan for improvement. Bill recently received very good evidence that Will had some major difficulties in supervising people. One of the supervisors who did not appear to be a part of the rumor campaign and was conscientiously concerned about the company gave Bill examples of the new man's mistakes. Bill felt he may have made a mistake in hiring Will.

Richard's responsibilities have also been

narrowed to more technical tasks. He is supervising the five-person repair crew, engineering some of the new products, examining the procedures for producing samples of new products, and beginning to examine a major redesign of the rough-mill area.

Major Competitor's Production.

The major competitor is Sand Crafters, Inc. A managerial person familiar with both operations provided these comments. Demand for Sand Crafters' products exceeded their capacity and this, in the person's opinion, was the main reason Artisan existed. Their sales were somewhat less than Artisan's, they had no debt, and their equipment was described as new. They were located in a small community where the workers were relatively skilled for this kind of business. The work force was primarily white male. The manager characterized the Artisan worker as about 2/3 as good as Sand Crafters. The workers in the third company in the industry were rated as 1/2. The quality of manufacture of Sand Crafters was considered first, Artisan second, and the third company a close third. Sand Crafters' weakness was in poor engineering of the products and an outdated approach to marketing. Sand Crafters schedules long runs in manufacturing with the objective of having three months' stock of top priority items. They do not use the EOQ Model because they are limited in their work-in-process space.

In describing the Artisan manufacturing system, the person noted that two-thirds of the equipment is idle at any time, and that neither capacity nor optimum production mix have yet been determined. The largest run size he claimed to have seen had been 250. Setup costs he estimated to average $30. He commented that this was the least directed operation he had ever seen, with the slowest pace and the lowest level of knowledge of this type of work. He felt its employees knew only the simple way of doing the job. Only one man in the company, for example, was able to count the board feet of lumber and there was no lumber rule in the plant. He stated that this was a skill that the smallest cabinet shop would have and that it was essential for any kind of usage control.

The Workforce.

Bill was greatly interested in the newest concept of management, frequently pointing to the latest book or sending a copy of an article to his managers or anyone with whom he was interacting. The behavioral writings made a lot of sense to him and he was very perceptive of behavioral processes in meetings or situations. The participative management systems and cooperative team environments were ones Bill wanted for Artisan. However he recognized his managers and the work force were not ready for this yet. His managers manipulated more than cooperated, and the workers were neither skilled nor very productive. When he discussed the workers' desires with the supervisors he was told they wanted a retirement program and higher pay, nothing else. Bill felt this was really what the supervisors themselves wanted.

As a basis for beginning change in this area, an outside consultant conducted an employee attitude survey in May 1977. All employees in the company were assisted in small groups in completing the written questionnaire. The questionnaire was designed: (1) to find out what they wanted, for example, more pay, retirement plans, more or less direction, etc.; (2) to gain insight into the probable impact of participative management moves; (3) to establish benchmarks of employee satisfaction so that changes over time could be monitored; (4) to develop an objective profile of the workers; and (5) to look for significant differences in attitudes between the various stratifications possible.

The survey included questions developed specifically for this situation as well as a highly regarded attitude instrument, the Job Descriptive Index (JDI). Although the wording is considered simple, many of the workers did not understand such words as "stimulating," "ambitious," or "fascinating," and it became necessary to read the entire questionnaire to them.

The study showed minorities accounted for 80% of the 300 employees; white females were the largest group at 40%. The workforce was 58% female, 57% white, and 39% over 45 years old. As many people have been with the company under two years as over 10 years— 24%. The pay was only a little above the legal minimum, but many workers felt fortunate to have their jobs. There did not appear to be a "morale" crisis; the five JDI measures located the company in about the middle of the norms. The supervisory group was highest in "morale" while management was lowest.

Exhibit 5-3 summarizes the Job Descriptive Index scores. The numbers in parentheses show the norms.

Employees were also questioned about a number of aspects of their work climate that could be improved. Exhibit 5-4 shows these questions.

Their expressed view of the organizational climate was relatively good. They claimed to enjoy their work, looked for ways to improve it, and felt expected to do a good job. They expecially felt their coworkers were good to work with and felt part of a team. They appeared to like their supervision.

Their views did not suggest need for a different manner of supervision. And they did not respond positively to the suggestions of being more in charge of themselves, did not feel strongly about having more of a say in how things are done, and didn't feel there were too many rules.

The survey revealed no critical problems, differences between groups were not extreme, and the resulting view of the worker was moderate. However the workers were relatively unsophisticated and there was concern they might not have expressed themselves on the instrument.

THE MEETING WITH BOB ON JUNE 10th

The last months of 1976 had been very good in spite of fears caused by the price increase and the changes in the sales organization, and had resulted in a $390,000 profit. Bob Atwood reported that the original plan for 1977 had been for no major changes—a regrouping, doing as in late 1976, just better. However there was no formal written plan. As actual sales in January and February ran well ahead of the prior year, production was allowed to stay higher than the plan. Bill believed Bob's estimate of sales at $6.5 million was very low. A quite conservative estimate, he felt, was $9.0 million. This level became accepted as the premise for production planning in the first part of the year. But March and April were disappointing and May was only fair. Bill still felt the $9 million was reasonable, as the normal retail sales patterns had been upset by inflation and the fuel crisis. But he recognized the risks and was concerned. He hoped the gift shows in July would settle what 1977 would hold.

On June 10, 1977, Bob Atwood had returned to Bill's office to press for some

EXHIBIT 5-3   SUMMARY OF JDI SCORES BY LEVEL (PERCENTILE)

| Group | Number | Overall | Attitude Towards: | | | | |
			Coworker	Work	Supervision	Promotion	Pay
(Maximum score)		25	54	54	54	27	27
Total Company	318	17.4	41.2	32.3	40.4	11.1	7.1
Management	7	15.9	38.0	39.4	48.0	18.7	15.9
(%)			(35)	(60)	(70)	(80)	(55)
Office	18	16.6	45.8	36.6	47.4	6.9	7.7
(%)			(60)	(50)	(65)	(50)	(25)
Supervision	13	19.7	46.8	39.2	46.1	16.1	12.2
Plant No. 1 Hourly	141	17.1	40.4	31.6	38.4	11.7	6.6
Plant No. 2 Hourly	101	18.1	39.8	31.3	42.6	11.0	5.9

decision on the inventory level. He wanted Bill to pull back on plans for 1977. As sales had been slower coming in and inventories had increased more than expected, Bob had become increasingly worried. The level on the last full inventory listing prepared about six weeks before stood at $800,000 in wooden goods. The current level was nearer $1,100,000. From a financial perspective Bob was willing to accept a level as high as $1,600,000. But this called for limiting production now. His report dated May 13th presented several alternative production levels for the fall, comparing particularly $600,000

EXHIBIT 5–4   RESULTS OF ATTITUDE SURVEY: MAY, 1977

What is your opinion on the following statements? Do you agree or disagree?	Average Employee Response
I enjoy taking the test.	3.97
My pay is fair for this kind of job.	2.26
My coworkers are good to work with.	4.14
My complaints or concerns are heard by management.	3.22
Things are getting better here.	3.45
The supervisors do a poor job.	2.35
I am fortunate to have this job.	3.95
Working conditions are bad here.	2.55
I benefit when the company succeeds.	3.11
I have all the chance I wish to improve myself.	3.19
The company is well run.	3.29
Communications are poor.	2.91
I don't get enough direction from my supervisor.	2.56
I enjoy my work.	4.13
I look for ways to improve the work I do.	4.21
I need more of a chance to manage myself.	3.11
I don't expect to be with the company long.	2.35
Morale is good here.	3.55
We all do only what it takes to get by.	2.19
I am concerned about layoffs and losing my job.	3.51
I like the way my supervisor treats me.	4.02
We need a suggestion system.	3.75
I want more opportunity for advancement.	3.86
My supervisor knows me and what I want.	3.56
We are not expected to do a very good job here.	2.01
There are too many rules.	2.58
I feel like part of a team at work.	3.82
The company and my supervisor seek my ideas.	3.06
I can influence dept. goals, methods and activities	3.01
There is too much "family" here.	2.77
This company is good for the community.	4.22

5 = Strongly agree
1 = Strongly disagree

and $720,000 per month. The advantages and disadvantages of $600,000 vs. $720,000 production levels are as follows:

Advantages and Disadvantages

Advantages of $600,000 Production Level:
1. Reduces scope of operation to afford high degree of control.
2. Maintains positive cash flow position for remainder of year.
3. Maintains more liquid corporate position.

Disadvantages of $600,000 Production Level:
1. More customer dissatisfaction from possible low service level.
2. Probable lost sales if orders increase.

Advantages of $720,000 Production Level:
1. High service level to accounts.
2. Low probability of decrease in service if orders increase.

Disadvantages of $720,000 Production Level:
1. Risk of inventory buildup.
2. Risk of being in a "lay off" situation if orders do not increase.

He advocated a $60,000 per month level.

Bob recommended they immediately cut production and make Richard Bare, the purchasing agent, production control manager with the responsibility for guiding the controlled inventory buildup. Since the desired total inventory level of $1,600,000 was twice the level shown on the last computer listing that included recommended run sizes (EOQs), he felt they could use this part of the computer system as a guide in selectively increasing the inventory. They could double either the Re-Order Points (ROPs) or the lead times in the computer, return the report, and use the new EOQs to double the inventory in a balanced form. Bob felt there had been unnecessary delay in making a decision and was impatient for Bill to put this to rest without further delay.

6

Organizations
You Have Known

The purpose of this exercise is to introduce you to the terminology of organization theory as it applies to actual organizations in your environment. In the normal course of your day you come into contact with many organizations or their products. In considering the variety of organizations that affect your life, reflect on the key characteristics of these organizations as described by an organization theorist. Such a description might include the goals of the organization, the extent of formalization and centralization, the environmental domains, and the type of technology used in the organization.

STEP 1: *Selecting Key Characteristics (30 min.)*

Listed below are concepts used in organization theory to describe organizations and a list of various organizations you may encounter in your everyday life. Working independently and using the concepts provided below, describe the four organizations assigned by your instructor. Compare and contrast the organizations based on your description of each. Depending on time constraints, you may need to do some research on the organizations to be better able to accurately describe all dimensions.

Structural Dimensions	Contextual Dimensions
Formalization	Size
Specialization	Technology
Standardization	Environment
Hieriarchy of authority	Domains
Decentralization	Complex / Simple
Complexity	Stable / Dynamic
Professionalism	Internal Culture
Personnel configuration	Symbols, rituals, values
Structure	Control Systems
Organic vs. Mechanistic	
Product, function, matrix	

Organizations		
Hospital	Automobile dealer	Fast food restaurant
Police dept.	Supermarket	Church
High school	Gas station	Bank
Airport	Newspaper	Construction company
Utility company	Radio station	
U.S. government	Library	

STEP 2: *Small-Group Discussion (20 min.)*

The class will be divided into small groups of two or three. Each group should discuss the exercise, comparing the individual descriptions of each organization. Work towards a consensus as to the most appropriate analysis.

STEP 3: *Class Discussion (15 min.)*

As a class, discuss each organization in terms of the concepts of organization theory. The

following questions may be useful in reviewing the exercise and the dimensions.

DISCUSSION QUESTIONS:

1. Which characteristics are most important
   in understanding organizations? Are the
   same concepts important for each of the
   four organizations selected for the
   exercise?
2. Do the characteristics seem to influence
   the method of operation in each organization? If so, give some examples.
3. Why would there be disagreements in
   describing the organizations by the concepts listed below? Is it possible the
   descriptions might change over time?
   Which characteristics would be affected
   and how?
4. How do the characteristics relate to the
   concept of organizations as open systems?
   Are there characteristics that can apply
   only to an organization that is an open
   system?

II

Design and Structure

7

The Cold Equations

He was not alone.

There was nothing to indicate the fact but the white hand of the tiny gauge on the board before him. The control room was empty but for himself; there was no sound other than the murmur of the drives—the white hand had moved. It had been on zero when the little ship was launched from the *Stardust*; now, an hour later, it had crept up. There was something in the supplies closet across the room, it was saying, some kind of a body that radiated heat.

It could be but one kind of a body—a living, human body.

He leaned back in the pilot's chair and drew a deep, slow breath, considering what he would have to do. He was an EDS pilot, inured to the sight of death, long since accustomed to it and to viewing the dying of another man with an objective lack of emotion, and he had no choice in what he must do. There could be no alternative—but it required a few moments of conditioning for even an EDS pilot to prepare himself to walk across the room and coldly, deliberately, take the life of a man he had yet to meet.

He would, of course, do it. It was the law, stated very bluntly and definitely in grim Paragraph L, Section 8, of Interstellar Regulations: *Any stowaway discovered in an EDS shall be jettisoned immediately following discovery.*

It was the law, and there could be no appeal.

It was a law not of men's choosing but made imperative by the circumstances of the space frontier. Galactic expansion had followed the development of the hyperspace drive and as men scattered wide across the frontier there had come the problem of contact with the isolated first-colonies and exploration parties. The huge hyperspace cruisers were the product of the combined genius and effort of Earth and were long and expensive in the building. They were not available in such numbers that small colonies could possess them. The cruisers carried the colonists to their new worlds and made periodic visits, running on tight schedules, but they could not stop and turn aside to visit colonies

First published in 1954

Written by Tom Godwin. Reprinted by permission of the author and the author's agents, Scott Meredith Literary Agency, Inc., 845 Third Avenue, New York, NY 10022.

scheduled to be visited at another time; such a delay would destroy their schedule and produce a confusion and uncertainty that would wreck the complex interdependence between old Earth and new worlds of the frontier.

Some method of delivering supplies or assistance when an emergency occurred on a world not scheduled for a visit had been needed and the Emergency Dispatch Ships had been the answer. Small and collapsible, they occupied little room in the hold of the cruiser; made of light metal and plastics, they were driven by a small rocket drive that consumed relatively little fuel. Each cruiser carried four EDSs and when a call for aid was received the nearest cruiser would drop into normal space long enough to launch an EDS with the needed supplies or personnel, then vanish again as it continued on its course.

The cruisers, powered by nuclear converters, did not use the liquid rocket fuel but nuclear converters were far too large and complex to permit their installation in the EDSs. The cruisers were forced by necessity to carry a limited amount of bulky rocket fuel and the fuel was rationed with care, the cruiser's computers determining the exact amount of fuel each EDS would require for its mission. The computers considered the course coordinates, the mass of the EDS, the mass of pilot and cargo; they were very precise and accurate and omitted nothing from their calculations. They could not, however, foresee, and allow for, the added mass of a stowaway.

The *Stardust* had received the request from one of the exploration parties stationed on Woden, the six men of the party already being stricken with the fever carried by the green *kala* midges and their own supply of serum destroyed by the tornado that had torn through their camp. The *Stardust* had gone through the usual procedure, dropping into normal space to launch the EDS with the fever serum, then vanishing again in hyperspace. Now, an hour later, the gauge was saying there was something more than the small carton of serum in the supplies closet.

He let his eyes rest on the narrow white door of the closet. There, just inside, another man lived and breathed and was beginning to feel assured that discovery of his presence would now be too late for the pilot to alter the situation. It *was* too late—for the man behind the door it was far later than he thought and in a way he would find terrible to believe.

There could be no alternative. Additional fuel would be used during the hours of deceleration to compensate for the added mass of the stowaway, infinitisemal increments of fuel that would not be missed until the ship had almost reached its destination. Then, at some distance above the ground that might be as near as a thousand feet or as far as tens of thousands of feet, depending upon the mass of ship and cargo and the preceding period of deceleration, the unmissed increments of fuel would make their absence known; the EDS would expend its last drops of fuel with a sputter and go into whistling free fall. Ship and pilot and stowaway would merge together upon impact as a wreckage of metal and plastic, flesh and blood, driven deep into the soil. The stowaway had signed his own death warrant when he concealed himself on the ship; he could not be permitted to take seven others with him.

He looked again at the telltale white hand, then rose to his feet. What he must do would be unpleasant for both of them; the sooner it was over, the better. He stepped across the control room, to stand by the white door.

"Come out!" His command was harsh and abrupt above the murmur of the drive.

It seemed he could hear the whisper of a furtive movement inside the closet, then nothing. He visualized the stowaway cowering closer into one corner, suddenly worried by the possible consequences of his act and his self-assurance evaporating.

"I said *out!*"

He heard the stowaway move to obey and he waited with his eyes alert on the door and his hand near the blaster at his side.

The door opened and the stowaway stepped through it, smiling, "All right—I give up. Now what?"

It was a girl.

He stared without speaking, his hand dropping away from the blaster and acceptance of what he saw coming like a heavy and unexpected physical blow. The stowaway was not a man—she was a girl in her teens, standing before him in little white gypsy sandals with the top of her brown, curly head hardly higher than his shoulder, with a faint, sweet scent of perfume coming from her and her smiling face tilted up so her eyes could look unknowingly and unafraid into his as she wanted for his answer.

Now what? Had it been asked in the deep, defiant voice of a man he would have answered it with action, quick and efficient. He would have taken the stowaway's identification disk and ordered him into the air lock. Had the stowaway refused to obey, he would have used the blaster. It would not have taken long; within a minute the body would have been ejected into space—had the stowaway been a man.

He returned to the pilot's chair and motioned her to seat herself on the boxlike bulk of the drive-control units that sat against the wall beside him. She obeyed, his silence making the smile fade into the meek and guilty expression of a pup that has been caught in mischief and knows it must be punished.

"You still haven't told me," she said. "I'm guilty, so what happens to me now? Do I pay a fine, or what?"

"What are you doing here?" he asked. "Why did you stow away on this EDS?"

"I wanted to see my brother. He's with the government survey crew on Woden and I haven't seen him for ten years, not since he left Earth to go into government survey work."

"What was your destination on the *Stardust?*"

"Mimir. I have a position waiting for me there. My brother has been sending money home all the time to us—my father and mother and I—and he paid for a special course in linguistics I was taking. I graduated sooner than expected and I was offered this job on Mimir. I knew it would be almost a year before Gerry's job was done on Woden so he could come on to Mimir and that's why I hid in the closet, there. There was plenty of room for me and I was willing to pay the fine. There were only the two of us kids—Gerry and I—and I haven't seen him for so long, and I didn't want to wait another year when I could see him now, even though I knew I would be breaking some kind of a regulation when I did it."

I knew I would be breaking some kind of a regulation—In a way, she could not be blamed for her ignorance of the law; she was of Earth and had not realized that the laws of the space frontier must, of necessity, be as hard and relentless as the environment that gave them birth. Yet, to protect such as her from the results of their own ignorance of the frontier, there had been a sign over the door that led to the section of the *Stardust* that housed EDSs, a sign that was plain for all to see and heed:

UNAUTHORIZED PERSONNEL
KEEP OUT!

"Does your brother know that you took passage on the *Stardust* for Mimir?"

"Oh, yes. I sent him a spacegram telling him about my graduation and about going to Mimir on the *Stardust* a month before I left Earth. I already knew Mimir was where he would be stationed in a little over a year. He gets a promotion then, and he'll be based on Mimir and not have to stay out a year at a time on field trips, like he does now."

There were two different survey groups in Woden, and he asked, "What is his name?"

"Cross—Gerry Cross. He's in Group Two —that was the way his address read. Do you know him?"

Group One had requested the serum; Group Two was eight thousand miles away, across the Western Sea.

"No, I've never met him," he said, then turned to the control board and cut the deceleration to a fraction of a gravity, knowing as he did so that it could not avert the ultimate end, yet doing the only thing he could do to prolong that ultimate end. The sensation was like that of the ship suddenly dropping and the girl's involuntary movement of surprise half lifted her from the seat.

"We're going faster now, aren't we?" she asked. "Why are we doing that?"

He told her the truth. "To save fuel for a little while."

"You mean, we don't have very much?"

He delayed the answer he must give her so soon to ask: "How did you manage to stow away?"

"I just sort of walked in when no one was looking my way," she said. "I was practicing my Gelanese on the native girl who does the cleaning in the Ship's Supply office when someone came in with an order for supplies for the survey crew in Woden. I slipped into the closet there after the ship was ready to go and just before you came in. It was an impulse of the moment to stow away, so I could get to see Gerry—and from the way you keep looking at me so grim, I'm not sure it was a very wise impulse.

"But I'll be a model criminal—or do I mean prisoner?" She smiled at him again. "I intended to pay for my keep on top of paying the fine. I can cook and I can patch clothes for everyone and I know how to do all kinds of useful things, even a little bit about nursing."

There was one more question to ask:

"Did you know what the supplies were that the survey crew ordered?"

"Why, no. Equipment they needed in their work, I supposed."

Why couldn't she have been a man with some ulterior motive? A fugitive from justice, hoping to lose himself on a raw new world; an opportunist, seeking transportation to the new colonies where he might find golden fleece for the taking; a crackpot, with a mission—

Perhaps once in his lifetime an EDS pilot would find such a stowaway on his ship, warped men, mean and selfish men, brutal and dangerous men—but never, before, a smiling, blue-eyed girl who was willing to pay her fine and work for her keep that she might see her brother.

He turned to the board and turned the switch that would signal the *Stardust.* The call would be futile but he could not, until he had exhausted that one vain hope, seize her and thrust her into the air lock as he would an animal—or a man. The delay, in the meantime, would not be dangerous with the EDS decelerating at fractional gravity.

A voice spoke from the communicator. *"Stardust.* Identify yourself and proceed."

"Barton, EDS 34G11. Emergency. Give me Commander Delhart."

There was a faint confusion of noises as the request went through the proper channels. The girl was watching him, no longer smiling.

"Are you going to order them to come back after me?" she asked.

The communicator clicked and there was the sound of a distance voice saying, "Commander, the EDS requests—"

"Are they coming back after me?" she asked again. "Won't I get to see my brother, after all?"

"Barton?" The blunt, gruff voice of Commander Delhart came from the communicator. "What's this about an emergency?"

"A stowaway," he answered.

"A stowaway?" there was a slight surprise to the question. "That's rather unusual—but why the 'emergency' call? You discovered him in time so there should be no appreciable danger and I presume you've informed Ship's Records so his nearest relatives can be notified."

"That's why I had to call you first. The stowaway is still aboard and the circumstances are so different—"

"Different?" the commander interrupted, impatience in his voice. "How can they be different? You know you have a limited supply of fuel; you also know the law as well as I do: 'Any stowaway discovered in an EDS shall be jettisoned immediately following discovery.'"

There was the sound of a sharply indrawn breath from the girl. *"What does he mean?"*

"The stowaway is a girl."

"What?"

"She wanted to see her brother. She's only a kid and she didn't know what she was really doing."

"I see." All the curtness was gone from the commander's voice. "So you called me in the hope I could do something?" Without waiting for an answer he went on. "I'm sorry—I can do nothing. This cruiser must maintain its schedule; the life of not one person but the lives of many depend on it. I know how you feel but I'm powerless to help you. You'll have to go through with it. I'll have you connected with Ship's Records."

The communicator faded to a faint rustle of sound and he turned back to the girl. She was leaning forward on the bench, almost rigid, her eyes fixed wide and frightened.

"What did he mean, to go through with it? To jettison me...to go through with it—what did he mean? Not the way it sounded...he couldn't have. What did he mean...what did he really mean?"

Her time was too short for the comfort of a lie to be more than a cruelly fleeting delusion.

"He meant it the way it sounded."

"No!" She recoiled from him as though he had struck her, one hand half upraised as though to fend him off and stark unwillingness to believe in her eyes.

"It will have to be."

"No! You're joking—you're insane! You can't mean it!"

"I'm sorry." He spoke slowly to her, gently. "I should have told you before—I should have, but I had to do what I could first; I had to call the *Stardust.* You heard what the commander said."

"But you can't—if you make me leave the ship, I'll *die.*"

"I know."

She searched his face and the unwillingness to believe left her eyes, giving way slowly to a look of dazed terror.

"You—know?" She spoke the words far apart, numb and wonderingly.

"I know. It has to be like that."

"You mean it—you really mean it." She sagged back against the wall, small and limp like a little rag doll and all the protesting and disbelief gone.

"You're going to do it—you're going to make me die?"

"I'm sorry," he said again. "You'll never know how sorry I am. It has to be that way and no human in the universe can change it."

"You're going to make me die and I didn't do anything to die for—I didn't *do* anything—"

He sighed, deep and weary. "I know you didn't, child. I know you didn't—"

"EDS." the communicator rapped brisk and metallic. "This is Ship's Records. Give us all information on subject's identification disk."

He got out of his chair to stand over her. She clutched the edge of the seat, her upturned face white under the brown hair and the lipstick standing out like a blood-red cupid's bow.

"Now?"

"I want your identification disk," he said.

She released the edge of the seat and fumbled at the chain that suspended the plastic disk from her neck with fingers that were trembling and awkward. He reached down and unfastened the clasp for her, then returned with the disk to his chair.

"Here's your data, Records: Identification Number T837—"

"One moment," Records interrupted. "This is to be filed on the gray card, of course?"

"Yes."

"And the time of the execution?"

"I'll tell you later."

"Later? This is highly irregular; the time of the subject's death is required before—"

He kept the thickness out of his voice with an effort. "Then we'll do it in a highly irregular manner—you'll hear the disk read first. The subject is a girl and she's listening to everything that's said. Are you capable of understanding that?"

There was a brief, almost shocked, silence, then Records said meekly: "Sorry. Go ahead."

He began to read the disk, reading it slowly to delay the inevitable for as long as possible, trying to help her by giving her what little time he could to recover from her first terror and let it resolve into the calm of acceptance and resignation.

"Number T8374-Y54. Name: Marilyn Lee Cross. Sex: Female. Born: July 7, 2160. *She was only eighteen.* Height: 5-3. Weight: 110. *Such a slight weight, yet enough to add fatally to the mass of the shell-thin bubble that was an EDS.* Hair: Brown. Eyes: Blue. Complexion: Light. Blood Type: O. *Irrelevant data.* Destination: Port City, Mimir. *Invalid data—*"

He finished and said, "I'll call you later," then turned once again to the girl. She was huddled back against the wall, watching him with a look of numb and wondering fascination.

"They're waiting for you to kill me, aren't they? They want me dead, don't they? You and everybody on the cruiser wants me dead, don't you?" Then the numbness broke and her voice was that of a frightened and bewildered child. "Everybody wants me dead and I didn't *do* anything. I didn't hurt anyone—I only wanted to see my brother."

"It's not the way you think—it isn't that way, at all," he said. "Nobody wants it this way; nobody would ever let it be this way if it was humanly possible to change it."

"Then why is it? I don't understand. Why is it?"

"This ship is carrying *kala* fever serum to Group One on Woden. Their own supply was destroyed by a tornado. Group Two—the crew your brother is in—is eight thousand miles away across the Western Sea and their helicopters can't cross it to help Group One. The fever is invariably fatal unless the serum can be had in time, and the six men in Group One will die unless this ship reaches them on schedule. These little ships are always given barely enough fuel to reach their destination and if you stay aboard your added weight will cause it to use up all its fuel before it reaches the ground. It will crash, then, and you and I will die and so will the six men waiting for the fever serum."

It was a full minute before she spoke, and

as she considered his words the expression of numbness left her eyes.

"Is that it?" she asked at last. "Just that the ship doesn't have enough fuel?"

"Yes."

"I can go alone or I can take seven others with me—is that the way it is?"

"That's the way it is."

"And nobody wants me to have to die?"

"Nobody."

"Then maybe—Are you sure nothing can be done about it? Wouldn't people help me if they could?"

"Everyone would like to help you but there is nothing anyone can do. I did the only thing I could do when I called the *Stardust.*"

"And it won't come back—but there might be other cruisers, mightn't there? Isn't there any hope at all that there might be someone, somewhere, who could do something to help me?"

She was leaning forward a little in her eagerness as she waited for his answer.

"No."

The word was like the drop of a cold stone and she again leaned back against the wall, the hope and eagerness leaving her face. "You're sure—you *know* you're sure?"

"I'm sure. There are no other cruisers within forty light-years; there is nothing and no one to change things."

She dropped her gaze to her lap and began twisting a pleat of her skirt between her fingers, saying no more as her mind began to adapt itself to the grim knowledge.

It was better so; with the going of all hope would go the fear, with the going of all hope would come resignation. She needed time and she could have so little of it. How much?

The EDSs were not equipped with hull-cooling units; their speed had to be reduced to a moderate level before entering the atmosphere. They were decelerating at .10 gravity, approaching their destination at a far higher speed that the computers had calculated on. The *Stardust* had been quite near Woden when she launched the EDS; their present velocity was putting them nearer by the second. There would be a critical point, soon to be reached, when he would have to resume deceleration. When he did so the girl's weight would be multiplied by the gravities of deceleration, would become, suddenly, a factor of paramount importance, the factor the computers had been ignorant of when they determined the amount of fuel the EDS should have. She would have to go when deceleration began; it could be no other way. When would that be—how long could he let her stay?

"How long can I stay?"

He winced involuntarily from the words that were so like an echo of his own thoughts. How long? He didn't know; he would have to ask the ship's computers. Each EDS was given a meager surplus of fuel to compensate for unfavorable conditions within the atmosphere and relatively little fuel was being consumed for the time being. The memory banks of the computers would still contain all data pertaining to the course set for the EDS; such data would not be erased until the EDS reached its destination. He had only to give the computers the new data; the girl's weight and the exact time at which he had reduced the deceleration to .10.

"Barton." Commander Delhart's voice came abruptly from the communicator, as he opened his mouth to call the *Stardust.* "A check with Records shows me you haven't completed your report. Did you reduce the deceleration?"

So the commander knew what he was trying to do.

"I'm decelerating at point ten," he answered. "I cut the deceleration at 17:50 and the weight is 110. I would like to stay at .10 as long as the computers say I can. Will you give them the question?"

It was contrary to regulations for an EDS pilot to make any changes in the course or degree of deceleration the computers had set for him but the commander made no mention of the violation, neither did he ask the reason for it. It was not necessary for him to ask; he had not become commander of an interstellar cruiser without both intelligence and an understanding of human nature. He said

only, "I'll have that given the computers."

The communicator fell silent and he and the girl waited, neither of them speaking. They would not have to wait long; the computers would give the answer within moments of the asking. The new factors would be fed into the steel maw of the first bank and the electrical impulses would go through the complex circuits. Here and there a relay might click, a tiny cog turn over, but it would be essentially the electrical impulses that found the answer, formless, mindless, invisible, determining with utter precision how long the pale girl beside him might live. Then five little segments of metal in the second bank would trip in rapid succession against an inked ribbon and a second steel maw would spit out the slip of paper that bore the answer.

The chronometer on the instrument board read 18:10 when the commander spoke again.

"You will resume deceleration at 19:10."

She looked toward the chronometer, then quickly away from it. "Is that when . . . when I go?" she asked. He nodded and she dropped her eyes to her lap again.

"I'll have the course corrections given you," the commander said. "Ordinarily I would never permit anything like this but I understand your position. There is nothing I can do, other than what I've just done, and you will not deviate from these new instructions. You will complete your report at 19:10. Now—here are the course corrections."

The voice of some unknown technician read them to him and he wrote them down on the pad clipped to the edge of the control board. There would, he saw, be periods of deceleration when he neared the atmosphere when the deceleration would be five gravities —and at five gravities, 110 pounds would become 550 pounds.

The technician finished and he terminated the contact with a brief acknowledgment. Then, hesitating a moment, he reached out and shut off the communicator. It was 18:13 and he would have nothing to report until 19:10. In the meantime, it somehow seemed indecent to permit others to hear what she might say in her last hour.

He began to check the instrument readings, going over them with unnecessary slowness. She would have to accept the circumstances and there was nothing he could do to help her into acceptance; words of sympathy would only delay it.

It was 18:20 when she stirred from her motionlessness and spoke.

"So that's the way it has to be with me?"

He swung around to face her. "You understand now, don't you? No one would ever let it be like this if it could be changed."

"I understand," she said. Some of the color had returned to her face and the lipstick no longer stood out so vividly red. "There isn't enough fuel for me to stay; when I hid on this ship I got into something I didn't know anything about and now I have to pay for it."

She had violated a man-made law that said KEEP OUT but the penalty was not of man's making or desire and it was a penalty men could not revoke. A physical law had decreed: *h amount of fuel will power an EDS with a mass of m safely to its destination;* and a second physical law had decreed: *h amount of fuel will not power an EDS with a mass of m plus x safely to its destination.*

EDSs obeyed only physical laws and no amount of human sympathy for her could alter the second law.

"But I'm afraid. I don't want to die—not now. I want to live and nobody is doing anything to help me; everybody is letting me go ahead and acting just like nothing was going to happen to me. I'm going to die and nobody *cares.*"

"We all do," he said. "I do and the commander does and the clerk in Ship's Records; we all care and each of us did what little he could to help you. It wasn't enough—it was almost nothing—but it was all we could do."

"Not enough fuel—I can understand that," she said, as though she had not heard his own words. "But to have to die for it. *Me,* alone—"

How hard it must be for her to accept the fact. She had never known danger of death; had never known the environments where the lives of men could be as fragile and fleeting as sea foam tossed against a rocky shore. She belonged on gentle Earth, in that secure and peaceful society where she could be young and gay and laughing with the others of her kind, where life was precious and well-guarded and there was always the assurance that tomorrow would come. She belonged in that world of soft winds and warm suns, music and moonlight and gracious manners and not on the hard, bleak frontier.

"How did it happen to me, so terribly quickly? An hour ago I was on the *Stardust,* going to Mimir. Now the *Stardust* is going on without me and I'm going to die and I'll never see Gerry and Mama and Daddy again —I'll never see anything again."

He hesitated, wondering how he could explain it to her so she would really understand and not feel she had, somehow, been the victim of a reasonlessly cruel injustice. She did not know what the frontier was like; she thought in terms of safe-and-secure Earth. Pretty girls were not jettisoned on Earth; there was a law against it. On Earth her plight would have filled the newscasts and a fast black Patrol ship would have been racing to her rescue. Everyone, everywhere, would have known of Marilyn Lee Cross and no effort would have been spared to save her life. But this was not Earth and there were no Patrol ships, only the *Stardust,* leaving them behind at many times the speed of light. There was no one to help her, there would be no Marilyn Lee Cross smiling from the newscasts tomorrow. Marilyn Lee Cross would be but a poignant memory for an EDS pilot and a name on a gray card in Ship's Records.

"It's different here; it's not like back on Earth," he said. "It isn't that no one cares; it's that no one can do anything to help. The frontier is big and here along its rim the colonies and exploration parties are scattered so thin and far between. On Woden, for example, there are only sixteen men—sixteen men on an entire world. The exploration parties, the survey crews, the little first-colonies—they're all fighting alien environments, trying to make a way for those who will follow after.

The environments fight back and those who go first usually make mistakes only once. There is no margin of safety along the rim of the frontier; there can't be until the way is made for the others who will come later, until the new worlds are tamed and settled. Until then men will have to pay the penalty for making mistakes with no one to help them because there is no one *to* help them."

"I was going to Mimir," she said. "I didn't know about the frontier; I was only going to Mimir and *it's* safe."

"Mimir is safe but you left the cruiser that was taking you there."

She was silent for a little while. "It was all so wonderful at first; there was plenty of room for me on this ship and I would be seeing Gerry so soon...I didn't know about the fuel, didn't know what would happen to me—"

Her words trailed away and he turned his attention to the viewscreen, not wanting to stare at her as she fought her way through the black horror of fear toward the calm gray of acceptance.

Woden was a ball, enshrouded in the blue haze of its atmosphere, swimming in space against the background of star-sprinkled dead blackness. The great mass of Manning's Continent sprawled like a gigantic hourglass in the Eastern Sea with the western half of the Eastern Continent still visible. There was a thin line of shadow along the right-hand edge of the globe and the Eastern Continent was disappearing into it as the planet turned on its axis. An hour before the entire continent had been in view, now a thousand miles of it had gone into the thin edge of shadow and around to the night that lay on the other side of the world. The dark blue spot that was Lotus Lake was approaching the shadow. It was somewhere near the southern edge of the lake that Group Two had their camp. It would be night there, soon, and quick behind the coming of night the rotation of Woden on its axis would put Group Two beyond the reach of the ship's radio.

He would have to tell her before it was too late for her to talk to her brother. In a way, it

would be better for both of them should they not do so but it was not for him to decide. To each of them the last words would be something to hold and cherish, something that would cut like the blade of a knife yet would be infinitely precious to remember, she for her own brief moments to live and he for the rest of his life.

He held down the button that would flash the grid lines on the view-screen and used the known diameter of the planet to estimate the distance the southern tip of Lotus Lake had yet to go until it passed beyond radio range. It was approximately five hundred miles. Five hundred miles; thirty minutes— and the chronometer read 18:30. Allowing for error in estimating, it could not be later than 19:05 that the turning of Woden would cut off her brother's voice.

The first border of the Western Continent was already in sight along the left side of the world. Four thousand miles across it lay the shore of the Western Sea and the Camp of Group One. It has been in the Western Sea that the tornado had originated, to strike with such fury at the camp and destroy half their prefabricated buildings, including the one that housed the medical supplies. Two days before the tornado had not existed; it had been no more than great gentle masses of air out over the calm Western Sea. Group One had gone about their routine survey work, unaware of the meeting of the air masses out at sea, unaware of the force the union was spawning. It had struck their camp without warning, a thundering, roaring destruction that sought to annihilate all that lay before it. It had passed on, leaving the wreckage in its wake. It had destroyed the labor of months and had doomed six men to die and then, as though its task was accomplished, it once more began to resolve into gentle masses of air. But for all its deadliness, it had destroyed with neither malice nor intent. It had been a blind and mindless force, obeying the laws of nature, and it would have followed the same course with the same fury had men never existed.

Existence required Order and there was

order; the laws of nature, irrevocable and immutable. Men could learn to use them but men could not change them. The circumference of a circle was always pi times the diameter and no science of Man would ever make it otherwise. The combination of chemical A with chemical B under condition C invariably produced reaction D. The law of gravitation was a rigid equation and it made no distinction between the fall of a leaf and the ponderous circling of a binary star system. The nuclear conversion process powered the cruisers that carried men to the stars; the same process in the form of a nova would destroy a world with equal efficiency. The laws *were,* and the universe moved in obedience to them. Along the frontier were arrayed all the forces of nature and sometimes they destroyed those who were fighting their way outward from Earth. The men of the frontier had long ago learned the bitter futility of cursing the forces that would destroy them for the forces were blind and deaf, the futility of looking at the heavens for mercy, for the stars of the galaxy swung in their long, long sweep of two hundred million years, as inexorably controlled as they by the laws that knew neither hatred nor compassion.

The men of the frontier knew—but how was a girl from Earth to fully understand? *H amount of fuel will not power an EDS with a mass of m plus x safely to its destination.* To himself and her brother and parents she was a sweet-faced girl in her teens; to the laws of nature she was *x,* the unwanted factor in a cold equation.

She stirred again on the seat, "Could I write a letter? I want to write to Mama and Daddy and I'd like to talk to Gerry. Could you let me talk to him over your radio there?"

"I'll try to get him," he said.

He switched on the normal-space transmitter and pressed the signal button. Someone answered the buzzer almost immediately.

"Hello. How's it going with you fellows now—is the EDS on its way?"

"This isn't Group One; this is the EDS," he said. "Is Gerry Cross there?"

"Gerry? He and two others went out in the helicopter this morning and aren't back yet. It's almost sundown, though, and he ought to be back right away—in less than an hour at the most."

"Can you connect me through to the radio in his 'copter?"

"Huh-uh. It's been out of commission for two months—some printed circuits went haywire and we can't get any more until the next cruiser stops by. Is it something important—bad news for him, or something?"

"Yes—it's very important. When he comes in get him to the transmitter as soon as you possibly can."

"I'll do that. I'll have one of the boys waiting at the field with a truck. Is there anything else I can do?"

"No, I guess that's all. Get him there as soon as you can and signal me."

He turned the volume to an inaudible minimum, an act that would not affect the functioning of the signal buzzer, and unclipped the pad of paper from the control board. He tore off the sheet containing his flight instructions and handed the pad to her, together with pencil.

"I'd better write to Gerry, too," she said as she took them. "He might not get back to camp in time."

She began to write, her fingers still clumsy and uncertain in the way they handled the pencil and the top of it trembling a little as she poised it between words. He turned back to the viewscreen, to stare at it without seeing it.

She was a lonely little child, trying to say her last good-by, and she would lay out her heart to them. She would tell them how much she loved them and she would tell them to not feel badly about it, that it was only something that must happen eventually to everyone and she was not afraid. The last would be a lie and it would be there to read between the sprawling, uneven lines, a valiant little lie that would make the hurt all the greater for them.

Her brother was of the frontier and he would understand. He would not hate the EDS pilot for doing nothing to prevent her

going; he would know there had been nothing the pilot could do. He would understand,
though the understanding would not soften
the shock and pain when he learned his sister
was gone. But the others, her father and
mother—they would not understand. They
were of Earth and they would think in the
manner of those who had never lived where
the safety margin of life was a thin, thin line
—and sometimes not at all. What would they
think of the faceless, unknown pilot who had
sent her to her death?

They would hate him with cold and terrible intensity but it really didn't matter. He
would never see them, never know them. He
would have only the memories to remind
him, only the nights to fear, when a blue-eyed
girl in gypsy sandals would come in his
dreams to die again—

He scowled at the viewscreen and tried to
force his thoughts into less emotional channels. There was nothing he could do to help
her. She had unknowingly subjected herself
to the penalty of a law that recognized neither
innocence nor youth nor beauty, that was
incapable of sympathy or leniency. Regret
was illogical—and yet, could knowing it to
be illogical ever keep it away?

She stopped occasionally, as though trying
to find the right words to tell them what she
wanted them to know, then the pencil would
resume its whispering to the paper. It was
18:37 when she folded the letter in a square
and wrote a name on it. She began writing
another, twice looking up at the chronometer
as though she feared the black hand might
reach its rendezvous before she had finished.
It was 18:45 when she folded it as she had
done the first letter and wrote a name and
address on it.

She held the letters out to him. "Will you
take care of these and see that they're
enveloped and mailed?"

"Of course." He took them from her hand
and placed them in a pocket of his gray uniform shirt.

"These can't be sent off until the next
cruiser stops by and the *Stardust* will have
long since told them about me, won't it?" she

asked. He nodded and she went on, "That
makes the letters not important in one way
but in another way they're very important—to
me, and to them."

"I know. I understand, and I'll take care of
them."

She glanced at the chronometer, then back
to him. "It seems to move faster all the time,
doesn't it?"

He said nothing, unable to think of anything to say, and she asked, "Do you think
Gerry will come back to camp in time?"

"I think so. They said he should be in right
away."

She began to roll the pencil back and forth
between her palms. "I hope he does. I feel
sick and scared and I want to hear his voice
again and maybe I won't feel so alone. I'm a
coward and I can't help it."

"No," he said, "you're not a coward.
You're afraid, but you're not a coward."

"Is there a difference?"

He nodded. "A lot of difference."

"I feel so alone. I never did feel like this
before, like I was all by myself and there was
nobody to care what happened to me. Always,
before, there was Mama and Daddy there and
my friends around me. I had lots of friends,
and they had a going-away party for me the
night before I left."

Friends and music and laughter for her to
remember—and on the viewscreen Lotus
Lake was going into the shadow.

"Is it the same with Gerry?" she asked. "I
mean, if he should make a mistake, would he
have to die for it, all alone and with no one to
help him?"

"It's the same with all along the frontier; it
will always be like that so long as there is a
frontier."

"Gerry didn't tell us. He said the pay was
good and he sent money home all the time
because Daddy's little shop just brought in a
bare living but he didn't tell us it was like
this."

"He didn't tell you his work was
dangerous?"

"Well—yes. He mentioned that, but we
didn't understand. I always thought danger

55

along the frontier was something that was a lot of fun, an exciting adventure, like in the three-D shows." A wan smile touched her face for a moment. "Only it's not, is it? It's not the same at all, because when it's real you can't go home after the show is over."

"No," he said. "No, you can't."

Her glance flicked from the chronometer to the door of the air lock then down to the pad and pencil she still held. She shifted her position slightly to lay them on the bench beside, moving one foot out a little. For the first time he saw that she was not wearing Vegan gypsy sandals but only cheap imitations; the expensive Vegan leather was some kind of grained plastic, the silver buckle was gilded iron, the jewels were colored glass. *Daddy's little shop just brought in a bare living*—She must have left college in her second year, to take the course in linguistics that would enable her to make her own way and help her brother provide for her parents, earning what she could by part-time work after classes were over. Her personal possessions on the *Stardust* would be taken back to her parents—they would neither be of much value nor occupy much storage space on the return voyage.

"Isn't it—" She stopped, and he looked at her questioningly. "Isn't it cold in here?" she asked, almost apologetically. "Doesn't it seem cold to you?"

"Why, yes," he said. He saw by the main temperature gauge that the room was at precisely normal temperature. "Yes, it's colder than it should be."

"I wish Gerry would get back before it's too late. Do you really think he will, and you didn't just say so to make me feel better?"

"I think he will—they said he would be in pretty soon." On the viewscreen Lotus Lake had gone into the shadow but for the thin blue line of its western edge and it was apparent he had overestimated the time she would have in which to talk to her brother. Reluctantly, he said to her, "His camp will be out of radio range in a few minutes; he's on that part of Woden that's in the shadow"—he indicated the viewscreen—"and the turning of

Woden will put him beyond contact. There may not be much time left when he comes in —not much time to talk to him before he fades out. I wish I could do something about it—I would call him right now if I could."

"Not even as much time as I will have to stay?"

"I'm afraid not."

"Then—" She straightened and looked toward the air lock with pale resolution. "Then I'll go when Gerry passes beyond range. I won't wait any longer after that—I won't have anything to wait for."

Again there was nothing he could say.

"Maybe I shouldn't wait at all. Maybe I'm selfish—maybe it would be better for Gerry if you just told him about it afterward."

There was an unconscious pleading for denial in the way she spoke and he said, "He wouldn't want you to do that, to not wait for him."

"It's already coming dark where he is, isn't it? There will be all the long night before him, and Mama and Daddy don't know yet that I won't ever be coming back like I promised them I would. I've caused everyone I love to be hurt, haven't I? I didn't want to—I didn't intend to."

"It wasn't your fault," he said. "It wasn't your fault at all. They'll know that. They'll understand."

"At first I was so afraid to die that I was a coward and thought only of myself. Now, I see how selfish I was. The terrible thing about dying like this is not that I'll be gone but that I'll never see them again, never be able to tell them that I didn't take them for granted, never be able to tell them I knew of the sacrifices they made to make my life happier, that I knew all the things they did for me and that I loved them so much more than I ever told them. I've never told them any of those things. You don't tell them such things when you're young and your life is all before you—you're afraid of sounding sentimental and silly.

"But it's so different when you have to die —you wish you had told them while you could and you wish you could tell them you're sorry for all the little mean things you ever did or said to them. You wish you could tell them that you didn't really mean to ever hurt their feelings and for them to only remember that you always loved them far more than you ever let them know."

"You don't have to tell them that," he said. "They will know—they've always known it."

"Are you sure?" she asked. "How can you be sure? My people are strangers to you."

"Wherever you go, human nature and human hearts are the same."

"And they will know what I want them to know—that I love them?"

"They've always known it, in a way far better than you could ever put into words for them."

"I keep remembering the things they did for me, and it's the little things they did that seem to be the most important to me now. Like Gerry—he sent me a bracelet of fire-rubies on my sixteenth birthday. It was beautiful—it must have cost him a month's pay. Yet, I remember him more for what he did the night my kitten got run over in the street. I was only six years old and he held me in his arms and wiped away my tears and told me not to cry, that Flossy was gone for just a little while, for just long enough to get herself a new fur coat and she would be on the foot of my bed the very next morning. I believed him and quit crying and went to sleep dreaming about my kitten coming back. When I woke up the next morning, there was Flossy on the foot of my bed in a brand-new white fur coat, just like he had said she would be.

"It wasn't until a long time later that Mama told me Gerry had got the pet-shop owner out of bed at four in the morning and, when the man got mad about it, Gerry told him he was either going to go down and sell him the white kitten right then or he'd break his neck."

"It's always the little things you remember people by, all the little things they did because they wanted to do them for you. You've done the same for Gerry and your father and mother, all kinds of things that

you've forgotten about but that they will never forget."

"I hope I have. I would like for them to remember me like that."

"They will."

"I wish—" She swallowed. "The way I'll die—I wish they wouldn't ever think of that. I've read how people look who die in space—their insides all ruptured and exploded and their lungs out between their teeth and then, a few seconds later, they're all dry and shapeless and horribly ugly. I don't want them to ever think of me as something dead and horrible, like that."

"You're their own, their child and their sister. They could never think of you other than the way you would want them to, the way you looked the last time they saw you." "I'm still afraid," she said. "I can't help it, but I don't want Gerry to know it. If he gets back in time, I'm going to act like I'm not afraid at all and—"

The signal buzzer interrupted her, quick and imperative.

"Gerry!" She came to her feet. "It's Gerry, now!"

He spun the volume control knob and asked, "Gerry Cross?"

"Yes," her brother answered, an undertone of tenseness to his reply. "The bad news—what is it?"

She answered for him, standing close behind him and leaning down a little toward the communicator, her hand resting small and cold on his shoulder.

"Hello, Gerry." There was only a faint quaver to betray the careful casualness of her voice. "I wanted to see you—"

"Marilyn!" There was a sudden and terrible apprehension in the way he spoke her name. "What are you doing on that EDS?"

"I wanted to see you," she said again. "I wanted to see you, so I hid on this ship—"

"You *hid* on it?"

"I'm a stowaway...I didn't know what it would mean—"

"Marilyn!" It was the cry of a man who calls hopeless and desperate to someone

already and forever gone from him. "What have you done?"

"I . . . it's not—" Then her own composure broke and the cold little hand gripped his shoulder convulsively. "Don't, Gerry—I only wanted to see you; I didn't intend to hurt you. Please, Gerry, don't feel like that—"

Something warm and wet splashed on his wrist and he slid out of the chair, to help her into it and swing the microphone down to her own level.

"Don't feel like that—Don't let me go knowing you feel like that—"

The sob she had tried to hold back choked in her throat and her brother spoke to her. "Don't cry, Marilyn." His voice was suddenly deep and infinitely gentle, with all the pain held out of it. "Don't cry, Sis—you mustn't do that. It's all right, Honey—everything is all right."

"I—" Her lower lip quivered and she bit into it. "I didn't want you to feel that way—I just wanted us to say good-by because I have to go in a minute."

"Sure—sure. That's the way it will be, Sis. I didn't mean to sound the way I did." Then his voice changed to a tone of quick and urgent demand. "EDS—have you called the *Stardust*? Did you check with the computers?"

"I called the *Stardust* almost an hour ago. It can't turn back, there are no other cruisers within forty light-years, and there isn't enough fuel."

"Are you sure that the computers had the correct data—sure of everything?"

"Yes—do you think I could ever let it happen if I wasn't sure? I did everything I could. If there was anything at all I could do now, I would do it."

"He tried to help me, Gerry." Her lower lip was no longer trembling and the short sleeves of her blouse were wet where she had dried her tears. "No one can help me and I'm not going to cry any more and everything will be all right with you and Daddy and Mama, won't it?"

"Sure—sure it will. We'll make out fine." Her brother's words were beginning to

come in more faintly and he turned the volume control to maximum. "He's going out of range," he said to her. "He'll be gone within another minute."

"You're fading out, Gerry," she said. "You're going out of range. I wanted to tell you—but I can't now. We must say good-by so soon—but maybe I'll see you again. Maybe I'll come to you in your dreams with my hair in braids and crying because the kitten in my arms is dead; maybe I'll be the touch of a breeze that whispers to you as it goes by; maybe I'll be one of those gold-winged larks you told me about, singing my silly head off to you; maybe, at times, I'll be nothing you can see but you will know I'm there beside you. Think of me like that, Gerry, always like that and not—the other way."

Dimmed to a whisper by the turning of Woden, the answer came back:

"Always like that Marilyn—always like that and never any other way."

"Our time is up, Gerry—I have to go now. Good—" Her voice broke in mid-word and her mouth tried to twist into crying. She passed her hand hard against it and when she spoke again the words came clear and true:

"Good-by, Gerry."

Faint and ineffably poignant and tender, the last words came from the cold metal of the communicator:

"Good-by, little sister—"

She sat motionless in the hush that followed, as though listening to the shadow-echoes of the words as they died away, then she turned away from the communicator, toward the air lock, and he pulled the black lever beside him. The inner door of the air lock slid swiftly open, to reveal the bare little cell that was waiting for her, and she walked to it.

She walked with her head up and the brown curls brushing her shoulders, with the white sandals stepping as sure and steady as the fractional gravity would permit and the gilded buckles twinkling with little lights of blue and red and crystal. He let her walk alone and made no move to help her, knowing she would not want it that way. She stepped into the air lock and turned to face him, only the pulse in her throat to betray the wild beating of her heart.

"I'm ready," she said.

He pushed the lever up and the door slid its quick barrier between them, enclosing her in black and utter darkness for her last moments of life. It clicked as it locked in place and he jerked down the red lever. There was a slight waver to the ship as the air gushed from the lock, a vibration to the wall as though something had bumped the outer door in passing, then there was nothing and the ship was dropping true and steady again. He shoved the red lever back to close the door on the empty air lock and turned away, to walk to the pilot's chair with the slow steps of a man old and weary.

Back in the pilot's chair he pressed the signal button of the normal-space transmitter. There was no response; he had expected none. Her brother would have to wait through the night until the turning of Woden permitted contact through Group One.

It was not yet time to resume deceleration and he waited while the ship dropped endlessly downward with him and the drives purred softly. He saw that the white hand of the supplies closet temperature gauge was on zero. A cold equation had been balanced and he was alone on the ship. Something shapeless and ugly was hurrying ahead of him, going to Woden where its brother was waiting through the night, but the empty ship still lived for a little while with the presence of the girl who had not known about the forces that killed with neither hatred nor malice. It seemed, almost, that she still sat small and bewildered and frightened on the metal box beside him, her words echoing hauntingly clear in the void she had left behind her:

I didn't do anything to die for—I didn't do anything—

8

Outdoor Outfitters, Ltd.

The early 1970s witnessed an explosion of interest in outdoor activites such as camping, backpacking, canoeing, and hiking. This trend substantially increased sales of recreation vehicles, including four-wheel drives, campers, and trail bikes. But Outdoor Outfitters, Ltd., a small chain of mountain equipment suppliers, was determined to carry only ecologically safe and sound items—those that are noiseless, nondestructive, and self-propelled. They furthered this image by sponsoring free outdoor country and bluegrass music concerts and other events. A recent catalog of Outdoor Outfitters, Ltd. carried this message:

WE HAVE COMPLETED OUR REMODELING!!!

Over the past few months, Outdoor Outfitters, Ltd. has been expanding (thanks to your patronage). During that time the store was a mess and service was a little. . .confusing, at best. But that's over with now.

We have enlarged and remodeled our showroom. The walls and display fixtures are done with some beautiful locally milled poplar boards and our stone work with local rip rap. We're ready for business now, so stop in and take a look at our new store.

Our People *Outdoor Outfitters, Ltd. is staffed by individuals who have been involved in outdoor activities for years. We actively use the equipment we sell and can give competent advice on its selection and usage. Educating the public is one of our main concerns and with this in mind, we sponsor educational seminars and trips throughout the year.*

Our Products *The companies. . .whose products we carry manufacture some of the finest outdoor recreation equipment in the world. From the Appalachians to the Himalayas, the products we handle have been tested and refined by generations of outdoorsmen.*

The term "leisure goods" is appropriate to recreation equipment since they are used in one's spare time. Hence, sales depend on the excess time available to the potential purchaser. While the work week has remained constant at 40 hours since World War II, the average work year has been reduced by longer vacations and additional paid

Reprinted by permission of Paul Miesing, Assistant Professor, School of Business, State University of New York at Albany.

holidays. Now up to one-third of the average American's time can be considered "free" or unoccupied. Much of this time is spent with the family, and leisure is now considered a necessity by many.

Recreation expenditures also depend on the money available to the potential buyer. Sales of these items generally keep pace with disposable income. Of these expenditures, approximately $12 billion a year is spent on sporting goods, with camping, skiing, and fishing equipment purchases equalling nearly $.5 billion each. Although growth for this industry is expected to surpass the economy as a whole, it should not match the rate experienced in the '60s and early '70s due to the dampening effects of inflation. (See Exhibit 8-1.)

Typically, buyers of leisure-oriented goods search for and demand information, are emotionally involved with their purchase, and have the option of postponing it. And since these goods satisfy needs for self-fulfillment and self-expression, there is little brand loyalty. Instead, purchasers are tremendously influenced by friends, experts, and magazine editorials. Furthermore, since first-time purchasers also tend to fall in the 19-24-year-old age group and are extremely fearful of making a wrong choice, these individuals are avid comparison shoppers, take longer to decide, and are price conscious. In short, the "right" equipment is usually one that is economi-

cally painless yet chic. On balance, the net result has been larger sales of quality and durable items, with the weakest sellers being the inexpensive ends of the lines.

In addition to time, money, and psychological fulfillment, demand for recreation equipment is also influenced by available "support" facilities, such as the mountains and streams of the nearby environment. Jefferson City, a middle-sized university town and headquarters for Outdoor Outfitters, Ltd., is well-suited for this since it is situated close to many national parks and national forests.

The area also draws thousands of visitors each year as a major tourist and recreational center. This attraction is reflected in the town's annual general merchandise sales (including variety and general stores) of around $50 million, with an identical amount attributed to department store sales. In addition, the median age—heavily influenced by the student population—is 28 for men and 30 for women, with approximately one-fourth of the workforce considered professionals and one-half considered white-collar.

Outdoor Outfitters, Ltd. was started in 1972 as the outgrowth of an M.B.A. thesis at the State University in Jefferson City. Having experienced several setbacks during 1973, it was sold by the founder in 1974. The company then began to reach a very good average annual growth rate as several additional

EXHIBIT 8-1   OUTDOOR OUTFITTERS, LTD.
Financial Statistics for Selected Firms For 1977

	5-yr. Avge. ROE	1-yr. Avge. ROE	5-yr. Avge. ROC	1-yr. Avge. ROC	Net Profit Margin	5-yr. Avge. Sales
AMF, Inc	13.3%	12.9%	8.9%	9.7%	3.3%	8.8%
Brunswick	12.3%	10.9	9.5	8.6	4.0	11.1
Fuqua	5.3	10.5	4.9	7.3	2.7	10.2
Recreation Industry Median	12.7	13.3	9.5	10.1	3.8	10.9
All Leisure Industry Median	15.1	17.5	11.1	12.7	5.4	11.2

ROE=return on equity
ROC=return on capital

stores were gradually opened along the foot-hills of the nearby mountain range, with Jefferson City serving as the center for these distant operations. However, sales at the Jefferson City store began to level off during the renovation in 1976 and 1977. Although some momentum was lost at this branch, it did not prevent the company as a whole from maintaining its above-average growth rate.

The location of the Jefferson City store was well-suited. The only local store carrying specialized recreation goods (except for several discount and general department stores), it was set in off the main thoroughfare through town—accessible, yet isolated. The store itself was somewhat disorganized, but this appearance only emphasized the casual atmosphere of the place.

With knowledgeable sales help, there was originally little need for direction by the managers. But the increase in size also brought about an increase in complexity, and so the acquirers decided to organize the operations by geographic area (see Exhibit 8-2) and to centrally manage the branches so as to achieve scale economies and greater purchasing power. The local managers retained the authority to stock, promote, and staff their branches within the budgetary guidelines. In addition, all the managers would attend monthly meetings that—among other things—determined the inventory to be purchased.

EXHIBIT 8–2 OUTDOOR OUTFITTERS, LTD.
Organization Chart

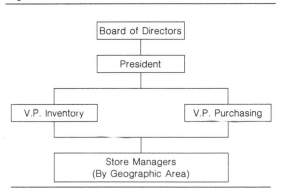

EXHIBIT 8–3 OUTDOOR OUTFITTERS, LTD.
Relative Productivity of Jefferson City Store

	Jefferson City Store	Average For Other Branches
Number Part-Time Employees	9	7
Number Full-Time Employees	2	2
Annual Employee-Hours	7,000	6,000
Sales per Employee-Hour	$32	$24

One aspect of this reorganization included a formal inventory control system, whereby items would be ordered monthly based on the prior year's sales. Actual stock levels were then recorded from sales tickets for the past week. Management planned to check this running tabulation periodically for accuracy of item, code number, color, and size, and to readjust any discrepancies. Examination of four random sales days revealed that, whereas the other branch stores averaged 4.5 recording errors per day, the Jefferson City store averaged 9 recording errors per day over the same period. (See Exhibit 8-3 for relative productivity estimates.)

Management also attempted to coordinate the stores with inter-company store transfers of merchandise. The company's purchaser relies heavily on reports from the manufacturers' representatives on which items are selling well, so he would determine each store's requirements and make allocations as he saw fit. Imbalances between local supply and demand required special shipping arrangements between branches, causing both delays and unnecessary expenses. Although the other stores averaged 7.5 such transfer requests per week, the Jefferson City branch made 11.5 inter-store transfer requests per week.

Special order requests also boosted costs. Generally under $50 each, every special order requires 15 minutes of processing time, both going out and coming in. In addition, costs add up for shipping and handling, telephone, administration, errors—and occasionally the cost of a customer failing to pick up a special order. As a result, management is considering instituting a service charge for special orders, or perhaps offering a discount to customers willing to switch preference toward items in stock. But so far, the sales help is reluctant to either request deposits for special orders or to recommend substitutions.

The Jefferson City store sales projections for 1978 have been lowered by 10% and profits by 20% based on early figures (at a time when other local businesses expect increased sales of 10%). The store's president wrote a recent memo, excerpted here:

Our current sales staff at the Jefferson City store consists of young, part-time individuals. As such, they continue to demonstrate an independence not welcome considering our recent setbacks. They are arrogant and impolite to customers. Their work pace is slow, and they avoid responsibility, claiming an unfamiliarity with our established procedures. They are obviously unaware of the costs involved for their practices. They continue to recommend items to our customers that they enjoy rather than attempt to sell what's on hand. This only leads to expensive imbalances in our inventory, inter-

store transfers, and special orders. In addition, they are sloppy and careless in their recording of items sold, further throwing off our inventory control. I really don't think they take this business seriously. Finally, they have demonstrated resistance to our improved system of operations and sabotage every new procedure we attempt to introduce. In short, they apparently do not have our interests at stake but only their own. With this in mind, I suggest we immediately replace the Jefferson City sales staff with more experienced full-time professional salesmen.

All these problems are now coming to a head. Management is contemplating further expansion by diversifying into such items as sportswear, cross-country skies, and even snowmobiles. In order to better implement this planned growth, management feels it needs to tighten the reins on the operations so that the various stores will be better coordinated. This need was particularly evident when the Jefferson City store introduced sports-shirts. Resentment from the sales help resulted in low sales, even though they might have earned a high commission on them.

9

How Sears Became a High-Cost Operator

In 1973, when Sears, Roebuck & Co. moved its headquarters, it seemed fitting that it was placed in the world's tallest building. Sears had always been associated with superlatives —biggest, best, and sharpest. The envy of its competitors, the huge retailer was second to none in its ability to ferret out innovative products and to get suppliers to provide them at the lowest cost. Its mail-order catalog was the largest of its kind, and its 860 stores, many of which were located in the first suburban shopping centers, represented the epitome of convenience. Its staff was huge—more than 400,000 employees—and where other retailers made do with just two buyers for a single line of merchandise, Sears could seek out sources with as many as 10.

But no one is envying the giant today. It has become the highest-cost mass merchandiser in the business, with general and administrative expenses siphoning off 29% of its sales dollars, compared with 23% for J. C. Penney Co. and 19% for K-Mart Corp. One competitor estimates that Sears would need to "weed out at least $100 million a year" to be competitive with low-cost retailers such as K-Mart. He guesses that, with Sears's "cumbersome" cost structure, Sears needs a 50% markup to make a profit on items that competitors need mark up only 35%.

Indeed, Sears's merchandising profit margin plunged to 2.2% in 1979 from 3.1% in 1976 and is expected to fall even further when 1980 figures are tallied. Its merchandising profits have slipped precipitously to $367 million in 1979 from $439 million in 1976 on stagnant annual sales of about $17 billion in the same period. In the first nine months of 1980, earnings plunged an additional 80% from the same period in 1979 on sales of $12 billion. Further, its credit-card operations lost $8.1 million in the first nine months of 1980. Wall Street has graded this performance by pushing the stock near its 20-year low.

TRIAL AND ERROR.

Indeed, the only bright spots in an otherwise dismal scene are Sears's insurance and real estate operations, areas that have little to do with the company's traditional retailing business. As if to underline the despair over its

Reprinted from the February 16, 1981, issue of *Business Week* by special permission, copyright © 1981 by McGraw-Hill, Inc.

core business, last year Chairman Edward R. Telling reorganized Sears into a semiholding company, in effect divorcing himself from the actual management of the troubled retailing operation. The rationale was that the move would allow Telling, a merchandising executive, to concentrate on new growth opportunities. Says Telling, "Businesses with the greatest growth potential and most promise will undoubtedly be those that have first call on assets."

Still, Sears's retailing operations account for 68% of overall revenues, and Telling cannot cut them off at the pockets without creating a fatal wound. The new managers of the operations have invested in some significant changes, such as centralizing purchasing stations, early-retirement incentives, and store modernization. And Telling is demonstrating a willingness to enter new retail growth areas: on Jan. 22, Sears announced the opening of five freestanding business machine stores that are to be the front-runners of a network of stores geared to capitalize on the growing interest in electronic equipment from both business managers and home users.

Whether the stores are successful or not, they represent a newly focused approach to revitalizing Sears's merchandising operations and a distinct change from the series of erratic and seemingly unrelated moves that Sears's managers have made in seeking financial recovery. Indeed, Sears's apparent trial-and-error approach to managing its way out of trouble has given aid and comfort to its competitors. As K-Mart and Dayton Hudson's Target Stores chain solidified their reputations as savvy discounters, and specialty shops such as Herman's and Toys Я Us wooed customers with in-depth inventories of single lines, Sears lost customers. A sample of its scattershot approach includes the following:

1. An attempt to lure more affluent people into its solid blue-collar customer base by stocking expensive, high-fashion merchandise. Ignoring its own image as the provider of merchandise for America's heartland, Sears also missed one of its great opportunities: capitalizing on the back-to-nature trend characterized by the *Whole Earth Catalog.* The company neglected to use its mail-order catalog to compete with sellers of health foods and simple tools. Meanwhile, the affluent showed little interest in clothing or jewelry sporting the Sears label, and its traditional customers were turned off by the new and higher prices.

2. Sears then decided to woo the specialty stores' customers by stocking products in depth. Customers still saw no reason to buy sporting equipment at Sears rather than at Herman's, for one, and grew even more confused about why to buy at Sears at all. Sears wound up with expensive inventory nightmares and no increased sales. "We tried to be too many things to too many people and got our merchandise stretched too thin," recalls a former Sears buyer.

3. K-Mart's customers became the next target. In 1977, as Telling became chairman, Sears embarked on an only-too-successful price war, shooting sales up 16%. But when the euphoria died down, management discovered that the price cuts had destroyed profits. Earnings for the merchandise group in 1977 fell more than 10%.

4. Suppliers became another target of Sears's floundering tactics. Expecting that Sears's buying muscle would keep suppliers in line, Telling ordered a get-tough policy with the company's suppliers, informing them that Sears would no longer inventory products that were slow sellers in the stores. Instead, suppliers found new customers and expanded their lines of branded merchandise. For example, in 1972 Sears accounted for 61% of Whirlpool Corp.'s sales. In 1979, sales of refrigerators, washers, and other appliances Sears bought from Whirlpool to sell under the Kenmore name accounted for only 47% of Whirlpool's sales.

Of all Sears's bad decisions, the erosion of supplier relationships may be the hardest to turn around. "We historically romanced our vendors," says one former buyer. "But since Telling's tough remarks in 1978, vendors are scrambling for non-Sears business, and Sears ends up with products that are the same as everyone else's. Why should a consumer then buy a Sears product when it could buy a branded product?"

TOP HEAVY.

At the root of most of these ill-conceived decisions lies an increasingly ponderous management structure. Sears until recently had an almost schizophrenic approach to management. It gave its field people virtual autonomy on promotional pricing, store size, product selections, and the like, yet it continually beefed up its corporate management staff in futile attempts to coordinate its diverse activities into a coherent whole. While the practice was relatively harmless during the days of unbridled growth, it created an almost knee-jerk reaction to solving problems: that of adding more managers. All through the 1970s, Sears continued to add executives, thus increasing its overhead at the same time it was superimposing a totally unwieldy hierarchy on the company.

For example, in 1976 Sears increased from five to nine its national merchandise groups, which handle buying, market development, promotion, and pricing. It created a new position, senior vice president of field, to coordinate the five territorial management teams that run Sears's vast network of stores and catalog houses. It even created a national retail sales staff to act as a liaison between headquarters and the field.

"Sears management structures on top of management structures have grown into a hindrance to timely decisions and good execution as well as an enormous cost burden," contends Louis W. Stern, a marketing professor at Northwestern University. Former Sears executives admit they and their colleagues

missed the boat. "We kept expecting our sales growth to resume the 10%-to-12% rate that we took for granted in earlier years," admits one high-ranking executive who just took early retirement. "We added more and more people . . . and found ourselves with an overhead monster we couldn't control or support."

Making matters worse, while Sears was adding layers of management, its store-level workforce was eroding, and its customer service was going sour along with it. Throughout the 1960s and early 1970s, Sears was able to entice experienced salespeople with lucrative incentive programs based on shares of Sears stock. Once the stock started sinking, however, the incentive evaporated with it, and salespeople began to leave. "With a few exceptions, you just don't find knowledgeable and attentive salespeople at Sears anymore," notes an industry consultant. "When I take something back that doesn't work, the Sears clerks nowadays tend to argue with me instead of readily replacing the item."

Belatedly, but nonetheless forcefully, Sears is grappling with its problems. Early last year, Telling sold his fellow directors on a massive early-retirement program aimed at managers older than 55. By year end, 1,600 of the 2,400 eligible employees took advantage of the plan, which provides three years of half pay in addition to normal pension benefits. The new vice president of field retired, and his job was eliminated. At the same time, Sears consolidated its nine merchandising groups into seven and dropped six of its 41 buying departments and five of its 46 field administrative units. The southwestern territory, which employed more than 300 people, was shut down altogether. Even the national retail sales staff was appreciably reduced. All told, by mid-1980 Sears's merchandising staff decreased to 288,000 employees. According to Telling, the reduction in executive staff will save some $125 million annually, after a write-off of $45 million.

Perhaps most significant, those who were left, combined with those hired to fill vacant positions, are much younger than their predecessors. It is no coincidence. Last year, in an attempt to infuse a more youthful orientation into what had become a stodgy management team, Telling promoted Edward A. Breenan, a 46-year-old territory manager, over the heads of several senior colleagues to become the new chairman and chief executive of the merchandise group. Brennan has, in turn, surrounded himself with a staff that is about 10 years younger than the former manager's. "I think the group will be far less set in beliefs, far more willing to take risks—all the advantages that youth brings will surface," Telling predicts.

PENICILLIN SHOTS.

Indeed, the new electronics stores represent a new risk, something that has been markedly absent from Sears. But the group's first priority still remains reducing operating costs. Last fall, for example, it quietly overhauled its time-worn merchandising format in which salespeople rang up sales at as many as 40 different locations in the store. Sears now uses centralized checkout stations in 4-6 clusters per store, an approach it expects will enable it to cut staff and to allow the remaining sales personnel to concentrate on serving customers.

This standardization of Sears stores is typical of what Brennan hopes to accomplish. "I feel very strongly that we need to approach the business as though we are a single store," he says. Although he insists that he recognizes that different territories do require different approaches, Brennan claims the similarities outweigh the differences. "We're not going to put together a snowblower sales program for Miami," he explains, "but we need consistency. If there is a right way to do something, then that right way should be used in New York, Los Angeles, and Miami."

Despite his protestations, however, Brennan will have to walk a very fine line between standardizing policies and removing decision-making even further from the pulse of the market. Centralized decisions can easily backfire when they are applied across the board to diverse markets and operations. For example, Sears has brutally cut back on promotional programs and trimmed advertising expenses to $532 million in 1979 from $571 million in 1978. The move has cut costs on lagging items but has also made deep inroads into the sales of items that were doing well. "It was like a clinic where the doctor would find the first patient had an infection and immediately order up penicillin shots for 650 other patients in the waiting room," complains one buyer who saw profits evaporate in her department when she cut advertising.

Not surprisingly, morale on the part of formerly autonomous field managers fell to an all-time low. "When I started out working in a store, we could call a lot of the shots and felt a tremendous pressure to perform well," says one Sears veteran. "Now the temptation is to blame someone in the tower if customers don't show up. People tend to get lethargic if they don't have the responsibility for making something work."

CONSOLIDATION.

Nonetheless, Brennan's apparent zeal for consolidation is rubbing off in the field, and not all managers are soured on it. William Bass, executive vice president, eastern territory, admits that his organization was a microcosm of the parent in its staffing procedures until 1977. "Then our gross margins started to suffer, and we stopped putting people on the payroll," he says. Instead, last year existing managers for the first time started a formal planning process, coupled with a microscope approach to costs. For example, even store engineers are now expected to prepare detailed plans of how to save energy costs on an item-by-item basis.

What is more, Bass is preparing to mirror Sears's corporate move last month to consolidate two departments—traffic, dealing with retail delivery, and logistics, which handled getting merchandise to stores or warehouses

—by combining his own traffic and logistics departments. Similarly, Sears has established a stronger corporate advertising department that Bass hopes will result in his being able to consolidate his own cadre of seven separate advertising staffs into a single, much smaller unit. "We've quit talking about headquarters and field, and now we're talking about Sears, about one program," he says.

Whether all field people will react with Bass's enthusiasm will probably rest on the success of Brennan's communications approach. Last fall Brennan staged a series of two-day meetings that for the first time in 30 years put Sears's top 125 corporate buyers in the same room with more than 1,000 key field people, including every store manager. Brennan himself conducted the meetings and brought along one of Sears's latest "recruits," actress Cheryl Tiegs of the new Sears Cheryl Tiegs signature line. Even some of Sears's crustier veterans claim the meetings generated some badly needed enthusiasm. For employees who could not attend, Brennan had parts of the meetings videotaped. Brennan also taped a separate message in which he made a pitch for salespeople to "act like you're happy the customer is there" and for store management to recognize that there is a "whole different world [of competition] out there selling our kinds of goods to our kinds of customers."

POLISHING ITS IMAGE.

But the biggest challenge facing Sears is to sharpen its fuzzy and much-tarnished image. Advertising and store displays are a vital route to accomplish this, and Brennan has turned responsibility for unifying them over to Robert E. Wood, II, aged 42, former manager of the home improvements merchandising group and grandson of General Robert Wood, the legendary head of Sears from 1928 to 1957. Wood intends to centralize the planning of local advertising as well as develop integrated national campaigns in Chicago.

Although Wood will make most of the campaign decisions, he insists that store managers will still have reasonable autonomy to promote specific items that sell well in their areas. "We have to integrate national advertising with local plans or run the risk of overkill on certain items and neglect of others," he concedes. In the past, Wood notes, local managers often interpreted plans for a national ad on a given product to mean that it is a high-priority item and should be promoted locally as well. They would thus spend local dollars on a message that was already getting to most customers. "We can't afford to duplicate what we do," he says.

But the jury is still out on whether Brennan will be able to get the proper blend of cost cutting and aggressive image rebuilding, of centralization and decentralization, of youth orientation and experience. Observers are unanimous in saying he faces a Herculean task. "Sears's reason for being was its exclusive products," says Ira Quint, a former Sears merchandising manager. "Expense controls don't give you a reason for being." And they do not attract customers, note other Sears watchers. "The company has positioned itself in such a nebulous way that I'm not sure the consumer wants to hear from Sears anymore," suggest Northwestern's Stern. Robert Kahn, a retailing consultant and director of Wal-Mart Stores, sums up: "Sears forgot its primary purpose is to please the customer by stocking the right goods and sticking by its principle of satisfaction guaranteed. Those things will be hard to regain."

10

Premium Fasteners, Inc.

Harry Simpson is unhappy with his job. Although he has been with Premium Fasteners for five years, he is now considering leaving the company because of the changes recently made. Basically, Harry is not prone to picking up and quitting. In fact, he had held only one other job since he graduated from high school 15 years ago. He left that job, not because he was overly unhappy with his work, but because he had recently married and had decided that he needed a better-paying position with greater job security. He found the job that fit his requirements at Premium Fasteners, Inc., which was known as Premium Nuts and Bolts.

At the time Harry joined the company, Premium was a small warehouser-distributor of a fairly complete line of industrial fasteners. The company was founded six years previously by the two Murphy brothers, Tom and Larry, who supplied small local automotive body shops and machine shops with their fastener needs. Originally they worked out of their family garage and the trunks of their cars. As their business expanded, they found that they could not meet the demand as a two-man operation. They then rented an old warehouse and set up shop.

When Harry was hired, the company consisted of seven workers in the warehouse, two salesmen, one bookkeeper-secretary, and the two owner-brothers. The organization was divided between the brothers into sales and administrative, and production. Under sales and administrative were the two salesmen and the bookkeeper-secretary, who was the wife of one of the brothers. Tom Murphy, who managed this area, spent most of his time out of the office functioning as a third salesman. The production side of the business consisted of one shipper-receiver, one clerk-typist, and five general production personnel, one of whom was Harry. Larry Murphy, who was responsible for this area, handled all the purchasing and scheduling, as well as lent a hand in the shop when there was a rush order or a backlog.

In general, the job of the five production workers involved picking, packing, and preparing a customer's order for shipment. The

Reprinted with permission of Macmillan Publishing Company from *Organizational Behavior Readings and Cases*, Second Edition, by Theodore H. Herbert. Copyright © 1981 by Theodore H. Herbert.

first step in the operation would be for the production worker to get a work order from the clerk-typist. He would then go to the storage racks, where the shipper-receiver had responsibility for placing the inventory. The next step would be to pick the items required on the order, take them to the work area, repackage them into small unit sizes, box the order, and take it to the shipper-receiver. The packer then had to return any excess to the inventory bins. Each worker had his own workbench, all of which were located in one part of the small warehouse.

The atmosphere was very congenial. All the workers were friendly and many socialized with each other after work. They all agreed that it was great to work for Larry Murphy. Besides giving his men a free hand in the performance of their jobs and chipping in when things became a little hectic, Larry always took his breaks with the guys; breaks usually occurred fairly randomly and lasted 10 to 20 minutes. Every once in a while he would join the crew, and they would all take in a ball game on Saturday. In addition, each morning Janet, Tom's wife and company bookkeeper, would brew a 36-cup pot of coffee for the whole staff.

Although the pay was not the highest, the Christmas bonus and the $100 gift for the birth of a baby were appreciated by all employees. They also did not really mind the two-week shutdown at Christmas, since it allowed time for hunting and visiting. Whenever the operation was a little slow, Harry and the other fellows usually found something to do, like straightening up the inventory bins or general maintenance and cleaning, to keep them busy.

The basic premise on which Premium Nuts and Bolts was founded stimulated a steady growth through the years; the major manufacturers of industrial fasteners did not find it feasible to package and ship their products in the small quantities required by many of the potential commercial users. This gave rise to many wholesalers, like Premium, who purchased from the major manufacturers in large lots and then repackaged and shipped in quantities to fit the needs of many light industrial concerns at a substantial profit. With the steady industrial growth in the area and their system of inventory control, Premium soon found itself in a position of not being able to fully supply the needs of its present customers as well as not being able to take advantage of the rapidly growing untapped market.

Not long after Harry joined the company, the production staff grew to 15, then 25, and kept growing. After three and a half years with Premium, Harry had seen the production staff grow from seven to 53, and he, as well as everyone else, realized that the facilities were inadequate. Orders were being received at a higher regular rate, and there was little time for socializing on the job. In order to help keep up with his work, Larry had hired a production supervisor, responsible for seeing that the work got done. Larry spent less and less time with the men on the floor. The production foreman, although well liked by the men, did not allow the freedom that Larry had given the men back in the old days. The men accepted this along with the role of the production supervisor. In general, with the exception of some added pressure, the performance of the job changed very little.

When Premium announced a name change to Premium Fasteners, Inc. and the move into a modern facility in an industrial park, nobody was surprised. The actual transition from the old location to the new location went extremely well. The sprawling 20,000-square-foot facility appeared more than adequate when compared to the old warehouse. Premium had installed the most modern equipment available and streamlined and mechanized the operations.

The plant was designed as a straight-line operation, with the flow designed around the major product groupings. The operations became highly structured, with departments being formed to specialize in the major areas of the production process. Each of the departments was supervised by a foreman (many of whom were hired after the move to the new facilities) who reported to the plant manager. Larry Murphy was now executive vice-president of Premium and practically all of his contact with the plant was handled through the plant manager.

Harry's job changed dramatically when the new facilities went into operation. Harry and the 100 other plant employees now performed specialized tasks. The flow through the plant started at receiving, where the fasteners were placed on a conveyor system that took them to a specific location according to their category. At these staging areas, an individual was responsible for removing the cartons and stacking them near the Boltrite packing machines. Once the fasteners were repackaged, they were again placed on the conveyor system where they were placed into inventory. At some later time the repackaged merchandise was then picked and shipped to Premium's customers.

Harry's new job was a first-class machine operator. In general it was his job to feed the nuts and bolts into the machine that would automatically weigh-count the quantity desired. The operation involved feeding the machine with bolts, manually folding the boxes and placing them in the machine, pressing a button, removing the full box, sealing the box, and placing the repackaged merchandise on a conveyor belt to be placed into inventory. The machine vibrated, and the clanging of loose nuts and bolts made the work area quite noisy.

The machines were also isolated from each other because they were strategically located through the plant. Harry now had very little contact with his co-workers. In fact, the only time he saw them was during the two 10-minute breaks and the 45-minute lunch. The only people he saw during the rest of the day were a boy, who stacked the newly arrived bolts next to the machine, and his foreman.

Jack Carmel was Harry's foreman; he had joined Premium shortly after the company moved into the new location. He did not get along very well with his men. He was very cold toward the men who worked for him and he showed little interest in anything besides work. He allowed them very little freedom in the day-to-day operation. In the eyes of his employees, Carmel was strictly a company man who would jump down their throats if they made any move that was not according to company policy. What was worse was that he was very rigid concerning the 10-minute breaks. It did not seem to matter to him that the lunch room and coffee machines were at the far end of the building. In fact, the men rather irreverently referred to Carmel as "the squirrel" because of his physical appearance and his uncanny knack of flitting around the department, always at the wrong moment.

Harry's relationship with the company changed as well. The factory workers were now on piecework. Harry viewed this new policy as insulting and somewhat degrading. The company also eliminated all bonuses and reduced the shutdown during Christmas.

After a year of working under the new conditions, Harry found himself contemplating switching jobs for the second time since he started working. Things just were not the same.

11

Olson's Locker Plant

Olson's Locker plant is located in Grand Island, Nebraska, a city of about 50,000 people. The locker plant was started in 1952 by Herb Olson when he came out of early retirement. He had been co owner and manager with his wife of a successful downtown hotel and restaurant until she died. He sold the business in 1950 at the age of 40. Two years later he decided to buy a small locker plant as a way to keep busy and increase his knowledge of the meat business.

For the first two years, all work was completed by Mr. Olson and an assistant who helped with the butchering. His clients were people who wished to have a hog or steer butchered, cut, and wrapped to order. The plant also had a small counter and meatcase in the front from which Mr. Olson sold meat to walk-in customers.

Olson's reputation for selling good meat at a fair price quickly spread. The business grew steadily. After 10 years he had 22 employees, and after 25 years he employs 70 people. The locker plant still does custom orders, but 70% of its business in 1978 is supplying meat to independent grocery stores, restaurants, and small markets in central Nebraska. Beef products account for 60% of the volume, pork the other 40%. The locker plant now handles about 35,000 lbs. of meat a day.

PLANT AND EQUIPMENT

As the volume of business increased, the locker plant became more mechanized. The plant is located in a single-story building with 7,000 square feet of work space. The building is divided into two parts. One side is used to kill and dress animals. The other side is used to cut and prepare finished meats for delivery to customers.

Mechanization has developed to the point where carcasses are now transported through the plant entirely by hooks and overhead rails. Workers use mechanical tools for several operations, such as power saws for splitting carcasses and a hydraulic winch to pull the skin from the carcass.

Employees range in age from 18 to 62. Workers on the shop floor are considered semiskilled and paid an hourly wage. The company is not unionized. Turnover is low.

Many employees have been with the company several years. Most do not have formal education beyond high school.

ORGANIZATION

The approximate organization structure for Olson's Locker Plant is shown in Exhibit 11-1. Herb Olson is owner and president. The management team includes a treasurer, sales manager, industrial engineer, plant superintendent and his assistant, and a personnel director. The treasurer keeps the financial records and also helps with the purchase of pigs and cattle. The sales manager has two salespeople reporting to him. The sales manager and one sales representative handle outside sales. The other salesperson handles sales over the counter. The industrial engineer just hired a new assistant to help with job measurement activities. All workers involved in the conversion of live animals to packaged meat report to the plant superintendent. The assistant superintendent assists with management of the plant and is in charge when the superintendent is absent.

The managers meet every Thursday evening to review their respective activities and to share information. This meeting is used to coordinate activities and to discuss solutions to unexpected problems. The management team is beginning to think that the organization needs to tighten up. A loosely run organization has been successful, but they are feeling the need to adopt more systematic procedures. The personnel director has been asked to establish written policies on matters such as hiring, firing, benefits, absences, and promotions. The personnel director has also requested permission to hire an additional person. The industrial engineer is also helping to systematize jobs and the work flow. The management team is quite satisfied with organization structure, but they sometimes wonder if they could be organized differently to improve efficiency.

THE PORK CONVERSION PROCESS

The process for converting live pigs into bacon and ham normally requires 14 operations. The dressing sequence begins by stunning the pig electrically. A rear limb is shackled, and the pig is elevated to an overhead rail where it is stuck and bled. The carcass is then dipped mechanically into a scalding tank for up to five minutes, where the hair is loosened. After scalding, pigs are moved mechanically to the dehairing area where the carcasses are scraped clean. The scraping process is partly accomplished by hand. After dehairing, the carcass is trans-

EXHIBIT 11-1   ORGANIZATION CHART FOR OLSON'S LOCKER PLANT

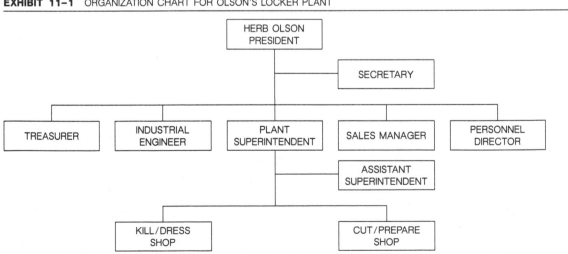

ferred to the singeing area. Singeing darkens the meat's outer edge and produces skin that has good leather quality. The carcass is then eviscerated. Next the carcass is skinned and the head is removed. Finally, the carcass is split in half with a handheld electric saw. At this point the carcass is inspected for disease and sent to the chilling room.

Pig halves are taken from the chilling room as needed by the meat-cutting operation. In this area, meat is thawed, cut into hams, bellies, and shoulders, injected with brine, boned, smoked, packed for sale or shipment, and rechilled.

A more detailed description of selected steps in the pork conversion process follows.

Skinning

Skinning is next to the last operation in the butchering and dressing process. The pig carcass hangs from the overhead rail, and the lower end is anchored by a hook in the jaw cavity to secure the carcass. The skin is cut open down the back of the front legs, down the back of the back legs, and down the middle of the belly. The legs are skinned out by hand with a sharp knife. An employee also loosens a fold of skin about three inches wide along each side of the belly cut. The knife should be used carefully and kept tight against the skin at all times. The fat is soft and easily cut. Gashes made by uncontrolled strokes of the knife do considerable damage to hams and bacons that are to be cured. A mechanical winch is then hooked to a fold of skin behind the neck, and it pulls the skin upward in a rapid motion, peeling it from the carcass. The carcass is then washed and moved to the next work station for splitting.

Brine Injection

Brine injection is the third procedure in the meat-cutting operation. After warming the carcass and cutting it into hams and shoulders, brine is injected into the meat. The purpose of the brine injection is to introduce a solution of salt, sugar, and nitrates into the meat. The salt acts as a preservative while the nitrates are used to retain the reddish color of the meat. The brine is injected by hand using a series of injection needles that are connected to a pumping machine. The brine ensures a more uniform cure and reduces the curing time to two or three days. Bellies are injected twice, once in the morning and again in the evening.

The injection requires modest skill. Operators are responsible to see that the quantity of solution does not exceed the limit set by federal law. They must also see that the brine is injected uniformly throughout the meat, and see that the needles are inserted into the arteries. The rate and pressure of the brine injection is controlled by the pumping machine.

Smoking

All pork products at Olson's Locker Plant are smoked during the conversion process. The purpose of smoking is to cook the raw meat and thus convert it to an edible product. The combination of heat and smoke causes a significant reduction in surface bacteria, so it is an important health item. Smoking also imparts a smoky flavor to the meat, which makes it more appealing to the customer. Smoking in the locker plant takes place in a separate smokehouse, which is actually an insulated room in which steam and smoke are introduced through a system of pipes. The smoke flavor is caused by the insertion of hickory, maple, and mahogany shavings in the fire that produces smoke. The minimum temperature for smoking a product can vary widely, depending upon the time available. Smoking at Olson's Locker Plant usually takes place at about 130° F. and lasts two days.

Smokehouse operators are responsible for deciding when a product is properly cooked. The final decision rests on the operator's judgment and is based on touch and appearance. Temperature, humidity, and other weather factors influence the required smoking time. There are many devices for measuring smokehouse conditions, but the final decision is based on personal experience and judgment.

Boning

The boning operation consists of trimming excess fat and cutting out the bones from hams and shoulders. Five employees are assigned to this task. They work around a large rectangular table. Boning the meat typically takes three times as long as trimming the fat and is the most difficult task. The workers along the boning platform are considered to be among the most skilled in the plant. Great dexterity is required to trim the fat and remove the bone with a minimum of waste. It takes a new person at least six months to gain proficiency in this task. Eight different methods of trimming and boning have to be learned to handle the various cuts of meat. Each ham within any category can present specific problems, depending upon size and the amount of fat and skin remnants. An experienced operator can tell immediately whether a ham will be difficult to work with. The criteria for assigning people to the boning operation are two years of experience working with meat and excellent manual dexterity.

OTHER TASKS

Industrial Engineering

In 1976, Mr. Olson hired an industrial engineer to improve internal efficiency. The industrial engineer works to establish production standards to control costs. He is also involved with production planning. The work includes studying the production operation throughout the plant, time and motion studies of each task, and suggesting new work procedures. The industrial engineer is also responsible for evaluating new equipment with respect to cost and labor savings. A monthly labor analysis report is also prepared for Olson and the plant superintendent.

The industrial engineering function encompasses several activities that require an engineering background. The industrial engineer's most important task is to develop production standards that measure productivity. Accurate production standards also help management schedule the flow of meat through the plant.

Purchasing and Selling

Herb Olson spends most of his time purchasing live animals and making sales to area stores. The company has two people making outside sales, but many buyers want to deal directly with Mr. Olson.

Livestock purchasing is tricky because there is no organized commodity market for meat in the area. Meat prices in the major centers (Omaha) fluctuate daily. Seventy percent of the cost of the finished product is the value of the livestock, so purchase price directly influences profit margins. Mr. Olson usually talks daily with meat brokers, local farmers, sale barns, and other sources of price information. He also negotitates directly with area farmers to buy livestock at a fixed price to reduce the risk for both sides. These purchases require Mr. Olson to visit farms and inspect the pigs.

Purchasing decisions are made quickly and informally. Formal confirmation is usually by letter, but the meat is often already shipped. Buyer and seller have to trust each other. Extensive experience is required to handle the purchase of livestock. Carcasses are also purchased from area slaughtering plants to handle unusual fluctuations in the demand for cut meat.

Mr. Olson stays in telephone contact with many buyers of his company's meat products. He visits stores on the way to visiting farms for the purchase of pigs and cattle. His salespeople also spend time telephoning and calling on local store buyers. An inside salesperson handles the sales paper work, and sells meat to customers over the counter. Mr. Olson stresses to the salesforce that they are to provide service to the customer no matter what the cost. He believes that as long as the company strives for perfection and customer satisfaction, the company will continue to grow and prosper.

Mr. Olson told an interviewer, "The most difficult part of my job is forecasting meat prices in the future. About 70% of the time I can predict whether prices will increase or decrease and make purchase contracts accordingly."

Order Assembly

The last step in the production sequence is the assembly of customer orders. Three people perform this operation. They assemble items from finished stock, move them to the packing area, check the assembled order against the customer's order, and arrange for shipment.

12

Creative Sentence Corp.

The purpose of this exercise is to illustrate the relationship between organization structure and technology. The nature of the transformation process (i.e., technology) will be analyzed as will the effect of size on the structure. Control and coordination mechanisms will be discussed as will developmental phases of the organization.

In this exercise you will be responsible for designing and operating a firm whose product is sentences. You will need to consider the organization size, structure, desired technology, and the relationship among the three. After completing one production period you will be allowed to assess the organization's effectiveness and make any changes you feel necessary for the second production period.

The success of each company is based on quality control, volume, efficiency, and organizational design. You will be scored on your productivity and profit. Productivity is measured by the number of words produced and used in sentences by your team, divided by the number of people on your team. Profit is the number of points earned minus the amount expended in purchases and "scrap."

$$P \text{ (words per person)} = \frac{\text{\# of words}}{\text{\# of people}}$$

STEP 1: *Group Planning Period (20 min.)*

The class will be divided into groups of various sizes, each group representing a company involved in manufacturing words that are then packaged into sentences. The success of each company is based on quality control, volume, efficiency, and organizational design.

During this planning period you should design your organization as you see fit for meeting the company's objectives. As there are a number of possible structures, you may wish to consider the following points:

a. What possible ways are there of achieving your organization's objectives? Consider the constraints placed on your organiza-

This exercise is based on Bernard M. Bass and Harold J. Leavitt, "Some Experiments in Planning and Operating," *Management Science,* 1963, 9, pp. 574-585.
Thanks to Lee Lyon for designing it.

tion (time, space, resources) in relation to your objectives.

b. In designing your organization, determine the basic division of labor, lines of authority and responsibility, and communication. Relate these to the company's objectives, tasks, and technology.

c. Consider the qualifications of each group member when designing and assigning jobs.

STEP 2: *First Production Run (20 min.)*

Read the rules and directions below. At the beginning of the first production period your group will be given a stack of index cards. Each card will have a single "resource word" and a number on it; the cards will be face down. The first card in the stack is "purchased" on credit for 10 points and can be turned face up as soon as the production period begins. Additional cards may be purchased and turned up at your discretion for a price of 10 points per card. The letters of the resource word serve as the raw materials available to produce new words that you will combine into sentences. For example, if the word is "architects," you can produce the words and sentence "She is a rich artist." The production process is illustrated in Exhibit 12-1.

STEP 3: *Production Break (10 min.)*

During this break evaluate the effectiveness and efficiency of your organization and determine any changes you may wish to make in the structure, job assignments, technology. Implement any changes during the next production run.

STEP 4: *Second Production Run (20 min.)*

Follow the same rules and directions as applied to the first production period.

STEP 5: *Final Tally*

While the auditor is compiling the final profit statements, each group should draw an organization chart that depicts the structure of its company during production runs #1 and #2. If changes in the structure were made during the break, draw separate charts for each production period.

STEP 6: *Class Discussion (20 min.)*

As a class, discuss the profit and production records of each company, the various structures and technologies used, and the relationships which appear between structure, technology, and size. The following questions may be helpful in focusing your discussion on these concepts.

EXHIBIT 12-1 MECHANICS OF SENTENCE CONSTRUCTION

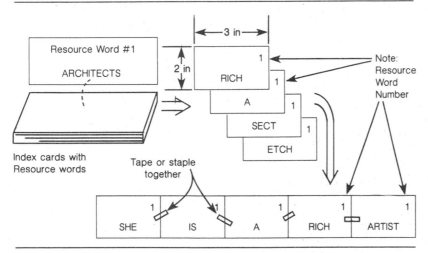

DISCUSSION QUESTIONS

1. What was the major difficulty in designing your organization for the first production run? What difficulties did you experience in the second design stage (after the production break)?
2. What type of structure did you begin with? In what way was it effective? Ineffective?
3. Did you change the structure, or any other aspect of your organization, for the second production run? Why did you make the changes? Did the changes make a positive or negative difference?
4. How did you determine if the organization was effective?
5. During which production period did the organization operate best? To what do you attribute this?
6. How did the discussion during the break progress? Was it orderly, frantic, were some people uninvolved or angered? What caused the reactions of the group? Did this affect the second production period?
7. How would you classify the technology you used? Describe the technology according to the studies discussed in class.
8. What effect did the size of the groups have?
9. Which group was most effective in terms of productivity and profit? How would you explain their success?
10. Based on this experience, how would you explain the relationship between size, productivity, and structure? What effect does technology have? Should one variable be more predominant when considering the design of an organization?

RULES

1. Only words from the same resource word can be used in a single sentence.

2. The same word cannot be produced more than once from a single resource word. A letter may not be used in a single word more times than it appears in the resource word; for example "artist" is legitimate, but "artistic" is not. It has too many i's.
3. Names and places are acceptable.
4. Excess words (those produced but not used in sentences) are considered excess inventory and are charged against your group by deducting 1 point per word from your total score.
5. Incorrect words (nonsense words, misspelled words, words using letters in violation of the rules) are analogous to "scrap" in manufacturing and will cost your team 2 points per word.

DIRECTIONS FOR PRODUCTION

1. "Purchase" your first resource word and begin manufacturing additional words. Write each word produced and the resource word card number on a separate piece of paper.
2. Using the words produced, make complete sentences by clipping the pieces of paper together. Your group receives 1 point for each word correctly used in the sentence.
3. An auditor will observe your production and score your output. However, your team must do the basic accounting. For each resource word you purchase you must record the number of words produced and the number of words used in sentences. As you purchase each word, turn in your accounting slip, excess words, and sentences to the auditor.

Word of advice: Work with only one resource word at a time to begin with. Keep in mind that you are buying your raw materials (resource words) on credit and all bills must be paid at the end of the game.

13

Aeronautical Systems Corporation

The Aeronautical Systems Corporation has experienced rapid growth in the past decade. Its current annual sales are approximately $250 million. The company employs 10,000 employees, a large proportion being highly talented engineers, technicians, and scientists. The company designs and manufactures complex custom-built electronics systems for the government, aviation firms, and other types of industrial organizations. Much of this work is done on a contract basis, where a number of companies are involved in the manufacture and construction of one major end product such as a missile, rocket or booster, or a new type of aircraft. This company also has standardized product lines that are produced and distributed by six United States divisions, a Canadian division, and an International division.

A basic company objective is constant product and systems innovation of a highly technical and complex nature in fields where there are few competitors. Top management believes in a highly flexible organizational structure, which—in large part—entails organizing activities around highly talented personnel, rather than fitting employees to an "ideal" organizational structure.

Following is an outline of the major manufacturing and distributing divisions and their major product lines:

  I. *Systems-Manufacturing Division, Los Angeles:*
    A. Space-Life-Support Systems
    B. Missile Systems
    C. Fluid Systems
    D. Flight-Electronics Systems
    E. Heat-Transfer Systems
    F. Environmental-Control Systems

  II. *Systems-Manufacturing Division, Phoenix:*
    A. Space-Power Systems
    B. Air-Pumping Systems
    C. Gas-Turbine Power Plants
    D. Pneumatic and Fluid-Control Systems

  III. *Research-Industrial Division, Los Angeles:* Manufactures and markets a line of industrial exhaust-driven turbo-chargers and specialized valves.

Permission granted for "Aeronautical Systems Corp."
from Richard Farmer and William Ryan.

IV. *Research-Aviation Service Division, Los Angeles:* Conducts airplane modification work—including structural and system changes—and distributes several lines of turbine-powered executive aircraft in the western states.

V. *Electric Division, New York:* Manufactures a line of specialized industrial generating equipment.

VI. *Air Cruisers Division, New Jersey:* Manufactures fabricated products, aircraft-escape devices, missile-recovery systems, etc.

VII. *Systems Manufacturing, Ltd. of Canada:* Manufactures avionic systems such as temperature controls and static inverters.

VIII. *Aeronautical Systems International, with head offices in Geneva:* Controls a series of technical sales offices in Europe, and is also the holding company of subsidiaries in Japan, Great Britain, and West Germany.

On most major contracts, more than one of the company's divisions are involved in the design, manufacture, and distribution of the systems or company end product. Divisions I and II, in particular, are highly interdependent and interrelated in much of their work. Divisions V and VIII are the most autonomous in terms of their product lines and operations. All the divisions, however, have some standardized products or systems, over which they have considerable operating autonomy.

DIVISIONAL ORGANIZATION

To quote a current company manual:

Each manufacturing division is responsible for its own financial statement and, therefore, enjoys a great deal of autonomy. The divisional manager, assisted by an assistant manager, has a complete organization of managers to control the operation of such departments as Engineering, Manufacturing, Quality Control, Quotation Administration, Accounting, Sales, and various service departments such as

Personnel, Administrative Service, and Plant Engineering and Maintenance. In addition to this basic functional organization, Divisions I and II are further divided into product-line organizations. Hence, the chief engineer, for instance, has a chief-product engineer over each product line. Similarly, the sales manager has complementary product-sales managers over each product line, and so on.

The history of the Aeronautical Systems Corporation is one of deliberately planned internal growth through continuous investment in research and development of new products to supplement and complement existing products and systems capabilities. This policy has resulted in an unusually wide product mix, with uniquely complementary characterisitics, that enables the development and production of complete, comprehensive accessory systems from components of various divisions and product lines. This practice has been exercised repeatedly and has established firm, practicable lines for inter-product group and inter-divisional collaboration in the creation of multiproduct systems.

CORPORATE ORGANIZATION

To quote the company manual:

The corporation or head-office management consists of a board of directors, a chairman of the board, a president and an executive vice-president. All divisional and subsidiary managers report to the executive vice-president. He is assisted in his task by several corporation vice-presidents and directors who are responsible for policy direction to the divisions relating to matters such as law, finance, accounting, public relations, industrial relations, contract and quotation administration, engineering, material, product planning, manufacturing, quality control, and sales and service. The vice-president of Sales also has a complete Corporation-Marketing Organization, which is responsible for the sale of the corporation's products from offices throughout the free world.

Some additional comment on the corporate-level marketing organization is warranted here. Under the vice-president of

Sales there are a number of salesforces organized on a customer basis; and within some of the customer groupings, there are also territorial breakdowns. For example, the following sales managers report to this vice-president:

1. Field Sales: Throughout the country, there are district sales offices, whose salespeople call on industrial customers.
2. Government Relations: This salesforce deals with government contracts.
3. Airlines: This salesforce deals only with airline companies; it consists of a number of regional offices.

Also reporting to the corporate vice-president of Sales are the manager of Engine Sales, whose salesforce calls on both the airlines and government customers, and the manager of Special-Systems Sales (mechanical, electrical, etc.), whose salesforce calls on all types of company customers. A director of Marketing Services also reports to this vice-president.

The head-office salespeople are the customer contacts for those systems and product lines that require joint developmental and manufacturing operations involving more than one division. These salespeople are the key disseminators of information between customers and those parts produced and sold to the customer. The divisional salespeople directly contact customers primarily where standardized products are involved and where the systems and products are under the autonomous control of a particular division.

PROGRAM ORGANIZATION

To quote the company manual:

For the development of larger systems involving components of various types and requiring the coordinated efforts of several product-line organizations and more than one division, some form of program organization is used. The extent and exact composition of the program organization will vary with the size and complexity of the program involved.

A complete program organization consists of the following major positions:

Program Manager
System-Project Engineer
Contract Administrator
PERT Coordinator
Reliability Coordinator
Maintainability Coordinator
Value-Engineering Coordinator
Quality-Control Coordinator
Support-Service Coordinator
Manufacturing Coordinator
Material Coordinator

The subdivisions within the program organization follow the functional-line organizational structure in each Manufacturing Division. They draw on the strength, skill, and experience of existing line-organization people, combining it into a highly specialized group with a program of centralized responsibility and authority that comes directly from division and corporate management. This program structure has proven highly successful on many major programs such as the recent F-111 aircraft, Gemini, Apollo and SPUR space programs, and many others.

PROGRAM MANAGER

To quote the company manual:

The program manager has complete responsibility for the development of the systems in the program and complete authority to implement all activities necessary to insure contract compliance. He has overriding authority to alter decisions and to recommend alternate action, if such will enhance contract compliance, improve product reliability or quality, reduce development of fabrication costs, or reduce the time to develop the systems. The program manager reports any conflict between programs, regarding utilization of manpower or facilities, to the appropriate division managers. The division managers take appropriate actions to resolve such conflicts. The program manager must resolve all internal program conflicts involving compromise of costs, performance, product quality or reliability, or program scheduling. He has authority to request such action as is required to resolve any conflicts. The program manager represents the primary liaison and coordination point between the manufacturing division(s) involved and the customer. He authorizes all personnel conferences and correspondence at the technical and administrative levels between the division(s) and the customer. The program manager participates in all personnel-performance reviews for all key program members. He may recommend personnel changes when and if he deems such action necessary to the successful accomplishment of program tasks. He continually keeps abreast of all program developments, significant accomplishments, and important problems. He reports general program progress to division management on a biweekly basis and is responsible to the customer for all contractual reporting.

14

Atlas Electronics Corporation (A)

COMPANY HISTORY

Atlas Electronics Corporation was organized by a group of engineers and scientists who pioneered electronic research and development for the Office of Scientific Research and Development during World War II. After the war, members of this group joined together to form a private company to continue their efforts.

From the start, Atlas earned a reputation among government and corporate customers as a leader in advanced electronic techniques and systems. Its present capabilities cover a wide spectrum of electronic applications and skills, including aviation systems, radar, space payloads, communications, and electronic warfare (reconnaissance and countermeasures). Atlas has continued to distinguish itself for advances in the state-of-the-art and for superior quality on numerous prototype and initial operational equipments developed for U.S. government agencies. Fully 95% of its business is on government R & D contracts, whether directly or for prime government contractors.

Atlas's success is largely due to the competence, dedication, and stability of its staff. Of its 3,000 employees, over half have engineering or scientific degrees. Approximately 15% of these have advanced technical or M.B.A. degrees or are working toward them. The primary resource of management is the brainpower of these men, who are professional specialists in diverse fields.

COMPANY ORGANIZATION

Atlas Electronics Corporation is a typical engineering company organized along functional lines. Its Functional Engineering Departments are oriented to various technical disciplines and are staffed with engineers, scientists, and technicians who work on developing advanced techniques and in the support of projects.

The departmental organization structure starts with the department head and goes down the line through the section heads, group leaders, and supervisory engineers, to the scientists, engineers, and technicians

This case was developed and prepared by W. R. Lockridge, C. S. Post Center, Long Island University. Reprinted by permission.

who are doing the detail work. The department heads report to John Doan, Executive Vice-President. Communications, approvals, and directions flow through this organization in an orderly manner. Each level is under the supervision of the level above it and normally will not operate without higher level approval and direction.

Atlas had three Functional Engineering Departments: an Antenna Department, a Receiver Department, and a Data Systems Department. Each of these is responsible for developing advanced techniques, performing engineering, and for giving support to R & D projects in its technical area. The organization of each of these departments is shown in Exhibits 14-1, 14-2, and 14-3.

In addition, Atlas has a Manufacturing Department (Exhibit 14-4), which does fabrication, assembly, and testing of production units. This department also reports to John Doan. Purchasing, accounting, personnel administration, and other services are performed by various company staff departments not shown in the exhibits.

From time to time, Atlas sets up an ad hoc Project Management to handle a large R & D contract. This is a semiautonomous group consisting of a project manager and other personnel drawn from the functional organizations in the company. It has complete responsibility for meeting all the requirements of the contract, but it gets the work

EXHIBIT 14-2 ATLAS ELECTRONICS CORPORATION (A) RECEIVER DEPARTMENT

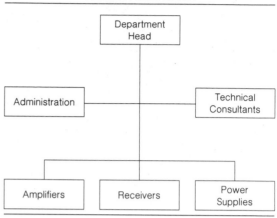

done in the Functional Departments. At the end of the project it is dissolved.

The Project Management assigns technical tasks to each supporting department to perform. To a limited extent, it is permitted to cut across organizational lines so that it can deal with the people doing the work without having to go through the whole hierarchy of their functional organizations. It handles scheduling and overall cost control; it deals with subcontractors and maintains liaison with customers; and it coordinates all the technical inputs and "hardware" from the supporting organizations into the overall system that is delivered to the customer.

The people who are transferred to the Project Management are mostly of a supervisory or senior category and report directly to the project manager. Their function is to advise him in their respective technical disciplines, to cooperate with him in managing the project, and to give "work direction"* to the personnel in the Functional Departments who are doing the work. The Project Management staff cannot directly supervise the work of the departmental personnel because these workers report in line to their department head. The department head may be on the same

---

*"Work direction": definition of the goals, specifications, and constraints (budget, schedule, etc.) for a technical task, as distinguished from detailed supervision of the work to perform it; the "what" to do, not the "how" to do it.

EXHIBIT 14-1 ATLAS ELECTRONICS CORPORATION (A) ANTENNA DEPARTMENT

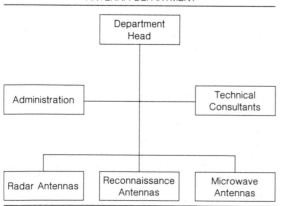

level or a higher level than the project manager. Consequently, the project manager has the problem of getting the utmost in effort from people who are responsible to someone else for pay raises, promotion, performance, and other aspects of line relationship.

SPYEYE PROJECT

As the result of a successful competitive proposal, the government has awarded Atlas an R & D contract for an airborne reconnaissance system called "Spyeye." The System consists of an antenna, a receiver, an amplifier, and visual read-out equipment. This is an advanced system requiring the development of specific equipment whose performance characteristics are beyond the existing state-of-the-art. Atlas agrees to produce a prototype model in nine months. Following acceptance by the government, it agrees to produce five operational systems within another six months.

The contract is for a firm fixed price of $6 million, of which $5.6 million is the estimated target cost and $400,000 is Atlas's fee. The contract has a profit-sharing incentive whereby the government and the contractor share any cost-saving below the $5.6 million on a 90/10% basis. It also provides penalties on the contractor for overrunning the cost, for late delivery, and for failure to meet per-

EXHIBIT 14-4 ATLAS ELECTRONICS CORPORATION (A) MANUFACTURING DEPARTMENT

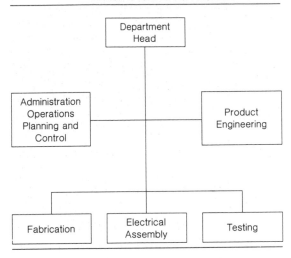

formance specifications. The government will debit Atlas dollar-for-dollar against its fee for any cost overrun, and will assess it $200 for every day of late delivery. Various penalties, up to 20% of the fee, are provided for failure to meet technical performance specifications.

PROJECT SUPPORT

The Spyeye project requires support from many functional areas throughout the company. It needs technical advice, engineering, and "hardware" from the reconnaissance section of the Antenna Department, the amplifier and receiver sections of the Receiver Department, the visual displays section of the Data Systems Department, and the fabrication, assembly, and testing facilities of the Manufacturing Department. (See Exhibits 14-1 through 14-4.)

ALTERNATIVES FOR PROJECT ORGANIZATION

Company management has to decide whether to organize Spyeye as an ad hoc Project Management, or to handle it through one of its Functional Departments. Two men are available to lead the project, but the one

EXHIBIT 14-3 ATLAS ELECTRONICS CORPORATION (A) DATA SYSTEMS DEPARTMENT

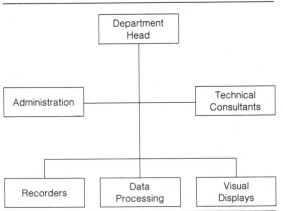

selected will depend on the choice of organization. These men are Howard Datson and Burt Saunderson.

Howard Datson, 55, is head of the Receiver Department. He has been with the company since its inception and has built his department to the largest in the company. Datson and his group were responsible for numerous innovations in the receiver line and have kept the company ahead of most of its competition in that field.

Datson put in a strong plea to the president, Homer Skillton, to let the Receiver Department manage Spyeye as a project within its functional organization. "My department has been in existence since this company started," he said. "We've a well-trained staff with a lot of managerial and technical know-how. We'll have to do the bulk of the development anyhow. And I'm sure we can handle the interfaces with the other departments without any trouble."

Datson went on to express some of his personal feelings about the alternative of setting up a Project Management. "You must recognize that we've built the reputation of this company on the technical capability and quality performance of its Functional Departments. I personally dislike becoming a 'service' organization to a group who will be here today and gone tomorrow. Also, it'll probably be managed by someone who is not as technically oriented as any of our department heads.

"One thing I want to make particularly clear," he continued, "nobody's going to come into my department and tell my men how they must do their work. They report to me and my supervisors and we're the ones who call the shots."

Burt Saunderson, 45, is a section head in the Antenna Department and has held that position for six years. He started as a project engineer 12 years ago and worked up through the group leader level to section head. A year ago he was relieved of his functional assignment and was appointed project manager in an ad hoc Project Management for an R & D

project called Moonglow. Moonglow was much smaller than Spyeye, but it had many of the same characteristics, such as the support from several different Functional Departments, a fixed price, and penalties for failure to meet cost, schedule, and performance specifications.

Saunderson and his Project Management group had successfully completed the Moonglow project. They had delivered the system on time, and the performance was satisfactory to the customer, although the equipment deviated slightly from the specification. They also had been able to increase the company's fee 1.5% by bettering the targeted cost. But Moonglow was now over and the people on it had to be reassigned.

While waiting for a new assignment, Saunderson served as bid manager on the Spyeye proposal to the government and was responsible for having come up with the reconnaissance system that the government finally bought. He felt he was the logical one to head up the Spyeye Project, if President Skillton decided to organize it as a Project Management. Accordingly, Saunderson sent a memorandum to Skillton outlining his reasons for this type of organization, which were, in essence, as follows:

1. The project involves four of the company's operating organizations. If management is established in any one of these, the company would have the awkward situation of one Functional Department directing the activities of others who are on a parallel with itself in the company organization structure.
2. The project involves more than mere technical development. Cost, schedule, and technical performance all must be evaluated and balanced to produce the optimum overall result. A Functional Department, steeped in its own technology and hampered by its organizational structure, would lack the objectivity to view the overall project problem in perspective and to meet the ever-changing

operational crises that arise from day to day.

3. The project does not involve pure research. It requires some innovation in the techniques area that can be done by the supporting Functional Departments. But someone will have to develop the overall system and that can best be done by a Project Management.

4. The project will add little to the long-range technical capability of the company. What it needs is an organization to "get the job done"—an organization that can use the technical support of the functional organizations without causing any permanent disruption in the company's organization structure.

President Skillton recognized that both men had good arguments.

15

Atlas Electronics Corporation (B)

SPYEYE PROJECT MANAGEMENT

President Skillton met with Executive Vice-President John Doan to discuss the Spyeye Project. "John, I've decided to organize Spyeye as a Project Management instead of assigning it to any of the Functional Departments. It's too big and too complex and it'll be in trouble from the start. I don't want to upset the stability of any department by temporarily expanding its personnel and giving it a coordinating job to handle." (See Exhibits 15-1 and 15-2.)

PROJECT MANAGER

"But this creates some problems on which I'll need your help," he continued. "The first is the selection of a Project Manager. He's got to be at home in the front office talking about budgets, time schedules, and corporate policies and also at home in the laboratory talking about technical research and development problems. Of course, we can't expect him to double as a member of top management and a scientist equally well, but he's got to know what can be done technically and be enough

EXHIBIT 15–1 ATLAS ELECTRONICS CORPORATION (B) SPYEYE PROJECT MANAGEMENT

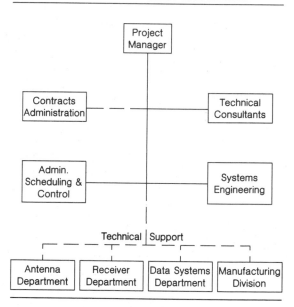

of a business man to get it done within the contract."

"I'm thinking of Burt Saunderson for the job. But I'd like your opinion of him. Burt's a

---

This case was developed and prepared by W. R. Lockridge, C.S. Post Center, Long Island University. Reprinted by permission.

graduate engineer with a B.S. and M.S. in electrical engineering. From his earliest training, he's dealt with scientific analysis. He's accustomed to working objectively with tangible things. But as a Project Manager, he'll have to marshall pieces of preliminary or tentative information, juggle several problems at once, compromise one requirement for the benefit of another, and make decisions that are often based on experience and judgment rather than on specific knowledge."

"Another thing," Skillton continued, "as a Section Head, Burt's accustomed to having direct-line authority over the people in his department doing the work. They do as he says. But as a Project Manager, he'll have to win the cooperation of the supporting department heads and their staffs to get things done. This kind of management means dealing with human nature, and Burt will have to put a lot of emphasis on human factors to succeed."

"Well, I feel his performance on the Moonglow Project shows he can do the job," Doan replied. "I'd rather have him than one of our department heads. Each of them is a professionally dedicated individual, highly skilled in the techniques of his field. What we need here is a different breed of cat—a manager who can run a business, rather than a professional who is endeavoring to optimize a technical advance."

PROJECT MANAGER AUTHORITY
President Skillton then raised another point. "No matter who we appoint, we've got to give

EXHIBIT 15-2   ATLAS ELECTRONICS CORPORATION (B) SPYEYE PROJECT

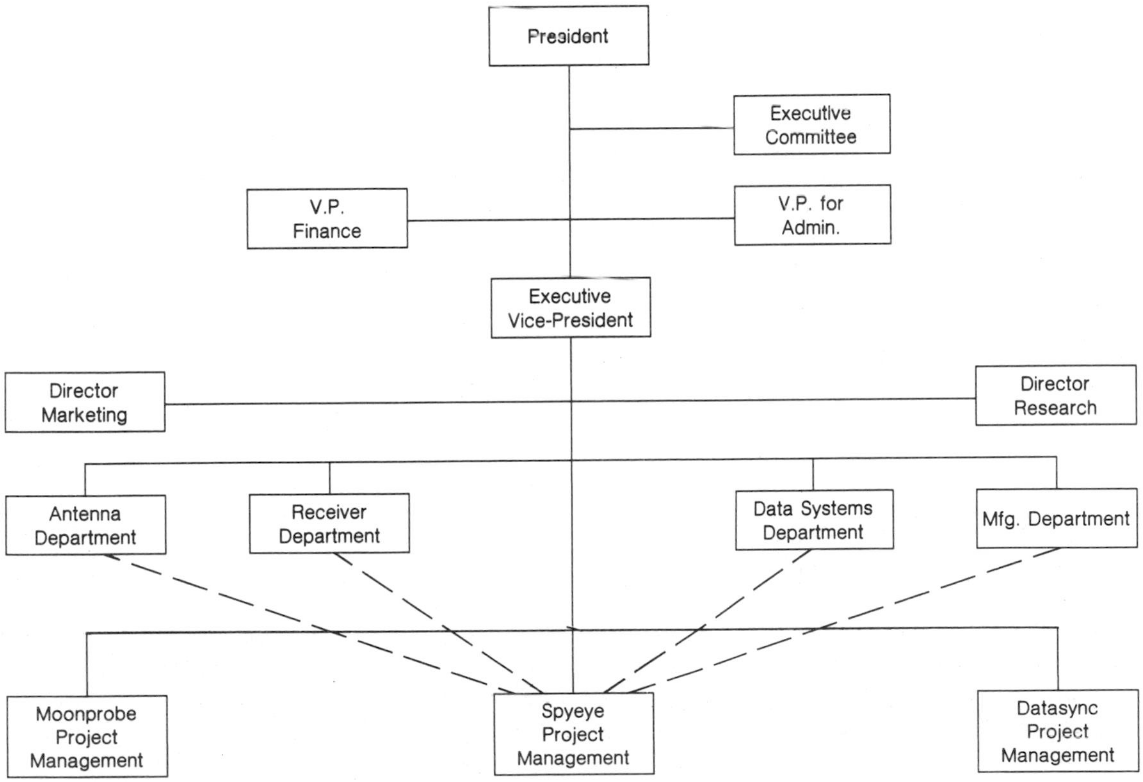

This chart indicates lines of responsibility only, not status.

him sufficient authority to get the job done. But we've a delicate situation here. We can't permit him to step in and tell a department head how to run his department. Yet we must give him sufficient status to compel their respect and cooperation. I'll have him report to you. This will place him on the same organizational level as the department heads who are supporting the Project."

"That's OK with me," Doan replied. "After all, I've other Project Managers reporting to me and I try to treat them and the department heads alike."

"Of course, Burt will have overall management of Spyeye and will assign technical tasks to each supporting department," Skillton continued. "But these will be in the nature of subcontracts with budgets and schedules that he'll have to negotiate with each department head and on which he'll obtain their commitment. He can tell them *what* to do, but not *how* to do it. This will keep design development in the Functional Departments where it belongs.

"But I'm not too happy about this arrangement," Skillton reflected, "because it gives the Project Manager little control. When Burt meets with a problem that requires some pressure on a supporting department, he'll have to come to you if he can't reach an agreement with the department head."

"Well, I'll have to assume that as my responsibility," Doan replied. "All the operations report to me and it's my job to see that any conflicts are resolved in the best interest of the company."

PROJECT STAFF

"Another problem we have to consider," Skillton continued, "is how we'll staff the Spyeye Project Management. Obviously, it should be with supervisory or senior technical people from the departments skilled in the project techniques. But each of these departments needs these people in its own operations. I don't want to step in and direct any department head to transfer people to the Project Management. Burt will have to con-

vince each department head that it's in the best interest of the company and the individual concerned to transfer him. Personally, I feel that it broadens a man's experience and capability to be assigned to a project for a while."

PROJECT SUPPORT

President Skillton meditated for a moment and then continued, "In mulling over the problem, John, it appears to me that if we could induce each department head to set up a Spyeye Support Group as a sub-project within his own department, responsible solely for support to the Spyeye Project Management, it would overcome some of the weakness of the ad hoc organization concept.

"This would, in effect, create a 'project within a project,' headed by a Project Leader who would take his 'work direction' from the Project Management staff rather than from his own departmental supervision. I think this would cut across the organizational lines to implement the interfaces between the Project Management and the supporting groups, and I feel it would inspire a team spirit on the project. At the same time, it would preserve the status of the Functional Department supervision, because detailed supervision of the work would remain with them. I want you to see if the Spyeye support can be organized in this manner," he concluded. (See Exhibit 15-3.)

EMPLOYEE MORALE

Skillton and Doan had another problem that neither of them had discussed: how to maintain employee morale under the structure of "two bosses" that the Spyeye Project Management created.

Jack Davis was a Group Leader in the Data Systems Department before he was transferred to the Spyeye Project Management. His new assignment required that he be the operational communications link between the project and his "home" department. He gave "work direction" to Abe Marks who was the

Project Leader heading up the Spyeye Project group in the Data Systems Department.

Jack and Abe were having lunch together in the company cafeteria. "I can't keep from wondering what'll happen to me when the project's over," Jack remarked. "Will I be transferred back to the Data Systems Department? If so, will I have lost ground by my temporary absence? Or will they assign me to another project? I don't see anything new coming in and I don't like it. Believe me, I keep looking around."

"I've my problems, too," Abe replied. "While I'm still in the department and report to Joe (his section head), I'm working exclusively on the Spyeye Project. I like the assignment. I feel I'm part of the project team, and when that equipment starts flying out there, I'm sure they'll give me credit for my part. But how does this affect my status and salary?

"When it comes time for rate review," he continued, "will Joe know how I'm doing? Burt knows more about my work than Joe does. Will they talk to each other, or will I be dropped in the crack?

"I'm in another bind," Abe added. "Often I have to decide what's best for the project as against what's best for the department. Should I do what the project needs to meet its contract or be loyal to the department's policies and standards? If I 'bite the hand that feeds me' where'll I wind up?"

"I guess these are some of the risks we have to take," Jack philosophised. "Some guys prefer the challenge of strict technical development. Others want the action of a project. Personally, I feel that this project assignment will broaden my experience, or I wouldn't have taken it. But I can't help but worry about what it'll do to my future."

Burt Saunderson didn't hear this conversation, but he knew that these feelings persisted with personnel working on the project, either on his staff or in the supporting departments. He wondered how he could induce these men to keep their "eye on the ball" and devote their full effort to the project when they were worrying about their personal futures.

PERFORMANCE PROBLEM

Seven months after the project started, Saunderson noted from his progress reports that the Receiver Department still failed to meet the technical performance specification on the receiver. The specification required a band spread from 1,000-10,000 mc. The breadboard model would only operate at 1,050-9,200 mc.

Time was getting short and he had to take prompt action. Investigation disclosed that it was doubtful if the circuit, as designed by the Receiver Department, would ever meet the specification. Consequently, it did not appear advisable to spend more time on it. Saunderson's technical staff advised him that the addition of another transistor on the lower end and the substitution of a 2QXR tube for a transistor at the upper end would cure the situation. Both of these would increase the cost and the tube would change the configuration of the "black box." His Project Administrator advised him that the project could absorb the cost and the customer said that the slight change in the configuration was not

EXHIBIT 15-3 ATLAS ELECTRONICS CORPORATION (B)
RECEIVER DEPARTMENT
SPYEYE PROJECT SUPPORT

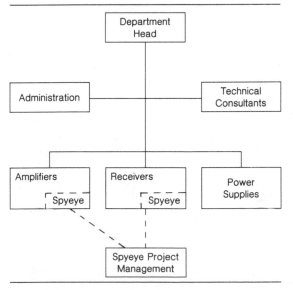

important. But here an obstacle arose. The Receiver Department was not satisfied with the quality of the 2QXR tube and refused to use it.

Saunderson met with Datson to discuss the problem. "Howard, we've got to do something to get that receiver up to spec. Time's getting short. We'll get socked $200 a day for late delivery and they'll take a slice of our fee for failure to perform. Now, I know you hate to use the 2QXR, but it'll do the job long enough to meet the life requirements and will satisfy the customer. We've got to give somewhere or we'll be in serious trouble."

"Yeah, I know how you feel," Datson replied, "but I've got to preserve the quality reputation of the company. After all, we obtained Spyeye because of our reputation for quality as much as for our technical competence and favorable price. If I do anything to impair that image it'll only hurt us in the long run."

16

Calgary Police Department

The function of the Calgary Police Department is to protect the life and property of the citizens and visitors to Atlanta. To achieve this goal we must effectively prevent crimes, make arrests and carry out the other related aspects of police work.

Chief Rousseau (1980)

RECENT HISTORY

James T. Rousseau was elected Chief of Police on February 2, 1962. He inaugurated a permanent recruit school. New types of radio equipment were purchased. The officers were given a much deserved day off each week. The headquarters building was redecorated to make working conditions better. The Detective Department was reorganized by division into robbery, larceny, burglary, homicide, vice, and miscellaneous squads. A wrecker was purchased to impound cars illegally parked, and a parking lot for these impounded cars was built.

In 1965 the first traffic policewomen were sworn in and given special training.

In 1966 the entire Calgary Police Department was reorganized into four divisions. These were Services, Uniform, Traffic, and Detective. Training and Detention were made separate divisions later. There was a superintendent in charge of each division.

In 1967 the County Police Department was absorbed into the Calgary Police Department. Police protection was extended to parts of the county outside the city that formerly had depended on the county police. The police department was now responsible for a geographical area almost twice as large.

Space problems were severely felt in 1971 and several departments had to be moved from headquarters. These problems were relieved in 1974 with the completion of a new headquarters building.

In 1973 there was a rise in racial and religious agitation. A Jewish temple was bombed and attacks against persons grew in frequency. The black civil rights and racial problem also became more significant.

THE COMMUNITY ENVIRONMENT

In 1980, the Calgary Crime Commission completed a study of the city's needs for police department services. The following are excerpts from the Crime Commission report.

Calgary's Youth

There is a serious need to focus the city's resources on the problem of preventing and controlling juvenile delinquency. We therefore recommend that the Calgary Youth Council be created as an official agency for this purpose. Membership would include the Superintendent of the Calgary Public Schools, the head of the Parks Department, the Chief of Police, a full-time executive director, a lay chairperson, and six lay members, for a total membership of 11.

The police department should be actively involved in the formulation and implementation of a community program of delinquency prevention and control. All available public and private resources should be fully used in such a program. It also should work with the public, private, and religious agencies devoted in whole or in part to delinquency prevention and coordinate the activities of these agencies to the extent desirable. Finally, it would collect, correlate, and disseminate information, statistics, and data on the subject of juvenile delinquency and make this information available to all agencies that might benefit from it.

Police in Low-Income Areas

There is a serious lack of understanding between residents of low-income areas and the police. All available means should be used to inform every citizen of the fact that the police serve not only to arrest and punish the lawbreaker, but also to protect the average citizen in his or her day-to-day life. The Calgary Police Department should send police counselors into problem areas to hold meetings and generally to inform the public of the protective role of the police. Neighborhood committees that include a police officer trained in social problem areas should be established. Existing independent neighborhood civic associations should also be used and a police counselor stationed in each Economic Opportunity Calgary neighborhood center.

Parks

One of Calgary's most serious problems with regard to juvenile delinquency and crime is that the most congested areas of the city have the fewest recreation facilities. Parks should be built in congested high crime areas of the city. Trained supervisory personnel must be provided. Equipment should be modern. More park police should be provided so that Calgary's people can enjoy their parks. Community centers should be kept open longer during the week and on weekends, particularly during the summer.

Organized Crime

The Commission has found that organized crime exists in Calgary on a local basis. More members of the Calgary Police Department should be trained to deal with the problems of organized crime. All law enforcement agencies in the Calgary area must constantly be on the alert for encroachments of organized crime on a local or national basis.

Care of the Alcoholic

Alcoholic offenders should be identified and a concerted effort should be made to remedy their addiction, thus eliminating the expense of their continued apprehension by the police, their imprisonment, and their trial before the Municipal Court. The Commission feels that this responsibility should belong to the City of Calgary.

Advancement

Police officers must be made secure in their jobs by an appropriate type of merit system. A cadet school for qualified high school graduates should be created, and there should be continued police training for recruit and veteran alike.

Modernization

The police department itself needs considerable modernization. The department should use all modern developments and law enforcement techniques, including such crime-fighting equipment as computers.

Police Department Study

The police department should be studied thoroughly by an independent professional agency to determine its present capabilities and its need for the immediate future. This study should evaluate and estimate Calgary's police requirements; it should appraise its organizational structure, personnel, equipment, and promotion system. On the basis of this study, there should be proposed a detailed plan of improvement to give the city and its citizens a modern police organization second to none.

Community Diversity

Different areas of the city have unique problems that do not seem to be recognized within the department. Similar services are provided throughout the city.

PRESENT ORGANIZATION STRUCTURE

In early 1980, the Calgary Police Department consisted of six divisions, each headed by a superintendent reporting to Chief Rousseau. The six divisions were: Service, Detective, Traffic, Uniform, Detention, and Training. The organization chart is shown in Exhibit 16-1.

Service Division

The Service Division, under the command of Superintendent Milton, is responsible for all the administrative aspects of the department. Superintendent Milton joined the department in 1950 and was named superintendent in 1975.

Specifically the division is charged with the compilation of criminal records (including the Royal Canadian Mounted Police reports), the transmitting and receiving of radio communications, and the telephone switchboard. The division is also responsible for all monies received by the department as well as the department's inventories, purchases, and maintenance.

The Service Division consists of the Crime Report Bureau, including Missing Persons Bureau, the Tabulation Room, and Communications. In addition, the division includes the Custodian's Office, Arsenal, and Maintenance Crew.

Detective Division

The Detective Division is headed by Superintendent Raymond Hill. Superintendent Hill joined the department in 1962 and was named Superintendent of the Detective Division in 1979.

The Detective Division is charged with the prevention of crime, the investigation of criminal offenses, the detection and arrest of criminals, and the recovery of stolen or lost property. The division consists of ten squads: Auto, Burglary, Homicide, Larceny, Robbery, Vice (includes Narcotic Investigations), Fugitive, Juvenile, Security, and Lottery. In addition, the Division includes the Identification Bureau and the General and Criminal Investigation Bureaus.

The most recent additions to the Detective Division are the Juvenile, Security, and Fugitive Squads.

The Juvenile Squad was formed in 1975 following rapid increase in the number of juveniles involved in illegal acts. The squad investigates cases in which children under 17 years of age are involved and assists other detective squads (when needed) to investigate crimes by juveniles. The division also works with the Juvenile Court authorities in the prevention of crime and rehabilitation of wayward children.

Sergeant Croy, who joined the department in 1962, heads the Juvenile Squad. Reporting to Sergeant Croy are nine persons.

The Security Squad consists of 12 officers and was formed in 1975. It operates under

EXHIBIT 16-1 ORGANIZATIONAL CHART FOR THE CALGARY POLICE DEPARTMENT

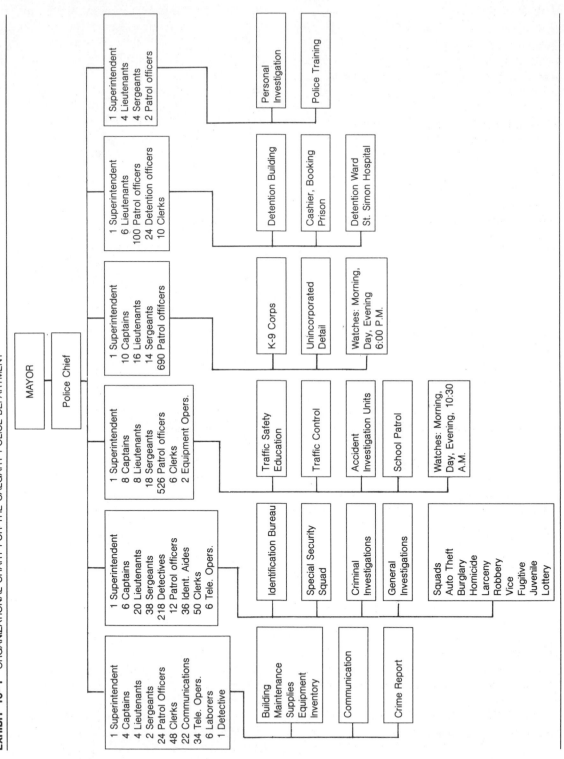

direct orders from the Chief of Police and the Superintendent of Detectives. The squad is charged with maintaining a constant check on the activities of subversive groups as well as keeping a check on any section of the city where racial tension exists or may start. The squad is also responsible for the safety of any visiting dignitaries (which includes working closely with other governmental agencies), investigating bombings, investigating internal problems that may arise within the department, and any other special assignments given by the Chief.

Lieutenant Madaline Barnett heads the Security Squad. Lieutenant Barnett is 32 years old. She joined the department eight years earlier as a uniformed officer patrolling a footbeat.

The Fugitive Squad was created in 1970. This squad specializes in the apprehension and prosecution of fugitives from penitentiary and justice. Lieutenant Benson heads this squad of 15 officers from Calgary plus 10 from other local jurisdictions.

Traffic Division

The Traffic Division promotes street and highway safety and the enforcement of vehicular traffic laws and regulations. In addition, the division is charged with handling large crowds who attend sports events, conventions, parades, circuses, and funerals. The Traffic Division consists of the following groups: Motorcycle, Accident Investigation, Foot Traffic, Parking Control, Radar Speed Control, and Helicopter Traffic Control. The division also includes School Police Officers, School Patrols, and the police wrecker.

Superintendent Spencer J. Lloyd heads the Traffic Division. He joined the department in 1952 and was named superintendent in 1980.

According to Chief Rousseau, if the Traffic Division can keep the number of fatalities low, the other traffic accident statistics will be reduced also. In pursuit of this goal, Chief Rousseau and Superintendent Lloyd meet weekly to discuss the current and projected traffic situation with representatives of the city, county, and provincial government agencies responsible for highways, the Calgary Safety Council, and several prominent citizens.

Uniform Division

The Uniform Division is charged with the protection of life and property, the prevention of crime, the detection and arrest of offenders, and the prevention of the public peace. Superintendent Samuel Locke is the commanding officer. He joined the department in 1949 and was named superintendent in 1966. Superintendent Locke's division consists of the following squads and bureaus: Radio Patrol; Motorcycle (nontraffic); K-9 Corps; Unincorporated Detail (see below); and Foot Patrols.

The Calgary Police Department furnishes, through the Uniform Division, services to the unincorporated area of Fulton County under a contract between the City of Calgary and Fulton County. The personnel and equipment comprising the Unincorporated Detail includes 4 captains; 2 lieutenants; 60 patrol officers; 16 patrol cars; 22 school traffic officers; and 8 motorcycles.

Detention Division

The Detention Division was established in 1973. Previously it was part of the service division. According to Chief Rousseau, during the racial problems of the early 1970's, 400 to 500 persons might be jailed at any one time. This created numerous problems that he believed could best be handled by a separate division.

Superintendent Jack Marston heads the Detention Division, which is responsible for the operations of the adjoining headquarters building and the detention ward at the Saint Simon Hospital, a large downtown public hospital. During 1980 about 155,000 people were processed by the Detention Division.

Superintendent Marston joined the department in 1955 and was named superintendent in 1966.

Training Division

The Training Division was created in 1974. Formerly it was part of the service division. The Training Division is responsible for police training and the investigation of applicants seeking to join the department. The division's commanding officer is Superintendent T. N. Danvers. He joined the force in 1950 and was appointed superintendent in 1973.

The division's principal training activity is a six-week school for new recruits conducted at least three times a year. Between 40 and 55 people attend each session, which is set up along the same lines as the RCMP's National Academy. Each session usually includes several officers from other departments, such as the airport or park police. These officers attend free of charge.

Other training activities include bimonthly discussion by each squad of the training keys prepared by the International Association of Chiefs of Police. These meetings are conducted by lieutenants and sergeants for the officers in their squads. Periodically, written examinations are given to all officers. These papers are graded and the results recorded in each officer's personnel file.

Watch System

The Police Department operates on the watch (shift) system. The watches are:

```
11 P.M.-7 A.M.  Morning Watch  ⎫
7 A.M.-3 P.M.   Day Watch      ⎬  Traffic
3 P.M.-11 P.M.  Night Watch    ⎭  Division

10 A.M.-6 P.M.  Traffic Watch  }  (intersection
                                  control)

8-9 A.M. & 2-4 P.M.  School Patrol
8 A.M.-4 P.M.        Office Personnel
12 P.M.-8 A.M.  ⎫
8 A.M.-4 P.M.   ⎬  Uniform &
4 P.M.-12 P.M.  ⎭  Detective
```

Each watch is covered by a captain from either the Uniform or Traffic Divisions, depending upon which one happens to be on duty at the time. "In this way," Chief Rousseau said, "I am able to have a superior officer responsible for whatever happens during the watch."

Districts

For patrol duty purposes, the City of Calgary is divided into four districts. Either 10 or 11 two-person patrol cars are assigned to each district during each watch. These cars are in constant radio communication with the central radio room located in the police headquarters building. Chief Rousseau refered to these patrol cars as his "mobile precincts." He believed it would take more funds to operate his department if it were organized on a precinct basis.

STRENGTHS AND WEAKNESSES OF THE CURRENT ORGANIZATION

Interview with Chief Rousseau:

Changes in Formal Structure   At the time I took over as chief, the service office operated out of the chief's office. In line with my desire to delegate authority, I created the Service Division and moved to the service and other divisions many of the management tasks formerly carried on by the chief's office. In the process I also abolished the two Deputy Chief of Police positions. Now, in my absence, the Superintendent of the Service Division acts as Chief.

Selection and Training   When I became Chief, I took action in two areas. First, I wanted to improve the training of police officers. I realized a number of officers did not fully realize what was demanded or expected of them. Second, I wanted to strengthen the moral courage and integrity of the department. While it is not always manifest, police officers are always under scrutiny and open to accusation. It appeared to me a number of officers were overly fearful of making mistakes or being falsely accused. I set out to correct this situation through training and clear-cut policies.

Our personnel department will accept applications only if our training division says that in their opinion the applicant will make a good police officer. Once the applicant is accepted and joins the force, s/he is assigned a counselor who is either a lieutenant or sergeant. The officers are encouraged to discuss with their counselor their problems. Also, we have squad meetings periodically to discuss the things on the officers' minds. I've told the counselors that if I get any reports of misconduct involving their advisees, I want to see the counselor. I want results.

The improvements over the last 10 years have been remarkable. We now have procedures and facilities for selection, training, and continuous officer testing and development. The ability of our officers is high.

Referring to the Crime Commission Report Now the Crime Commission has recommended we get more involved in prevention activities for juvenile and organized crime. The Mayor has told me to follow up these recommendations, but not to go over my budget allocation. In a sense our 6 P.M. detail has functioned as our crime prevention detail. Moreover, the Commission report seems to be calling for more than the normal concept of a police officer's function. How should I organize for crime prevention? How many officers should I assign to this task? What kind of officers should they be? What are some of the things these officers should be doing? These are all questions I must resolve quickly.

Other Problems The police department is becoming very large. Size is a problem. Police officers get lost in the bureaucracy. They have trouble identifying with the purpose of the organization. I wonder if a "precinct" form of organization (self-contained area police units) would be better? In addition we have so much paperwork. Millions of pieces of paper are processed each year. No one likes it.

Coordination between divisions is poor. Each division is becoming a separate organization, doing its own business. For example, one division doesn't know what another is doing when working in schools or low-income areas. They don't communicate with one another. Other examples: a patrol officer will write up a burglary, and never hear back from the detective division. Job openings are usually filled from within the same division. Personnel rotation is poor. Police officers can spend their careers in one activity.

We would like to install a large centralized computer in the Service Division to handle paperwork and do statistical analyses. We are afraid it may be unreliable, and that it will make the Police Department more bureaucratic and impersonal. Could computers be installed in each division?

17

Club Méditerranée

Sipping a cognac and smoking one of his favorite cigars on his way back to Paris from New York on the Concorde, Serge Trigano was reviewing the new organization structure that was to be effective November 1981. In the process, he was listing the operational problems and issues that were yet to be resolved. Son of the chief executive of the "Club Med," Serge Trigano was one of the joint managing directors and he had just been promoted from director of operations to general manager of the American zone, i.e., responsible for operations and marketing for the whole American market. Having experienced a regional organization structure that was abandoned some four years ago, he wanted to make sure that this time the new structure would better fit the objectives of Club Med and allow its further development in a harmonious way.

COMPANY BACKGROUND AND HISTORY

Club Med was founded in 1950 by a group of friends led by Gérard Blitz. Initially, it was a non-profit organization, set up for the purpose of going on vacation together in some odd place. The initial members were essentially young people who liked sports and especially the sea. The first "village," a tent village, was a camping site in the Balearic Isles. After four years of activities, Gilbert Trigano was appointed the new managing director. Gilbert Trigano came to Club Med from a family business involved in the manufacture of tents in France, a major supplier to Club Med. With this move, and in the same year, the holiday village concept was expanded beyond tent villages to straw hut villages, the first of which was opened in 1954. Further expanding its activities, in 1956 Club Med opened its first ski resort at Leysin, Switzerland. In 1965, its first bungalow village was opened, and in 1968 the first village started its operation in the American zone. Club Med's main activity, which it still is today, was to operate a vacation site for tourits who would pay a fixed sum (package) to go on vacation for a week, two weeks, or a month

This case was prepared by Professor Jacques Horovitz as a basis for class discussion rather than to illuminate either effective or ineffective handling of an administrative situation. Copyright © 1981 by IMEDE (International Management Development Institute), Lausanne, Switzerland. Not to be used or reproduced without permission.

and for whom all the facilities were provided in the village. Club Med has always had the reputation of finding beautiful sites that were fairly new to tourists (for instance, Moroccan tourism was "discovered" by Club Med) and that offered many activities, especially sports activities, to its members.* In 1981, Club Med operated 90 villages in 40 different countries on five continents. In addition to its main activity, it had extended to other sectors of tourism in order to be able to offer a wider range of services. In 1976, Club Med acquired a 45% interest in an Italian company (Valtur) that had holiday villages in Italy, Greece, and Tunisia, mainly for the Italian market. In 1977 Club Med took over Club Hotel, which had built up a reputation over the last 12 years as a leader in the seasonal ownership time-sharing market. The result of this expansion had been such than in 1980 more than 770,000 people had stayed in the villages of Club Med or its Italian subsidiary, whereas there were 2,300 in 1950. Most members were French in 1950, and in 1980 only 45% were French. See Exhibit 17-1. In addition, 110,000 people had stayed in the apartments or hotels managed by its time-sharing activity. In 1980, Club Med sales were actually about 2.5 billion French francs and its cash flow around 170 million French francs. The present case focuses exclusively on the organization structure of the holiday village operations and not on the time-sharing activities of the company.

SALES AND MARKETING

In 1981 Club Med was international with vacation sites all over the world, and so were its customers. They came from different continents, backgrounds, market segments, and did not look for the same thing in the vacation package. Club Med offered different types of villages, a wide range of activities to accomodate all the people who chose to go on a package deal. The Club offered ski villages, i.e., hotels in ski resorts for those who

*When going on vacation to any of Club Med's villages, one becomes a "member" of Club Med.

EXHIBIT 17-1 MEMBERS OF CLUB MED ACCORDING TO COUNTRY OF ORIGIN (1979) (EXCLUDING VALTUR)

France	301,000	43.1%
USA/Canada	124,000	17.8%
Belgium	41,600	6 %
Italy	34,400	4.9%
W. Germany	34,100	4.9%
Switzerland	18,500	2.6%
Austria	6,800	1 %
Australia	18,400	2.6%
Others	84,900	12.1%
Conference & seminars*	34,700	5 %*
	698,500	100 %

*Most seminars are in France for French customers.

liked to ski; straw-hut villages with a very Spartan comfort on the Mediterranean, mainly for young bachelors; hotel and bungalow resort villages with all comfort open throughout the year, some with special facilities for families and young children. An average client who went to a straw-hut village on the Mediterranean usually did not go to a plush village at Cap Skirring in Senegal (and the price was different too), although the same type of person might go to both.

A family with two or three children who could afford the time and money needed to travel to a relatively nearby village with a baby club was less likely to go to a village in Malaysia due to the long journey and the cost of transportation. Broadly speaking, a whole range of holiday makers were represented among the Club's customers. However, there was a larger proportion of office workers, executives, and professional people and a small proportion of workers and top management. The sales and marketing of the Club, which began in Europe, had expanded to include two other important markets: the American zone, including the U.S., Canada, and South America, and the Far Eastern zone, including Japan and Australia. The Club's sales network covered 29 countries; sales were either direct through the club-owned offices, 23 of which existed at the moment (see Exhibit 17-2 for countries where the Club owns commercial offices as well as villages and operations) or indirect through travel agencies (in France Havas was the main retailer). Originally, all the villages were aimed at the European market; in 1968 with the opening of its first village in America, the Club broke into the American market and opened an office in New York. Since then, the American market had grown more or less independently. Some 80% of the beds in the villages located in the American geographical

EXHIBIT 17-3 NUMBER OF VILLAGES BY TYPE AND SEASON*

	Sea			Mountain	Total
	Huts	Bungalows	Hotels		
Summer season	14	31	26	10	81
Winter season	0	19	11	23	53

Source: Club Méditerranée Trident N123/124 Winter 80-81, Summer 81.

area were sold to Club members in the United States and Canada; 65% of French sales, which represent 47% of the Club's turnover, were direct by personal visits to the office, by telephone or letter. However, in the U.S., direct sales accounted for only 5% of the total, the remaining 95% being sold through travel agencies. These differences were partly explained by national preferences, but also by a deliberate choice on the part of the Club. Until the appointment of Serge Trigano to lead the U.S. zone, all sales and marketing offices reported to a single world-wide marketing director.

THE VILLAGE

Club Med had around 90 villages and it was growing fast. In the next three years (1981-84) about 20 new villages were scheduled to open. At Club Med a village was typically either a hotel, bungalows, or huts, usually in a very nice area offering vacationers such activities as swimming, tennis, sailing, water skiing, windsurfing, archery, gymnastics, snorkling, deep sea diving, horseback riding, applied arts, yoga, golf, boating, soccer, circuits, excursions, bike riding, and skiing. There were also usually on site a shop, a hairdresser, even some cash changing, car renting, etc., and a baby or mini club in many places. Club Med was well known for having chosen sites that were the best in any country where they were, not only from a geographical point of view, but also from an architectural point of view and the facilities provided. Exhibit 17-3 shows the number of villages

EXHIBIT 17-2 COUNTRIES OF OPERATIONS (BEFORE NEW STRUCTURE)

Country	Separate Commercial Office	Country Manager	Country Manager Supervising Commercial Operations	Villages
Germany	X			
Switzerland	X	X		X
Turkey			X	X
Italy	X	X		X
Venezuela	X			
Belgium	X			X
Mexico			X	X
USA	X	X		
Bahamas		X	same as U.S.	X
Haiti		X	same as U.S.	X
Brazil			X	X
Japan	X			
Great Britain	X			
Tunisia			X	X
Morocco		X		X
Holland	X			
Greece	X	X		X
Israel			X	X
Malaysia	X	X		X
France	X	X		
New Zealand	X			
Australia	X			X
Egypt		X		X
Singapore	X			
Canada	X			
Tahiti		X		X
South Africa	X			
Spain	X	X		X
Senegal		X	same	X
Ivory Coast		X		
Mauritius		X	same as Reunion	X
Sri Lanka		X	same as Mauritius	X
Guadeloupe		X	same as U.S.	X
Martinique		X	same as U.S.	X
Reunion Island		X		X
Dominican Republic		X	same as U.S.	X
United Arab Emirates				X

that were open during the winter or summer season by type.

Essentially, there were three types of villages. The hut villages, which were the cheapest, open only during the summer season, and which started Club Med, and which were on the Mediterranean did not offer all the comfort that the wealthy traveler was used to (they had common showers, for example). Then there were bungalows or hotels or "hard type" villages, which were more comfortable with private bathrooms. Most were still double-bedded, which meant that two single men or women would have to share the same bedroom. In a village, there were two types of people. The GMs, or "gentils membres," who were the customers, usually came for one, two, three, or four weeks on a package deal to enjoy all the facilities and activities of any village. The GOs, or "gentils organisateurs," helped people make this vacation the best; there were GOs for sports, for applied arts, for excursions, for food, for the bar, as disk jockeys, as dancing instructors, for the children or babies in the mini-clubs, for maintenance, for traffic, for accounting, for receptions, etc. [Although the GOs were specialized by function, they also had to be simply "gentils organisateurs," i.e., making the GM's life easy and participating in common activities, such as arrival cocktails, shows, games, etc.] On average, there were 80 to 100 GOs per village.

There was a third category of people who were behind the scene: the service people, usually local people hired to maintain the facilities, the garden, to clean up, etc. (about 150 service people per village). They could also be promoted to GOs.

Every season, i.e., either after the summer season from May to September and winter season in April, or every six months, all the GOs would be moved from one village to another; that was one of the principles of the Club since its inception, so that nobody would stay for more than six months in any particular site. The village chief of maintenance was an exception. He stayed one full year; if a village was closed in the winter, he remained for the painting, the repair, etc. The service people (local people) were there all year around or for six months, if the village was only open in the summer (or winter for ski resorts). Exhibit 17-4 shows a typical organization structure of a village from the GO's point of view.

Under the chief of the village there were several coordinators: one for entertainment, responsible for all the day and night activities (shows, music, night club, plays, games, etc.); the sports chief who coordinated all the sports activities in any particular village; the maintenance chief who would see to the maintenance of the village, either when there was a breakdown or just to repaint the village or keep the garden clean, grow new flowers, etc., and who was assisted by the local service people; the food and beverage chief who

EXHIBIT 17-4   ORGANIZATION CHART OF A TYPICAL VILLAGE

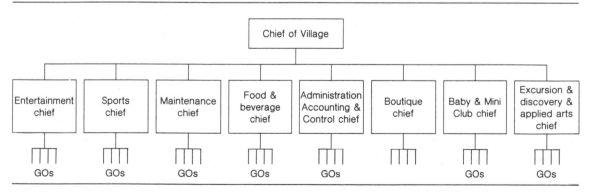

coordinated the cooking in the different restaurants and was responsible for the bar. Usually there was a bazaar for miscellaneous, a garment boutique, and a hairdresser under a boutique's coordinator. There was a coordinator for the baby club (if existent) within the village to provide the children with some special activities; this coordinator was also responsible for the medical part of the village (nurses and doctor). Many times there was a doctor on site, especially when a village was far from a big town. There was a coordinator of excursions and applied arts. Its services would help the GM to go somewhere or propose accompanied excursions (one, two, three days) for those who wanted it, or try with the help of a GO to make a silk scarf or pottery. There was a coordinator of administration, accounting, and control who dealt with cash, telephone, traffic, planning and reception, basic accounting, salaries for GOs and service personnel, taxes, etc. The services of food and beverages and the maintenance were the heaviest users of local service personnel.

COMPANY ORGANIZATION STRUCTURE

Exhibit 17-5 shows the organization structure of Club Med's holiday village activity just before Serge Trigano's appointment as Director of the U.S. zone. (The rest—time-sharing activities—are additional product-market subsidiaries.)

There were several joint managing directors who participated in the Management Committee. Essentially, the structure was a functional one with a joint managing director for marketing and sales, another one for operations, and several other function heads for accounting, finance and tax. Exhibit 17-6 shows how the operations part of the organization was structured.

Essentially the structure was composed of three parts. As there was an entertainment chief in the village, there was a director of entertainment at head office; the same was true of sports. There were several product directors who mirrored the structure of the village. There were country managers in certain countries where the Club had several vil-

EXHIBIT 17-5 ORGANIZATION CHART—BEFORE NOVEMBER 1981
HOLIDAY VILLAGES ACTIVITY ONLY

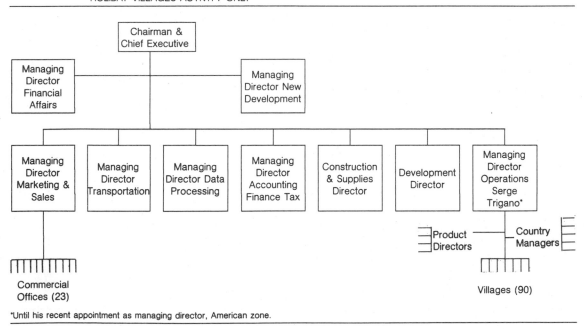

*Until his recent appointment as managing director, American zone.

lages in operation, and then there were the 90 villages. All reported to Serge Trigano.

THE ROLE OF THE PRODUCT DIRECTORS

Product directors were responsible for the product policy. They made decisions with respect to the policy of Club Med in all the villages, such as the type of activities that should be in each village, and the maintenance that should be done. They recruited and trained the various GOs needed for their domain (i.e., sports GOs, entertainment GOs, administration GOs, cooks, etc.). They staffed the villages by deciding with the director of operations which chief of village would go where and how many people would go with him. They made investment proposals for each village either for maintenance, new activities, extension, or renovation purposes. They also assumed the task of preparing the budgets and controlling application of policies in the villages by traveling extensively as "ambassadors" of the head office to the villages. Each one of them was assigned a certain number of villages. When visiting the village, he would go there representing not his particular product but Club Med's product as a whole. Also, each of them, including the director of operations, was assigned on a rotating basis the task of answering emergency phone calls from any village and making emergency decisions, or taking action if necessary. Exhibit 17-7 presents examples of product organization. In the new regional

EXHIBIT 17-6 ORGANIZATION CHART—JUST BEFORE THE NEW MOVE (NOV. 1981)

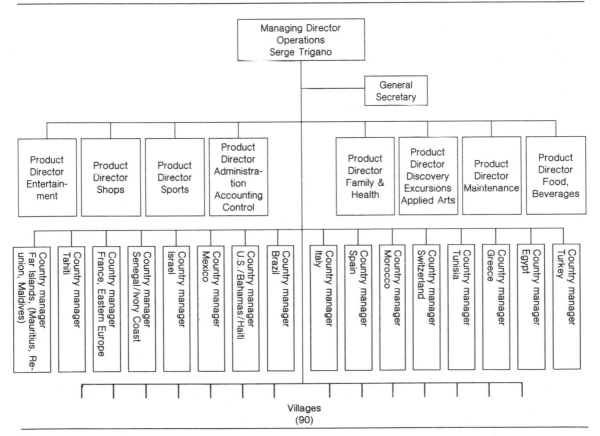

EXHIBIT 17-7 EXAMPLES OF PRODUCT MANAGEMENT

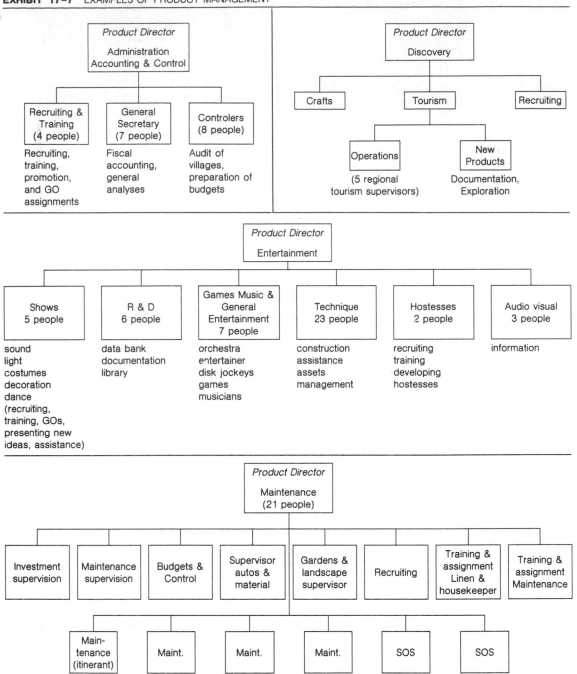

structure, their role and place were questioned.

THE ROLE OF THE COUNTRY MANAGER

Country managers were mainly the ambassadors of Club Med in the countries where Club Med had village(s). Usually they were located in countries with more than one village. They would handle political relations themselves, maintaining lasting relationships with elected bodies, mayors, civil servants, regional offices, etc. They would introduce to the new team coming every six months what the country had to offer, its constraints, local mores, the local people to be invited, local artists to be invited, the traps to be avoided, the types of suppliers, the type of local events that might be of interest for the village (so that the village would not forget, for instance, national holidays, etc.). They would try to get Club Med more integrated politically and socially in the host country, in particular in less developed countries where there was a gap between the abundance and richness of the Club compared to its immediate environment. They also had an assistance role such as getting work permits for GOs and also finding suppliers; sometimes, in fact, the country manager had a buyer attached to his staff who would purchase locally for the different villages to get economies of scale. In addition, the country managers personally recruited and maintained lists of the service personnel available to Club Med. They would negotiate the salaries, wages, and working conditions of the service personnel with the unions so that the village wasn't involved every six months in a renegotiation. Also, they might have an economic role by helping develop local production or culture as the Club was a heavy buyer of local food and products. They could also act as a development antenna looking for new sites or receiving proposals from local investors and submit them to head office. They would handle legal and tax problems when Club Med had a local legal entity, and maintain relationships with the owners of the land, hotels, or bungalows when Club Med—as was often the case—was only renting the premises.

PROBLEMS WITH THE CURRENT STRUCTURE

The current structure had been set up about four years ago. It had also been the Club Med's structure before 1971, but in between (1971-1976) there had been a change in the operations side only that had involved setting up area managers; instead of having one director of operations, there had been five directors who had under their control several countries and villages. From 1971 to 1976, there had been no country managers and each of the area managers had had about 10 or 15 villages under his supervision. This structure was changed in 1976 because it seemed to have created several Club Meds in one. The area managers had started to try to get the best chiefs of village and people for their area. As a result, GOs were not moving around every six months from one area of the world to another as was the policy, and area managers started giving different types of services to their customers so that, for instance, a Frenchman going to one of the zones one year and to another the next year would find a different Club Med. These reasons had led to the structure presented in Exhibit 17-6 for the operations. But until now marketing had always been world-wide.

Of course, the structure in operation until now had created the reverse problem: it seemed to Serge Trigano and others that it was too centralized. In fact, Serge Trigano had a span of control (which is rarely achieved in industry) of 90 chiefs of village plus 8 product directors and 14 country managers, all reporting to him from all over the world. There was an overload of information, too much detail and too many issues being entrusted to him, which would be worse as time would go by since Club Med was growing and doubling its capacity every five years. Besides the problem of centralization and information overload, another problem seemed to appear because Club Med's operations had not adapted enough to the international character of its customers. Most of the GOs were still recruited in France whereas now 15-20% of the customers came from the American zone. France was not even the best location to find GOs, who often needed to speak at least one other language. They had to be unmarried, under 30, they had to change countries every six months, and they had to work long hours and be accessible 24 hours a day, seven days a week, for a relatively low salary. The feeling was that maybe one could find happier and more enthusiastic people in Australia or Brazil than in France. Too much centralization, information overload, and lack of internationalization in operations were among the big problems in the current structure. Also, there was a feeling that a closer local coordination between marketing and operations could give better results since customers seemed to concentrate on one zone (American in the U.S., European in Europe) because of transportation costs, and a coordination might lead to a better grasp of customer needs, price, product, offices, etc. For example, when Club Med was smaller and operating only in Europe, departure to its villages was possible only once a week. As a result, reception at the village, welcome, and departure was also once a week. Lack of local coordination between operations and marketing had created arrivals and departures almost every day in certain villages, overburdening GO smiles and organization of activities. As another illustration, the American customer was used to standard hotel services (such as bathroom, towels, etc.), which may differ from European services. Closer local ties might help the Club respond better to local needs.

Centralization had also created bottlenecks in assignments and supervision of people. Every six months everybody—all GOs—was coming back to Paris from all over the world to be assigned to another village. Five or ten years ago, this was in fact a great happening that allowed everybody to discuss with the product people, see headquarters, and find friends who had been in other villages. But now with 5,000 GOs coming almost at the same time—and wanting to speak to the product directors—reassigning them was becoming somewhat hectic. It was likely to be even worse in the future because of the growth of the company.

PLANNING AND CONTROL

The planning cycle could be divided into two main parts: first, there was a three-year plan started two years ago, which involved the product directors and the country managers. Each product director would define his objectives for the next three years, the action programs that would go with it, and propose investments that he would like to make for his product in each of the 90 villages. All the product directors would meet to look at the villages one by one and see how the investment fitted together as well as consider the staffing number of GOs and service personnel in broad terms for the next three years. Of course, the big chunk of the investment program was the maintenance of the facilities since 55% of the investment program concerned such maintenance programs. The rest was concerned with additions or modifications of the villages, such as new tennis courts, a new theater, restaurant, revamping a boutique, etc. The country managers were involved in that same three-year plan. First of all they would give the product directors their feelings and suggestions for investments as well as for staffing the villages. In addition, they would provide some objectives and action programs in the way they would try to handle personnel problems, political problems, economic problems, cultural and social integration, sales of Club Med in their country, and development.

Besides this three-year operational plan, there was the one-year plan that was divided into two six-month plans. For each season a budget was prepared for each of the villages. This budget was mostly prepared by the product director for administration accounting, and it concerned the different costs, such as goods consumed, personnel charges, rents, etc. This budget was given to the chief of the village when he left with his team. In addition to this operational budget, there was an investment budget every six months that was more detailed than the three-year plan. This investment budget was prepared by the maintenance director under the guidance of and proposals from the different product directors. It was submitted to the operations director and then went directly to the chief executive of the company. It had not been unusual before the three-year plan had been controlled that the proposals that product directors were making to the maintenance director were three times as high as what would be in fact given and allowed by the chief executive.

On the control side, there was a controller in each of the villages (administrator chief of accounting and control) as well as central controllers who would be assigned a region and would travel from one village to the other. But the local controller and his team in fact were GOs like any others and they were changing from one village to another every six months. There was a kind of "fact and rule book" that was left in the village so that the next team would understand the particular ways and procedures of the village. But, generally speaking, each new team would start all over again each time with a new budget and standard, rules, and procedures from central head office as well as with the help of the fact and rule book. These two tools—the three-year plan and the six-month (a season) budgets—were the main planning and control tools used.

OBJECTIVES AND POLICIES

Five objectives seemed to be important to Serge Trigano when reviewing the structure.

One was that the Club wanted to continue to grow and double its capacity every five years, either by adding new villages or increasing the size of the current ones.

The second objective, which had always guided Club Med, was that it would continue

to innovate, not to be a hotel chain but to be something different as it had always been and to continue to respond to the changing needs of the customers.

A third objective stemmed from the fact that Club Med was no longer essentially French; the majority of its customers did not in fact come from France. As a result, it would have to continue to internationalize its employees, its structure, its way of thinking, training, etc.

The fourth objective was economic. Costs were increasing, but not all these costs could be passed on to the *gentils membres* unless the Club wanted to stop its growth. One way of not passing all costs to the customer was to increase productivity by standardization and by better methods and procedures.

The fifth objective was to retain the basic philosophy of Club Med: to keep the village concept an entity protected as much as possible from the outside world, but integrated in the country in which it was; to keep the package concept for GMs; and finally to retain the social mixing. Whatever your job, your social position, etc., at Club Med you were only recognized by two things: the color of your bathing suit and the beads you wore around your neck that allowed you to pay for your scotch, orange juice, etc., at the bar. Part of the philosophy, in addition, was to make sure that the GO's nomadism would continue: change every season.

THE PROPOSED NEW STRUCTURE

With these objectives in mind, the new structure to be effective November 1981 had just been sketched as shown in Exhibit 17-8.

The idea would be to move the operations and marketing closer together in three zones. One would be America (North and South), another Europe and Africa, and the third (in the long run when this market would be more developed) the Far East. In each area, a director would manage the operations side (the villages) and the marketing side (promotion, selling, pricing, distributing Club Med's concept). In fact, most of the American GMs were going to the American zone villages, most of the European GMs to the European zone, and most of the Asian GMs to the Asian zone. As the cost of transportation from one zone to another was increasing, people could not afford to go very far.

This was the general idea and now it had to be pushed further. Among the main interesting and troublesome aspects of the new structure were the following: how to keep the Club Med from separating into three different entities with three different types of products with this structure? Should such an occurrence be avoided? It seemed that this should not be allowed; that's why the structure that had been there four years ago with five regions failed. It had transformed Club Med into five mini Club Meds, although even at that time the five area managers did not have marketing and sales responsibility. In addition to this major issue of how to preserve the unity and uniqueness of Club Med with a geographic structure, several other questions were of great importance:

- Who would decide what activities would take place in a village?
- Who would decide the investments to be made in a village?
- Who would staff a village?
- Would there be a central hiring and training of all GOs or only some of them?
- How would the geographic managers be evaluated in terms of performance?
- If they wanted to continue with the GOs and give them the right and the opportunity to move every six months from one part of the world to another, how would the transfer of GOs be done?
- How should the transfer of GOs be coordinated?
- Should there be some common basic procedures, like accounting, reporting, etc., and in that case, who would design and enforce those procedures?
- How could there be some coordination and allocation of resources among the three regions? Who would do it? How would it be done?

EXHIBIT 17–8 THE PROPOSED STRUCTURE

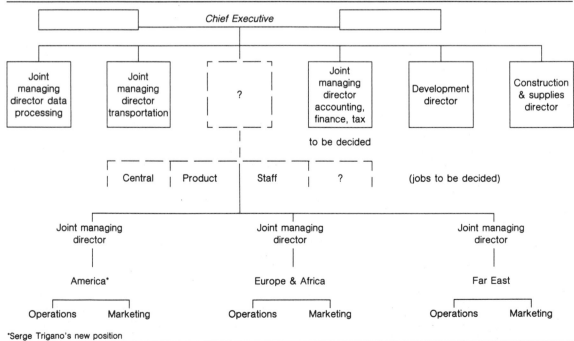

*Serge Trigano's new position

Also of importance was the problem of transition.

- What would happen to the country managers?
- What would happen to the product directors?

- What would happen to central marketing and sales?

These were some of the questions that bothered Serge Trigano on the flight to Paris from New York.

18

Organizational Coordination

The purpose of this exercise is to analyze the coordination and integration mechanisms in organizations. One purpose of structure is to provide horizontal and vertical linkages between organizational subcomponents. Linkage is the sharing of information to achieve coordination within the organization. Vertical mechanisms for coordination, such as vertical information systems, rules and procedures, and plans and schedules, link the lower and upper levels of the organization. Horizontal linkages such as task forces, committees, liaison roles, and full-time integrators provide coordination across departments.

STEP 1: *Determination of Linkage Mechanisms (20 min.)*

The organization chart (Exhibit 18-1) is of Condensed Products, Inc., a medium-size manufacturing firm. For each coordination problem below, indicate the type of linkage mechanism that you think would be most appropriate. Outline your reasons for selecting the mechanism and indicate which organizational positions would be involved.

STEP 2: *Class Discussion (10 min.)*

The following questions may be useful in focusing your discussion on conceptual material presented in previous lectures.

1. Is it possible that more than one type of linkage would be appropriate? How did you determine which would be most effective?
2. In addition to using an appropriate linkage mechanism what else is necessary for effective coordination and integration of functions?
3. Would a different organizational structure (matrix or product) require different linkage mechanisms for the same situations? Give an example.
4. What effect do the internal and external environments have on the need for coordination and integration? Would these also affect the types of linkages selected? In what way?

COORDINATION PROBLEMS

1. The salesforce has discovered that many customers are dissatisfied with the quality of the newest product being offered by the company. The product was the result of an idea initiated by the research division. The research division designed the product that was then forwarded to production.

Numerous delays were caused by incomplete designs, lack of parts necessary to complete the product, and failure to meet safety and quality checks. Initial sales indicate there may be a large demand for the product (initial marketing research indicated the same). However, the complaints being received require immediate attention in order for sales not to be affected. In addition to solving this problem the plant manager wants to avoid similar incidents in the future.

2. Recently the Director of Data Processing attended a conference on management information systems. She returned feeling the operations of Condensed Products would be better coordinated and controlled if such a system were installed. The system she has in mind would require input of quantitative data from various units into the computer system. The data could be analyzed and compiled into weekly reports that would indicate production rates, expenses incurred, and specific departmental records (e.g., turnover, sales records, budget information, monitoring of stock levels). The Director realizes she must submit a proposal that outlines the potential of the system and provides for (1) the short-term task of assessing the needs and use in each department and (2) the long-term implementation and coordination in each area.

3. The President has been receiving individual weekly written reports from each vice-president outlining the week's activities, problems, and successes. Occasionally the report of one department would be useful to another vice-president, but only if the information were received in a timely fashion. It is also evident from past experience that some of the legal entanglements that are currently in court could have been avoided if the company's general counsel

EXHIBIT 18-1 ORGANIZATION CHART FOR CONDENSED PRODUCTS, INC.

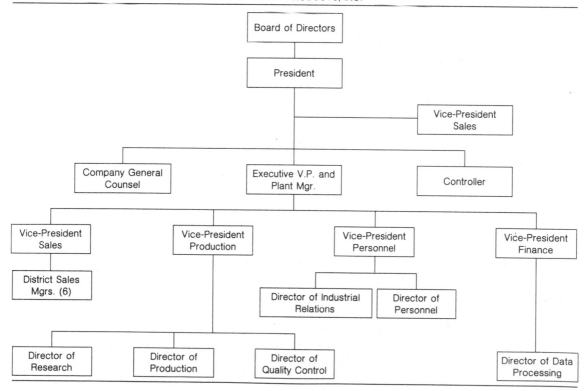

had been aware of problems earlier. The vice-presidents don't anticipate the speed with which a minor irritation can grow into a major lawsuit.

4. The local union, which represents the majority of the production employees, has just released its latest points to be included in the new contract. One issue that appears feasible is to enlarge the employee cafeteria. The Director of Industrial Relations feels this will need only the approval of the plant manager and can actually proceed before the contract negotiations begin.

5. A rash of in-house thefts of office equipment and small tools has been discovered during the annual inventory of plant equipment. Though the company policy explicitly states the ramifications for stealing, several departments have allowed employees to borrow materials overnight, or for a weekend, in order to do company business at home. The plant manager has received the itemized listing of losses and is appalled at the extent of the losses.

6. The Board of Directors has agreed to begin acquisition procedures for a similar company in a neighboring state. The Board has decided that the President will be responsible for all phases of the acquisition, including determining how the new company will merge with the current organization, at least in terms of operating. It has been agreed that the new acquisition will remain separate, but will be reporting to the President. The concern of the Board is that the President will frequently be out of town and, when the new company is acquired, the President will have two companies to monitor and twice as many positions reporting to him. There is also some concern as to whether the two companies should merge some activities.

7. The six district sales managers have been with the company for varying lengths of time and have differing levels of ability. The six have semi-annual meetings to discuss problems and issues in sales techniques. One manager has suggested that the group get someone who is knowledgeable about sales techniques and can give some training on sales. The group has agreed that a "short course" would be helpful, but isn't quite sure how to go about getting approval or even if the company would fund it. There may even be similar programs offered by the company personnel department, but none of the district sales managers is familiar with the internal staff development opportunities.

III

Internal Organization Processes

19

The Welfare Department

Rozalind Stamos, Director of the Intake Section of the Lincoln County Welfare Department, prepared to confront the group leaders of her section—Alan Short and Susan Evans. She had about reached the end of her rope over the conflict between the two groups. Alan and Susan each supervised six intake workers involved in a pilot project to provide direct service to applicants for welfare, as well as to reduce the pay-out to recipients.

The state welfare department had approved a one-year trial of "Roz's brainchild." She had hand-picked the 12 most productive, enthusiastic, and personable caseworkers, and the two best group leaders, for this experiment. Caseworkers were to work with each applicant to determine the type and duration of assistance necessary for the client to become self-supporting; to help secure the indicated services (training, child support, housing, etc.); to provide personal support; and to negotiate a predetermined termination date. As an experienced social worker, Roz was confident that the program would help teach the truly needy necessary survival skills, provide temporary financial

help, and eventually reduce the amount of aid actually paid to welfare recipients.

Roz thought she had done everything "by the book." Alan and Susan helped select their caseworkers. Everyone pitched in during the move to the new facilities, laughing and joking with each other as they determined the arrangement of desks, dividers, telephones, etc. The caseworkers, clerks, and receptionists brought in champagne and snacks in celebration of the new venture. It all seemed like one big happy family—then.

Now, six weeks later, caseworkers from one group aren't speaking to those of the other, Alan and Susan no longer lunch together, and Roz can't remember the last time anyone laughed. Simon, the receptionist, has just left Roz's office. There are 15 people waiting in the Intake lobby, and not one caseworker will answer his calls. He reported that three workers from each group were out of the office on home visits, but that the other six refused any new cases. The workers in Alan's group told him to assign all new cases to people in Susan's group until the case loads were more even, and Susan's people told her they wouldn't see anyone until Alan's people did. He didn't know what to do, and was almost shaking with frustration.

Roz invited Alan and Susan into her office, closed the door, and demanded, "What is going on out there? I feel I'm running a kindergarten. What is wrong with your people?"

Alan responded, "My people are justifiably refusing to carry the whole department any longer. They break their backs working with an intake for an hour—convincing her to get into a training program; setting up an appointment with Legal Aid to file for child support; calling a friend in Food Stamps; getting a rent payment from the township; and finally securing a pre-dated withdrawal from the client. When they get back to their desks they find notes indicating that the next two intakes are theirs. They look over and see three people in Susan's unit sitting there with clean desks and smug smiles on their faces. It's not fair for my people to do what they are supposed to and Susan's to just glide by."

"Whoa, wait just a minute," Susan said, holding up her hand. "Why should my people do double work just because they are more efficient than yours? Intakes are assigned alternately, but equally. If Marie can complete hers in 20 minutes, why should she take two more just because it takes Sydney an hour to do one? That would mean that Marie would be seeing three times as many people. That is what isn't fair."

At this point, Roz interceded and asked, "How is it that there is such a difference between the groups in the amount of time spent on an intake? We have a checklist for all the possible service. Alan, why do your people take so long?

"Possibly because they are doing a good job," Alan retorted. "They spend time with each person, they listen, they care. They don't just go through the checklist—they look for ways to really help people. When they make home visits they often end up taking children to the clinic, or the whole family to the grocery. They are acting in the real spirit of this program—not just going through the motions. Look at the stats—you'll find that at least 50% of the time my people get voluntary withdrawals. Susan's average is less then 20%. That's the difference."

"Look," Susan replied, "there are some cases where a voluntary withdrawal is not appropriate. Some people really need long-term help. Others are never going to agree to withdraw, so it is just a waste of time to try to convince them. My workers know that. Maybe what we need is for them to teach your group how to judge people more accurately."

"Fat chance! My workers won't be caught dead with your bunch of goldbricks. They want to help people, but they won't be walked on any longer, and I support them."

"Save me from the world-savers," said Susan, *sotto voce.*

20

The University Art Museum

Visitors to the campus were always shown the University Art Museum, of which the large and distinguished university was very proud. A photograph of the handsome neoclassical building that housed the Museum had long been used by the university for the cover of its brochures and catalogues.

The building, together with a substantial endowment, was given to the university around 1912 by an alumnus, the son of the university's first president, who had become very wealthy as an investment banker. He also gave the university his own small, but high quality, collections—one of Etruscan figurines, and one, unique in America, of English pre-Raphaelite paintings. He then served as the Museum's unpaid director until his death. During his tenure he brought a few additional collections to the museum, largely from other alumni of the university. Only rarely did the museum purchase anything. As a result, the museum housed several small collections of uneven quality. As long as the founder ran the museum, none of the collections was ever shown to anybody except a few members of the university's art history faculty, who were admitted as the founder's private guests.

After the founder's death, in the late 1920s, the university intended to bring in a professional museum director. Indeed, this had been part of the agreement under which the founder had given the museum. A search committee was to be appointed, but in the meantime a graduate student in art history who had shown interest in the museum and who had spent a good many hours in it, took over temporarily. At first, she did not even have a title, let alone a salary. But she stayed on acting as the museum's director and over the next 30 years was promoted in stages to that title. But from the first day, whatever her title, she was in charge. She immediately set about changing the museum altogether. She catalogued the collections. She pursued new gifts, again primarily small collections from alumni and other friends of the university. She organized fund raising for the museum. But, above all, she began to integrate the museum into the work of the university. When a space problem arose in the years immediately following World War II,

From *Management Cases* by Peter F. Drucker. Copyright © 1977 by Peter F. Drucker. By permission of Harper & Row, Publishers, Inc.

Miss Kirkhoff offered the third floor of the museum to the art history faculty, which moved its offices there. She remodeled the building to include classrooms and a modern and well-appointed auditorium. She raised funds to build one of the best research and reference libraries in art history in the country. She also began to organize a series of special exhibitions built around one of the museum's own collections, complemented by loans from outside collections. For each of these exhibitions she had a distinguished member of the university's art faculty write a catalogue. These catalogues speedily became the leading scholarly texts in the fields.

Miss Kirkhoff ran the University Art Museum for almost half a century. But old age ultimately defeated her. At the age of 68 after suffering a severe stroke, she had to retire. In her letter of resignation she proudly pointed to the museum's growth and accomplishment under her stewardship. "Our endowment," she wrote, "now compares favorably with museums several times our size. We never have had to ask the university for any money other than for our share of the university's insurance policies. Our collections in the areas of our strength, while small, are of first-rate quality and importance. Above all, we are being used by more people than any museum of our size. Our lecture series, in which members of the university's art history faculty present a major subject to a university audience of students and faculty, attracts regularly 300-500 people; and if we had the seating capacity, we could easily have a larger audience. Our exhibitions are seen and studied by more visitors, most of them members of the university community, than all but the most highly publicized exhibitions in the very big museums ever draw. Above all, the courses and seminars offered in the museum have become one of the most popular and most rapidly growing educational features of the university. No other museum in this country or anywhere else," concluded Miss Kirkhoff, "has so successfully integrated art into the life of a major university and a major university into the work of a museum."

Miss Kirkhoff strongly recommended that the university bring in a professional museum director as her successor. "The museum is much too big and much too important to be entrusted to another amateur such as I was 45 years ago," she wrote. "And it needs careful thinking regarding its direction, its basis of support, and its future relationship with the university."

The university took Miss Kirkhoff's advice. A search committee was duly appointed and, after one year's work, it produced a candidate whom everybody approved. The candidate was himself a graduate of the university who had then obtained his Ph.D. in art history and in museum work from the university. Both his teaching and administrative record were sound, leading to his present museum directorship in a medium-sized city. There he converted an old, well-known, but rather sleepy museum to a lively, community-oriented museum whose exhibitions were well publicized and attracted large crowds.

The new museum director took over with great fanfare in September, 1971. Less than three years later he left—with less fanfare, but still with considerable noise. Whether he resigned or was fired was not quite clear. But that there was bitterness on both sides was only too obvious.

The new director, upon his arrival, had announced that he looked upon the museum as a "major community resource" and intended to "make the tremendous artistic and scholarly resources of the Museum fully available to the academic community as well as to the public." When he said these things in an interview with the college newspaper, everybody nodded in approval. It soon became clear that what he meant by "community resource" and what the faculty and students understood by these words were not the same. The museum had always been "open to the public" but, in practice, it was members of the college community who used the museum and attended its lectures, its exhibitions, and its frequent seminars.

The first thing the new director did, however, was to promote visits from the public schools in the area. He soon began to change the exhibition policy. Instead of organizing small shows, focused on a major collection of the museum and built around a scholarly catalogue, he began to organize "popular exhibitions" around "topics of general interest" such as "Women Artists through the Ages." He promoted these exhibitions vigorously in the newspapers, in radio and television interviews, and, above all, in the local schools. As a result, what had been a busy but quiet place was soon knee-deep in school children, taken to the museum in special buses that cluttered the access roads around the museum and throughout the campus. The faculty, which was not particularly happy with the resulting noise and confusion, became thoroughly upset when the scholarly old chairman of the art history department was mobbed by fourth-graders who sprayed him with their water pistols as he tried to push his way through the main hall to his office.

Increasingly, the new director did not design his own shows, but brought in traveling exhibitions from major museums, importing their catalogue as well rather than have his own faculty produce one.

The students too were apparently unenthusiastic after the first six or eight months, during which the new director had been somewhat of a campus hero. Attendance at the classes and seminars held in the art museum fell off sharply, as did attendance at the evening lectures. When the editor of the campus newspaper interviewed students for a story on the museum, he was told again and again that the museum had become too noisy and too "sensational" for students to enjoy the classes and to have a chance to learn.

What brought all this to a head was an Islamic art exhibit in late 1973. Since the museum had little Islamic art, nobody criticized the showing of a traveling exhibit, offered on very advantageous terms with generous financial assistance from some of the Arab governments. But then, instead of invit-

ing one of the University's own faculty members to deliver the customary talk at the opening of the exhibit, the director brought in a cultural attache of one of the Arab embassies in Washington. The speaker, it was reported, used the occasion to deliver a violent attack on Israel and on the American policy of supporting Israel against the Arabs. A week later, the university senate decided to appoint an advisory committee, drawn mostly from members of the art history faculty, which, in the future, would have to approve all plans for exhibits and lectures. The director thereupon, in an interview with the campus newspaper, sharply attacked the faculty as "elitist" and "snobbish" and as believing that "art belongs to the rich." Six months later, in June 1974, his resignation was announced.

Under the bylaws of the university, the academic senate appoints a search committee. Normally, this is pure formality. The chairperson of the appropriate department submits the department's nominees for the committee who are approved and appointed, usually without debate. But when the academic senate early the following semester was asked to appoint the search committee, things were far from "normal". The dean who presided, sensing the tempers in the room, tried to smooth over things by saying, "Clearly, we picked the wrong person the last time. We will have to try very hard to find the right one this time."

He was immediately interrupted by an economist, known for his populism, who broke in and said, "I admit that the late director was probably not the right personality. But I strongly believe that his personality was not at the root of the problem. He tried to do what needs doing and this got him in trouble with the faculty. He tried to make our museum a community resource, to bring in the community and to make art accessible to broad masses of people, to the blacks and the Puerto Ricans, to the kids from the ghetto schools and to a lay public. And this is what we really resented. Maybe his methods were not the most tactful ones—I admit I could have done without those interviews he gave. But what he tried to do was right. We had better commit ourselves to the policy he wanted to put into effect, or else we will have deserved his attacks on us as 'elitist' and 'snobbish.' "

"This is nonsense," cut in the usually silent and polite senate member from the art history faculty. "It makes absolutely no sense for our museum to try to become the kind of community resource our late director and my distinguished colleague want it to be. First there is no need. The city has one of the world's finest and biggest museums and it does exactly that and does it very well. Secondly, we here have neither the artistic resources nor the finanical resources to serve the community at large. We can do something different but equally important and indeed unique. Ours is the only museum in the country, and perhaps in the world, that is fully integrated with an academic community and truly a teaching institution. We are using it, or at least we used to until the last few unfortunate years, as a major educational resource for all our students. No other museum in the country, and as far as I know in the world, is bringing undergraduates into art the way we do. All of us, in addition to our scholarly and graduate work, teach undergraduate courses for people who are not going to be art majors or art historians. We work with the engineering students and show them what we do in our conservation and restoration work. We work with architecture students and show them the development of architecture through the ages. Above all, we work with liberal arts students, who often have had no exposure to art before they came here and who enjoy our courses all the more because they are scholarly and not just 'art appreciation.' This is unique and this is what our museum can do and should do."

"I doubt that this is really what we should be doing," commented the chairman of the mathematics department. "The museum, as far as I know, is part of the graduate faculty. It should concentrate on training art historians

in its Ph.D. program, on its scholarly work, and on its research. I would strongly urge that the museum be considered an adjunct to graduate and especially to Ph.D. education, confine itself to this work, and stay out of all attempts to be 'popular,' on both campus and outside of it. The glory of the museum is the scholarly catalogues produced by our faculty, and our Ph.D. graduates who are sought after by art history faculties throughout the country. This is the museum's mission, which can only be impaired by the attempt to be 'popular,' whether with students or with the public."

"These are very interesting and important comments," said the dean, still trying to pacify. "But I think this can wait until we know who the new director is going to be. Then we should raise these questions with him."

"I beg to differ, Mr. Dean," said one of the elder statesmen of the faculty. "During the summer months, I discussed this question with an old friend and neighbor of mine in the country, the director of one of the nation's great museums. He said to me: 'You do not have a personality problem, you have a *management* problem. You have not, as a university, taken responsibility for the mission, the direction, and the objectives of your museum. Until you do this, no director can succeed. And this is *your* decision. In fact, you cannot hope to get a good man until you can tell him what your basic objectives are. If your late director is to blame—I know him and I know that he is abrasive—it is for being willing to take on a job when you, the university, had not faced up to the basic management decisions. There is no point talking about *who* should manage until it is clear *what* it is that has to be managed and for what.' "

At this point the dean realized that he had to adjourn the discussion unless he wanted the meeting to degenerate into a brawl. But he also realized that he had to identify the issues and possible decisions before the next faculty meeting a month later. Here is the list of questions he put down on paper later that evening:

1. What are the possible purposes of the University Museum:

   ■ to serve as a laboratory for the graduate art-history faculty and the doctoral students in the field?
   ■ to serve as major "enrichment" for the undergraduate who is not an art-history student but wants both a "liberal education" and a counter-weight to the highly bookish diet fed to him in most of our courses?
   ■ to serve the metropolitan community—and especially its schools—outside the campus gates?

2. Who are or should be its customers?

   ■ the graduate students in professional training to be teachers of art history?
   ■ the undergraduate community—or rather, the entire college community?

   ■ the metropolitan community and especially the teachers and youngsters in the public schools?
   ■ any others?

3. Which of these purposes are compatible and could be served simultaneously? Which are mutually exclusive or at the very least are likely to get in each other's way?

4. What implications for the structure of the museum, the qualifications of its director, and its relationship to the university follow from each of the above purposes?

5. Do we need to find out more about the needs and wants of our various potential customers to make an intelligent policy decision? How could we go about it?

The dean distributed these questions to the members of the faculty with the request that they think them through and discuss them before the next meeting of the academic senate.

21

Measuring Organizational Effectiveness

Organizational effectiveness is the degree to which an organization realizes its goals. Various approaches to assessing effectiveness include whether the organization achieves its goals in terms of desired levels of output; whether the organization obtains the resources necessary for high performance; and whether the internal activities and processes of the organization reflect an internal health and efficient use of resources.

The organizations listed below operate with different goals in mind and assess their effectiveness at meeting these goals in different ways. The purpose of this exercise is to illustrate the relationship between goals and effectiveness and methods for measuring effectiveness.

STEP 1: *Determining Goals and Assessing Effectiveness (20 min.)*

For each organization below list two possible goals and the approach which might be used to assess the organization's effectiveness at meeting these goals.

STEP 2: *Small-Group Discussion (15 min.)*

Working in groups of three, discuss the goals you have identified and the measures necessary to determine the effectiveness of the organization in meeting these goals.

STEP 3: *Group Presentation (10 min.)*

Each group should select from the list one organization and corresponding set of goals and effectiveness measures to share with the class. In explaining your choice, indicate why other types of measures would or would not be just as useful in measuring organizational effectiveness.

STEP 4: *Class Discussion (15 min.)*

Review and discuss the goals and measures identified by the members of the class. The following questions may be helpful in integrating this exercise with previous class discussions regarding goals and effectiveness.

DISCUSSION QUESTIONS

1. Did the goals and measures of effectiveness tend to be stated in quantitative or qualitative terms? Which is easier to observe?

2. Is it possible to have multiple measures for one goal? If so, give an example. Do multiple measures guarantee a better assessment of achieving goals?

3. How does efficiency relate to the goals and effectiveness measures identified by the exercise? Are there different determinations for efficiency? Such as?

4. When determining measures of effectiveness, who did you decide would be applying such measures? Top management? Employees? Customers? Does it matter?

5. In which domain is each goal? How does this translate into the measurements you selected?

		Goals	*Effectiveness Measures*
1.	Automobile Manufacturer		
2.	Post Office		
3.	Professional Hockey Team		
4.	Local Newspaper		
5.	Farmer		
6.	High School		
7.	Labor Union		
8.	Community Theater Group		
9.	Local Chamber of Commerce		

22

Identifying Organizational Goals

The purpose of this exercise is to understand the types of goals that organizations pursue and how these goals are used by the organization. This exercise consists of two parts. Part A will focus on the organizational goals reported by American managers to be important. Part B will require you to research an actual organization to determine its official and operative goals.

PART A. ASSUME YOU ARE THE MANAGER OF A SMALL- TO MEDIUM-SIZE BUSINESS.

STEP 1: *Team Formation (5-10 min.)*

The class will be divided into teams of two people each. Individually each person will study the eight goals listed and the examples.

STEP 2: *Ranking the Objectives (15 min.)*

Working independently, rank the eight goals in order of importance (1 being most important). Enter your rankings under the column labeled "individual." Discuss and compare each ranking with your teammate and determine a team ranking. Enter this ranking under the column labeled "team."

STEP 3: *Comparison and Discussion (10 min.)*

Your instructor will identify the ranking for each goal based on "Organizational Goals and Expected Behavior of American Managers." Discuss your ranking and your team's compared to the research findings. The following questions may be considered.

DISCUSSION QUESTIONS

1. How do you account for the difference between yours, your team's, and the research findings' rankings? The similarities?
2. Would managers of large firms rank the

This exercise is based on Robert Doktor, Alfred Edge, Lane Kelley, "Planning Objectives," *Experiencing Management: Active Learning for Large Classes* (Honolulu: Management Publishing Co., 1980), 11-16; and Douglas T. Hall, et. al. "Goal Analysis," *Experiences in Management and Organizational Behavior* (NY: John Wiley & Sons, Inc., 1975), 168-170.

objectives differently? Would it make a difference if the firm was successful vs. less successful?

3. How would an organization attempt to meet each of these goals? How would its effectiveness at meeting each be assessed? What purpose do these goals serve? Are they realistic?

PART B. SURVEY OF OFFICIAL AND OPERATIVE GOALS

The following exercise involves identifying the official and operative goals of an actual organization. For the purposes of this exercise use the following definitions.

Official goals are the formally identified purposes of the organization. Official goals are spoken or written and often appear in official organizational material (e.g., annual report, policy manual). Official goals may appear vague and directed to appeal to the public and the organization's constituents.

Operative goals are the "real" goals of the organization, as reflected in the behavior and operations of the organization. Operative goals are not necessarily similar to the official goals and may even conflict. Operative goals provide the framework for making the day-to-day operating decisions.

STEP 1: *Assignment of Organization and Guidelines*

Your instructor will assign an organization for which you will investigate and determine its official and operative goals. Sources you may wish to consult include: published material on the organization; interviews with employees and top managers; the organization's manual, which outlines policies, procedures, rules; and personal observation of the operation.

STEP 2: *Data Collection and Analysis*

Using the suggestions above, collect the data necessary to determine the public and "real" goals of the organization. Make separate lists of each type, noting the sources that support your interpretation. Compare your lists and note any discrepancies. In reviewing the two sets of goals, can you point to actual actions or operations that indicate support of the goals? Actions that are contrary? How do you explain the inconsistencies?

EXHIBIT 22-1 WORKSHEET: IDENTIFYING ORGANIZATIONAL GOALS

Goals	Individual Ranking	Team Ranking	Research Ranking
Industrial Leadership Example: To be number one in their industry.			
Organizational Efficiency Example: To achieve a given production level with fewer inputs.			
Social Welfare Example: To contribute to the quality of life in the community.			
Organizational Stability Example: The ability to absorb minor shocks.			
High Productivity Example: To produce a large number of products at a low cost.			
Employee Welfare Example: To provide the employees with a safe and healthy work environment.			
Profit Maximization Example: To make the most money possible.			
Organizational Growth Example: To develop the organization.			

STEP 3: *In-class Small-Group Discussions*

The class will divide into small groups and discuss the data gathered by each person. Discuss the goals you identified, your classification of the goals, and differences noted between goals and actions.

STEP 4: *Class Discussion*

As a class, discuss goals and their role in organizations. The following questions may be helpful in relating the topic to the data you collected for this exercise.

DISCUSSION QUESTIONS

1. In the small-group discussions, were there instances in which you disagreed with someone's interpretation and classification of data? Would this be possible within the organization itself? If so, what would be the cause and how should the difference be resolved?

2. Can an organization be effective if it has conflicting goals? Which goals should have precedence?

3. Who determines the goals for the organization? How and when are goals changed?

4. What provides the most accurate basis for determining what an organization is trying to accomplish?

5. How are the goals you identified for the assigned organization similar or different from the goals discussed in Part A of this exercise? Are those in Part A official or operative goals?

23

Layoff at Old College

Memorandum: Office of the College President
To: College Budget Committee
Subject: Next Year's Budget Preparation

In my continuing effort to hold down the costs of running the college, I am ordering you to identify existing academic programs that will be subject to reduction or elimination. In order to support the academic programs that have proven to be effective and cost beneficial I am asking you to identify the five departments/programs/activities (D/P/A) of the lowest priority in the college. Elimination or reduction of these activities should result in a reduction of no less than 10% of your budget for this past year as a base. If the five D/P/A of the lowest priority do not amount to a 10% reduction in your budget, continue listing D/P/A until the 10% reduction is achieved.

The following criteria will be used in developing your reductions:

1. No across-the-board reduction (i.e., 10% from each D/P/A).
2. Assume that statutes and regulations can be changed to achieve the reduction (i.e., Faculty can be dismissed despite tenure status).
3. Identify exactly which D/P/As are to be reduced.
4. Identify the number of Faculty and Clerical/Technical (T/C) positions that would be eliminated/abolished.
5. Submit the information to my office immediately.

The proposed changes may result in radical changes in the character and objectives of the college. Consider carefully whether a program is absolutely essential for a well-rounded college experience. Maintain the basic integrity of the college but at the same time carry out your duty. Whatever reductions you impose must be determined by a well-reasoned, thorough, and sensitive assessment of the potential implication of such reduction. There should be no illusion, however, that the required cuts can be accomplished in a painless or popular way.

Signed /S/ the College President
Attachment

Reprinted with permission of Allen J. Schuh, Professor, California State University at Hayward.

REASON FOR THE BUDGET REDUCTION

The College President's memorandum ordering the reduction in personnel is a result of the tremendous recent and sustained drop in student enrollments, while at the same time the costs to maintain departments/programs/activities have substantially increased. The President has decided that not every college can be all things to all people and Old College simply can't provide every course or major that the faculty and students might like. There is a need to increase the efficiency of the college and now is the time to make the required reductions. It should be noted that personnel salaries compose over 80% of the total cost of running the college.

TIMEFRAME

The President will allow the reduction to be phased in over a three-year period if necessary to allow the laid-off people an opportunity to secure other employment. Also, each college job generates approximately a half position in the local community. The college is a major employer in the local geographical area. A phase-in over several years would also allow students in the affected areas to complete current graduation requirements. Appropriate admissions policies and criteria would be revised to limit access of new students to the threatened departments/programs/activities.

ORIGINAL MISSION OF THE COLLEGE

Upon its founding, Old College was expected to provide: (a) a general education for undergraduates, primarily in the first two years of college, (b) a wide range of academic majors and minors for students pursuing a baccalaureate degree, and (c) job-related education for potential teachers and other students seeking a variety of public and private employment. It was hoped that masters degrees might also be offered in a limited number of fields. The most prestigious occupational training programs such as dentistry, medicine, engineering, and law would never be attempted. Also, no programs in agriculture or natural resources, architecture and environmental design, or home economics would ever be offered.

At the founding ceremony, the trustees declared:

Students selecting Old College for their major educational experience will know and feel the spirit, imagination, and traumas of mankind, they should be able to understand and apply the method of scientific inquiry, they should know man as he is, and they should discover, develop, and practice their talents and interests through original expression. Thus, an array of offerings in Humanities, Physical and Life Sciences, Social Sciences, and Expressive Arts would be presented and retained for the enrichment of students at least for their first two years of college experience.

Job-related courses and programs should be offered to strengthen and extend the occupational opportunities of students in school-based services, client-oriented professions, management of public and private organizations, and quantitative data-processing occupations.

Upper division and graduate programs should be offered and sustained that will lead to an academic major or minor or to a master's degree, to prepare students for doctoral programs in other universities, proceed to teaching positions in secondary schools and community colleges, proceed to advanced occupational training programs in fields such as law, engineering, dentistry, and medicine elsewhere.

Specialized academic training is to be offered in ways that enrich the lives of the students and/or serve their communities.

LOCATION, HISTORY, AND PHYSICAL FACILITIES

Old College is located in a picturesque setting with rolling hills. Trees, grass, and flowering shrubs abound on the campus. The college strives to maintain a friendly atmosphere with close student-faculty relations, an emphasis on student self-government, and community involvement. The college has been in existence for 20 years. The peak enrollment occurred eight years ago and has since dropped 20%.

The physical facilities include large modern buildings for instruction, a bookstore, library, administration building, student health center, cafeteria, athletic stadium, theater and television facility, a foreign language laboratory, a computer center, and an on-campus ecological field station.

The educational emphasis stresses small class size and easy student access to professors. The curriculum presents a balanced approach of liberal arts and applied degrees in undergraduate and graduate programs. There are extension and summer sessions, and late afternoon and evening classes. The college operates on the quarter system. The programs of the college are accredited by the appropriate associations.

CHARACTERISTICS OF THE STUDENTS

The total enrollment is 9,800 students—49% men and 51% women. Only about 1% of the students are from foreign countries. The undergraduates make up 70% of the students while the remaining 30% are graduate students. The average student age is 27 years. Undergraduate courses are 90% of the curriculum (many graduate students take undergraduate courses to meet the prerequisites for graduate study in a field other than that for which they hold an undergraduate degree). Fifty-five percent of the students carry 12 or more units per term, which is considered full time attendance. The ethnicity breakdown has been estimated at approximately:

EXHIBIT 23–1 STAFF ORGANIZATION CHART FOR OLD COLLEGE

Area		Number of Positions
I.	Instructional Administration	36
	School (Administrative unit above the department level) Offices Clerical/Technical	
	Assistance to Administration	25
	Faculty Teaching Courses	403
	Clerical/Technical Assistance to Teaching Faculty	94
	Subtotal	558
II.	Academic Support	
	Library	63
	Audio-Visual	14
	Computer Center	33
	Subtotal	110
III.	Student Services	
	Social and Cultural Development	9
	Counseling	13
	Testing	3
	Placement	7
	Housing	2
	Disabled Students	2
	Equal Opportunity Program	15
	Financial Aids	13
	Health Services	21
	Subtotal	85
IV.	Institutional Support	
	Executive Management	26
	Financial Operations	35
	Personnel	7
	Logistical Services	
	Business Management	20
	Security	13
	Motor Pool	4
	Admissions and Records	48
	Plant Operations	165
	Community Relations	5
	Subtotal	323
	Total College Personnel	1,076

Comment: Approximately $30 million is required to meet this payroll. These salaries account for over 80% of the total cost of running the college for one year.

72% Caucasian, 14% Black, 6% Oriental, 4% Chicano, 1% Filipino, 1% Central-Latin-South American, 1% Native American, 1% Other.

EXHIBIT 23-2 RELEVANT STATISTICS BY DEPARTMENT

Department	A	B	C	D	E	F	G	H	I	J	K	L	M	N	O	P	Q
Black Studies	1	1	0	4.4	2.0	.5	.0	1.56	130	0	14.0	0	0	211.4	113.7	21.5	18.6
English	18	0	.3	18.2	18.3	2.0	.0	4.15	312	46	18.8	0	1	202.2	115.3	16.3	18.0
Foreign Languages	19	1	0	13.7	20.0	1.75	1.0	3.50	155	10	11.5	9	0	198.4	135.2	14.0	12.8
History	21	0	0	17.2	21.0	2.0	.0	4.31	284	44	16.6	1	0	196.6	119.1	19.9	20.5
Philosophy	9	0	0	6.2	9.0	1.0	.0	1.45	65	0	10.8	2	1	196.4	105.3	20.9	16.4
Speech	9	0	1	9.5	10.0	3.0	.0	2.4	63	26	33.4	2	0	195.1	113.7	17.7	15.9
Biology	15	0	.7	16.1	15.7	3.0	5.5	4.11	534	71	42.9	5	4	212.2	128.7	14.7	16.6
Chemistry	11	0	.3	11.4	11.3	2.0	5.5	2.83	106	15	17.6	6	3	220.3	147.4	14.8	14.9
Geology	6	0	0	5.8	6.0	1.0	1.5	1.33	47	0	39.8	2	4	217.9	151.9	14.2	17.1
Health Sciences	1	0	0	1.3	1.0	0	0	.25	15	0	54.0	0	8	—	—	24.6	16.4
Mathematics	27	0	0	27.1	27.0	3.0	0	6.62	215	37	11.1	15	0	204.0	127.7	18.8	19.3
Nursing	4	3	.7	6.3	7.7	1.0	0	1.4	342	0	93.9	0	7	213.1	123.7	8.9	8.9
Physical Science	1	0	0	.5	1.0	0	0	.1	3	0	0	0	5	—	—	19.9	14.3
Physics	4	0	0	5.3	4.0	1.0	2.0	1.19	31	7	21.0	6	2	199.2	88.7	17.3	17.7
Statistics	8	2	.3	11.4	10.3	1.5	.5	2.78	48	26	9.8	16	1	199.4	132.6	19.3	19.6
Anthropology	8	0	.7	6.2	8.7	1.25	.25	1.76	100	33	19.5	1	5	196.7	157.2	18.6	17.3
Geography	7	0	.7	4.3	7.7	1.0	.5	1.25	123	18	46.2	0	3	201.3	130.4	18.7	14.2
Human Development	4	0	0	6.8	4.0	1.75	0	1.98	517	0	69.7	1	0	195.5	115.6	19.3	20.1
Mass Communication	3	0	.3	6.4	3.3	1.0	.75	1.61	84	0	54.6	0	2	196.1	120.6	20.9	17.1
Mexican-American Studies	1	0	0	.6	1.0	0	0	.13	18	0	6.2	0	2	196.7	112.1	19.6	11.3
Native-American Studies	0	1	0	.7	1.0	0	0	.15	0	0	0	0	0	—	—	17.0	10.4
Political Science	10	0	.7	7.9	10.7	1.75	0	1.98	343	18	38.1	1	3	195.6	114.3	21.3	14.5
Psychology	18	0	0	16.6	18.0	3.0	1.0	4.07	527	0	40.0	7	2	194.9	114.5	23.8	19.2
Sociology	13	0	0	16.0	13.0	2.5	.5	3.89	491	29	36.2	3	3	197.7	109.9	20.0	21.2
Art	15	0	0	11.6	15.0	2.0	4.5	3.02	457	0	53.9	0	0	201.1	110.7	15.6	13.4
Drama	3	0	.3	3.8	3.3	1.0	3.5	.83	10	0	42.8	0	1	217.5	120.6	16.4	13.5
Music	22	0	0	13.6	22.0	2.5	4.5	3.45	228	42	64.8	0	0	208.6	139.8	13.5	10.1
Accounting	11	0	.3	27.7	113	2.0	0	6.13	696	139	75.6	3	4	205.6	129.2	20.3	22.3
Management Sciences	14	4	0	28.5	18.0	1.5	0	6.31	717	143	86.3	3	4	205.6	129.2	21.0	21.6
Marketing	4	0	.3	6.3	4.3	0	0	1.19	135	26	86.7	3	4	205.6	129.2	23.7	21.8
Criminal Justice	1	0	1	4.9	2.0	0	0	.77	0	0	50.8	0	4	—	—	25.8	28.1
Economics	9	1	.7	17.5	10.7	1.0	0	3.88	99	19	7.1	3	3	201.2	111.2	22.7	24.6
Educational Psychology	20	0	0	15.0	20.0	3.0	0	3.67	0	556	85.9	0	0	—	—	13.0	12.5
Physical Education	21	0	.7	26.5	21.7	3.5	3.7	5.26	348	37	38.9	1	4	205.3	126.9	14.8	14.3
Public Administration	2	3	2	7.7	7.0	1.0	0	2.10	0.	291	69.0	0	0	—	—	14.6	17.1
Recreation	1	1	0	3.1	2.0	1.5	0	.79	356	0	66.1	0	2	196.5	116.2	19.7	16.3
School Administration	5	0	0	2.0	5.0	.5	0	.59	0	0	56.5	0	0	—	—	11.2	7.8
Teacher Education	28	0	.7	19.0	28.7	4.0	.5	5.83	0	471	16.8	0	0	—	—	15.7	12.8
General Studies	0	0	0	2.5	0	0	0	.99	0	0		0	0	—	—	18.4	12.9
Women's Studies	0	0	0	.2	0	0	0	.05	0	0	—	0	0	—	—	22.3	14.2

Titles for Column Headings A to Q:

A Number of tenured faculty in the department. Tenure is not permanent employment in a university. Tenure is only in a department or teaching service area. Professors have tenure only if there is work and they commit no illegal, immoral, or incompetent act. If the teaching service area or department is eliminated, faculty lose all job rights.

B Number of faculty seeking tenure in the department. Typically a few members of the teaching faculty are new to the college and are seeking a tenured position. These faculty are evaluated for a period of up to seven years and are subject to yearly evaluation on their publications, teaching, committee work, and work in the community.

C Number of temporary faculty who teach in the department (not tenure track). These are lecturers or temporary faculty who are usually Ph.D. candidates at other local universities.

D Number of faculty positions that should exist in the department if all departments were held to a standard student-faculty ratio of 18:1. Since the college receives its money from the State Legislature on a ratio of one full-time faculty position for each 18 full-time equivalent students (usually expressed as 18:1) it could be a rough justice practice to require all departments to meet that ratio. Departments should use this ratio as a reference each year as they consider their teaching load. Classes that are small should be combined. A professor might even view his/her own contribution from this perspective. If one course has only 10 students, another class better have at least 26 to offset the smaller expensive offering. Any department that consistently falls below 18:1 is simply not paying its share.

E Total number of faculty in the department (the sum of A, B, and C)—the total number of full-time teaching positions in the department now. No provision is made here to alert the reader of pending retirements or separations. These data are just as they appear on the course control computer printout.

F Number of clerical positions in support of teaching faculty who work in the department. Clerical employees receive permanency after one year in their job. A clerical's permanency is to the whole college. Thus, if a particular clerical position is eliminated, the person would not necessarily separate from the university. Possibly that person would bump a person of less seniority in another part of the campus. Typing is the same anywhere on campus, thus the situation is not the same as with faculty. With faculty, a sociologist can't always teach biology or accounting. But clerical duties are essentially the same everywhere.

G Number of technical positions working in the department. Technical support to faculty positions are glass blowers in chemistry, specimen preparers in biology, or piano tuners in music. Thus, while they have permanency rather than tenure, a highly skilled technician has fewer transferable skills to an entirely new area. We have no experience record to suggest what exactly will happen with the technical support positions in a layoff.

H Percentage of courses taken by students in comparison to the college as a whole. This is a popularity ratio arrived at by counting the number of students taking a course in the department and expressing it as a ratio to the total enrollments in the college.

I Number of undergraduate degrees awarded in the past five years. Self explanatory. What isn't here is whether this number is increasing, steady, or declining over the years.

J Number of graduate degrees awarded in the past five years. Self explanatory. See I above.

K Percentage of courses taken by students who major in the department. This is a concentration ratio that counts all students taking courses in a department and then checks their college major. A department with a low percentage is essentially a service department to other majors. To some extent, such service to others insures one's own survival. A high ratio shows that the majority of students taking courses there are their majors. A department with a high ratio could be eliminated without affecting many people other than those being eliminated.

L Number of other departments that require students in their major to take courses in the department. Some departments offer courses highly regarded by the other departments. For example, a course in statistics is required by over a third of the departments on the campus, but no one but geographers are required to take a geography course. Obviously, any department with a zero in this column is more vulnerable to elimination than those with a higher number.

M Number of other departments where a student in this major will have to take at least one course. This octopus variable shows how broad a background in other departments the major in this department is required to have for graduation. Health Sciences is well wired politically because it requires their students to have courses in eight other departments. These other departments are apt to come to their assistance if anyone would suggest they be eliminated.

N Number of units a student in this major takes on the average before graduating (186 quarter units are required for graduation). Frequently students transfer from another college or change majors and so accumulate a larger number of units than needed before graduating.

O Number of units a student takes here at Old College who majors in this department before graduating with an undergraduate degree (i.e., units not transfered in from another college). Self explanatory.

P The average student-faculty ratio for this major at 18 comparable institutions. Self explanatory.

Q The approximate student-faculty ratio for this department last academic year. These data were calculated for three regular academic quarters plus the summer session. No information is available on whether the ratio is raising, stable, or falling over the last five years.

24

Denver Department Stores

In the early spring of 1974 Jim Barton was evaluating the decline in sales volume experienced by the four departments he supervised in the main store of Denver Department Stores, a Colorado retail chain. Barton was at a loss as to how to improve sales. He attributed the slowdown in sales to the current economic downturn affecting the entire nation. However, Barton's supervisor, Mr. Cornwall, pointed out that some of the other departments in the store had experienced a 15% gain over the previous year. Cornwall added that Barton was expected to have his departments up to par with the others in a short period of time.

BACKGROUND

Jim Barton had been supervisor of the sporting goods, hardware, housewares, and toy departments in the main store of Denver Department Stores for three of the 10 years he had worked for the chain. The four departments were situated adjacent to each other on the ground floor of the store. Each department had a head salesclerk who reported to Mr. Barton on merchandise storage and presentation, special orders, and general department upkeep. The head salesclerks were all full-time, long-term employees of Denver Department Stores, having an average of about eight years' experience with the chain. The head clerks were also expected to train the people in the department they supervised. The rest of the staff in each department was made up of part-time employees who lived in or near Denver. Most of the part-time people were students at nearby universities who worked to finance their education. In addition there were two or three housewives who worked about 10 hours a week in the evenings.

All sales personnel at Denver Department Stores were paid strictly on an hourly basis. Beginning pay was just slightly over the minimum wage and raises were given based on length of employment and work performance evaluations. The salespeople in the housewares and sporting goods departments were paid about 40¢ an hour more than the clerks in the other departments because it was thought that more sales ability and experience were needed in dealing with the people who shopped for items found in those departments.

As a general rule the head salesclerk in each department did not actively sell, but kept the department well stocked and presentable, and trained and evaluated sales personnel. The part-time employees did most of the clerk and sales work. The role of the salesclerk was seen as one of answering customer questions and ringing up the sale rather than actively selling the merchandise, except in the two departments previously mentioned where a little more active selling was done.

The salesclerks in Barton's departments seemed to get along well with each other. The four department heads usually ate lunch together. If business was brisk in one department and slow in another, the salespeople in the slower area would assist in the busy department. Men clerks often helped the

women clerks in unloading heavy merchandise carts. Store procedure was that whenever a cash register was low on change a clerk would go to a master till in the stationery department to get more. Barton's departments, however, usually supplied each other with change, thus avoiding the longer walk to the master till.

Barton's immediate supervisor, Mr. Cornwall, had the reputation of being a skilled merchandiser and in the past had initiated many ideas to increase the sales volume of the store. Some of the longer-term employees said that Mr. Cornwall was very impatient and that he sometimes was rude to his subordinates while discussing merchandising problems with them.

The store manager, Mr. Blanding, had been with Denver Department Stores for 20 years and would be retiring in a few years. Earlier in his career Mr. Blanding had taken an active part in the merchandising aspect of the store, but recently he had delegated most of the merchandising and sales responsibilities to Mr. Cornwall. (Exhibit 24-1 is an organizational chart of the store.)

EXHIBIT 24–1   DENVER DEPARTMENT STORES ORGANIZATIONAL CHART

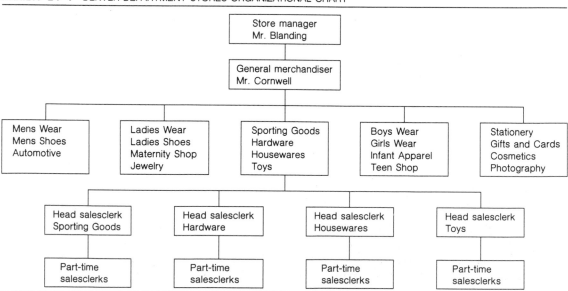

SITUATION

Because of Mr. Cornwall's concern, Barton consulted with his department supervisors about the reason for the declining sales volume. The consensus reached was that the level of customer traffic had not been adequate to allow the departments to achieve a high sales volume. When Barton presented this problem to Mr. Cornwall, Cornwall concluded that since customer traffic could not be controlled and since the departments had been adequately stocked throughout the year, the improvement in sales would have to be a result of increased effort on the part of the clerks in each department. Cornwall added that if sales didn't improve soon the hours of both the full- and part-time salesclerks would have to be cut back. Later Barton found out that Cornwall had sent a letter around to each department informing employees of the possibility of fewer hours if sales didn't improve.

A few days after Barton received the assignment to increase sales in his department Mr. Cornwall called him into his office again and suggested that each salesperson carry a personal tally card to record his daily sales. Each clerk would record the sales he made and at the end of the day the personal sales tally card would be totaled. Cornwall said that by reviewing the cards over a period of time he would be able to determine who were the "dead wood" and who were the real producers. The clerks were to be told about the purpose of the tally card and that those clerks who had low sales tallies would have their hours cut back.

Barton told Cornwall he wanted to consider this program and also discuss it with the head salespeople before implementing it. He told Mr. Cornwall that the next day was his day off but that when he returned to work the day after he would discuss this proposal with the head salesclerks.

Upon returning to the store after his day off, Mr. Barton was surprised to see each of his salespeople carrying a daily tally sheet.

When he asked Mr. Cornwall why the program had been adopted so quickly, Cornwall replied that when it came to improvement of sales, no delay could be tolerated. Barton wondered what effect the new program would have on the personnel in each of his departments.

When Mr. Cornwall issued the tally cards to Barton's salespeople, the head salesclerks failed to fill them out. Two of the head clerks had lost their tally cards when Cornwall came by later in the day to see how the program was progressing. Cornwall issued the two head clerks new cards and told them that if they didn't "shape up" he would see some "new faces" in the departments.

The part-time salespeople filled out the cards completely, writing down every sale. The rumor that those clerks who had low sales tallies would have their hours cut spread rapidly. Soon the clerks became much more active and aggressive in their sales efforts. Customers were often approached more than once by different clerks in each department. One elderly lady complained that while making her way to the restroom in the back of the hardware department she was asked by four clerks if she needed assistance in making a selection.

When Barton returned the day after the institution of the program the head salesclerks asked him about the new program. Barton replied that they had no alternative but to follow Cornwall's orders or quit. Later that afternoon the head clerks were seen discussing the situation on their regular break. After the break the head clerks began waiting on customers and filling out their sales tally cards.

Not long after the adoption of the program, the stock rooms began to look cluttered. Unloaded carts lined the aisles of the stock room. The shelves on the sales floor were slowly emptied and remained poorly stocked. Sales of items that had a large retail value were especially sought after and the head salesclerks were often seen dusting and rearranging these more expensive items. The head clerk's tally sheets always had the greatest amount of sales when the clerks compared sheets at the end of each day. (Barton collected them daily and delivered them to Cornwall.) The friendly conversations among salespeople and between clerks and customers were shortened and sales were rung up on the cash register and completed in a much shorter time. Breaks were no longer taken as groups and when they were taken they seemed to be much shorter than before.

When sales activity was slow in one department, clerks would migrate to other departments where there were more customers. Sometimes conflicts between clerks arose because of competition for sales. In one instance the head clerk of the hardware department interrupted a part-time clerk from the toy department who was demonstrating a large and expensive table saw to a customer. The head clerk of the hardware department introduced himself as the hardware specialist and sent the toy clerk back to his own department.

Often customers asked for items that were not on the shelves of the sales floor. When the clerk looked for the item it was found on the carts that jammed the stock room aisles. Some customers were told the item they desired wasn't in stock and later the clerk would find it on a cart in the stock room.

When Barton reported his observations of the foregoing situations to Mr. Cornwall, he was told that it was a result of the clerks adjusting to the new program and to not worry about it. Cornwall pointed out, however, that sales volume had still not improved. He further noted that the sum of all sales reported on the tally sheets was often

$500 to $600 more than total department sales according to the cash register.

A few weeks after the instigation of the tally card system Cornwall walked through the hardware department and stopped beside three carts of merchandise left in the aisle of the stock room from the morning of the day before. He talked to the head clerk in an impatient tone and asked him why the carts weren't unloaded. The clerk replied that if Mr. Cornwall had any questions about the department he should ask Mr. Barton. Cornwall picked up the telephone and angrily dialed Barton's office. Barton told him that the handling of merchandise had been preempted by the emphasis on the tally card system of recording sales. Cornwall slammed down the receiver and stormed out of the department.

That afternoon, as a result of a request from Barton, Blanding, Cornwall, and Barton visited the four departments. After talking with some of the salespeople, Mr. Blanding sent a memo announcing that the tally card program would be discontinued immediately.

After the program had been terminated, salesclerks still took their breaks separately and conversations seemed to be limited to only the essential topics needed to run the department. Barton and the head salesclerks didn't talk as freely as they had before and some of the head clerks said that Mr. Barton had failed to represent their best interests to Cornwall. Some of the clerks said that they thought that the tally card system was Barton's idea. The part-time people resumed the major portion of the sales and clerking job and the head clerks returned to merchandising. Sales volume in the departments didn't improve.

25

The Fat Boy Program

Nonprofit organizations envy and emulate profit-making organizations. They envy, for they believe that profit-making organizations have concrete, measurable goals. They emulate as they try to develop such goals.

One such attempt was the Management Control System (MCS) introduced in the late 1950s within a large subordinate command of the U.S. Air Force. The MCS was a complicated system that involved measuring activities thought to be important, such as aircraft hours flown, aircraft in commission, numbers of re-enlistments, and so on. These measurements were made comparable by assigning "points" according to the degree of accomplishment. For example, if an air base re-enlisted only 50% of those eligible, it could receive 10 points, whereas if it re-enlisted 60%, it could receive the maximum number of points, say, 100. This system allowed higher commanders to indicate areas where they felt effort should be expended and to emphasize the importance of these areas. Therefore, some officers believed that an air base could be controlled by selecting areas and by exercising judgment in weighting the points to be assigned and awarded. Com-

manders had been relieved of their commands after their bases had earned below a certain number of points.

To make the system less susceptible to wide fluctuations, which might cause a commander to suffer because of transient phenomena, points were assigned on a running quarter basis (that is, three months were averaged), even though each area was measured monthly. As the current month was added, points earned three months before were dropped. Additionally, the practice of having a maximum and a minimum for each area prevented a commander from being unduly penalized for an extraordinarily bad month or rewarded for a fortuitously good month.

Consequently, each month there were very few areas where any action could be taken to improve the score of a base. In many areas maxima had been earned; in others the base might be below the minimum, and no foreseeable effort could bring performance up to the level where more points would be earned.

One month Colonel Jacob Lembeck was discussing the forecasted quarterly MCS score with his comptroller, Mr. Leon Counter.

Permission granted for "The Fat Boy Program" from Richard Farmer and William Ryan.

Colonel Lembeck was concerned that there were very few areas where an improvement could be forecasted. "Damn it, Counter, there must be more we can do. You tell me that we have to sit here and take a score that is 15 points lower than last month's. I just can't believe it. I can't take a low score."

"There *is* one area. That is the weight control, or Fat Boy, program. As you know, the commanding general is concerned about overweight. Everyone has to be weighed monthly as part of the physical fitness program. If we have more than 10 people out of 5,000 overweight, we will get only 10 points.

If we can cut this figure to five, we will get the maximum, 40 points."

Colonel Lembeck ordered each of the 15 overweight airmen to be weighed daily and their weights reported to him. On the last day of the month, he had all those who were still overweight report to the steam room in the base gymnasium. Colonel Lembeck, a former All-American tackle, took the group into the steam room and stayed with them for eight hours. At the end of this time, only five persons were over the weight limit. The base earned the maximum number of points for its weight control program.

26

A New Division

At the Craig Company, a new division was formed that would be responsible for the corporate mining investments overseas. The objectives were to oversee mining investments in Africa; protect the company's interests in mining investments under construction in South America; and market iron ore thoughout the world, especially in the Far East and in Europe. The long-term organizational goals were to maintain or augment dividend income from the African investments that were under increasing African political pressure to reduce dividends or reinvest in Africa; to handle all legal, financial, and managerial responsibilities involved in an iron-mine investment under construction in South America; to continue to market iron ore, and to develop new markets for the ore.

Senior management decided to locate the division headquarters at the main office, in a 30-story building located in a major international capital. The corporate offices were on floors from the sixth through the sixteenth; but because of shortage of office space, a decision was made to locate the new division on the second floor. The existing offices of the president and vice-president were on the fourteenth floor. The offices of the Market Research section, composed of five people, were on the eleventh floor; part of the Commercial staff (four people) was on the sixth floor; the Engineers (five people) and the Financial group (six individuals) were quickly moved to the second floor. The subgroups of the division were separated from each other physically by location on different floors of the building.

Since the new division was crucial to the operations of the total organization, the president was to be the chief executive officer with his vice-president assisting him. Each of the new division's separate activities was to be headed by a managing executive who would supervise the people under him. Each of these executives was to report directly to the president or, in his absence, to the vice-president.

The president determined that the prime short-term goals of the new division were to

Robert E.C. Wegner/Leonard Sayles, *Cases in Organizational and Administrative Behavior*, copyright © 1972, pp. 197-204. Reprinted by permission of Prentice-Hall, Inc., Englewood Cliffs, NJ.

concentrate on marketing iron ore and to handle all details for the mine under construction. Management determined that a total work force of about 25 people would be adequate to accomplish all the work.

Before discussing the actual operation of the new division, it is necessary to make a few comments about the jobs of the president and vice-president of Craig Company. Because of the international operations of the company, both these men spent less than half their working time in their offices at corporate headquarters.

During the periods when the president and vice-president were in the office they were diligently preparing reports on their previous trips, catching up with correspondence that had accumulated during their absence, and making plans for the next trip. The periods spent in the office were short, two weeks at most, therefore both men tried to accomplish as much work as possible by giving dictation not only to their own secretaries but also to the supervisors' secretaries. The supervisors resented having their secretaries involved in this way because their own work fell behind. In order to complete the work, some overtime was required by the secretaries. The typing quality of the work for the executives was poor, because the secretaries who were enlisted often did not understand the dictation given by the officers and therefore did not type letters up to the quality standards expected by these men. The low-quality work was returned to the secretaries for retyping. Letters and reports were retyped two or three times, and occasionally some work was redone four or five times.

The executives as well as the secretaries became irritated, and such irritation manifested itself among the girls by crying, grumbling, and refusing to work overtime, and by the executives in vocal outbursts. After a few months, one excellent secretary requested a transfer. Her reason for this request was that she had never before been a secretary to several people simultaneously, and she did not intend to begin now!

All groups should have moved to the new offices in September, but the offices on the second floor required major renovation before they could be occupied. From September until January no decision was taken on the floor-plan arrangement of the new offices. The president wanted to be consulted on all phases of the layout planning. But during those months he was away on business trips about 60% of the time, so there was little opportunity to discuss with him the details of the floor plan. The vice-president traveled with the president; consequently he could not be apprised of the layout planning being done by the engineers. No other group was requested to help with the layout, or make any decision on the plan, although all groups made suggestions.

At the time the division was formed, all employees were asked by the president whether a transfer would be acceptable. If anyone refused to leave his or her existing job, no penalty was assessed. Some who were invited did not accept because they believed —or so they said—that the new organization would not afford them the best opportunities. These people were not questioned further as to the reasons for their decision. Among those who joined the group were certain individuals who were dissatisfied with their present positions and had requested transfers. There were also others who had been suggested for transfer by their superiors because of unsatisfactory performance in their present positions. A few of these were accepted because they had the talents required, even though they had not done acceptable work in other positions. One or two had a long history with the company and previously had done fine work.

One transferee, a Market Research analyst, had been transferred from two other divisions prior to joining the Overseas Investment group. In the past he had done some superb analyses, but developed a reputation for being difficult to work with. He preferred to work alone, producing volumes of work some of which proved difficult to read because of unusual grammar and syntax. His approach to a job was imaginative and considered brilliant by his co-workers. He had never been promoted to a supervisory position when younger people around him were moved up. He claimed that the other employees had taken advantage of his special knowledge and used his work to advance their own interests. After a short period of time in each division, say three months, he became increasingly close-mouthed about the work he was doing and sent progress reports and final reports of his work not to his immediate supervisor for inspection, but to the senior man of the division.

Often the supervisor objected; but the analyst continued the practice. Resentful of his behavior, the supervisor refused salary increases or job promotions for this analyst. This had been his typical history prior to entering the new division. It was hoped that by transferring him, he would find satisfaction in the job and the company would benefit from his work. In the new division he was to report to the president. His job was analyzing and reporting on potential markets. Since the president was often absent, the analyst was subjected to little supervision and was soon working on pet projects unrelated to the work of the division.

From September to January he did almost no work that could have been useful to the president, and continually irritated the Marketing personnel who requested assistance from him and were refused; moreover, he constantly criticized the work of others. Eventually there was little conversation between the analyst and the others in the division. He claimed that his reason for not complying with their requests was that the work had not been initiated by the president who was, in fact, his boss.

OPERATIONS OF THE NEW DIVISION

Work efficiency in the new division was not high when the group was formed. Output was far less than expected. Most of the employees had not previously worked under the direction of executives; neither had the subgroups worked with their supervisors before. For some people, the type of work was different from what they had done previously. Also, employees were located on four separate floors.

Primarily the work involved calculation and accumulation of engineering, financial, and marketing data, and writing reports for the division executives and for the senior management. Advice on decisions approved or actions initiated by the division executives was relayed to the other workers vocally; however, when these men were out of the city, communication was in writing or by telephone. Frequently the executives made overseas telephone calls to keep the chief accountant, chief engineer, or other employees fully apprised of their activities.

Reports from subordinates were mailed to the executives when the latter were absent from the city. Reports from corporate headquarters were also mailed to the executives. Reports written by subordinates, however, were sent to the president and vice-president upon request and without approval of the traveling executives. Conflicts resulted when the travelers did not accept the conclusions in the reports, and in several instances subordinates were asked to retrieve the reports from the senior management so that they could be altered. The subordinates were greatly embarrassed on these occasions.

Communication between the offices in the building was accomplished almost entirely by telephone. A memorandum of instruction for normal day-to-day activity was time-wasting and unnecessary. Excessive time was consumed by the president, vice-president, and the division executives in traveling by elevator to the appropriate floors to give instructions, comment on work in process, provide trade-offs, or simply to observe what was going on. Often several trips each day were necessary for these purposes. In addition, employees were constantly traveling from floor to floor to pass on information, provide trade-offs, gossip, and report to the executives.

Telephones provided the most convenient way to communicate, but confusion and misunderstanding persisted. Errors in office correspondence and in reports to the president and vice-president became common. The uncovering of these errors resulted in anger or a feeling of frustration among the employees. Arguments between the subgroups that had cooperated to produce the reports became more frequent. Eventually the president and vice-president lost confidence in the work of the subordinates, and consequently also in the work of the division executives.

All groups attempted to take extra care to catch errors before the work left the office; yet, regardless of the amount of time devoted to eliminating errors, the instances of such errors did not diminish to any great extent. The total amount of work that would normally be expected ebbed as the writers and editors slowed in their output. Reports were produced late. A general lack of confidence in the work pervaded the entire office. The executives did not trust the subordinates, and the subordinates believed that the executives were exaggerating small errors. High-quality work, a goal of the executives and senior management, was not being produced.

Corporate management (the chairman of the board and some of the directors) also began to doubt the quality of work and pressured the president to insist on better performance from the new division. The result of this was that the president and vice-president became vocally abusive to division executives and employees, and to each other. Naturally enough, the problems continued.

As September passed into October, then November, there was a steady deterioration in work quantity and quality. Many employees spent considerable time just grousing together. The length of time spent traveling between floors to pass on information increased. One division executive began to arrive at work late and to leave early. His sub-ordinates eased up on their work until he arrived, then slowed up again after he left. He began complaining to almost everyone who would listen. Some of his comments were, "The company has been unfair to me before on my job, and now they have shifted me to a new position where I won't be able to use my knowledge effectively." Or, "Now that I have this new job, which is a promotion, I expected to get a pay raise." Or, "The boss isn't here, and I don't know what I am supposed to do. He won't be back for a week."

In the four months that the division continued working on the four floors, morale among the employees disintegrated. A divisional esprit de corps had not developed. The few groups of three to five people who worked together on one floor developed strong subgroup strengths. They worked together all day, and even had lunch together as often as possible. Each group was composed of people who did similar work. A kind of professionalism developed among the groups, especially in their supervised relationship with the division executives.

The president was absent from the office because he had to travel, but he was also "absent" from the employees because he believed that a certain distance should be kept between the supervisor and subordinates. He disliked administrative and personnel work, and avoided these activities as often as possible. It was his intention to have the vice-president handle these functions. The vice-president had a reputation for getting along with most people and tended to supervise using the "be good" approach, but he was not in the office enough to be effective. The president was autocratic in his dealings with subordinates and disdainful of the assistantship-type function of some groups, such as the corporate Personnel Department.

At the time the new division was formed, the vice-president was requested to fill out a job description of his work in the new division. The request emanated from the corporate Personnel Department. After completing the job description form, he asked the president to evaluate it. The president signed the form with the comment that the description of work was too elaborate, but that he would sign it anyway. Some months later, when the vice-president took an action with which the president disagreed, the latter questioned why the action had been taken without requesting permission. The reply was that the decision area for that work lay with the vice-president. The vice-president reminded the president of the job description. The president then remarked that what was on the description form was for the Personnel Department, but that the form had nothing to do with what his job in the division was, so "forget the job description!"

The subgroups began to operate almost as separate companies with their own goals and objectives. After a few months, the differentiated groups increased the inter-group conflicts as trade-offs became difficult because of the physical barrier imposed by work done on separate floors. The flow of work, insufficient from the outset, decreased as conflicts increased and confusion between the groups arose. No cohesion between the subgroups existed, and inner subgroup cohesion developed to an excessive degree as the supervisors of each subgroup tended to represent only their subordinates' interests.

As this unhappy and unproductive situation wore on, top corporate management began to wonder whether the forming of the new division had been such a good idea in the first place. There was more and more talk that a complete reorganization of the new division was in the cards and, as rumor had it, "heads would roll." The president, vice-president, and division executives, feeling insecure about their jobs, were even more irritable and thus also inefficient.

27

Making of a Bad Cop

What makes a policeman go sour? I can tell you. I was a Denver policeman until not so long ago. Then I quit so I could hold my head up.

Don't get me wrong. I'm not trying to shift the burden of responsibility for the burglaries, break-ins, safe jobs and that sort of thing. That is bad, very bad. But I will leave it to the big shots and the newspapers and the courts to say and do what needs to be said and done about that.

My concern is about the individual officer, the ordinary, hard-working, basically honest but awfully hard-pressed guy who is really suffering now.

Young fellows don't put on those blue uniforms to be crooks. There are a lot of reasons, but for most of the guys it adds up to the fact they thought it was an honorable, decent way of making a living.

Somewhere along the line a guy's disillusioned. Along the way the pressures mount up. Somewhere along the way he may decide to quit fighting them and make the conscious decisions to try to "beat" society instead.

But long before he gets to that point, almost as soon as he dons the uniform, in fact, he is taking the first little steps down the road that does, for some, eventually lead to the penitentiary.

Let me back up a little. I want to talk about how you get to be a policeman, because this is where the trouble really starts.

Almost any able-bodied man can become a policeman in Denver. If he is within the age brackets, if he is a high school graduate, if he has no criminal record, he is a cinch.

There isn't much to getting through the screening, and some bad ones do get through. There are the usual examinations and questionnaires. Then there is the interview. A few command officers ask questions. There is a representative of civil service and a psychiatrist present.

They ask the predictable questions and just about everybody gives the predictable answers: "Why do you want to become a policeman?" "I've always wanted to be a policeman. I want to help people." Five or ten minutes and it is over.

Five or ten minutes to spot the sadist, the psychopath—or the guy with an eye for an easy buck. I guess they weed some out. Some others they get at the Police Academy. But

Reprinted by permission of *The Denver Post*.

some get through.

Along with those few bad ones, there are more good ones, and a lot of average, ordinary human beings who have this in common: They want to be policemen.

The job has (or had) some glamour for the young man who likes authority, who finds appeal in making a career of public service, who is extroverted or aggressive.

Before you knock those qualities, remember two things: First, they are the same qualities we admire in a business executive. Second, if it weren't for men with these qualities, you wouldn't have any police protection.

The Police Academy is point No. 2 in my bill of particulars. It is a fine thing in a way. You meet the cream of the Police Department. Your expectations soar. You know you are going to make the grade and be a good officer. But how well are you really prepared?

There are six weeks at the academy—four weeks in my time. Six hectic weeks in which to learn all about the criminal laws you have sworn to enforce, to assimilate the rules of evidence, methods of arbitration, use of firearms, mob and riot control, first aid (including, if you please, some basic obstetrics), public relations, and so on.

There is an intangible something else that is not on the formal agenda. You begin to learn that this is a fraternity into which you are not automatically accepted by your fellows. You have to earn your way in; you have to establish that you are "all right."

And even this early there is a slight sour note. You knew, of course that you had to provide your own uniforms, your own hat, shoes, shirts, pistol and bullets out of your $393 a month.

You knew the city would generously provide you with the cloth for two pair of trousers and a uniform blouse.

What you didn't know was that you don't just choose a tailor shop for price and get the job done.

You are sent to a place by the Police Department to get the tailoring done. You pay the price even though the work may be ill-fitting. It seems a little odd to you that it is always the same establishment. But it is a small point and you have other things on your mind.

So the rookie, full of pride and high spirit, his head full of partly learned information, is turned over to a more experienced man for breaking in. He is on "probation" for six months.

The rookie knows he is being watched by all the older hands around him. He is eager to be accepted. He accepts advice gratefully.

Then he gets little signs that he has been making a good impression. It may happen like this: The older man stops at a bar, comes out with some packages of cigarets. He does this several times. He explains that this is part of the job, getting cigarets free from proprietors to resell, and that as a part of the rookie's training it is his turn to "make the butts."

So he goes into a skid-road bar and stands uncomfortably at the end waiting for the bartender to acknowledge his presence and disdainfully toss him two packages of butts.

The feeling of pride slips away and a hint of shame takes hold. But he tells himself this is unusual, that he will say nothing that will upset his probation standing. In six months, after he gets his commission, he will be the upright officer he meant to be.

One thing leads to another for the rookies. After six months they have become conditioned to accept free meals, a few packages of cigarets, turkeys at Thanksgiving, and liquor at Christmas from the respectable people in their district.

The rule book forbids all this. But it isn't enforced. It is winked at on all levels.

So the rookies say to themselves that this is OK, that this is a far cry from stealing and they still can be good policemen. Besides, they are becoming accepted as "good guys" by their fellow officers.

This becomes more and more important as the young policeman begins to sense a hostility toward him in the community. This is fostered to a degree by some of the saltier old hands in the department. But the public plays its part.

Americans are funny. They have a resentment for authority. And the policeman is authority in person. The respectable person may soon forget that a policeman found his lost youngster in the park, but he remembers that a policeman gave him a traffic ticket.

The negative aspect of the job builds up. The majority of the people he comes in contact with during his working hours are thieves, con men, narcotics addicts, and out and out nuts.

Off the job his associations narrow. Part of the time when he isn't working, he is sleeping. His waking, off-duty hours do not make him much of a neighbor. And then he wants to spend as much time as he can with his family.

Sometimes, when he tries to mix with his neighbors, he senses a kind of strain. When he is introduced to someone, it is not likely to be, "This is John Jones, my friend," or "my neighbor"; it is more likely to be, "This is John Jones. He's a policeman."

And the other fellow, he takes it up, too. He is likely to tell you that he has always supported pay increases for policemen, that he likes policemen as a whole, but that there are just a few guys in uniform he hates.

No wonder the officer begins to think of himself as a member of the smallest minority group in the community. The idea gradually sinks into him that the only people who understand him, that he can be close to, are his fellow officers.

It is in this kind of atmosphere that you can find the young policeman trying to make the grade in the fraternity. But that is not the whole story.

A policeman lives with tensions, and with fears.

Part of the tensions come from the incredible monotony. He is cooped up with another man, day after day, doing routine things over and over. The excitement that most people think of as the constant occupation of policemen is so infrequent as to come as a relief.

Part of the tensions come from the manifold fears. I don't mean that these men are cowards. This is no place for cowards. But they are human beings. And fears work on all human beings.

Paramount is the physical fear that he will get hurt to the point where he can't go on working, or the fear that he will be killed. The fear for his family.

There is the fear that he will make a wrong decision in a crucial moment, a life-and-death decision. A man has been in a fight. Should he call the paddy wagon or the ambulance? A man aims a pistol at him. Should he try to talk to him, or shoot him?

But the biggest fear he has is that he will show fear to some of his fellow officers. This is the reason he will rush heedlessly in on a cornered burglar or armed maniac if a couple of officers are present—something he wouldn't do if he were alone. He is tormented by his fears and he doesn't dare show them. He knows he has to present a cool, calm front to the public.

As a group, policemen have a very high rate of ulcers, heart attacks, suicides, and divorces. These things torment him, too. Divorce is a big problem to policemen. A man can't be a policeman for eight hours and then just turn it off and go home and be a loving father and husband—particularly if he has just had somebody die in the back of his police car.

So once again, the pressure is on him to belong, to be accepted and welcomed into the only group that knows what is going on inside him.

If the influences aren't right, he can be hooked.

So he is at the stage where he wants to be one of the guys. And then this kind of thing may happen: One night his car is sent to check on a "Code 26"—a silent burglar alarm.

The officer and his partner go in to investigate. The burglar is gone. They call the proprietor. He comes down to look things over. And maybe he says, "Boys, this is covered by insurance, so why don't you take a jacket for your wife, or a pair of shoes?" And maybe he does, maybe just because his partner does, and he says to himself, "What the hell, who has been hurt?"

Or maybe the proprietor didn't come down. But after they get back in the car his partner pulls out four $10 bills and hands him two. "Burglar got careless," says the partner.

The young officer who isn't involved soon learns that this kind of thing goes on. He even may find himself checking on a burglary call, say to a drugstore, and see some officers there eyeing him peculiarly.

Maybe at this point the young officer feels the pressure to belong so strongly that he reaches over and picks up something, cigars perhaps. Then he is "in," and the others can do what they wish.

Mind you, not all officers will do this. Somewhere along the line all of them have to make a decision, and it is at that point where the stuff they are made of shows through. But the past experience of the handouts, the official indifference to them, and the pressures and tensions of the job don't make the decision any easier.

And neither he nor the department has had any advance warning, such as might come from thorough psychiatric screening, as to what his decision will be.

Some men may go this far and no further. They might rationalize that they have not done anything that isn't really accepted by smart people in society.

This is no doubt where the hard-core guy, the one who is a thief already, steps in. A policeman is a trained observer and he is smart in back-alley psychology. This is especially true of the hard-core guy and he has been watching the young fellows come along.

When he and his cronies in a burglary ring spot a guy who may have what it takes to be one of them, they may approach him and try him out as a lookout. From then on it is just short steps to the actual participation in and planning of crimes.

Bear in mind that by this stage we have left all but a few policemen behind. But all of them figure in the story at one stage or another. And what has happened to a few could happen to others. I suppose that is the main point I am trying to make.

28

Chicago Police Force

The City of Chicago's police force is one of the nation's largest. Its 10,500 sworn officers patrol an area of 224 square miles with a population of 3,550,000. Located on the southwest shores of Lake Michigan, the city is divided into 21 approximately equal population districts. Despite continued growth of the city and a rise in nationally reported crime, the Chicago Police Department has experienced a steady decrease in reported crime over the past two years.

DEPARTMENT ORGANIZATION

The three primary units of the department are the Bureaus of Field Services, Staff Services, and Inspectional Services (see Exhibit 28-1 for a condensed organization chart). Each is headed by a Deputy Superintendent of the Police Department. (All positions in the Chicago Police system above that of captain are exempt. That is, these positions do not have civil service tenure, but are filled at the discretion of the Superintendent, and he has the authority to return the individual to the rank of captain should he deem this to be in the best interests of the Police Department.) The following paragraphs briefly describe the functions of each of these bureaus.

Bureaus

Bureau of Field Services   By far the largest bureau, it has approximately 80% of the department's human resources. It is directly responsible for protecting the life and property of the citizen and for apprehending criminals. It is divided into four units, Patrol, Traffic, Detective, and Youth, whose principal functions are discussed below.

Patrol Division   Containing over 8,000 personnel, it is the city's first line of defense against crime. Headed by a Chief, it is divided into six areas, each headed by an Area Deputy. An area contains three to four districts, each containing a station house and headed by a District Commander. A district is subdivided into a number of beats (20-35) of approximately equal police work load, each of which is manned 24 hours a day by an

Written by F.W. McFarlan and T.C. Raymond. Reprinted with the permission of the U.S. Department of Justice. Prepared for the Management Institute for Police Chiefs with funds provided under a grant support under the Law Enforcement Act of 1965.

149

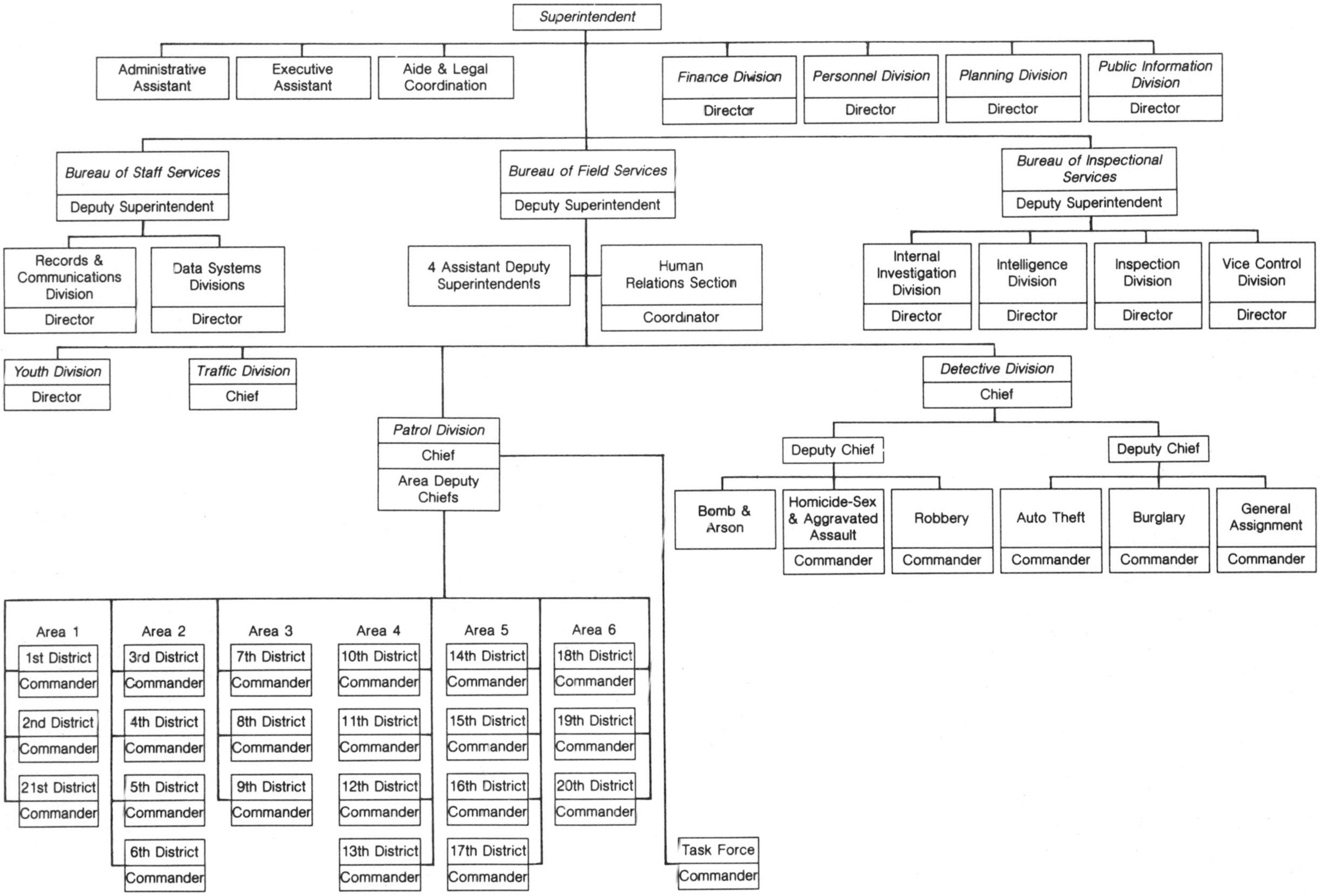

EXHIBIT 28–1 CHICAGO POLICE DEPARTMENT ORGANIZATION CHART

assigned patrol car. In addition, there is a city-wide "Task Force" that provides a "blitz" type reserve force to assist district personnel in special problem areas.

Organizationally, the personnel in each district are divided into three eight-hour watches, each headed by a watch commander, a captain. Watches begin at 12:00 P.M., 8:00 A.M., and 4:00 P.M., and are rotated every 20 days. Approximately 60-100 people are assigned to each watch. In the 18th District, for example, a typical watch has 96 officers including a captain, three lieutenants, seven sergeants, and 85 patrolmen. Because of days off, furloughs, sick leaves, etc., only 50%-60% of this number are normally available for duty on any given day.

While the District Commander has the overall responsibility for crime detection and prevention in his district, as well as administrative responsibility for his men, the Central Headquarters Communications Center assigns patrol cars to specific calls in the district. Often, only after a car has returned to the District Station House at the end of the watch is the Commander aware of how his people spent their time during the day. The Commander does, however, determine how the watch resources will be divided between patrol cars, plainclothes work, and miscellaneous other assignments. It is by this division of available resources that the District Commander can affect to a certain degree the amount of crime in his district. Because of the strong seasonality and time patterns associated with certain crimes, the Commander has the flexibility to schedule more personnel on one shift than on another, stagger vacation schedules, and move subordinates from regular beats to special assignments. For example, crimes of armed robbery are four times as likely on warm summer nights as they are on cold winter afternoons. Thus the Commander will schedule his district to most effectively match requirements with available personnel.

Traffic Division A completely autono-

mous division, it uses nearly 10% of the people in the department. It is decentralized under the jurisdiction of six area headquarters. Its field personnel are responsible for investigating accidents, selective enforcement of moving violations, parking enforcement, and the direction of downtown traffic.

Detective Division Employing 1,300 personnel, it is divided into six major areas: robbery, homicide and sex, burglary, auto theft, bomb and arson, and general assignment. The detectives operate out of special area headquarters and work under the direction of section commanders quartered at Central Headquarters. While preliminary investigations of complaints are made by patrolmen on the beat, detectives are assigned to conduct followup investigations on an individual case basis.

Youth Division Consisting of 400 personnel, it is primarily concerned with juvenile delinquency. Its functions are to prevent and suppress delinquent behavior; to aid and assist other units in the proper disposition of apprehended juveniles; to assemble and disseminate information relevant to gang activities; and to observe gang movements.

Bureau of Staff Services Employing approximately 1,600 persons, it provides technical and material tools to assist the Bureau of Field Services in accomplishing its tasks. Specialized services of this bureau include: training sessions, records and communications, a crime laboratory, central services, automotive maintenance, radio maintenance, and the building maintenance division.

Of particular interest are the operations of the communications section located in a large room on the second floor of 13-story central headquarters. This section is responsible for handling all telephone requests for service and for dispatching an appropriate number of patrol cars to the scene. To handle this task, the section is organized as follows: the entire city has been divided into eight zones of approximately equal service requirements. These zone boundaries are constructed so that, to the extent possible, they respect district boundaries. (Six districts operate in two radio zones each. The primary factor for this is alignment of Bell Telephone exchanges with radio zones.) The vast majority of each zone's service calls are handled 24 hours a day by three three-person officer groups (each group working eight hours). Seated together at a large desk in the communications center, each officer has a large glass street map of the zone in front of him or her. On the map are drawn the district boundaries lying within the zone and border lines for the beats within each district. In the middle of each beat is a small electric light bulb representing the patrol car assigned to the beat. A light that is turned off means the patrol car is not available for service, either because it is on special assignment, or, perhaps, because it is not even on the road.

All regular Bell Telephone calls originating within the zone are automatically sent to this desk by special telephone circuiting. In cases where all three telephones for the zone are busy, the calls are referred, after 10 seconds, to a traffic overflow desk. If the nature of the incident is such that it can safely be responded to upon receiving the call, the dispatcher will fill out a radio ticket on the call including the following information.

1. Name and address of caller.
2. Type of call (armed robbery, burglary, etc.).
3. Time call is received, time car is dispatched, and time of the car's return to service are electrically stamped on the card by the dispatcher.

Then, scanning the map in front of him, the dispatcher will select a patrol car to handle the job and then radio instructions to this car to proceed to the location, together with a description of the type of problem that awaits

him. The radio dispatchers are especially selected experienced officers who have spent a long time in the districts in which they are now assigning cars. This background is considered vital for the job because they must:

1. Decide on the appropriate level of response to the situation (one, two, or more cars).
2. Select the specific car to handle the assignment. Making this decision requires a detailed knowledge of the pattern of one-way streets confronting a car as it moves to the destination, and the overall flexibility left in the district for rapid handling of possible subsequent calls.

Following the assignment, the dispatcher then notes the specific car assigned to the job on the ticket and puts the ticket in a box to his immediate right. When the patrol car has finished the job and telephoned a report of the case to the central office, he then radios the dispatcher that he is free. (Car availability lights are controlled by putting the radio ticket into a slot corresponding to the car number. When the radio ticket is in the slot the light is automatically turned "Out"—designating that the car is not available for service call.) The dispatcher turns the car's light on on the map, stamps the time the job was completed on the ticket, and forwards the ticket on a route which will eventually carry it to Data Processing.

Bureau of Inspectional Services With 400 employees, the Bureau provides the department with a variety of internal and external services. It periodically inspects the several units, installations, equipment, and records to insure compliance with established regulations and procedures. It conducts field operations to produce intelligence on organized crime and subversive activities. It maintains a continuing estimate of the vice situation and the department vice control effort.

DATA PROCESSING

The Chicago Electronic Data Processing center is organizationally a staff activity and reports to the Deputy Superintendent of the Bureau of Staff Services who, in turn, reports to the Superintendent. The EDP Center is headed by a civilian with a broad background in EDP and, specifically, in police EDP operations. The Center currently operates on a budget slightly greater than $1,000,000. Of this amount approximately 65% is spent on personnel and the remainder on equipment.

Of the 110 people who are currently employed in the EDP area 93 are keypunch, computer and punched card equipment operators, and supporting personnel (people who code certain source documents in a form suitable for keypunching. For example, on radio tickets they assign an appropriate number indicating the type of call it was [burglary 026, etc.]). These people are divided into three shifts of approximately equal length and, with the exception of the machine operators, maintain a 24-hour-a-day operation Monday through Saturday. The computer and punched card machine operators' time is scheduled for 24-hour-a-day, seven-day-a-week operation. The remaining 17 personnel are systems analysts and programmers who provide the continuing rework and program maintenance support. They normally work a 9:00 to 5:00 day.

The Chicago Computer Center has an 80K IBM 1410 computer. Peripheral equipment attached to the machine includes six high-speed tape drives, and a 1301 disk storage unit containing 28,000,000 characters of storage. Twelve IBM 1014 remote terminals, located in the headquarters outside the computer room, are available to immediately access information stored on the 1301 disk storage unit. Ten of these terminals are located in the Communications Center (one for each zone and one for each of two city-wide frequencies) and two in the Field Inquiry section. Off-line equipment in the center includes 12 keypunches, six key veri-

fiers, and one each of the following: sorter, collator, reproducer, interpreter, and accounting machine. As of June 1966, the Center was barely holding its own by operating 24 hours a day, seven days a week; thus it was recognized that a decision to expand the system would have to be made in the immediate future.

COMPUTER REPORTING

Computer usage in the department falls primarily into two major areas. The first is the provision of real-time information concerning the status of cars and individuals to the patrolman on the beat who has made an arrest or is investigating a suspicious incident. The second is the provision of various management reports to key supervisory personnel down through the District Commander level. (In addition, there are a number of more routine staff activity applications such as payroll and automotive repair accounting that are not discussed here.) Both of these application areas are described in some detail below.

Real-Time Information Retrieval

Field personnel have almost immediate access to computer files containing data on wanted persons and stolen vehicles. A patrolman, desiring special information, radios the radio dispatcher in the communications center and tells him the information he wants. An IBM 1014 terminal (10 in total) is located beside the radio dispatcher's desk. (The terminal's physical appearance is very similar to that of a typewriter.) The dispatcher types in the necessary information concerning the person or vehicle. When he has finished typing the message (roughly 10-20 seconds), he presses a release key that causes the computer to stop whatever task it is currently doing, retrieve the necessary information, and type it out on the terminal. Depending on the nature of the request, the computer will require between two and 20 seconds to get the information. The radio dispatcher then relays this information to the patrolman. The following paragraphs describe some of the specific questions that may be asked:

Warrant Is there a warrant out for the person's arrest (other than traffic warrant)? After a police warrant has been taken out in court and approved by a judge, it is sent to the Warrant Section of the Field Inquiry unit which forwards a copy to the EDP Center. The information on the warrant is keypunched on cards and fed into the computer for storage on the 1301 disk file. The following information is included:

1. Name, address, birthdate, sex, race, height, and weight of wanted person.
2. Warrant number (generated by warrant section).
3. Date warrant issued and district in which it is to be served.
4. Charge for which warrant issued.
5. Any known aliases of suspect.

At present there are some 30,000 warrants on file. About 33,000 warrants are issued each year and of these nearly 26,000 are served. Sixty percent of all warrants issued are served within a week. After three years, if a warrant has not been served it is automatically dropped from the file.

When a warrant has been served, the district station house teletypes this message to the warrant section. This information is then sent to the EDP Center which deletes the warrant from the file. Since not all warrants are picked up by this process, a supplemental check is made every month. A list of warrants outstanding for more than 45 days in a district is sent to the district for confirmation. This list is nearly always checked and returned to the EDP Center within a week, where appropriate corrections on the computer file are then made.

It should be noted that the computer program used to generate information in response to inquiries is enormously complex and often more than one name will be provided when a request is made. Two principal reasons account for this:

1. To speed computer search processing time, when a specific name is being searched for in the files, it is condensed to just its consonants. Thus, for example, the names Black and Block both appear as BLCK to the computer. Thus a request for information on a person named Black may produce information on both names.
2. When the computer fails to find a name that perfectly agrees with that provided by the patrolman, it will relax some of the constraints on the typed information on the assumption that either it or the patrolman may not have all the facts straight. For example, it will look to see if it has Harry Blacks who match all the descriptions except for the address, and if it finds several it will print them out. There is a whole hierarchy of constraint relaxations that are included in the computer program.

As a result the patrolman may get either a positive identification of a person, a list of "possibles," or a message stating that the computer has no record of this individual. In the latter cases he must further interrogate the suspect to get a positive linkup or a list of "possibles."

Traffic Warrants Another file that can be examined is the traffic warrant file. This file is somewhat smaller than the warrant file and at the present time contains some 10,000 names. Roughly 100 warrants per day are issued. The file is purged on a regular basis.

Stop Order Another file available is the stop-order file. This includes names of people whom detectives want to talk to in connection with a possible active role in a criminal act, parole violators, prison escapees, and Service AWOLs. Due to the tensions attendant to an arrest and the possibility of unfortunate errors occurring in the heat of the moment, no "just-to-talk-to's" are added to the file. It currently contains about 1,800 names with 50 names being added per day. This file is also purged on a regular basis.

License Revocation   A fourth file that is checked is the driver's license revocation file. Once a week a list of newly revoked and suspended drivers' licenses is sent to Chicago from the Bureau of Motor Vehicles in Springfield. These include licenses revoked or suspended in Cook County and the four surrounding counties. Approximately 1,000 to 2,000 such items are received per week. At the present time some 40,000 revocations are in the computer memory. No effort is made to purge this file.

License Suspension   This is very similar to the license revocation file. At present there are some 13,000 names on file. Included in the file record is the termination date of the suspension. On this date, the computer automatically erases this record from computer memory.

These files are widely used during the day, although there is extensive peaking of usage at certain hours of the day. There are over 2,400 inquiries on a typical day, of which nearly half are about people.

In addition to information on persons, a computer file on stolen cars is also maintained. When a car is reported stolen and this is verified by a patrolman, he calls the communications center and provides the following information:

1. Year and make of car.
2. State in which car is licensed and license number.
3. Patrol beat making the call.

The dispatcher then types this information on the console terminal and it is stored in computer memory. The patrolman will then fill out a more detailed case report, a copy of which is forwarded through channels to Data Processing. The following supplementary information on this case report will then be added to the computer record. This will include:

1. Name, address, and telephone number of owner.
2. Date and time car was stolen.
3. City license number.
4. Vehicle identification number, style, and color.

If this report is not received within a week, the temporary steal record will be wiped out of computer memory; this information will be sent to the appropriate district station house. Once the permanent record has been prepared it will stay on the computer either until the car has been recovered (90% of reported auto thefts are recovered in Chicago) or until three years have elapsed. There are over 30,000 reported auto thefts in Chicago each year and the file currently has approximately 25,000 vehicles listed in it.

When a patrolman discovers a stolen car he will radio this information to the communications dispatcher who will type a "temporary recovery entry" into the computer indicating that the car has been recovered. It will not be dropped from the computer file, however, until a copy of the patrolman's report has been received in Data Processing, and a card summarizing the information punched and read into the computer.

To assist officers in identifying the cars, every day a "Daily Hot Sheet" listing the license number of the 550 most recently reported and unrecovered auto thefts is prepared by the computer. This is then printed on the back of the "Chicago Police Department Daily Bulletin," a two-page information sheet distributed to every officer in the department. At the end of the week a supplemental sheet of the 1,100 most recently reported and unrecovered auto thefts is prepared and distributed.

When an officer wishes to interrogate the

file, he radios the dispatcher and gives the information. The radio dispatcher then types in this information and will get a response. Over 1,300 inquiries of this type were received on a recent Thursday. It is estimated that the total information retrieval function is currently consuming up to seven hours of computer running time each day.

Management Reporting Tools

In addition to its real-time information retrieval activities, the computer center also prepares a number of reports for the Patrol Division. The more significant of these are described below.

Summary of Radio Dispatch Tickets

Prepared daily, this report is distributed to all personnel in the Patrol Division down through the level of District Commander. This report summarizes the information on all radio dispatch cards prepared the previous day and is ready for distribution at 9:00 A.M. In discussing the report with the EDP Manager, the following points seemed particularly noteworthy to the casewriter:

1. The same report is distributed to all District Commanders.
2. For each crime classification three statistics are reported; incidents today, cumulative incidents, last period to date. (To overcome the comparison problems inherent in comparing crime in a month with four weekends to those in a month with five weekends, Chicago's basic reporting system is based on a year that is divided into 13 28-day periods.)
3. Last year's temperature range and precipitation for the same police period date last year are reported on the top of the report.
4. Major classifications on the report include the following:
   a. Major index crimes (number of homicides, rapes, serious assaults, robberies, burglaries, thefts, and auto thefts).
   b. Total nonindex crimes (includes such items as theft under $50).
   c. Miscellaneous noncriminal (cat on roof, water seepage, etc.).
   d. Total traffic accidents in District.
   e. Total police service. This is the sum of the four previous categories of incidents.
5. Since the basic data source for this report is the radio dispatch tickets, the report includes crimes that may later be unfounded (reclassified to another category) following a detective's investigation. It, however, excludes crimes that were unfounded by preliminary investigation (patrol car does not release itself for duty on another incident until it has completed a preliminary investigation of the incident and has radioed any reclassification data back to the communications dispatcher).

A copy of the "Summary of Radio Dispatch Cards" report for June 9, 1966, is included as Exhibit 28-2. Normally 6,000 to 7,000 tickets are prepared each day.

Weekly Analysis of Radio Dispatches

At the end of the week (Wednesday at 12:00 P.M.), the radio dispatch tickets for the entire week are analyzed and a summary report of this analysis is mailed out along with the Daily Summary of Radio Dispatched Tickets the following morning. A copy of the report distributed on June 2, 1966, is included as Exhibit 28-3. In discussing the report with the EDP manager, the casewriter noted the following items of interest:

1. The same crime categories were used in this report as in the daily report.
2. No absolute number of incidents figures were contained on the report, only a percentage analysis.
3. The top of the report ranked the districts in relation to their percentage performance improvement over the same week last year. For example, looking at Exhibit 28-3, the sixth district recorded a 75.9%

EXHIBIT 28-2 SUMMARY OF RADIO DISPATCH CARDS

(includes crimes that may be later unfounded but excludes crimes unfounded by preliminary investigation)

Weather on same police period date last year:			Precipitation - None		Police Period* Date:		15-P06-66	
			Temperature Range - 61-76		Calendar Date:		09 JUN 1966	

		Area 1		Areas	Area 6			Citywide
Districts	21	1	2	2-5	18	19	20	Total
Homicide:								
Today	0	0	0		0	0	0	1
This period to date	1	1	2		0	1	0	12
This period last year to date*	0	0	2		0	0	0	8
Last period to date*	0	0	3		0	0	0	8
Rape:								
Today	0	0	0		0	0	1	5
This period to date	6	0	16		6	6	7	106
This period last year to date*	10	0	21		4	2	3	104
Last period to date*	2	1	12		6	3	2	78
Serious Assault:								
Today	0	0	1		0	0	0	20
This period to date	20	5	54		17	10	17	429
This period last year to date*	22	6	61		23	7	16	417
Last period to date*	27	4	41		15	8	4	336
Robbery:								
Today	1	1	7		5	0	4	46
This period to date	59	22	140		53	21	27	806
This period last year to date*	59	8	122		51	14	12	732
Last period to date*	41	14	101		31	12	25	635
Burglary:								
Today	3	0	9		6	7	12	128
This period to date	74	21	129		109	100	145	1,882
This period last year to date*	79	29	89		98	96	137	1,826
Last period to date*	104	35	96		93	105	125	1,759
Theft ($50 and over):								
Today	7	1	7		5	2	5	52
This period to date	44	40	47		68	61	71	736
This period last year to date*	53	62	36		86	83	106	897
Last period to date*	45	69	45		68	46	62	765
Auto Theft:								
Today	3	2	5		4	2	4	103
This period to date	69	34	84		67	78	108	1,526
This period last year to date*	53	35	99		108	63	87	1,523
Last period to date*	51	20	93		81	56	92	1,476
Total Index Crimes:								
Today	14	4	29		20	11	26	355
This period to date	273	123	472		320	277	375	5,497
This period last year to date*	276	140	430		370	265	361	5,507
Last period to date*	270	143	391		294	230	310	5,057
Total Nonindex Crimes:								
Today	17	15	36		19	22	28	400
This period to date	375	235	579		425	394	474	7,473
This period last year to date*	354	278	465		422	361	481	7,045
Last period to date*	328	251	517		444	359	476	7,097
Miscellaneous Noncriminal:								
Today	132	92	199		168	184	180	2,880
This period to date	2,670	1,491	4,777		3,198	3,588	4,077	59,662
This period last year to date*	2,585	1,302	4,145		3,069	3,100	3,398	53,582
Last period to date*	2,296	1,510	3,903		2,953	2,998	3,432	50,922
Traffic Accidents:								
Today	28	42	16		31	27	52	684
This period to date	219	272	225		307	263	454	6,176
This period last year to date*	180	292	245		251	255	443	5,904
Last period to date*	196	320	262		329	270	460	6,524
Total Police Service:								
Today	191	154	280		238	244	286	4,319
This period to date	3,537	2,121	6,053		4,250	4,522	5,380	78,808
This period last year to date*	3,395	2,012	5,285		4,112	3,981	4,683	72,038
Last period to date*	3,090	2,224	5,073		4,020	3,857	4,678	69,600

EXHIBIT 28-3 WEEKLY ANALYSIS OF RADIO DISPATCHES

*District Percent of Change Over Prior Year**   *Police Week 01-07/P06/66 vs 01-07/P06/65*

Homicide		Rape		Ser Assault		Robbery		Burglary		Theft		Auto Theft		Index		Non Index		Misc Noncr		Traffic Acc		Total Serv	
Dist	%	Dist	%	Dist	%	Dist	%	Dist	%	Dist	%	Dist	%	Dist	%	Dist	%	Dist	%	Dist	%	Dist	%
13 -	100.0	15 -	100.0	18 -	76.9	8 -	87.5	8 -	51.6	16 -	64.7	18 -	52.4	18 -	27.4	1 -	14.8	18 -	.6	19 -	20.4	18 -	1.4
1	.0	21 -	66.7	16 -	66.7	20 -	37.5	11 -	28.6	15 -	64.3	16 -	31.6	8 -	25.0	13 -	7.1	21	2.8	1 -	16.8	17	.9
3	.0	3 -	50.0	1 -	60.0	15 -	33.3	17 -	24.3	17	56.0	7 -	24.5	17 -	25.0	19 -	7.1	12	3.4	6 -	13.3	12	2.9
5	.0	19 -	50.0	7 -	36.4	10 -	19.4	12 -	17.5	9 -	50.0	3 -	21.2	16 -	18.5	7 -	1.4	6	5.0	17 -	12.5	1	3.2
6	.0	12 -	33.3	12 -	28.6	3 -	17.5	1 -	16.7	1 -	38.5	5 -	20.0	12 -	14.5	20 -	1.3	11	6.3	11 -	9.0	11	3.8
8	.0	2 -	8.3	14 -	20.0	11 -	2.7	21 -	16.2	13 -	36.0	6 -	18.4	1 -	6.8	16 -	1.1	17	7.4	2 -	7.0	6	4.3
9	.0	1	.0	11 -	13.0	12	.0	15 -	11.1	18 -	34.9	2 -	9.3	7 -	6.0	11	.5	16	9.1	8 -	5.6	21	4.9
11	.0	4	.0	2 -	10.3	17	.0	7 -	9.6	6 -	31.2	10 -	8.3	15 -	2.3	17	3.4	14	9.3	12 -	5.5	16	6.3
12	.0	6	.0	8	.0	21	5.7	14	.0	8 -	31.2	12 -	3.7	11 -	1.0	8	6.1	5	10.7	15 -	4.1	7	8.2
14	.0	9	.0	10	5.0	18	7.4	18	7.0	5 -	26.7	9	.0	21	.7	14	6.1	7	11.1	14 -	3.1	14	8.3
15	.0	14	.0	13	5.9	6	22.2	16	11.5	12 -	25.0	13	2.3	9	1.3	6	7.0	15	11.3	13 -	1.8	13	8.5
16	.0	16	.0	9	20.0	9	25.0	9	14.8	21 -	18.5	17	5.9	3	5.4	18	7.4	13	11.4	3	.0	8	8.7
17	.0	17	.0	21	20.0	2	26.3	19	26.3	10 -	18.2	4	10.0	10	5.6	3	8.2	1	12.7	10	.0	15	9.6
18	.0	13	33.3	19	40.0	7	37.9	20	27.3	19 -	14.3	19	10.7	5	6.0	10	10.7	9	14.7	9	4.2	10	10.2
19	.0	11	50.0	5	57.1	13	41.7	10	27.7	20	.0	14	11.5	13	10.3	5	10.8	19	15.9	4	4.7	19	10.4
20	.0	7	66.7	20	66.7	5	75.0	13	31.0	7	7.7	8	16.7	19	11.5	9	12.5	8	16.4	5	9.6	9	12.7
2	100.0	5	100.0	3	70.0	19	80.0	4	35.0	3	22.2	1	35.7	6	14.7	15	20.0	3	16.6	7	9.8	3	14.1
4	100.0	8	100.0	6	100.0	4	125.0	5	46.2	2	66.7	15	35.7	14	17.1	21	20.7	10	17.7	20	10.9	10	14.7
7	100.0	18	100.0	17	200.0	14	150.0	3	47.8	14	72.7	21	39.3	2	20.4	2	26.3	2	18.1	21	12.0	2	17.8
10	100.0	10	120.0	15	400.0	1	300.0	2	55.0	11	91.7	11	42.9	20	28.1	4	28.6	4	18.5	16	13.5	20	19.0
21	100.0	20	300.0	4	800.0	16	400.0	6	75.9	4	140.0	20	56.4	4	51.7	12	29.5	20	22.4	18	17.4	4	20.3

District Percent of City Wide Total   *Police Week 01-07/P06/66*

Homicide		Rape		Ser Assault		Robbery		Burglary		Theft		Auto Theft		Index		Non Index		Misc Noncr		Traffic Acc		Total Serv	
Dist	%	Dist	%	Dist	%	Dist	%	Dist	%	Dist	%	Dist	%	Dist	%	Dist	%	Dist	%	Dist	%	Dist	%
1	.0	1	.0	1	1.0	1	2.0	1	1.1	1	4.7	1	2.6	1	2.1	1	3.1	1	2.4	1	3.6	1	2.5
2	16.7	2	20.0	2	13.0	2	17.6	2	7.1	2	7.4	2	5.3	2	9.0	2	7.8	2	8.3	2	3.9	2	8.0
3	16.7	3	7.3	3	8.5	3	8.0	3	7.7	3	3.3	3	5.6	3	6.7	3	6.4	3	8.3	3	5.4	3	7.8
4	16.7	4	.0	4	4.5	4	2.2	4	3.1	4	3.6	4	4.5	4	3.5	4	4.1	4	3.0	4	4.1	4	3.2
5	.0	5	1.8	5	5.5	5	3.4	5	4.3	5	3.3	5	6.5	5	4.7	5	3.8	5	4.2	5	6.3	5	4.4
6	.0	6	1.8	6	2.0	6	2.7	6	5.8	6	3.3	6	4.2	6	4.2	6	3.9	6	3.3	6	3.6	6	3.4
7	16.7	7	9.1	7	7.0	7	9.8	7	5.4	7	4.2	7	5.0	7	6.0	7	6.2	7	6.4	7	5.4	7	6.3
8	.0	8	1.8	8	1.5	8	.2	8	1.7	8	3.3	8	4.8	8	2.5	8	4.0	8	3.2	8	5.6	8	3.4
9	.0	9	.0	9	3.0	9	2.4	9	3.5	9	1.8	9	3.7	9	3.1	9	4.6	9	4.6	9	5.5	9	4.6
10	16.7	10	20.0	10	10.5	10	6.1	10	6.8	10	2.7	10	6.0	10	6.5	10	5.3	10	6.0	10	4.9	10	5.9
11	.0	11	10.9	11	10.0	11	8.8	11	7.4	11	6.8	11	6.8	11	7.6	11	6.0	11	6.0	11	5.2	11	6.0
12	.0	12	3.6	12	5.0	12	5.6	12	3.8	12	5.3	12	3.5	12	4.3	12	3.9	12	3.9	12	3.8	12	3.9
13	.0	13	7.3	13	9.0	13	8.3	13	6.3	13	4.7	13	6.1	13	6.6	13	5.2	13	5.6	13	4.0	13	5.5
14	.0	14	.0	14	2.0	14	1.2	14	3.6	14	5.6	14	4.0	14	3.4	14	4.0	14	4.4	14	4.7	14	4.3
15	.0	15	.0	15	2.5	15	1.0	15	3.6	15	1.5	15	5.2	15	3.2	15	4.1	15	3.8	15	4.3	15	3.8
16	.0	16	.0	16	.5	16	1.0	16	3.3	16	1.8	16	1.8	16	2.0	16	2.6	16	2.1	16	5.3	16	2.4
17	.0	17	.0	17	1.0	17	.2	17	3.2	17	3.3	17	2.5	17	2.3	17	2.6	17	2.4	17	4.9	17	2.6
18	.0	18	3.6	18	1.5	18	7.1	18	5.2	18	8.3	18	4.1	18	5.3	18	6.2	18	5.2	18	4.7	18	5.3
19	.0	19	1.8	19	3.5	19	2.2	19	5.5	19	8.9	19	4.2	19	4.8	19	4.9	19	5.9	19	4.0	19	5.6
20	.0	20	7.3	20	2.5	20	1.2	20	8.0	20	9.4	20	8.3	20	6.8	20	6.4	20	6.7	20	7.5	20	6.7
21	16.7	21	3.6	21	6.0	21	9.0	21	3.5	21	6.5	21	5.3	21	5.5	21	5.1	21	4.4	21	3.4	21	4.5

* % of change in excess of 1000 plus or minus

represent a complete picture of the patrol increase in burglaries this period as opposed to a year ago. This was the largest percentage increase in burglaries in the city. Conversely, in traffic accidents their performance this year was much better than last year as they achieved a 13.3% reduction to rank third from the top in the city in terms of improvement.

4. The bottom part of the report indicates the percent of the total city's crime activity in each category that occurred in each district. For example, in the week ending June 2, 55 reported rapes occurred in the city, one in the sixth district. Therefore, the sixth district is credited with having 1/55 or 1.8% of the city's total activity in this category.

Police Period Crime Summary This report, frequently referred to as "The Bible," is distributed on the Monday following the close of a period not only to the people receiving the other two reports, but to many others including the press. Crime categories are broken down in much greater detail in this report than in the others. Unlike the previous two reports, this report is based not on radio dispatch tickets but on case reports. These case reports are prepared by the patrolman handling the incident, and subsequent to review in the District and Area offices are sent to the detective division which sends a copy to the EDP Center where the key classification information is entered into the computer. To assure that all cases originating in the period are reported, all radio dispatch cards prepared for criminal offenses are assigned a "Records Division Number." This number is also given to the officer preparing the case report.

A list of all "Records Division Numbers" issued during the period is stored in the computer. Seven days before the end of the period, this list is checked against the file of cases submitted, and a list of cases due but not yet submitted is prepared and sent to the several district station houses for immediate action. The average time for a report to reach

EDP after the patrolman has completed handling the incident is three days although in peak work periods this may be as many as seven days. Some 35,000 to 40,000 case reports are submitted each period.

An additional data input is generated by the Detective Division. Approximately 15,000 incidents a period are followed up with a detective's investigation. After the completion of the investigation (in some cases this may take 90 days or more) a final report is prepared, one copy of which is sent to EDP. This may result in a reclassification of a crime (an armed robbery may be reclassified as a burglary, etc.). In this case the current period's armed robbery total will be reduced by one for the appropriate district and the burglary figure increased by one. Because of reclassifications the current period's total for the categories in question will not always be an accurate representation of the period's reported crime activity. A further distortion will occur because some crimes occurring close to the end of the period will not be written up in time to be included in the period's statistics.

Patrol Division Operations Report The above three reports are referred to as the crime statistics reports. In addition to these reports two "operations" reports are prepared each period that provide statistics concerning the patrol activities on individual beats, watches, districts, areas, and finally for the city as a whole. These reports highlight performance on so-called preventable crimes (i.e., if a patrolman had been visible in the vicinity, the crime would not have occurred). There are certain crimes that are classified as non-preventable. For example, a homicide in which a man murders his wife would be classified as non-preventable. Exhibit 28-4 is a sample Patrol Division Operations report for the first two beats of the first watch in the 14th district.

The statistics for each watch and district are determined by adding together the individual beat statistics (no sample of this report is shown since it is entirely analogous to the

EXHIBIT 28–4   PATROL DIVISION OPERATIONS REPORT

Criminal Incidents		Beat 1 — Incidents Handled in this Beat by this Car	Beat 1 — Total Incidents in this Beat — This Period	Last Period	This Period Last Year	Beat 2 — Incidents Handled in this Beat by this Car	Beat 2 — Total Incidents in this Beat — This Period	Last Period	This Period Last Year
Serious Assault	Street								
	Other								
Minor Assault	Street						2	1	
	Other								
Armed Robbery	Street								
	Other			1					
Strong Arm Robbery	Street								
	Other								
Residential Burglary	Entry Ground Level								
	Entry - Other	1						1	
Non-Residential Burglary	Tavern and Liquor Sales			1					
	Supermarkets and Gas Stations								
	Other							1	
Auto-Theft	Street	2				1	3	1	
	Parking Lot								
	Other								
Theft From Auto	Street								
	Parking Lot								
	Other								
Theft-Auto Accessories	Street			1					
	Parking Lot								
	Other								
Purse Snatching	Street								
	Other								
Bicycle Theft									
Other Theft									
Other Crimes		1	2			1	7	1	
Total		4	5			2	12	5	

Other Incidents	Beat 1 — Total Incidents in this Beat — This Period	This Period Last Year	Incidents Handled in any Beat by this Beat Car	Average Time in Minutes per Incident Handled	Beat 2 — Total Incidents in this Beat — This Period	This Period Last Year	Incidents Handled in any Beat by this Beat Car	Average Time in Minutes per Incident Handled
Curfew Violations								
Traffic Accidents	9		3	137	8			
Auto Recoveries	2		1	59	2			
Misc. Non Criminal								
Disturbances	14		13	20	10		6	46
Sick and Injured					2			
Suspicious Persons	3		2	30	3		1	4
Other	33		28	49	28		9	13
Total	61		47	46	53		16	25

Time on Call	Beat 1 — Incidents Handled — Criminal	Other	Time in Hours	% of Total Hours	Beat 2 — Incidents Handled — Criminal	Other	Time in Hours	% of Total Hours
This Beat Car		22	17	22.7	2	8	3	4.6
Other Beat Cars - This District	3	21	38	50.7	10	22	30	46.2
Other Units this District		11	5	6.7		10	5	7.7
Task Force Units								
Other Department Units	1	7	15	20.0		13	27	41.5
Total - This Beat	4	61	75	100.0	12	53	65	100.0
This Beat Car in this Beat		22	17	36.2	2	8	3	20.0
This Beat Car in other Beats	6	25	25	53.2	5	8	10	66.7
This Beat Car on Assists	1	8	5	10.6	2	5	2	13.3
Total - This Beat Car	7	55	47	100.0	9	21	15	100.0

The information given above for the second beat may be interpreted as follows:

1. Twelve criminal incidents occurred on this beat between midnight and 8:00 A.M. this period as opposed to five in the previous period. (This is a relatively new report and has not been in effect long enough to have statistics generated for this period last year.) Of these 12 incidents, two were handled by the car assigned to the beat and 10 by another car assigned to the district. No criminal incidents on this beat were handled by Task Force units or department units from other districts.

2. A total of 53 other (non-criminal) incidents occurred this period on the beat including eight traffic accidents, two auto recoveries, 10 disturbances, two sick cases, three suspicious people, and 28 miscellaneous incidents. Eight of these incidents were handled by the car assigned to the beat. These incidents together with the two criminal incidents required three hours to handle, which was 4.6% of the total service time required on the beat during the period. Similarly, 22 other incidents and 10 criminal incidents on the beat were handled in 30 hours by the other beat cars assigned to the district; 10 incidents requiring five hours were handled by other units in the district (traffic, juvenile, etc.) and 13 incidents taking a total of 27 hours were handled by units from other districts.

3. The patrol car assigned to the beat spent 15 hours handling a total of 30 incidents. Ten of the incidents occurred on this beat and 13 on other beats. The remaining seven incidents involved helping another car on an assignment (this is called an "assist").

4. Statistics regarding the time to handle the 16 "other" incidents in which the car was not on an assist are as follows: An average 46 minutes was required to handle each of six disturbances, four minutes to handle a suspicious person, and an average of 13 minutes for each of nine miscellaneous incidents.

beat report). These reports of course do not represent a complete picture of the patrol car's activity since statistics on other items important to the operation of a patrol car are not included. These would include premise checks, plant checks, automobile trouble, court appearances, and lunch hours.

District and Area Patrol Division Operations Reports This is also a period report and is in many ways similar to the previous report. In addition to being a more aggregative report, it includes some additional important information that is described in

Exhibit 28-5. Semi-annually the city moves from a winter patrol beat pattern to a summer patrol beat pattern. At that time the crime patterns in the various beats are reviewed to make sure that they still represent an equal police work load. To provide more meaningful data to work with, the computer processes a file containing the radio dispatch ticket data for the past six months. At the time the ticket was entered into the file it was given a nine-digit code, representing the block in the city where the crime occurred. The computer processes the tickets to come up with an activity index for each block of the city. In developing this index all incidents are not given equal weight. Part I crimes are given a weight of four, Part II crimes are given a weight of three, and miscellaneous calls a weight of one.

This material is then sent to the Planning Section which, taking into account natural boundaries (one example would be a major highway), one way streets, etc., develops a series of beats of approximately equal size. This information is then reviewed with Area and District Commanders and appropriate changes are made.

In conjunction with this, the Arrest File (a computer record of arrests by block) is then scanned to see to which beat-watch-district (BWD) combination the 250 two-man cars should be assigned. Each multiple arrest in the BWD is counted as one point, each armed arrest as one point, and each arrest with resistance as one point. Thus, for example, a multiple arrest in which there was armed resistance would be given a score of three. After these computations are completed, the list is sorted by score so that the BWD with the highest score is at the top. The first 250 BWDs on the list are then assigned two-man cars.

EXHIBIT 28–5 PATROL DIVISION OPERATIONS REPORT

Criminal Incidents	Total Incidents in This District This Period	One Man Beat Cars				Two Man Beat Cars				Other Arrests			
		Incidents Handled in any District	Avg. Time in Mins. Per Inc. Handled	Arrests Made		Incidents Handled in any District	Avg. Time in Mins. Per Inc. Handled	Arrests Made		Task Force		Other Units This District	
				Cases	Persons			Cases	Persons	Cases	Persons	Cases	Persons
Serious assault	56	47	97	12		11	80	2		1		2	
Minor assault	76	63	89	14		12	76	4				3	
Armed robbery	45	44	86	5		4	73						
Strong arm robbery	48	46	76	3		2	95	1					
Residential burglary	91	89	73	1		2	65	1					
Non-residential burglary	35	35	97	2									
Motor vehicle theft	75	73	65	1		1	71					2	
Theft from motor vehicle	31	23	66										
Theft of motor vehicle accessories	42	38	62	1		1	45					1	
Purse snatching	13	12	69										
Bicycle theft	14	13	90										
Other theft	149	134	76	15		3	96	1				5	
Other Crimes	180	153	88	25		11	62	1		2		4	
Sub-total	855	770	80	79		47	74	10		3		17	
% of total police service	15	21		32		9		20		100		41	
Other Incidents													
Curfew violations													
Traffic accidents	375	52	80	9								1	
Vehicle recoveries	47	41	81	2		1	3					1	
Misc. non-criminal													
Disturbances	1503	1077	30	97		364	26	26				6	
Sick and injured	397	26	50	1		3	57	1					
Suspicious persons	168	132	26	8		25	20						
Other	2173	1576	44	48		96	47	13				16	
Sub-total	4663	2904	39	165		489	30	40				24	
% of total police service	85	79		68		91		80				59	
Total police service	5518	3674	48	244		536	34	50		3		41	

Time on Call	Criminal					Other				
	Incidents Handled		Total Time in Hours	% of Total Hours	Avg. Time per Inc. Handled	Incidents Handled		Total Time in Hours	% of Total Hours	Avg. Time per Inc. Handled
	On Call	On View				On Call	On View			
Beat Cars in their own Beat	232	23	333	23.9	78	1019	77	662	15.2	38
Beat Cars in Other Beats-This District	442	42	651	46.8	80	1982	196	1405	32.3	38
Other Units of this District in this District	20	9	29	2.1	62	767	75	967	22.2	68
Task Force Units in this District	3		2	.1	59					
Other Department Units in this District	74	10	99	7.1	70	487	60	531	12.2	58
Assits made by one man cars	289	79	262	18.8	42	1348	286	740	17.0	27
Assists made by two man cars	19	3	15	1.1	41	65	13	48	1.1	37
Total-This District	1079	166	1391	100.0	67	5668	707	4353	100.0	40
Assists made to one man cars	316	80	298		45	1229	222	695		28
Assists made to two man cars	90	24	66		35	385	102	215		26

Features of this report to be noted include:

1. Breakdown of incidents handled by one-man and two-man cars.
2. Indications of the number of incidents handled that resulted in arrests and the number of persons arrested (this last feature has only recently been added and hence does not appear on the Exhibit). For example, 47 incidents of serious assault were handled in district 21 by one-man beat cars during the period. It took an average of 97 minutes to handle each incident and 12 of them resulted in arrests being made.
3. Breakdown between number of incidents handled by beat cars as a result of a radio call and those that the patrolman observed happening and immediately intervened.

29

University Control Graph

The purpose of this exercise is to develop control graphs for the participants' university. The control graph illustrates the concepts of both amount and distribution of control in organizations. The questions are worded in exactly the same way as control graph research. For use with non-university organizations, titles in the question should be replaced with titles appropriate to the organization under consideration.

STEP 1: *Answer Control Graph Questions (5 minutes)*

Each student in the class and the instructor should complete the control graph questions below.

1. In general, how much influence would you say each of the following persons or groups *actually have* on what happens in your university?

	Almost no influence	A little influence	Moderate influence	Quite a lot of influence	A great deal of influence
The President	1	2	3	4	5
Deans	1	2	3	4	5
Department Heads	1	2	3	4	5
Professors	1	2	3	4	5
Students	1	2	3	4	5

2. In general, how much influence would you say each of the following persons or groups *should have* on what happens in your university?

	Almost no influence	A little influence	Moderate influence	Quite a lot of influence	A great deal of influence
The President	1	2	3	4	5
Deans	1	2	3	4	5
Department Heads	1	2	3	4	5
Professors	1	2	3	4	5
Students	1	2	3	4	5

STEP 2: *Calculate Influence Scores (10 minutes)*

Volunteers from the class should gather information from all students about their scores. The scores may be written on a piece of paper or the volunteers may wish to have a show of hands. From this information the average score for each hierarchical level for each question can be calculated.

The instructor's response should be kept separate from student responses in these calculations.

STEP 3: *Draw Control Graphs (5 minutes)*

Students' average scores for the "actually

162

have" and "should have" curves should be drawn on the chalkboard as illustrated in the graph below. The vertical axis reflects the amount of influence and the horizontal axis shows the hierarchy levels. The "actual" control should be written as a solid line and the "should have" as a dashed line. A separate graph should be used for the instructor's scores.

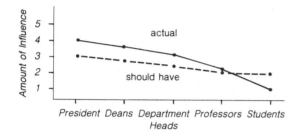

STEP 4: *Discussion (15 minutes)*

At this time the class should discuss and interpret the results of the control graph. The following questions may facilitate discussion.

1. Does the slope of the curves indicate a democratic or autocratic organization?
2. Are the slopes the same as would be expected in manufacturing organizations, in municipal governments, or other organizations?
3. Does the instructor's perception of control differ from the students'? Why would this be? Which is more accurate?

4. Which curve reflects the most total control for the university? What does greater total control mean for university functioning?
5. Which of the curves reflects the most skewed distribution of control? The most even distribution of control? What does distribution of control mean for university functioning performance?
6. Would the university be more effective if it conformed to the amount of control that students think each hierarchical level "should have?"

STEP 5: *Variation (20 minutes)*

Variations of the above exercise can be repeated to illustrate that overall control is not a unidimensional phenomenon in organizations. Influence and control may differ considerably depending on specific issues. For example, administrative versus academic domains of control may produce wide variation in perceived influence. The above questions (Step 1) can be changed to ask how much influence each of the following persons or group have on the content of courses taught in this university? This would reflect the academic domain. Questions could also be asked with respect to pay raises, or changes in organization structure that are in the administrative domain. These variations would help participants map influence throughout the university for specific issue areas.

30

The Bogged-Down Bus Business

Not even when its lunar module landed on the moon did Grumman Corp. receive as much publicity as it has in recent weeks. The frames of its proud new Flxible buses began to crack and the buses were taken off the streets of New York, Chicago, and Los Angeles for repairs. "We're going to fix them so well," proclaims Grumman Chairman John C. Bierwirth, who has not lost his sense of humor, "that when the worlds collide the only thing left standing on earth will be our frames."

Could be, but that solves only one problem. The really serious cracks are in the bus industry itself, which until recently seemed on the verge of a comeback. For years, as millions deserted public transportation for private cars, transit-bus manufacturing was a marginal business, producing only a few thousand vehicles a year, most of them to replace their worn-out predecessors. But the industry had one thing going for it: a very good bus. With millions now forced back to buses by the soaring cost of automobile driving, that bus might have generated respectable profits.

But after a lengthy and expensive effort by

government and industry, the good bus is being sent to the junkyard. In its place the country is getting an attractive but costly and ridiculous urban tank, a bus strong enough to remain intact rolling down a mountainside and yet so vulnerable that it can be crippled by a pothole or shut down by an overworked air conditioner. It's also a bus that may never be profitable to manufacture.

In this fiasco, there is plenty of blame to go around. One group of culprits includes politicians of the Nixon and Carter Administrations, who became too deeply involved in bus designing. Another is a militant clique of handicapped people who forced their demands on the politicians. The industry is culpable, too, for going along with the new-bus concept and—in Grumman's case—for delivering a defective product.

A SENSIBLE-SHOES APPROACH

Although hardly glamorous, the traditional American transit bus is an admirable piece of work, capable of withstanding the daily punishment of stop-and-start traffic over broken city streets. In 1959 General Motors introduced the New Look bus, and to avoid anti-trust action later agreed to sell components so that two competitors could make it as well, American Motors and the then independent Flxible Corp. (It's pronounced "flexible"; the first *e* was dropped years ago for trademark reasons.)

New Looks are those familiar vehicles that still make up the greatest part of the nation's fleet of 54,500 transit buses and have over the years proved an excellent sensible-shoes kind of transportation—sturdy and relatively cheap.

Nonetheless, John A Volpe, Secretary of Transportation in the first Nixon Administration, ruled that the New Look would have to go. Volpe's department wanted to standardize bus production, so that city transit authorities could no longer demand custom features that were driving up costs. Since federal grants at that time paid for two-thirds of each bus —a proportion since increased to four-fifths—that was a reasonable enough argument. A second consideration was dubious, however. The number of bus rides was still declining, from 5.8 billion a year in 1965 to 4.5 billion in 1972. The department wanted a pretty bus, to woo people out of their cars. But 1972 was the nadir for ridership, and the subsequent rebound, to 5.6 billion riders in 1979, suggested that wooing wasn't necessary.

The department offered the three manufacturers about $24 million to start working on prototypes of its dream vehicle, to be called the Transbus. It soon became apparent that Transbus would not be cheap—that standardization would come at the Cadillac rather than the Chevrolet level. For example, in some cities children stick their arms and heads out of bus windows and get injured. Only a few cities have had a serious problem with such recklessness, but everyone would get the extraordinarily expensive solution: all the windows would be permanently sealed. That meant that the slightest malfunction in the air conditioner would send the bus to the repair shop.

As Transbus evolved on the drawing board, it ceased being a transportation project and started to become a social project. "The middle class had their cars," says one participant in the planning. "We were going to do something for the people we started referring to as the 'yophus,' the young, old, poor, handicapped, and unemployed." The department insisted on a floor no more than 22 inches from the ground, so old people could get on more easily and so a ramp could be dropped to the curb for wheelchairs to be rolled aboard.

Humane idea though it was, the low floor presented insuperable engineering problems. Even as the three manufacturers produced prototype Transbuses, they were certain the vehicles would not survive in service. The power train and other vitals were so perilously close to the ground they could easily rupture on a bumpy road. Moreover, the manufacturers doubted that they could get Transbus into production. One of the realities of transit-bus manufacture is that the volume is so small that suppliers are reluctant to tailor parts. Bus makers settle for axles, tires, and other parts designed primarily for trucks. The low-slung Transbus had to run on very small wheels; otherwise, the wheel housing would have protruded deeply into the interior. Firestone Tire & Rubber Co. agreed to make a few special tires for the prototypes, but was not interested in full-scale production.

By July 1976 it was clear that Transbus had broken down, and even many of its promoters in the Transportation Department were willing to abandon it and look for other solutions. Transit agencies offered to provide door-to-door van service to accommodate the handicapped. But several organizations representing the handicapped, whose leaders included vocal Vietnam veterans, rejected the idea. They demanded, as a matter of civil rights, to be "mainstreamed" and given access to mass transportation. They protested on the steps of the Capitol and sat in at the department. "They'd be wheeled into your office one after another, each successive one in more pitiable shape than the last," says Robert Hemmes, who was director of the project in the early 1970s. "It was very effectively arranged." (Hemmes presided over another transportation debacle of the 1970s, an enormously expensive monorail for university students at Morgantown, West Virginia.)

The politicians gave in. In 1977, Brock Adams, then Secretary of Transportation, ordered that after September 30, 1979, the matching funds be provided only for Transbuses. There was just one hitch: no U.S. manufacturer would produce them. Adams, furious, tried to find a manufacturer in Europe. No takers there either.

SHORT PEOPLE SHORT-CHANGED

A costly compromise was worked out. For several years GM had been working on an alternative, the Advanced Design bus. Except for its higher floor, it was much like Transbus. For the handicapped, GM offered a different solution: equip the bus with an elaborate lift to pick wheelchairs up from the sidewalk. Although it stopped short of endorsing the Advanced Design as the ultimate bus, the department put out another edict with far-reaching consequences: after July 2, 1979, any city that wanted to order a bus without a wheelchair lift would have to pay 100% of the price. Flxible said that it, too, was prepared to make an Advanced Design bus. American Motors had decided to get out of the bus business.

GM's Advanced Design bus, called the RTS II, started coming off the assembly line in Pontiac, Michigan, in 1977. Flxible's version, the 870, began to roll off its line in Delaware, Ohio, in 1978. Both vehicles are handsome, with clean lines and smooth sides. But otherwise it is hard to see how they improve the lot of the ordinary bus rider. Short people are actually worse off on at least some of the Advanced Designs. The rails that standing passengers hang on to are higher than those on the New Look buses.

The most advanced thing about the Advanced Design buses is the cost of buying and operating them. They sell for close to $150,000, or almost twice as much as a New Look bus sold for five years ago. In the same period truck prices have risen only 40%. The price of the new buses includes no less than $10,000—and as much as $14,000—for that mandatory wheelchair lift. It generally includes an electronic frill: a $4,000 to $6,000 computer-controlled sign that flashes the bus's destination above the front window.

Gas mileage has dropped considerably. With all its extra features the RTS II weighs 3,000 pounds more than the GM New Look. Transit authorities in Philadelphia estimate that a fleet of 298 RTS IIs requires an outlay of at least $1 million more a year for fuel than an equivalent number of New Look buses. The wheelchair lift alone adds 750 pounds to the weight. Lifts are also delicate contraptions. Edward R. Stokel, who runs GM's bus business in the U.S., estimates that for every 15 lifts a transit authority will have to hire an additional mechanic.

The GM lift is also complicated to operate. The driver has to stop the bus and walk to the rear door to activate the mechanism with the ignition key. Flxible uses a similar system installed in the front steps. It's more efficient because the driver can operate it from his seat, but also likely to cost more to maintain. The front right-hand corner tends to be the most banged-up part of a bus.

Distressingly few of the handicapped are using the lifts. In Philadelphia, whose experience is typical, the 298 lifts are used a total of eight times a week. "When we first introduced them last summer, everyone in a wheelchair took a ride," says David L. Gunn, general manager of the Southeastern Pennsylvania Transportation Authority. "The novelty wore off." For the money spent on those lifts, Philadelphia could provide van service with attendants to help the many handicapped who cannot get down the stairs of their homes to reach the bus stop.

When lift-equipped buses begin to arrive

in New York City this spring, they are likely to get their first test in combat conditions. Substantial numbers of handicapped people may try to board buses that are crowded much of the day. Will there be a backlash against the handicapped? Will some bus riders decide that the lifts are just one more irritating delay in an already declining service and find other transportation? Or will the drivers simply pass the wheelchairs by?

NOT-SO-MIGHTY ROHR

Of the two Advanced Design buses, the General Motors RTS II has held together much better on the street. In the early models the air conditioners kept breaking down, mostly because the compressor was too close to the engine and overheated, but GM has fixed that and some other bugs. For the most part, the 5,183 RTS IIs in service are performing well.

Not so the 2,656 Grumman Flxible 870s that have been delivered. They, too, have had some relatively minor problems—such as inadequate air conditioning in early models —but one serious flaw as well, an undercarriage so insubstantial that dozens have cracked after only a short time on the street. The original mistake was not Grumman's, but that of Rohr Industries, a California aerospace company that owned Flxible when the 870 was designed. Grumman, a Long Island aerospace company, purchased Flxible from Rohr for $55 million in 1978. When Grumman bought Flxible, says Chairman Bierwirth, it was not troubled that the cars another division of Rohr had made for San Francisco's BART rail system had been plagued by defects.

Rohr, it is clear in retrospect, underdesigned the 870. Because the manufacturer has to pay a penalty to the purchasing city if the bus is delivered at more than 25,500 pounds ($3 for every pound of overweight), Rohr engineers created a lightweight undercarriage, based on an A-shaped frame rather than the traditional rectangle. Before Grumman bought Flxible, its engineers checked out the 870 and pronounced its parts, including the A-frame, A-OK.

They were wrong. Atlanta, the first customer, complained of cracks in the engine cradle. "Flxible would weld them and they'd break again, as many as five times," says Jim Huggins, director of maintenance for the Atlanta transit system.

A flutter of apprehension followed as Flxible got ready to send the 870 into New York City. Flxible had won a contract to supply 1,327 buses, a sale Grumman believed would help give Flxible its first profitable year since the New Look went out. But transit men consider New York's potholes the most brutal in the nation. The city's Metropolitan Transit Authority hired Stephen H. Crandall, a professor of mechanical engineering at MIT, to test-ride the 870 on the mean streets of Brooklyn and the Bronx. He, too, said the bus could take it.

The first of the buses reached New York in July 1980, and by autumn the cracks appeared. On close inspection, cracks were found in the frames of buses on the streets of Los Angeles, Chicago, and Hartford as well. What went wrong? "It's a matter of metal fatigue," explains Robert G. Landon, a Grumman executive brought in to run Flxible in 1978. He charitably adds: "The engineers knew how much stress the bus would be going through, but they missed on how frequently the bus would be taken to the high-stress point." The frames of Flxible buses in the field are now being strengthened at five sites around the country.

GM receives an immediate benefit from Flxible's troubles: New York canceled its order for 477 buses not yet built and gave the order to GM instead. Without that sale GM's bus factory would have run out of work by the first week of June.

WASHINGTON'S LARGESS IS LIMITED

The future is not encouraging. Theoretically, there is a market for as many as 6,000 new transit buses a year. A bus lasts about a dozen years, which means the existing fleet should be replaced at the rate of about 4,500 new buses a year. With ridership now back to where it was in 1965 and rising by 5% annually, there may in time be a demand for perhaps 1,000 or so additional buses a year. The market prospects outside the U.S. for American buses are not promising. Europe has many well-established manufacturers, and the Advanced Design is too expensive for most other parts of the world.

The total market is likely to be much smaller than those projections suggest. Congress has appropriated only limited funds to buy the $150,000 buses Washington helped create. Over the past few years bus deliveries have averaged only about 3,500, with GM's truck and coach division and Flxible each accounting for about 40%. The remaining 20% has been divided among several foreign competitors. These include General Motors of Canada, which now makes a version of the New Look bus that includes a wheelchair lift. The market is unlikely to grow much. The best guess by transit agencies and manufacturers is that the Reagan Administration will reduce operating subsidies, estimated at about $850 million in the current fiscal year. With less operating money, cities will not be adding new routes and expanding their fleets.

The industry expects that the Administration will not try to cut back on capital grants for buses; about $930 million has been appropriated for this year. But not all of that will go for vehicles. Some will be used to reconstruct antiquated repair shops. More cities are likely to follow the lead of Philadelphia, which plans to rebuild 270 buses at a cost of up to $50,000 each to stretch out their lives for another five years. That, of course, will cut into the replacement market.

Both GM and Flxible, moreover, will have difficulty holding their market shares as foreign competitors move in to exploit their vulnerability. The Europeans claim they can supply buses that are cheaper to operate, even though their buses too must include

wheelchair lifts. The only way a transit authority can get around accepting a wheelchair lift is to forfeit the federal grant. As far as the American Public Transit Association can tell, no city has yet decided to go it alone.

Neoplan, a West German bus manufacturer, is building a plant in Lamar, Colorado, where it will assemble New Look buses with lifts. Atlanta expects to receive 50 vehicles this summer and Milwaukee has signed up for 46. Another West German company, MAN, has been selling an "articulated" bus, that is, a conventional transit bus with a 15- or 20-foot-long caboose attached to the main body with an accordion-like connector. Seattle has 151 in service, San Diego 45, and Washington, D.C., 43. Those were made in Germany, but U.S. customers have spoken so well of the articulated bus—which carries more passengers and boosts productivity—that MAN is building a plant in Cleveland, North Carolina.

AT LEAST THEIR PLANES FLY

Neither GM nor Flxible is likely to earn a profit on its Advanced Design project. Landon of Flxible says the 870 can make money with a volume as low as 1,500 vehicles a year, and he expects to make a profit in 1981. But that's operating profit. Grumman has already written off $87 million over the three years from 1978 to 1980, including the purchase price of Flxible and a reserve of $7 million to cover repairs of the cracked frames. After taxes, Flxible has cost Grumman $50 million in earnings it probably will not recover. In 1980, losses from Flxible reduced Grumman's earnings by 30¢ a share, to $2.35. GM invested $50 million in new tools to make the RTS II. To amortize that, GM will have to sell 2,400 buses a year for a time. Later the breakeven point will drop to 2,000 but even that figure seems out of reach. "The demand isn't there, the funds aren't there," says Robert W. Truxell, general manager of GM's truck and coach division.

As GM's executives scan the horizon, the

bus business is so tiny—well under 1% of corporate sales—that its troubles don't even show up as a blip. For Grumman the injury is not very great either. The design flaw is embarrassing, but that will not materially hurt Grumman's military-airplane business.

But an opportunity has been lost. The bus business could have been made sound; instead, it was sent on an absurd route. If the industry had one of those fancy electronic destination signs above the front window, it would be flashing NOWHERE.

31

The Queen Elizabeth Hospital

The Queen Elizabeth Hospital was founded in 1894 under the name of the Montreal Homeopathic Hospital (the name was changed in 1951). The hospital has been at its present location in the west end of Montreal since 1927. The catchment area consists of approximately 200,000 persons, the majority of whom live in middle-class residential districts. There are over 250 beds in the hospital and the number has grown only very slightly over the past 10 years*.

The hospital is classified as an acute general hospital center. Most types of surgery are performed and the institution is considered to have a first-class psychiatric staff. In recent years there has been a shortage of nursing staff and psychiatric beds. The public demand for outpatient services has grown much more quickly than the hospital resources available to deal with it. For example, the total nursing staff has grown from 221 in 1972 to 232 in 1973 whereas in the same period emergency admissions have increased

over 10%, and the percentage increases in ambulatory visits, diagnostic radiology services, laboratory units, and social service contracts were 10%, 22%, 17%, and 16% respectively.

Of the 102 full-time members of the medical staff, 46 are directly associated with the Faculty of Medicine at McGill University as Associate Professors, Assistant Professors, Lecturers, or Demonstrators. The Queen Elizabeth's institutional affiliations are numerous.

In 1973 the Queen Elizabeth was requested by the provincial government to close its obstetric facilities. This case looks at the decision-making process involved in the termination of obstetric care and the conversion of facilities to other uses.

KEY PARTICIPANTS AND ADMINISTRATIVE BODIES

The discussion of administrative structure will be limited to a consideration the key entities involved in the decisions to close and transform the obstetric facilities at the hospital. The organization chart (Exhibit 31-1)

---

*"The Hospital's aspirations are not directed to expansion but toward higher standards of performances within our resources." From *Presentation to McGill Teaching Hospital Council*, June 18, 1974, p.4.

Written by Danny Miller. Reprinted with permission of the author.

illustrates many of the important formal inter-relationships in authority and accountability amongst these bodies.

The key participants in this case include:

1. *The Department of Social Affairs* of the Province of Quebec issued directives concerning the consolidation of obstetric services and the closing of facilities at the Queen Elizabeth. The resulting changes in function and budget had to be approved by this government ministry.
2. Several members of the *McGill University Faculty of Medicine* played an advisory role in the reorganization of obstetric resources among seven English-speaking hospitals in the Montreal area (including the Queen Elizabeth). Dr. Lee, the Associate Dean of Community Medicine, was particularly active in helping the various hospitals assess their obstetric facilities.
3. *The Board of Directors* and the *Executive Committee of the Council of Physicians and Dentists* in the Queen Elizabeth were responsible for ratifying the key decisions made regarding obstetrics by the committees within the hospital, within the framework, of course, of the government's directives.
4. *The Executive Director* of the hospital,

EXHIBIT 31–1   QUEEN ELIZABETH HOSPITAL OF MONTREAL CENTRE, ORGANIZATION & OPERATIONS CHART

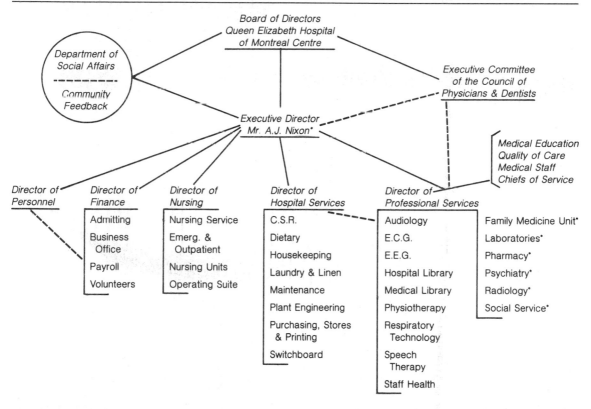

June 3, 1974.

Solid line ——————— denotes direct accountability.

Broken line —————— denotes staff relationship (communications and advisory capacity) with no direct accountability.

*Departments that report to Executive Director for administrative matters.

Mr. Nixon, coordinated the various decision-making bodies, was influential in suggesting administrative procedures and committees to facilitate decision-making, and was instrumental in helping devise solutions to the transition problem. Mr. Nixon sat on the committees mentioned in (3) and (5) and reported to the Board.

5. *The Property, Space Utilization, and Equipment Committee* (not shown on the organization chart) reported to both the Executive Committee of the Council of Physicians and Dentists and to the Board of Directors of the hospital. This committee was the most important decision-making body to deal with the problem of what to do with the obstetric facilities. The members of the committee included: the Executive Director (Mr. Nixon), the Director of Professional Services (Dr. Nancekivell), the Chairman of the Executive Committee of the Council of Physicians and Dentists, the Physician in Chief (Dr. Palmer), the Chief of Obstetrics and Gynecology (Dr. Catterill), the chiefs of the other medical departments (e.g., surgery, radiology, psychiatry), the Director of Nursing (Miss Bryant), the Nurse Coordinator of the Family Medicine Unit, and the Maintenance Supervisor. Because he had the greatest amount of relevant expertise, Dr. Catterill was particularly active on this committee.

THE DECISION-MAKING CLIMATE

Mr. Nixon was convinced that the decision-making approach in hospital centers should be as participative as possible and that the advice of experts was essential in making complex decisions. He maintained that because decisions in one area influence many other departments in the hospital, it was mandatory for many people to be consulted before taking action. Mr. Nixon's belief in participative decision-making set the climate in which the closing of the Obstetric Unit was carried out.

Mr. Nixon also stressed his interest in rationalizing the planning, decision-making, and transition processes in the hospital. As a senior executive with much management experience, Mr. Nixon had evolved guidelines for drafting proposals and resolving issues. He encouraged the use of cost benefit analysis, clear objectives, longer time horizons, and the generation of alternative solutions in decision-making. He also emphasized the importance of the practicality of solutions, the need to pay attention to details and potential problems in implementation, and the importance of social psychology in organizational behavior.

THE DECISION TO CLOSE THE OBSTETRICS DEPARTMENT

The Department of Social Affairs had become increasingly concerned about the effectiveness of the obstetric units within the Province. It appeared that there was an excess number of maternity beds and that infant and maternal mortality rates were unduly high. A subsequent study by the Department revealed that hospitals with small obstetric units (less than 1,000 deliveries per annum) had by far the highest mortality rates and were less efficient financially. The conclusion was reached that 3,000 deliveries per unit would be the minimum acceptable number to yield better quality care at a lower cost. The Department decided to consolidate the 26 obstetric units in Greater Montreal into 9 to 12 centers, each having a neonatal intensive care unit.

The process was well under way by February 1973 when the Deputy Minister of Social Affairs requested the help of McGill University in examining the obstetric units of hospitals associated with McGill. Dr. Lee, the Associate Dean of Community Medicine at McGill, was asked to submit his recommendations on how to consolidate obstetric facilities. Seven English-language hospitals were subsequently visited and appraised by Dr. Lee, who had considerable familiarity with the problem.

Because their obstetric unit was relatively small, the Queen Elizabeth Hospital was one of the seven to be affected by the plans of the Department. The number of deliveries there had declined from 1,267 to 1,182 between 1969 and 1972, and approximately 30 of the 44 beds in the Obstetrics and Gynecology area were devoted to obstetrics.

Early in March, Mr. Nixon attended a meeting with members of the McGill Faculty of Medicine (including Dr. Lee) and the administrators of the other six hospitals. The government's consolidation plans were discussed and the hospital representatives were informed that only about half of the seven hospitals would be allowed to retain their obstetric units (no names were mentioned). None of the seven hospitals handled the minimum 3,000 deliveries. The reactions of the administrators were diverse; some were much against closing their units while others were receptive to the idea. Mr. Nixon adopted the latter posture.

On March 20, the bi-weekly meeting of the Property, Space Utilization, and Equipment (P.S.E.) Committee took place. Mr. Nixon discussed his meeting with the representatives of McGill and the other hospitals and mentioned the Department's proposed plan to close the obstetric facilities. Dr. Catterill, the Chief of Obstetrics and Gynecology, was asked to head a committee with Mr. Nixon, Miss Bryant (the Director of Nursing), and Dr. Palmer (the Physician in Chief). The committee was to prepare recommendations on the issue for presentation to the Council of Physicians and Dentists, the Hospital Board, and McGill.

The Executive Director, most of the medical staff, and the nursing staff had long known the government's plans to consolidate obstetric facilities in the province. Thus, although no formal plans had been considered before the setting up of this committee, the hospital administration and medical personnel were aware that changes were in the wind.

On March 29 Dr. Catterill submitted a report to Mr. Nixon summarizing two options that he felt were open to the Queen Elizabeth

in response to the government's directives. Exhibit 31-2 shows this report.

In late March, Dr. Catterill met with representatives from the McGill Faculty of Medicine. His impression of the obstetrics situation is recorded in the minutes of the April 2nd meeting of the P.S.E. Committee as follows:

Obstetric Beds. Dr. Catterill stated that four obstetric units of the seven in the English sector will be closed. The names of these four are not known. He was not sure whether they will be closed 3 + 1, or all four at once. The final decision will be made in July. It looks as if we will be asked to close our unit since our facilities do not seem adequate for the required number of deliveries. However, Dr. Catterill felt we could reach the minimum requirement with cramping and some reconstruction. It is undecided as to what will happen to the beds that are closed. Should this happen, gynecology may be closed out elsewhere and we then might have to increase our gynecology beds. Dr. Catterill will be meeting with Dr. Lee shortly, and will report further at our next meeting.

Discussions with Dr. Lee in early April confirmed Dr. Catterill's conclusion that the appropriate action to take would be the closure of obstetric facilities at the hospital. The Board of Directors were informed of this development during the month and so was the Executive Committee of the Council of Physicians and Dentists. Each of these bodies voiced some complaints regarding the potential loss of obstetric facilities (so did the Director of Nursing) but by and large they accepted the development as a fait accompli. Only token resistance was offered.

On May 3, the Deputy Minister of the Department of Social Affairs sent a letter to the President of the Board of Directors of the Queen Elizabeth requesting the hospital to close their obstetric services. (See Exhibit 31-3.)

The decision process up to this point was fairly clear cut. The government decided that obstetric resources could be more effectively allocated. McGill Faculty of Medicine personnel and several key people in the Queen

EXHIBIT 31-2 DR. CATTERILL'S REPORT

RETAIN QUEEN ELIZABETH HOSPITAL OBSTETRICAL UNIT

Utilizations of at least 40 of the 44 beds on the present obstetrical floor at an ideal 85% occupancy rate, thus handling approximately 3,000 deliveries annually. This Unit would serve the west end of the city and could remain associated with clinics in St. Henri and Pte. St. Charles as well as Elizabeth House for unmarried girls. Neonatal problems would be handled in the Neonatal Unit of the Montreal Children's Hospital.

Difficulties:
1. There are only three delivery rooms; four would be necessary to handle this volume.
2. There are only four labor rooms; would need to increase to six or eight.
3. Lack of Recovery Room.
4. Nursery area is barely adequate.
5. Loss of present gynecology beds that are now an integral part of the obstetrical floor. This would necessitate providing gynecology facilities elsewhere.

Impression:
Our present obstetrical volume (1,200 deliveries annually) could be increased to 2,000 without major changes becoming necessary, but beyond that, the above deficiencies could create extreme problems.

DISBAND QUEEN ELIZABETH HOSPITAL OBSTETRICAL UNIT

At present there are 44 beds on the obstetrical floor, of which 15 to 18 are used for gynecology. With the loss of the Obstetrical Unit, 26 beds would be effectively freed.

Without capital outlay, the obstetrical area on the third floor could be used for:

1. *A Complete Gynecology Unit*
   The 26 beds could be available as replacements for gynecology beds closed or displaced in other hospitals as the result of enlarged obstetric units.

2. *Combined Gynecology-Surgical Specialty Unit*
   The specialty beds now on the second floor could be relocated on the obstetrical floor, thus releasing beds for the ICU and Coronary Care areas.

3. *Combined Gynecology-Urology Unit*
   Urology Unit could be relocated on the third floor, with an increase in the number of beds now allocated to Urology. This would provide a more functional Urology Unit in close association with Gynecology and provide sufficient beds for residency training in Urology.

In the above plans, the present delivery rooms would be available for minor surgical and gynecological procedures, particularly on an outpatient basis. Nurseries could be used for holding areas (Surgical Day Center).

Difficulties:
Staffing problems (Nursing and Anesthesia).

Impression:
The loss of the Obstetrical Unit would seem to be the more practical and economical plan of the two. In this way a pressing need for a Surgical Day Center area would be realized, long on the list of priorities at the Queen Elizabeth Hospital.

Respectfully submitted,
T.B. Catterill, F.R.C.O.G., F.R.C.S.(C)
Obstetrician and Gynecologist-in-Chief

EXHIBIT 31-3 RECOMMENDATION TO CLOSE QUEEN ELIZABETH HOSPITAL OBSTETRIC SERVICE

Mr. J.R. Houghton
President
Board of Governors
Queen Elizabeth Hospital
2100 Marlowe Avenue
Montreal, Quebec

Mr. President:

As you no doubt know, the Ministry of Social Affairs has just completed the analysis of the needs in obstetrics and postnatal sector. Following this study, the Ministry does not deem it desirable, from an economics and medical level, to maintain small obstetrics departments such as yours.

Consequently, we request you to take the necessary measures, in view of the closing of your obstetrics department around October 15, 1973.

We appreciate the quality of services rendered the population during many years and we request you to increase your services in the spheres where the needs appear to increase rapidly.

Please note that the Ministry has requested the following Hospital Centres in your region to increase the capacity of their obstetrics services: St. Mary's, Jewish General.

The Ministry is presently studying a project aimed at developing obstetrics services of the Royal Victoria Hospital. In view of the considerable time necessary for the full realization of this project, the Montreal General Hospital will continue to offer obstetrics services until it is possible for the Royal Victoria to receive a larger number of patients, in more modern quarters.

The Ministry trusts your institution will contribute important assistance to Physicians and other groups concerned, in order to facilitate the putting into effect of the changes involved by these decisions.

The Ministry personnel is disposed to meet with you to discuss dispositions relative to these changes. Dr. Stanly Knox has been assigned to act as representative of the programmation with your Board of Governors.

Please accept, Mr. President, the expression of my best regards.

JACQUES BRUNET, M.D.
Deputy Minister
cc: Dr. A. F. Nancekivell
    Dr. T. B. Catterill

Elizabeth Hospital agreed with this decision. Only a small amount of resistance to the potential closing facilities at the Queen Elizabeth was expressed by the Board and the Council of Physicians and Dentists. Then a directive came from the Deputy Minister of Social Affairs instructing the hospital to terminate its obstetric services. Thus, although the final decision came from outside the hospital, the key parties concerned—the Executive Director and the Obstetrician and Gynecologist-in-Chief—were receptive to

THE DECISION ON
RESOURCE REALLOCATION

The key issues after May 3 were how and when to phase out obstetrics and more importantly, how to reallocate the resources set free. Mr. Nixon stated that the key criteria were the beds of the community, and the hospital's ability to use existing (or retrained) personnel in the new undertaking. That is, it was agreed that any new service would have to both satisfy pressing social needs and assure complete utilization of idle resources —staff, space, beds and equipment. The facilities to be vacated upon the elimination of obstetric services consisted of 3 delivery rooms, 4 labour rooms, 3 nurseries, and about 30 beds.

Around the middle of May, the P.S.E. Committee began to tentatively discuss the mechanics of the phasing-out process and various suggestions were received on the alternative uses of facilities. Problems of staff training and space and bed utilization were mentioned. Since it was agreed that the committee should develop concrete plans to present to the government, all Chiefs of Service were asked to study the problem to present their perspectives at the next P.S.E. meeting.

At that meeting, which took place on May 28, Dr. Catteril suggested that since the Obstetrics and Gynecology issue had not been completely settled in *all* seven hospitals, plans for the reallocation of facilities on the 3rd floor (the area of the Obstetrics Department) should be postponed until the needs of the community became better known. Dr. Palmer, Physician-in-Chief, thought it would be best to have a plan ready to present to the Department of Social Affairs as soon as possible.

Mr. Nixon suggested that the 3rd floor would lend itself to surgery procedures and a Day Care Centre. (This idea had been discussed several times over the past few years by surgical representatives on the Council of Physicians and Dentists.) The need for such facilities had become increasingly evident with growth of emergency and outpatient services.

Dr. Catterill suggested having Gynecology on one floor—the 3rd—and giving up present Gynecology beds on the 6th floor to other services. He also stated that there could be room left over for a Urology ward on the 3rd floor. The possiblity of relocating Psychiatry on the 3rd floor was considered but since this would increase its capacity by only two beds some felt such a move would not justify the cost of the relocation. The option was kept open, however.

More suggestions were offered at this meeting of May 28th but they were essentially in the same vein as above. The meeting closed without reaching any firm conclusions on the issue, although the various proposals were not fundamentally different. The P.S.E. Committee stated that it would remain open to further suggestions.

In early June the Committee decided on a closing date for Obstetric Services. October 19th was chosen after considering existing commitments to patients.

By mid July the P.S.E. Committee had refined its ideas on the proposed use of the Obstetric facilities. Dr. Catterill's submission outlines the proposed changes in Exhibit 31-4.

On July 20th, the P.S.E. Committee met to make a final decision on the matter. The resolution varied only slightly from Dr. Catterill's July 16 proposal in that it was decided to move E.N.T. (Ear, Nose and Throat, a surgical sub-specialty) to the third floor. Delivery rooms were to be used for the Surgical Day Center and 30 beds were to be devoted to Gynecology.

Mr. Nixon informed the Board of these recommendations and Dr. Nancekivell (Director of Professional Services) called a meeting of the Executive of the Council of Physicians and Dentists before the end of the month to discuss the recommendations and seek ratification.

The final decisions concerning the use of vacated obstetric services fulfilled the two original requirements: the hospital would be better able to meet community needs for emergency and outpatient surgery services, and the facilties could be adapted to this new service with minimal cost. The Day Care Center would also reduce operating costs by eliminating the need for overnight hospital stays. Further, the additional 15 to 30 gynecology beds would help meet the increased demand that would occur with the closing of services elsewhere.

IMPLEMENTATION

Late in the summer, Mr. Nixon began planning the implementation of the new facilities. At the P.S.E. Committee meeting of September 10, it was recommended that a committee be formed to organize the Surgical Day Care Center. The committee was comprised of the professionals most familiar with the medical requisites of such a unit.

While some members of the nursing staff were a little reluctant to change their work areas, retraining of Nursing personnel in O.R. procedure went very smoothly. The Director of Nursing supported the changes not only because she approved of the rationalization of the city's obstetric resources but also because she felt that the nursing services in the Queen Elizabeth's obstetric unit had been uneconomical because of the spatial layout of facilities. She suggested that the nursing staff in general were receptive to the changes because they had been advised of events at an early stage (before the government's edict arrived) and were assured in a series of group discussions (which had taken place from April to October) that individual skills and preferences would be considered in the relocation of staff.

Most of the medical specialists in Obstetrics and Gynecology were to maintain their affiliation with the Queen Elizabeth with respect to their Gynecology practices but were to start to perform deliveries at two other major hospital centers (The Royal Victoria and St. Mary's). Some of these physicians expressed remorse at having to leave the hospital for their obstetrics practice but it is believed that most did not feel seriously inconvenienced at having to do so.

On September 25, the P.S.E. Committee discussed some of the specific details which had to be settled before the Day Care Center could open in early November. The points raised centered on the disposal of old equipment, the oxygen and suction to be installed, the precise staffing requirements, the surgi-

---

EXHIBIT 31–4 PROPOSED REQUIREMENTS AND CHANGES FOR THE 3rd FLOOR

1. Delivery Room Area to be used as follows:		C	Infertility Center - hopefully to move to larger quarters in out-patient area
Delivery Room No. 1	Minor Out-Patient surgery under general anaesthesia (gynecology, general surgery, etc.) cystoscopies excluded	4. Obs-Gyn Bed Changes	
Delivery Room No. 2	Recovery Room	1.	Loss of 6 Gyn beds on 6th Floor
Delivery Room No. 3	Out-patient surgery under local anaesthesia (Cases presently being done in Emergency Area)	*2.	35 gynecology limit on 3rd Floor
		*3.	Remaining 10 beds for Urology (male and female)
2. Labor Rooms (4)	Admission Area for out-patient surgery		
3. Nurseries			
A or B	Out-Patient surgical admission and late recovery area to replace Room 237 when 2nd Floor O.R. changes are made and to relieve eventual congestion in labor room area (#2 above)		

*The present complement of gynecology beds is 21, with frequent overflow to the Obstetrical area.

After October 15, there will be three further Staff members requiring gynecology facilities. If one considers that 3.5 beds are required per gynecologist, we will then have to supply 9 staff members and the Infertility Center; thus the need for 35 beds.

T. B. Catterill, M.D.
July 16, 1973

EXHIBIT 31–5 NIXON'S REPORT

October 22, 1973.

Dr. Jacques Brunet
Deputy Minister
Ministry of Social Affairs

Dear Sir:

In accordance with your letter of May 3, the Queen Elizabeth Hospital of Montreal Center Obstetrics Department closed at 12:00 noon October 19, 1973.

The phasing-out of this Department has moved ahead as planned. The delivery room area will be used as a Day Center for elective Medical/Surgical minor procedures.

The Gynecology Department will have access to 30 beds and the sub-specialties of Surgery will have access to the balance of 15 beds. The only expense that we will incur in this change will be the purchase of Medical/Surgical supplies for the Day Care Center, at approximate cost of $9,000.00

All our Nursing Staff and other employees have been relocated satisfactorily without any disruption to their service.

The projected 1973 operating cost of our third floor including the Case Room and Delivery Room area is $427,441.00.

The 1974 budget estimate for the third floor including the Day Care Center is $350,225.00; a net saving of approximately $77,216.00.

We are constantly reviewing the need for beds in our Family Medicine Unit and Department of Psychiatry. Presently we are able to meet both these Departments' bed requirements, although pressure is mounting from Psychiatry for more beds.

We would appreciate receiving confirmation of these changes from your Department.

Albert J. Nixon
Executive Director

---

cal supplies required, the scheduling of personnel resources, and so forth. It was suggested that a committee be formed to look after any problems in implementing the Surgical Day Care Center. The Chiefs of Services were asked to nominate representatives of their departments to sit on this committee.

On October 19, 1973 the Obstetrics Department was closed. On October 22, Mr. Nixon sought confirmation for the changes from the Department of Social Affairs. (See Exhibit 31-5.)

The Day Care Center opened, as planned, in early November, 1973.

32

Memorial Hospital

The purpose of this role-playing exercise is to illustrate and reinforce concepts relating to organizational decision-making processes. Organization decision-making may follow several models depending on the organizational situation. The following exercise will challenge you to analyze the organization setting, determine the goals of the organization and the path for achieving those goals, identify the problem, and propose a solution. Upon completion of the role-playing exercise the class will discuss the decision-making models as they relate to the situation presented.

STEP 1: *Volunteers (5 min.)*

The instructor will ask for six volunteers from the class to be the "actors" in this role-playing exercise.

STEP 2: *Introduction of Background Material (5-10 min.)*

The volunteers will leave the room and receive descriptions of their individual roles. They will not be able to discuss their roles with each other. While the volunteers are reading their roles the rest of the class should read the background material below.

STEP 3: *Committee Meeting (15 min.)*

Returning to the front of the classroom, the volunteers will meet as the Pediatric Ward Administrative Committee, with the nurse and social worker as guests. The group will attempt to reach a decision on the issue presented by Mrs. Mills and Mr. Brown while the remainder of the class observes the decision-making process.

STEP 4: *Class Discussion (20 min.)*

In reviewing the group role-playing session as a class, consider the following discussion questions as they relate to material previously presented in classroom lectures.

This exercise is based on "Strategies of Changing: A Multiple-Role Play" in *The 1973 Annual Handbook for Group Facilitators,* John E. Jones and J.W. Pfeiffer, editors, LaJolla, CA: University Associates, Inc., 1973, and "You Are Bob Waters, Assistant Administrator at Unity Hospital," distributed by the Intercollegiate Case Clearing House, Soldiers Field, Boston, MA 02163.

DISCUSSION QUESTIONS

1. What are the goals of the hospital? Does each person involved in the decision-making process agree on one set of goals? On how to meet these goals?
2. What is the problem the hospital is facing? What are the possible solutions? How was the committee meeting influenced by each person's interpretation of the problem and solution?
3. How would you analyze the hospital's problem situation in terms of social factors, political factors, uncertainty, constituencies?
4. Which model of organization decision-making did you see operating in your group? Would another model have been more appropriate based on the organization's situation? Why or why not?
5. Did you see evidence of coalition building taking place? When can this be effective in decision-making? When is it harmful to the process?
6. If this problem were to be presented to Dr. Peterson for him to solve as an individual, what process would you suggest he use for reaching a decision? Would his solution be an organizational decision even though he is responsible for the final recommendation?

The Pediatric Ward, Memorial Hospital

The Pediatric Ward Administrative Committee meeting will start in a few moments. The Administrative Committee consists of Dr. Peterson, Chief Resident in Pediatrics, Mr. Perez, Assistant Administrator of the hospital, Mrs. Axel, Head Nurse of the Pediatric Ward, and Mr. Jones, Assistant Head Nurse of the ward. Two additional people will be present at today's meeting, Mrs. Mills, a nurse on the ward, and Mr. Brown, a social worker.

Memorial Hospital is located on the near west side of a large city in Ohio. Over the last 10 years, the neighborhood has changed to predominantly blue-collar and minority residents, and the economic status of the neighborhood has decreased. Local residents are the primary clientele of the hospital.

The pediatric ward, along with other wards, faces a continuing shortage of financial resources. The hospital is supported by county taxes, but resources never seem adequate to provide all the services needed. The pediatric ward has adopted techniques that enable staff to accomplish more work. Older children are typically harnessed to little chairs in front of TV sets or placed in cribs to watch TV. Infants lie in cribs with bottles tied to the side of the crib. The bottles can be popped into the children's mouths without having to take them out of the crib. The nurses are kept busy filling out reports in the nursing station, which is closed from the wards, although they do make regular tours through the ward every 30 minutes or so. Nurses aides check on the children and do the routine tasks of sweeping the floor and making beds.

The nurse and social worker who have asked to attend today's administrative committee meeting are concerned about the changing conditions on the ward. They have asked for an opportunity to express these concerns. (Information for specific roles will be distributed by the instructor.)

33

Infinite Processes, Inc.

The purpose of this exercise is to illustrate various decision-making processes used within and among groups with limited resources and information. Each group will be responsible for developing supportive arguments to be used by a representative to a committee charged with decision-making. The deliberations of the committee will be observed by the class and will be the basis for class discussion.

STEP 1: *Orientation (10 min.)*

The class will be divided into five groups. As a group you are representing one of the five research divisions of Infinite Processes, Inc. Your group is responsible for a major research proposal that is coming up for discussion at the research committee meeting. Each group member should read the background material on Infinite Processes, Inc. below. Your instructor will give your group detailed information on your specific research proposal and brief background data on the other four projects to be discussed at the committee meeting.

STEP 2: *Development of Supportive Arguments (15 min.)*

Each group is to spend this time developing supportive arguments as to why their research project should receive top priority in terms of development.

STEP 3: *Select Representative (5 min.)*

Each group will select one member to serve as the divisional research manager to represent their project at the meeting of the research committee. The committee is composed of the five divisional research managers and the vice-president for research.

STEP 4: *Research Committee Meeting (30 min.)*

The vice-president for research will convene the committee meeting and charge the group with determining the priority for research expenditures. The class will observe the discussion, but may not participate or make comments. The committee will then discuss

By Joseph A. Raelin, Director, and Claudia Harrison, Research Associate, Institute for Public Service. Copyright © 1982, Institute for Public Service, Boston College, Chestnut Hill, MA 02167. By permission.

the projects and reach a decision to present to the vice-president.

STEP 5: *Presentation of Decision (10 min.)*

The Committee will present its decision to the vice-president who will have the final decision-making authority. Upon hearing the vice-president's decision, each divisional manager will then return to his/her group and describe the meeting and explain the decision as if the action had not been observed.

STEP 6: *Discussion (15 min.)*

The class as a whole should reflect back over the meeting of the research committee and discuss what happened. The representatives are encouraged to discuss their feelings toward the process used by the committee, their reaction to the final decision, and their return to their group. The observers should reflect on the process observed and their feelings regarding the presentation by their representative. The instructor and students may also wish to compare their observations to theories of decision-making and intergroup behavior as illustrated in lectures or readings. The following questions may help guide that discussion.

DISCUSSION QUESTIONS

1. What criteria did the decision-makers use in making their decision? Were the criteria explicit or implicit? Did they seem to change?
2. Did coalitions emerge? Was there evidence of bargaining taking place? If so, how far into the discussion did this occur?
3. Were there phases in the decision process? If so, identify these.
4. How do you think this process might have differed if there had not been a time limit on the meeting? If the vice-president had been involved in the discussion?
5. Was the decision consistent with the goals of Infinite Processes, Inc.?

INFINITE PROCESSES, INC.

As a large diversified conglomerate, worldwide activities at Infinite Processes, Inc. span five major industries. The corporate divisions, which are organized along industry lines, form the basis for operations. Business is carried out in each divisional entity under its own name, within its own individual organizational structure. Divisional or company titles and principal industries are as follows: Vellein Metrics—Telecommunications; Dynamo-electrics—Electronics; Carboneer, Inc.—Oil, Gas, and Alternative Energy; Silage Systems—Food Processing; and Pulse Dynamics—Electromedical Equipment.

Two major corporate priorities are the development of new initiatives and growth through internal operations. Believing that technology is the key to the future, Infinite Processes, Inc. seeks to be a leader in technological development. Aggressive growth goals have been consistently met by the corporation as a whole. Growth has occurred at a 10-year compounded rate of 10% for consolidated sales, net income, and earnings per share. Future growth is targeted at this same 10% rate. The long-term objective is to develop a corporation that has a strong base in those industries that show future growth potential, especially through technological development.

The nature of competition, primarily a function of the specific industry, varies greatly among divisions. In general, Infinite Processes, Inc. faces competition both from other large conglomerates and from smaller enterprises with single lines of business. Significant factors that affect the degree of competition vary across industry lines. For example, technological innovation, quality, and reliability are the principal factors in the telecommunications industry. Pricing and distribution are the key factors in the food processing industry. The single most significant factor in oil, gas, and alternative energy is pricing.

It is acknowledged in the corporate world that Infinite Processes, Inc. has been successful primarily because of its R & D. In particular, it has been extremely effective in moving seemingly inconspicuous ideas very quickly into full-scale development and ultimately into the marketplace before the competition "knew what was happening." Further, the company seems to be able to apply its principles of R & D management to any kind of industry, hence its success as a conglomerate. Originally a small electronics component operation, Infinite Processes is now one of the most respected technological concerns in the country.

Projects Under Consideration

At the time of this case, five industrial R & D projects, one from each division within Infinite Processes, Inc., have been designated as worthy of consideration for full-scale commercialization. However, due to a crunch on cash flow precipitated by a dogged recession, the director of research at corporate headquarters can choose only one of these projects for immediate funding. The remaining four must be ranked for secondary consideration should a reversal in the

current sales drag occur.

At Infinite Processes, Inc., the R & D function is centrally coordinated for purposes of budget control. R & D operations, however, are carried out at the divisional facilities. A corporate research committee, which is under the immediate control of the director of research, who presides at all meetings, makes all R & D budget allocation decisions. The committee is composed of the divisional R & D managers.

Each project presented for consideration represents the top priority of its divisional management, i.e., projects have already undergone a similar process within the divisions. The projects are all at the end of Stage 2 development, and are under review for continuation to full-scale commercialization. The research committee has assembled to review the data on the five projects and to hear the arguments of the respective divisional R & D managers. Final decision-making authority rests with the director of research. (Specific information on the five R & D projects will be distributed by the instructor.)

IV

Organization Dynamics

34

Canco Incorporated

Canco Incorporated is one of the largest diversified organizations in Canada. Recently, the president, Stan Elkins, met with his executive committee for a three-day discussion of strategies that need to be implemented in order for Canco to remain competitive in the next decade. The committee includes Stan and 14 executive vice-presidents who serve as the policy board for the vast organization of 40,000 employees located in 87 different facilities throughout the world. Last year, sales exceeded $3.0 billion, which was an increase of $400 million over the previous year.

Before attending the three-day discussion sessions, Stan had been reviewing and analyzing notes he had carefully taken at an executive training program one month ago. The program was presented by consultants over a five-day period for chief executive officers of $1-billion organizations and focused on the processes of management by objectives (MBO). The articulate and convincing trainers had been so impressive that Stan invited one to spend a day at Canco to discuss MBO. The training experience and personal discussions convinced Stan that

MBO was what Canco needed to plan, organize, and coordinate for the next decade of growth and competition. Thus, Stan wanted to share his enthusiasm with the executive committee and encourage them to begin implementing MBO within their respective areas of responsibility.

The executive committee met with Stan on the first day of the discussion meetings and focused on the only agenda item for the meetings, MBO. The discussion immediately focused on MBO's applicability to Canco. The majority of executives questioned Stan's rationale for interest in MBO. These discussions became very intense. A capsule portion of one of the most heated exchanges is the following:

STAN: Jim, you are just not listening to what I am saying about MBO. I know that it is not a "cure-all," but it sure is better than waiting for our competition to devour us in crucial markets.

JIM: I'm aware of crucial market penetration, but I'm also afraid that we have not carefully diagnosed our organization, goals, and personnel. Who should be involved in MBO?

The source for this case could not be identified.

How should it be implemented? When? What goals are we attempting to achieve with MBO? Should it be implemented the same way with each of our plants? How much will it cost? What kind of commitment is needed for success? Where has it worked? Stan, these are only a few questions among the many that we must react to on the front end. Ignoring them just doesn't make good sense.

STAN: Your questions are well thought out and are important, but they mask or can retard the need to respond to competitive pressures. If we were to answer every important question before taking action, our organization would never act. The realities of our business force us to act. The reactive organizations are those attempting to surpass our performance. I'm just not willing to be a reactive president in these times of change, shortages, and increased regulatory pressures.

RALPH: Stan, haste can lead to waste and expectations that are not achieved. I know that MBO is a vogue, but I also am aware of the lack of good evidence to justify its widespread usage. Can't we answer some of the important questions before committing ourselves to this major change and development program?

STAN: I didn't know you had already traced the evidence of MBO. I want you to understand that thousands of organizations have used MBO successfully because its benefits outweigh its costs. For us to disregard this as evidence is a serious mistake that indicates somewhat of an insecure feeling on our part.

MELISSA: Stan, you're the one who's asked us to be careful before jumping on a "fad" or "bandwagon." I just don't believe that we have been careful enough. To commit 4,000 managers to MBO without a thorough analysis of problems or potential problem areas is dangerous. Many of these managers may not

be suited for MBO and will require extensive training in goal-setting. Have you considered this possibility?

STAN: Melissa, I do not want to commit one manager to MBO unless the program is completely supported by this committee. The evidence I have examined clearly indicates that top-level executive support is a must for a successful MBO program. Training is a continual process in this company. Why are you so interested in MBO training? We always train, and this is one of the reasons we are attractive as an organization to potential managers. Let's not present a "red herring" in the form of training. Canco employment at the managerial levels requires training even without MBO. Training and development throughout a person's career are needed and provided in this organization.

JIM: Stan, the engineers, technicians, research and development scientists, and accountants will laugh you out of this idea. They just plain resist control, and MBO is control.

This type of debate occurred over the full three-day discussion session. Stan insisted that MBO was *the* program for Canco and wanted to begin implementation at the top echelons within three weeks. At the close of the discussions, Stan informed the committee that as soon as the standard operating procedural details were worked out, MBO instructional material would be provided to them. The vice-president of personnel at corporate headquarters, Tom Murchison, was designated the coordinator of Canco MBO programs. Stan set up a timetable for Canco training and implementation that covered 10 months. He expected every manager of the approximately 4,000 to be aware of and involved in MBO activities within 10 months after the program was initiated at the top echelon in the company.

35

School of Education: Case of a Contracting Organization

"How negative do you feel today, Slocum?" inquired Johnson, who was the assistant dean for programs and chairman of the reorganization committee, half in jest and half seriously of the educational administration professor. The school reorganization committee was meeting to discuss problems arising from the recent reorganization of the school.

The school had begun as a Department of Education and Psychology within a small teachers college. In 1964, Psychology became a separate department, followed in 1967 by the Elementary and Secondary Education Departments. Special Education, Educational Administration, and Counselor Education were separated out in 1970. Finally in 1973, the Student Teaching Department was formed (see Exhibit 35-1).

EXHIBIT 35-1 SCHOOL OF EDUCATION: CASE OF A CONTRACTING ORGANIZATION
ORGANIZATION CHART, AUGUST 1979

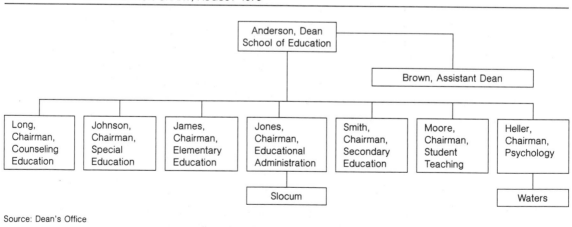

Source: Dean's Office

Written by Mahoud A. Moursi and Susan K. Smith. Reprinted with permission of Mahmoud A. Moursi, Professor, Central Michigan University.

Dr. Anderson had been dean since 1967. Prior to that he was Chairman of the Department of Education and Psychology. Having been at the university since 1948, he was now nearing retirement. A man of integrity, he was respected by most of his faculty.

The Dean had tried to persuade the School of Education faculty to reorganize in 1972 and 1975. He had proposed combining the departments of Elementary Education, Secondary Education, and Student Teaching to form a Teacher Education Department. The other departments were to remain intact. Both attempts at reorganization failed in the face of considerable faculty opposition.

By 1979, when the Dean made his third attempt at reorganizing the school, condi-

tions had changed. Student credit hours (SCH) within the school had decreased by 14% since 1975. Full-time-equated (FTE) faculty positions had decreased 6%. The Department of Psychology was the only department that was growing. Their SCHs had increased 12% and their FTE 32% since 1975 (see Exhibit 35-2). If the Department of Psychology was excluded from the School of Education figures, the school decrease in SCH for 1975-80 was 27%, and the decrease in FTE was 20% (see Exhibit 35-3).

The Provost supported the reorganization. The university had originally been a teachers college, but changes in the job market and accompanying changes in student career interests had resulted in the development of

EXHIBIT 35-2 SCHOOL OF EDUCATION: CASE OF A CONTRACTING ORGANIZATION
ON CAMPUS SCH[1] PRODUCTION, FTE[2] TEACHING POSITIONS, 1975-1980

	1975-76	1976-77	1977-78	1978-79	1979-80	% Change 1975-80
SCHOOL Education SCH	89,600	87,184	86,229	84,620	77,339	−14%
FTE	141.71	137.71	138.32	134.53	133.28	−6%
DEPT Counselor Education SCH	4,758	4,345	3,505	3,432	3,173	−33%
FTE	10.79	8.96	8.47	7.17	7.13	−34%
DEPT Elementary Education SCH	12,679	12,401	12,284	11,835	10,707	−16%
FTE	22.20	19.80	20.04	19.47	19.80	−11%
DEPT Educational Administration and Library Science SCH	6,163	4,911	5,092	4,436	3,823	−38%
FTE	10.78	11.38	11.45	10.33	10.14	−6%
DEPT Psychology SCH	31,065	33,422	35,689	36,318	34,560	+12%
FTE	37.01	39.92	46.19	47.61	48.92	+32%
DEPT Secondary Education SCH	10,324	9,696	7,903	7,623	6,715	−35%
FTE	16.70	15.37	13.10	11.79	11.64	−30%
DEPT Special Education SCH	7,200	6,787	6,730	6,405	5,983	−17%
FTE	10.51	10.13	9.98	10.77	10.29	−2%
DEPT Student Teaching SCH	17,411	15,622	14,971	14,372	12,210	−30%
FTE	33.22	31.05	28.12	26.26	24.99	−25%

[1]SCH: student credit hours
[2]FTE: full-time-equated
Source: Office of University Planning and Research

a new mission for the university. The education of teachers was no longer the basic purpose of the university. Rather, the professional education of business men and women was the university's new mission.

Since the university used a "student driven" model, declining enrollment in the School of Education had resulted in a decreased allotment of full-time-equated teaching positions to the school. Under these circumstances, contracting the organization from seven to three departments, was an appropriate response from the point of view of the Provost's office.

The decrease in FTE faculty positions was causing problems for the school since 85% of its faculty were tenured. Four departments, Counselor Education, Secondary Education, Elementary Education, and Educational Administration, were fully tenured. Most of the faculty had been with the school for many years (see Exhibit 35-4).

In August 1979, the Dean proposed a more sweeping reorganization than he had in 1972 and 1975. Not only were Special Education, Student Teaching, Secondary Education, and Elementary Education to be combined into Teacher Education, two of the remaining three departments, Counselor Education and Educational Administration, were to be combined into Educational Services (name changed later to Counseling, Educational Administration, Library Materials, and Community Leadership). The Psychology Department, as before, was to remain untouched.

The reorganization would require some people to move to different buildings so that members of the same department could be together (see Exhibit 35-5).

An implementation committee, chaired by the Dean and consisting of representatives from each of the departments, was charged with developing a proposal on which the faculty could vote on November 9.

The proposal was based on the Dean's recommendation, and presented only one reorganization plan. The committee had added a transitional structure, departmental units, to the Dean's proposal (see Exhibit 35-6).

The units, corresponding to the former departments, would be headed by unit coordinators. According to the proposal, the continuation of the units depended upon the departmental task forces created to develop departmental procedures. Each department would also be directed to form a program task

EXHIBIT 35-3 SCHOOL OF EDUCATION: CASE OF A CONTRACTING ORGANIZATION
SCH[1] AND FTE[2] OF SCHOOL OF EDUCATION, EXCLUDING PSYCHOLOGY DEPARTMENT

| Year | 1975-80 | | | | | Differences: |
	1975-76	1976-77	1977-78	1978-79	1979-80	1975-80
School SCH	89,600	87,184	86,229	84,620	77,339	−12,261
Psych SCH	31,065	33,422	35,689	36,318	34,560	+3,495
School-Psych SCH	58,535	53,762	50,540	48,302	42,779	−15,756
% Decrease, SCH	—	8%	6%	4%	11%	−27%
Psych. as % of Total School SCH	35%	38%	41%	43%	45%	
School FTE	142	138	138	135	133	−9
Psych FTE	37	40	46	48	49	+12
School-Psych FTE	105	98	92	87	84	−21
% Decrease, FTE	—	7%	6%	5%	3%	−20%
Psych as % of Total School FTE	26%	29%	33%	36%	37%	

[1]Student credit hour
[2]Full-time-equated

Source: University Office of Planning & Research

force charged with reviewing programs and curriculum. The task forces would have time limits within which to complete their work. In addition, an ongoing School Organization Committee would be formed and charged with resolving problems that arose out of the reorganization.

The proposal was voted upon in November and passed 61 to 27. Most of the support for the proposal came from the two departments least affected by the change: psychology and student teaching.

Psychology was not really involved since that department was not changed and members did not interact very much with the rest of the school faculty.

Student teaching consisted primarily of off-campus faculty who supervised student teachers in various locations throughout the state. As a result, they were more aware of the need to update the school's curriculum and were supportive of the Dean's desire to make programmatic changes in the school. They had attempted to bring about changes in curriculum themselves but had been rebuffed by the on-campus faculty.

Johnson: All right, let's get going. Last week we looked over Wells and Moody Hall to see where we could put people and I think...

Slocum: Forget it. The people in my department are not going to move out of Wells into Moody Hall. They like the offices they have

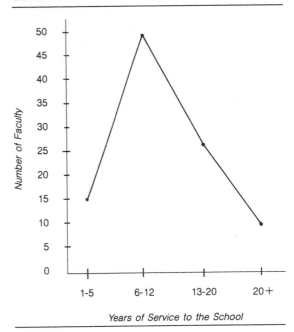

EXHIBIT 35–4   FACULTY TENURE, FALL 1980

now; they've been there a long time and they don't want to move in with those guys in Moody Hall. Some of them are even afraid of the rats "psych" has over there. We didn't want to go in with Counselor Education in the first place. I've been a professor of Educational Administration throughout my career. Now I'm a professor of Counseling, Educational Administration, Library Media, and

EXHIBIT 35–5   DEPARTMENTAL LOCATIONS

| *Pre-reorganization: Location of Departments* | | |
Fenwick	*Wells*	*Moody*
Psychology Special Education	Student Teaching Secondary Education Elementary Education Education Administration and Library-Media	Counseling Education

| *Post-reorganization: Location of Departments* | | |
Fenwick	*Wells*	*Moody*
Psychology	Teacher Education Student Teaching Secondary Education Elementary Education Special Education	C.E.A.L.M.C.L.[1] Counseling Education Educational Administration Library-Media

[1]Counseling, Educational Administration, Library Media, and Community Leadership.

Community Leadership. The other people in my profession don't even know what that is! Another thing, we don't have anything in common with those counselors. They're all wrapped up in people and their emotions. We take a straightforward, objective view of problems. We're concerned with systems, not individuals.

Johnson: I know there are problems with putting those two departments together, but each one is too small to continue as a separate entity. With decreasing resources the Dean had to get rid of the small departments. I'll admit I thought he should have put Counselor Education in with the school psychologists in the Psychology Department. They at least have something in common.

Waters: No way. The school psychologists are in my department and they wouldn't

stand for it. The credentials of school psychologists and counselors are completely different. School psychologists have much more extensive training requirements than counselors. Putting those two groups together wouldn't work at all. You know, someone should have paid more attention to how this whole thing was going to come out. There is a lot more involved in change than just drawing boxes on an organization chart. This reorganization has had a big impact on people: both faculty and staff.

Johnson: Let's get back to the space problems. The Dean wants Educational Administration to move into Moody and Special Education to move out of Fenwick into Wells. That way each of the departments will have all their people in the same building.

Smith: Well I hate to break this up, but I have

EXHIBIT 35-6   SCHOOL OF EDUCATION: CASE OF A CONTRACTING ORGANIZATION
ORGANIZATION CHART, AUGUST 1980

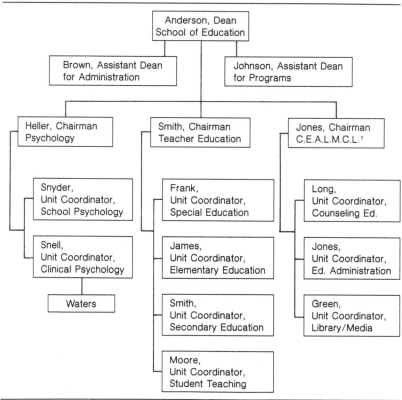

[1]Counseling, Educational Administration, Library Media, and Community Leadership.

a class at 11 and I have to get back to Wells Hall. It would sure help if we had release time to work on these committees. Some of my people are complaining about the way the departmental task forces are cutting into their class preparation time.

Johnson: OK, we'll meet again next week. Wait a minute, Smith, and I'll walk to Wells with you. I need to stop at the Dean's office.

Later on their way across campus, Smith, who was chairman of the new Department of Teacher Education and former chairman of the Secondary Education Department, asked Johnson how the faculty in Special Education felt about the reorganization.

Johnson: They're very concerned. As you know, a lot of them are relatively young and new to the University. Going from a department of 7 to one of 56 is quite a change. They are especially concerned about getting tenure. The rest of the faculty in the teacher education department don't know them very well and they are not that familiar with special education. How are the special education faculty going to be evaluated? Also, it's well known that Secondary Education has four more tenured positions than it should have according to the Provost's office, and that when people leave those positions, they won't be replaced. It looks to me as though it's going to be hard for any of my people to get tenure and if anyone has to be laid off, they'll be the first to go.

Smith: Well, I hope it doesn't come to that. Although do you realize that in 1971, 2,300 people were recommended for certification and this year we're only recommending 900? What concerns me are these confounded units. Here I am, chairman of the department, and the unit coordinators are acting like department chairmen. They're signing drop and add cards, approving budgets, and recruiting staff. The units are acting just like mini-departments.

Johnson: That's because this is a year of transition. The units are supposed to fade away after this year, according to the Dean. Not everyone agrees with that though.

Smith: That's for sure. Some of my faculty maintain these units can go on forever if the department decides to keep them. To hear them talk, there hasn't been any change at all.

Johnson: Then what's the point of the reorganization?

Smith: Beats me, but keeping these units is a neat way to finesse the reorganization.

Johnson: Why do you suppose psychology wasn't touched by any of this?

Smith: Rumor has it that the Dean didn't want to do anything that might encourage them to leave the school. After all, they're the only department that's growing and if they went to Liberal Arts, we would lose a lot of FTE.

Meanwhile, two of the Counseling Education faculty were discussing the reorganization over their morning coffee.

Miller: I'm supposed to go to one of those task force meetings again this afternoon. What a waste of time!

Terry: And all for nothing, too. The only money the reorganization saves is a couple of department chairperson's salaries, and that doesn't amount to anything.

Miller: Let's face it. The real reason the Dean wanted this reorganization is so that he can go out in a blaze of glory!

Terry: That's for sure. We don't have a thing in common with those guys from educational administration. I hope they never do move over here.

Later that day, Johnson, who had become the second assistant dean as a part of the reorganization, met with the Dean.

Dean: How did your meeting go this morning, Mike?

Johnson: About the same. Slocum is dragging his feet and we can't seem to resolve the space issue. Educational Administration probably isn't going to move unless you tell them they must.

Dean: It's frustrating to have all this resistance. They don't seem to realize how important this is to the school. We need to cut costs and the reorganization will allow us to reduce administrative expenses. More than that, it will permit us to be more flexible. We have to expand our mission beyond that of educating the classroom teacher. We could be educating people who are training personnel outside the classroom, such as in the private sector. Also, with the emphasis on "mainstreaming" we need to have special education faculty interacting with elementary education and secondary education.

Johnson: I agree with your reasons for reorganizing, Dean, but unless you take a stronger stand it's not going to happen. There are many people opposing the change, and unless you use stronger leadership, these committees are going to study it to death.

The next morning the Dean met with the other assistant dean, Dr. Brown, who was also a professor of psychology.

Dean: Good morning, Louise. I wanted to speak with you about the reorganization. You talk to a lot of people. How do you think it's going?

Brown: Well, in teacher education it's beginning to come along. The chairman has a nice informal way about him that will bring those people around eventually. Jones, on the other hand, is coming on rather strongly.

Most of the people in his department are maintaining their old territorial boundaries and hoping the reorganization will go away.

Dean: What do you think about the relocation of educational administration to Moody at this point?

Brown: Financially, it has to be done. We must reduce some of these administrative expenses. I hope you are successful in persuading them to move. If you force them, however, I am afraid they may bring in the faculty union.

After Dr. Brown left, the Dean pondered his options. Should he continue to let the departmental task forces and School Organization Committee try to resolve the problems of the unit structure and the allocation of space, or should he play a stronger role in the process? He would be retiring in a year or two, and he wanted to accomplish the reorganization before leaving. The Dean thought about how he had devoted his entire professional life to the growth and development of the school. Now he had one more task, getting the organization into a stronger position to cope with its changing environment. He needed that reorganization! How could he get it?

36

A Crisis Change Program

The Parks and Recreation Department in a major city was well known for its lack of progressive accomplishment. The director was an easygoing man who had worked for the city for 30 years. He got along well with people and had many close friends in his department and in the city government. However, he did little to improve his department. When the director retired, the city manager and the city council decided that it was time to bring in a dynamic new director who could turn the department around and produce visible results that the public would recognize.

A new director was found who seemed to fit the needs of the city manager and city council perfectly. He was a large man (about 6'4" and stocky) who seemed to have an unlimited supply of energy and innovative ideas. He was quite knowledgeable in the field of parks and recreation, and he was dedicated to making a name for himself (he was in his mid-30s) by making his Parks and Recreation Department a model for other cities.

CHANGES UNDER THE NEW DIRECTOR

The changes made by the new director came fast and furious. New parks, new equipment, and new recreation programs began to appear. Even though many of the changes were not budgeted, the director became known as a wheeler-dealer who could bargain and make special deals to get whatever was needed. However, the rapid changes and the new director's style also began to result in a number of serious problems. Shortly after he arrived, the new director had fired several key people in the organization and replaced them with younger, more dynamic persons. The firings, along with the autocratic style that he used to get things done, quickly resulted in considerable internal turmoil. He was also beginning to get a lot of negative reactions from other department heads because of what they began to label as his "wheeler-dealer style of crisis management." This was particularly true of the purchasing department because the new director was

From W. L. French, J. E. Dittrich, and R. A. Zawacki, *The Personnel Management Process: Cases in Human Resources Administration*, copyright © Houghton Mifflin Co., 1982. Used with permission.

continuously short-changing the system to get changes funded and implemented more rapidly.

CRISIS SITUATION

After about a year and a half under the new director, the situation reached a crisis stage. In addition to the internal problems, a local newspaper began a series on the Parks and Recreation Department with the obvious goal of getting the director fired. Trust began to break down in the department because the information from the newspaper stories was being supplied by department members as well as by the employees who got fired. This resulted in a state of near paranoia in the department. Rumors became rampant and genuine communication and problem-solving deteriorated because no one knew for sure who was involved in supplying the newspaper with material. Employees became divided on the issues—some agreeing that the director should be fired and others supporting the director because he had accomplished many improvements in the Parks and Recreation programs and facilities.

CHOOSING AN INTERVENTION STRATEGY

The city manager had been aware of the problems in the Parks and Recreation Department for some time and had tried to work with the director in solving them. However, little progress was made. The city manager was now faced with the dilemma of deciding what to do about the situation. He believed that the Parks and Recreation director had tremendous potential if he could develop a more appropriate management style and resolve some of the pressing organization problems, so he decided to hire a consultant to work with the director and give the director one more chance to turn the situation around.

The city manager, consultant, and director met, and the city manager made it clear that he believed the problems could be resolved but that it should also be clear that this was a last-chance approach for the director. Because of the limited time and funds available to improve the situation, a short-range strategy was worked out that included the following:

1. Phase I (three weeks). The consultant would spend time building rapport with the director and Parks and Recreation division heads.
2. Phase II (two weeks). An analysis would be made of the internal operations of the department. The consultant used an approach he called an "organizational physical." An organizational physical consists of a computer-based questionnaire given to all employees and a sampling of personal interviews from all levels of an organization. The questionnaire and interviews provide a profile of the whole organization, each division, and each supervisor's work group.
3. Phase III (two weeks). A comprehensive report would be prepared showing the findings from the organizational physical. The consultant would then review the findings first with the director, then with the director and city manager, and finally with the director and his five division heads. The consultant would also meet with each division head to review the results for his division. In addition, the consultant would meet with the supervisors in groups to give them their profiles and discuss what to do with the information.
4. Phase IV. A decision would be made on the most appropriate action to take next.
5. Phase V. Six weeks after Phase IV, the consultant would conduct a sampling of interviews to determine what progress had been made.

WHAT ACTUALLY HAPPENED

The director reluctantly agreed to the program and expressed strong feelings that he was fed up with having to work under such adverse conditions where other department heads, the press, some citizens (he and his family were sometimes harassed by citizens calling his home), and now the city manager were all out to get him. The city manager tried to explain that he hired the consultant because he believed in the director, but the director wasn't convinced of the city manager's intentions.

The consultant spent considerable time with the director listening to problems and talking about different management approaches and their consequences. He gradually gained the director's confidence until the results came back from the organizational physical. The results confirmed the suspicions about the internal problems and the negative reaction to the director's management style. When the consultant reviewed the results with the director, the director became very angry and denied the results. After a three-hour discussion, the consultant finally said that the prospects for change really boiled down to one thing: the director's willingness to accept responsibility for his part of the problems.

THE DIRECTOR BEGAN TO CHANGE

The consultant continued the feedback part of Phase III, which resulted in several of the division heads and supervisors making significant changes in response to the findings. However, the major issue was whether the director would change. After several weeks, the director began to mellow, and he gradually accepted responsibility for his part of the problems. He and the consultant then began to explore ways to rebuild the department and to change the director's management style.

CHOOSING A ONE-SHOT STRATEGY TO TURN THE SITUATION AROUND

Unfortunately, the funding for the consultant was almost depleted, and the consultant and director were faced with the dilemma of having to choose one strategy that would have the greatest potential for turning the situation around. It was decided that the best strategy would be to work with the top management team (the director and the five division heads) and try to build them into an effective team in hopes that unity and organization at the top would begin to bring unity in the rest of the departments. The choice was a high risk one because the funding allowed for only one more day of consulting time to accomplish such a difficult objective. However, the director felt that without a team effort at the top, his chances for turning the situation around were next to zero, so he decided to go with the strategy.

THE TEAM-BUILDING WORKSHOP

The consultant decided that because of the open hostility and lack of trust among the top management team, the best approach would be to spend one other half day for a team-building workshop. During the personal interviews, the consultant primarily explained what would happen at the workshop, asked for commitment to accomplishing the workshop objectives, discussed potential problems that might occur in the workshop, and expressed a strong belief in the director's commitment to making constructive changes in the organization and his management style. The interviews alleviated many of the concerns of the division heads that the workshop would be a disastrous, head-rolling fiasco.

TEAM-BUILDING DESIGN

An off-site location was selected for the workshop. The workshop began at 12:00 P.M. with a catered lunch and was to end by 5:00 P.M. The agenda for the workshop was:

- Lunch
- Introduction by the department head
- Overview of the agenda, workshop objectives, and ground rules by the consultant

- Review of the major strengths and problems in the top management team by the consultant
- Additions to the strengths and problems made by the team members
- Prioritizing the problems and selecting the most important ones to resolve
- Solving the problems and assigning responsibilities for follow-up
- Workshop wrap-up

WHAT HAPPENED AT THE TEAM-BUILDING WORKSHOP

As the workshop began, the tension was very high, and most of the division heads were visibly nervous. The director broke the ice by admitting to many of the problems he had caused and by expressing a desire to use more of a team approach to managing the department. The consultant then introduced some ideas on healthy and unhealthy ways for teams to work together. He then asked the team members to agree on some ground rules for how they wanted to work together during the workshop and for what they would do if any of the members became unconstructive. This exercise began to open the group up, and one of the managers said that while they had some constructive ground rules to work from, he would like to get some things out in the open. This led to each manager expressing concerns about the director and the other managers. The openness of all members, including the director, made it possible to clear the air about a number of apprehensions and differences the managers had. Many difficult issues were brought out, but the gist of the process was to produce a marked change in caring and trust and a willingness to work together among the team members.

The remainder of the meeting went smoothly, and all the agenda items were accomplished. The group also agreed to a plan for how they would restructure their staff meetings so they would operate as an executive team. They also agreed to confront each other when any of them, including the director, began to do anything to hamper their ability to work as a team. At this point the director was so elated with the results that he suggested that they have another similar session at which the group would, as a team, establish the objectives for the department so that they would all be working toward the same goals. There was unanimous agreement to the recommendation, and the meeting ended on a high note.

PROGRESS SINCE THE CRISIS WORKSHOP

The consultant did a follow-up report six weeks after the workshop. The report showed that considerable progress had been made. For example, the management team completed its objectives and began to work very effectively as a decision-making team. Also, the director made a conscientious effort to improve his management style, and most employees were aware of the changes, although a few employees felt that he either had mellowed too much or that he was still just as overpowering as before. Two serious problems remained, however. First, the newspaper campaign continued. This caused some internal morale and communications problems and undermined external relations with the public and the city council. The other problem was that, while the director began to change, many of the other department heads in the city would not change their attitudes toward him because of past encounters. Therefore, even though the criticism of the Parks and Recreation director diminished considerably, the city manager was still getting pressure from some of the other department heads to look for a new Parks and Recreation director.

37

Mail Route Improvement vs. The Manana Principle[1]

"Postal proposal rejected," said the headline, and the opening statement of the newspaper article left no doubt: "The U.S. Postal Service has rejected as 'garbage' a computerized route system for mail trucks that a Kansas State University professor says would save millions of dollars." Dr. Leonard W. Schruben, a research agricultural economist who had developed the LOCKSET method some eight years ago while at Stanford University, was stunned. During his years of experience with the method he had found no case in which the dispatching methods used by firms or government agencies had resulted in a routing with fewer miles than was discoverable by an appropriate version of LOCKSET.

About two years ago he had focused his attention on the U.S. Postal Service, which operates one of the nation's largest truck

A pilot study for the Topeka postal district showed that the routes designed by the computer outperformed the manually designed mail distribution system. He was certain that if the Postal Service implemented his method, substantial cost savings could be realized without any reduction in service.

Postal officials, who had participated in his work, had repeatedly expressed their confidence in the study's success, and Schruben simply did not understand the Postal Service's decision. What had gone wrong?

THE TRUCK DISPATCHING PROBLEM

Basically, the truck dispatching problem can be defined as the optimization of routes for a fleet of trucks used for delivery from a central depot to a large number of delivery points. It is designed to allocate loads to trucks in such a manner that all demands are supplied and that the total mileage covered is minimized.

There are several different operations research methods available to solve carrier routing problems, none of which has been found to be very successful by practitioners.

[1]One of the most subtle forms of resistance to change is to ostensibly accept and encourage the innovator, to publicly proclaim support of innovative goals, and while doing that to build in various safeguards devised to control, delay, and to ultimately nullify real change. We call this tactic, which leads innovative action to peter out while at the same time giving the organization the public semblance of progressiveness, the manana principle.

Reprinted with permission of Karl Dickel and James W. Gentry, Professor, Oklahoma State University.

The typical method in use is still one of trial and error. The dispatcher looks at a map, picks out routes consistent with available carrier capacities, and then by trial and error attempts to find shorter routes.

THE LOCKSET METHOD

Schruben's LOCKSET method is based upon an algorithm first developed by Clarke and Wright, and uses a sequential procedure to solve carrier routing problems. It starts from an initial solution in which each delivery is made on a one-stop route. Then, a successive aggregation of routes is carried out according to the highest distance-saved coefficient, which is the time saved by combining two routes as opposed to making two separate trips. The procedure is very flexible and many restrictions can successfully be built into the algorithm (travel time and truck capacity restrictions, special equipment trucks, bulk deliveries, road conditions, etc.).

LOCKSET tends to provide a "good" rather than an optimum solution. Since the procedure consecutively "locks" points into routes, it excludes them from further consideration; thus it is possible to preclude the best solution. On the other hand, LOCKSET reduces the number of possible alternatives considerably. An exact method would require the calculation of $\frac{1}{2}n!$ different combinations for a problem with n delivery points. Analyzed with LOCKSET, the same problem needs only $\frac{1}{2} \cdot n \cdot (n-1)$ calculations, or $1/(n-2)!$ of the explicit enumeration approach. Thus, the greater the magnitude of the problem, the greater the relative efficiency of LOCKSET. For instance, a problem with only 15 delivery points requires a mere 105 distance-saved coefficients compared with an astronomical 654 billion possible alternatives.

SUCCESSFUL INDUSTRIAL APPLICATIONS

The technique's performance has been tested against results of dispatching methods used by firms of different sizes, with various delivery configurations and different numbers and capacities of trucks. For example, LOCKSET was used to route trucks for a Massachusetts feed manufacturer, a Pennsylvania grocery chain, an Iowa meat packer, a Minnesota dairy, a Nebraska milk hauler, a Kansas soft drink bottler, as well as a California egg distributor. In none of the cases did the management procedure use a shorter set of routes than was discovered by LOCKSET.

Typically, the application of LOCKSET did not result in a drastic change in the routes, while distance savings ranged between 8% and 12%. In some cases, however, savings up to 20% were realized. Interestingly, small operations experienced the largest savings. Yet, distance savings are not the only outcome, as LOCKSET has provided a variety of other valuable results, such as:

1. reduction in fleet size
2. better utilization of available truck capacities,
3. balancing of routes,
4. marginal delivery costs for existing as well as new customers,
5. optimal location of outside storage facilities, and
6. evaluation of driver performance.

EXPERIENCES WITH KANSAS SCHOOL DISTRICTS

The reorganization of school bus routes in several Kansas school districts has been one of the most extensive applications of LOCKSET so far, and it illustrates the method's first application by a governmental agency.

In the 1970-71 school year, the 308 Kansas school districts spent almost $15 million for busing pupils to and from schools. In many districts the transportation item is second only to teacher salaries, thus representing an important area for potential cost savings.

The service requirements for busing school children is very restrictive, compared with most commercial operations, and those differences necessitated modification in the procedures successfully used to solve commercial problems.

By 1973, LOCKSET had been adopted by 10 school districts and the computer routes met or exceeded all standards of the manual routes. The saving in total mileage usually amounted to about 10%, and the reduction in the number of buses was even more substantial (between 10% and 30%). In general, the average length of ride could be reduced. In some cases, the computer-designed routes increased the longest ride for students but in no case did a student have to ride longer than the maximum 60 minutes allowed by state regulations. In most situations, computerized routes tended to shorten long rides more than lengthen short rides. Waiting periods for pupils could be reduced and a better coordination of class and bus schedules could be obtained.

All parties agreed that the computer may neglect consideration of the human element, and that the final analysis had to be left to human judgment. If necessary, the computer had to be overruled. As an example, in Unified District 224 with two schools in Clifton and Clyde, the computer proposed that one of the families in each district should switch schools. The children involved asked to remain with their old school friends and teachers. After deliberation by the Board of Education, the computer was overruled. Due to this procedure, there was generally no dissatisfaction or rejection of the new routes by the pupils and their parents.

The cost to install the LOCKSET method in a district ran from $1,500 to $5,000, depending on the size of the district and the number of routes. Annual maintenance of the system was estimated to run $1,000 to $3,000. All districts were able to save a multiple of these costs. For instance, the study for district 383, Manhattan, cost $3,000 and resulted in saving more than $9,000 in the first year of operation. Furthermore, three of the 22 buses in use could be eliminated. In the succeeding years, savings could be improved even further.

Following these successful applications,

Schruben offered the Kansas school system an interesting alternative: for $400,000, a statewide reorganization of bus routes could be carried out that would save the state an estimated one million gallons of gasoline a year. However, this proposal did not produce any definite action. While many superintendents appeared before legislative committees to advocate a comprehensive statewide study, there was noticeable reluctance to employ the method independently. Some superintendents felt that it was either "inappropriate" or "too costly" for them, and some also feared that parents might regard a change in bus scheduling as unnecessary. Yet Schruben blamed the failure of his proposal on bureaucracy. He supposed that the reluctance of school districts to employ his study was primarily caused by the fact that the state funds most of the school district's transportation costs. Up to now, only a few more school districts have revised their transportation schedules on a voluntary basis.

THE POSTAL PROPOSAL

On January 21, 1976, Schruben made a report available to the general public in which he claimed that the U.S. Postal Service could save more than $40 million annually, without any reduction in service, if they reorganized their mail delivery routes by his method. Further savings, he said, could be realized with comparatively minor adjustments in schedules and by selected closings.

Coincidentally, Edward V. Dorsey, a senior assistant postmaster general for operations, happened to visit Kansas City on the same day to talk to area postal managers about the grave financial situation of the U.S. Postal Service and to ask for ideas from the managers on things they could do to cut costs. "We've got to use every measure we can to reduce costs," he said, and he added that costcutting programs could include abandoning Saturday delivery, limiting special delivery services, or not processing mail as fast as is now done.

Schruben's study had been initiated in

June 1974 when the Postal Service granted him authority for access to Highway Contract Route records at the Topeka Sectional Center Facility (SCF). The Topeka SCF is one of 545 in the United States and it serves the 133 post offices with zip codes whose first three digits are 664, 665, 666, and 668. All sorting other than bulk mail for the individual post offices is done at the facility. At the time of the study the SCF used 32 trucks, of which 14 served "main" routes originating in Topeka. The other 18 trucks served "subroutes" originating from 9 outlying transshipment stations. The trucks run to the end of the line when dropping mail in the morning and return to their point of origin in the evening to complete the daily pickup leg. To meet service standards, all mail has to leave Topeka by 4:15 A.M., and the latest delivery time has to be 6:30 A.M. for first-class mail, 7:30 A.M. for second class, and 9:00 A.M. for third-and fourth-class mail.

Both Leonard Stadler, manager of logistics for the Topeka center, and Ralph Kingman, director of mail processing, aided Schruben in the procurement of necessary data and showed great interest in the study. On October 7, 1975, more than one year after the work had begun, Schruben submitted a first draft of the manuscript to them, soliciting their comments and requesting their review. A week later, Schruben and his assistant held a conference with Kingman and Stadler, in which every route was individually reviewed. Stadler suggested a few changes that were made on the spot. After that, the postal representatives agreed that the computer routes would perform successfully, and authorization to publish the report was given some weeks later.

THE RESULTS OF THE STUDY

"Computer designed routes would provide better service than manually designed routes in most cases," Schruben said in his press release. "Computerized routes would result in earlier mail delivery to many communities in the Topeka mail distribution center. In no case would mail be delivered later than with manually designed routes."

As the report showed, only 20 of the 32 trucks were needed, resulting in the reduction of 150,000 miles and a savings of $80,000 a year. The average arrival time of first-class mail in the morning was reduced from 6:00 A.M. to 5:47 A.M., for second-class mail from 6:18 A.M. to 6:01 A.M., and for third-and fourth-class mail from 6:51 A.M. to 6:27 A.M.

"If the Topeka routes were typical of other mail distribution centers in the U.S.," Schruben concluded, "annual savings of approximately $500,000 and $40 million, respectively, for Kansas and the nation could be passed on to those who use the mail." Compared with his experience with other delivery routing systems, he found that the design of the Topeka manual routes was equal to or better than that of many private businesses and other government agencies. Even so, the computer-designed routes offered substantial savings of about 20%, and preliminary results of a second study indicated similar savings for the star routes at Springfield, Ill.

An estimated $7,500 annually would be needed to develop and maintain computer routes for mail distribution centers like that in Topeka, and "who can't afford to spend $7,500 to make an $80,000 saving in transportation costs?" In addition, further savings could be possible by discontinuing or consolidating smaller post offices, and the computer could help estimate both potential savings and changes in service associated with each such closing or consolidation.

Finally, the report suggests revising the method of awarding mail routes. "Route design and bidding procedures deprive the Postal Service of possible benefits by excluding contractor participation in route design. Contractors now bid on the routes and the lowest qualified bidder for each route is awarded the contract. Judgment as to the number and design of routes depends entirely on the skill and experience of the officer designing the routes. It is not tested by the bidding process, so it may result in inefficient route design and unnecessarily high costs." Schruben believes that computerized routing could encourage participation by contractors in route design if bidding were conducted in the same manner as real estate bidding often is, allowing an individual to bid on an entire tract rather than small, individual parcels.

THE RESPONSE

"I believe the study has merit," Stadler said to journalists, "and I think the computer would be faster and more accurate, but I don't believe the savings would be as great as he quotes."

"From the time the study was made, there have been several thousand miles reduced manually. Four of the trucks have been eliminated since that time."

"And some things would be more inconvenient. For instance, from what I have seen, it would require a big truck, like a semi, to pick up mail at St. George. That would be too inconvenient—it's just too large a truck to back in and everything there."

"Finally," Stadler said, "figuring the mileage of the trucks isn't feasible because they are let on bids. We don't care how many trucks someone says they're going to use, if they give us one bid. If we furnished our own trucks, that would be a different story."

The report as well as Stadler's statements received great publicity and, as Schruben says, "a number of people commenting to me were glad that the Postal Service showed promises of modernization and a willingness to explore new ideas that might result in savings."

On February 2, 1976, William R. Roberts, Wichita postal district manager, sent a letter to R. P. Koenigs, director of the central region logistics division, in which he criticized Schruben's study most severely. Some days later, the same letter was released to the press.

"Schruben's bulletin was immediately followed by many newspaper articles and TV coverage that was unfavorable to the U.S. Postal Service, but very favorable to Professor Schruben," Roberts said. "A partial review of the proposal by the Wichita postal district, however, does not substantiate Professor Schruben's highly publicized potential cost savings to the USPS. In fact, additional routes would be required to make his proposal usable."

"The problem was not the computer. It was the lack of essential data, incomplete understanding of our transportation schedules and frequencies by programmers (probably students), a lack of knowledge of our service requirements, and a few other minor problems. The result was 'garbage in and garbage out' of the computer."

His criticism was followed by an enumeration of problem areas that he found made the computer routes unworkable. Most important of all, he said, the proposal did not allow service standards to be met and it contained erroneous mileage figures for most truck routes. As an example, he pointed out that the study had neglected to mention that first-class post offices are required to receive mail from trucks leaving Topeka prior to 4:00 A.M., and that it showed mileage figures of 126.2 instead of 13.0 miles or 77.8 instead of 17.9 miles. However, the most aggravating error, he stated, was the attempt to send a mail truck from Grantville to Tecumseh, over the Kansas river where there is no bridge. "In view of the above problems and erroneous data," he concluded his letter, "further analysis of this highly publicized report is not deemed necessary."

SCHRUBEN BACKS HIS PROPOSAL

"I have checked every substantive statement critical of the study that you mentioned in your letter to R. P. Koenigs. Without exception, each one is false," Schruben countered in a letter to Roberts on February 12, 1976, and the subsequent enumeration of incorrect conclusions reads like a lecture to Roberts.

"Nowhere does the report state the early trucks (those leaving Topeka prior to 4:00 A.M.) are not needed. I do not understand how anyone could read the report and reach any other conclusion."

"You confuse route lengths with distance mail travels from Topeka. The mileage figures you labeled erroneous are distances mail travels from Topeka to the last stop, even though it may be carried by as many as three different trucks on three different routes before it arrives at its final destination. This is clearly spelled out in the report."

"There is no inference in the report that the computer would route a truck from Grantville to Tecumseh over a river where there is no bridge. The computer used actual routes in laying out routes and takes into account road conditions. If it is necessary to backtrack to find a bridge or a freeway exit five miles down the road, the computer schedules accordingly. That was the case in the Grantville to Tecumseh link. The extra miles are because there is no direct bridge between these two locations."

"It is most unfortunate that you did not fully acquaint yourself with the plan. By your own admission, your comments are based on a 'partial analysis' and a 'quick summary' of the report. A complete analysis and summary could have prevented erroneous interpretations and shown two public institutions cooperating to save taxpayers and postal users money without diminishing services."

"Because of the implications for my reputation and that of the University in the publication of your letter, we deem it essential to make public a summary of the above. Also, any further public statements by you that are not factual will of course be closely examined for effect on my reputation and that of the University."

The public reaction to this dispute may be reflected in a statement on *The Salina Journal's* Page of Opinion: "There's considerable evidence that Postal Service officials

wouldn't recognize a good postal service plan if it kicked them in the shins. And like most bureaucrats, they don't want 'outsiders' telling them how to run their Service, even if they don't know how themselves."

Subsequently, Schruben was not given any other opportunity to talk to area postal managers. "They frankly refused to talk to me," he said. "Obviously some people had gotten cold feet, and I would not be surprised if there has also been some pressure from superiors. Stadler's change, for instance, is a clear symptom for me."

THE FINAL REJECTION

On February 17, 1976, E. V. Dorsey sent a letter to Duane Acker, President of Kansas State University, in which he expressed the Postal Service's appreciation of Professor Schruben's work, and explained their objections to the plan. "There are some misunderstandings on his part (both qualitative and quantitative) which render his work less immediately applicable than might otherwise be the case," he said.

"First, I would like to emphasize that the transportation costs are generally irrelevant to the analysis of a recommendation to close or retain a small post office."

"Professor Schruben's work assumes that minimization of vehicle miles results in an optimum network. This is not always correct. There are many instances (including some in the Topeka area) where a higher mileage solution results in both a lower cost and lower energy utilization solely because it allows use of smaller vehicles on long mileage elements of the operation.

"Finally, the models are vastly more expensive to utilize than Professor Schruben estimates. I can only assume that Professor Schruben failed to include the labor costs of data collection in his estimate of $7,500 per location. Even so, his point that computer-assisted scheduling is financially attractive, albeit overstated, is still valid.

"The Postal Service is already highly committed to the concept of computer-assisted scheduling technology. Where the state of art has proven adequate, we have moved aggressively to implement its use. The Postal Service is currently recovering in excess of $3 million annually from our efforts, and the trend is dramatically upward."

A later inquiry about the savings potential of Schruben's plan made by Senator Robert Dole (Kansas) rendered a similar reply from the U.S. General Accounting Office. The letter, postmarked April 30, 1976, said further that "it appears that the Topeka study has paralleled the work of the Service. Although the Topeka study and the Service's Star Route Simulator both propose using computer assistance for improving star routes, these efforts were pursued independent of each other. Service headquarters officials stated they were not aware of the Topeka study until January 1976."

On May 18, 1976, the Postal Service released a final statement to the press. It concludes: "The conclusion that the Postal Service rejected out of hand Dr. Schruben's proposal for a computerized routing system for mail trucks is simply not true. Dr. Schruben's plan was carefully weighed by postal officials, and was found not applicable to our needs."

38

Municipal Light

In 1902 the citizens of Hamilton passed a proposal to develop a source of hydroelectric power for street lights and other public purposes. Up until that time all power had been supplied by private companies. During the first half of the twentieth century, a number of dams and steam-generating plants were developed in order to supply a large portion of Hamilton's power needs. The existence of Municipal Light also served as a rate regulator for electric power purchased from private companies. Since its beginning in 1902, Municipal Light has developed into one of America's most efficient electric utilities, powered almost entirely by nonpolluting hydroelectric generating facilities. This self-supporting, tax-paying utility maintains rates that are among the nation's lowest (less than half the national average), with but two rate increases in 66 years. In addition to low rates, Municipal Light provides a spectrum of consumer services: electric range, electric water heater, and electric heating system repair service at no charge—except for parts; advice on heating and air conditioning; free estimates on electric heating costs; advice on use and care of electric appliances; recipes and other household hints; advice on adequate wiring; 24-hour emergency light trouble service; and water-heater rental as low as $1.25 monthly. As a consequence, Municipal Light has built up a good image in the minds of consumers for low rates and free services.

Municipal Light employs approximately 1,800 women and men for the Hamilton service area and the hydroelectric projects. Employees have considerable pride in their organization and enjoy the company's good image with customers. Many jobs have been passed from father to son, and in a number of instances three generations are represented on the Municipal Light payroll. In many cases, several members of the same family are currently working in the organization. Obviously, many traditions and norms have evolved over time with respect to employee relations—among peers as well as among superiors and subordinates. Approximately 700 of the 1,800 employees are represented by the International Brotherhood of Electrical Workers.

In 1972 Charles Newman was appointed

From *Experiential Exercises and Cases in Management* by Fremont E. Kast and James A. Rosenzweig, copyright © 1976 McGraw-Hill Book Co. Reprinted with permission.

superintendent of Municipal Light. He was a retired Air Force brigadier general with a distinguished military career and experience in managing large-scale weapon procurement programs. The appointment was controversial because many Municipal Light workers, as well as some members of the city council, contended that the superintendent should have had experience in an electrical utility. The mayor and a majority of the council, however, felt that managerial skills were transferable and that Mr. Newman was the right person for the job at that particular time. They were concerned that Municipal Light was entering a new era in which the emphasis would have to be placed on cost savings in order that rates could be held down to the current very attractive levels. In this context, the new superintendent accepted a mandate that emphasized public responsiveness, and he implemented programs designed to develop a greater sensitivity to the needs of Municipal Light's customers and owners and to provide them with more effective, efficient service.

An outside consulting firm—Donner, Blitzen, and Associates—was hired to conduct a comprehensive study of the organization—the first in its 70-year history. A year later, the study conclusions pointed the way toward an annual saving of over $2 million for the utility's rate payers, plus substantial increases in the speed and efficiency of customer service. An automated customer information system (CIS) was designed to provide near-instantaneous customer data from a control computer. By eliminating duplicate filing systems and reducing incidents of error, CIS would save an estimated $1 million annually. A proposed management reporting system involved a broad range of coordinated reports to assist Municipal Light managers in evaluating performance and analyzing work procedures on a regular, systematized basis. Another recommendation involved a work management system to establish a project priority and scheduling procedure together with more precise work control and documenta-

tion in the engineering and operations area of the utility. A proposed organization and systems planning and coordination report would provide the necessary research capability and control to coordinate the new and ongoing utility programs. It was anticipated that implementation of all the recommendations should take approximately three years.

Municipal Light receives over 18,000 telephone calls a day for service and information, plus several hundred of an administrative nature. In April 1974, an automated centrex telephone system replaced equipment that had been installed in 1935. The new electronic switching means faster, more efficient service for Municipal Light customers.

Automation, plus implementation of the Donner, Blitzen, and Associates study, has resulted in certain personnel changes, reductions in some areas, and additional hiring in others. When the automation program was first started in 1970, the utility made a firm commitment to all personnel that there would be no layoffs or reductions in salary—a commitment that Municipal Light has stood by during the past years. To retain personnel for certain jobs in the utility, a skill redistribution program was created as an ongoing effort. To complement the skill redistribution program as well as to provide opportunities for all personnel to upgrade performance in various disciplines, Municipal Light established a training division in June 1973. The newly formed section was authorized to ascertain training needs in the utility and to develop appropriate courses to augment the already established tuition reimbursement and other education programs. Courses have been conducted in office and technical skills as well as in the management area.

Municipal Light has a firm commitment to Hamilton's Affirmative Action Program. The target for reaching minority parity within the service area is 1975, while 1978 is the goal set for equal representation of women. In 1974, women were admitted to training programs in the electrical trades, an area from which they had been historically excluded. This program was coordinated with the International Brotherhood of Electrical Workers, the Civil Service Commission, and the Hamilton personnel department.

In 1972, Superintendent Newman established a Citizens Policy Advisory Committee, consisting of 14 members who represented a wide spectrum of the community. Their recommendations have been included in policy deliberations on matters such as rates, generation and research, street lighting, underground policy, energy marketing, finances, and environmental impact.

On Wednesday, November 22, 1972, the following story appeared in the Hamilton *Harbinger.*

NEWMAN SUSPENDS 16 AT MUNICIPAL LIGHT

PRIVATE DETECTIVES TURN UP "ABUSES"

City Light Superintendent Charles Newman disclosed yesterday he has suspended 16 field employees and reprimanded two for abusing coffee break periods.

Newman said he hired a private detective firm to shadow Municipal Light crews for one week after getting complaints from citizens that some men were taking extended coffee breaks at their Hamilton cafés.

The investigation also turned up possible abuses of coffee break times by "15 to 18" employees of the Hamilton Engineering Department, according to George Everest, principal assistant city engineer for operations.

However, Everest said he cannot say if there are any actual violations in his department until he has had each reported case checked out. This is being done now.

The three cafés involved, Everest said, are near 2d Avenue and Barstow Street, 7th Avenue N.E. and Interlake Way, and N. 34th Street and Stevens Way N.

Newman said two Municipal Light employees were suspended for 10 days without pay, five were suspended for two days and nine for one day. Two others received letters of reprimand.

The superintendent said at least one of the disciplined employees was also disciplined in a similar investigation three years ago for the same thing.

Everest said his department also has to discipline employees from time to time for coffee break time abuses.

The private detective agency placed the three locations under surveillance during the work week of October 30 through November 3 and made its reports according to vehicle license numbers.

The private eyes timed the length of time crews spent in the cafés. Normal time allowed for coffee breaks is 15 minutes in the forenoon and afternoon, Everest said.

Newman said: "We talked to our people involved and they admitted the abuses. The severity and frequency of the violations varied."

Newman stressed that the infractions involved only a small minority of Municipal Light workers and "I continue to be amazed at the dedication of 99% of our employees."

He said those abusing lunch or coffee break periods not only are gypping the city, "they are also cheating on their fellow employees."

"I will not stand for this."

He said most of the violators "had been around for a while." He said that if any "extenuating circumstances" turn up later, the disciplinary actions will be rectified.

"We're not against coffee breaks—just the abuse of them" Newman declared.

The president of the security agency involved maintained that his agents did not spy upon employees of the utility. Their job was to check only on vehicles and that this task fell within their overall contract of protecting Municipal Light facilities and equipment. Citizen reaction was quick and varied. Some supported management in its efforts to "shape up" employees. Others felt that this goal, however meritorious, was overshadowed by the sneaky tactics used. They emphasized that control and discipline should be handled within the organization via normal managerial procedures.

This episode touched off a series of disputes within the organization, some of which were given publicity in the press. Two of the four city council members who voted against the superintendent at his confirmation hearing in 1972 said publicly that Newman hadn't done badly. One stated, "On balance, I would have to say he's done a good job." Another observed, "I like a number of things he's done, changes that I favored such as reducing personnel and opening up the utilities operations. I also hear about morale problems among the rank-and-file workers. There are pluses and minuses...." The majority of the council who supported Newman in the beginning reaffirmed their position by stating, "Yes, we think he is doing a good job, making the kinds of changes we wanted to see." In December 1973, supervisory personnel—not Newman—suspended six more utility workers for coffee break abuses. This time, supervisory personnel did the surveillance rather than the security firm. Newman stated, "Those who were abusing their privileges were being unfair to their fellow workers. I felt that the previous management had failed to stop such abuses and that I must. Letters from the public supported the disciplinary actions 50 to 1."

During this period, a new discipline code was written, at the request of employees, to make penalties more equitable. According to Newman, union leadership failed to attend drafting sessions. The code was put into effect on March 21, 1974. In early April, two foremen were suspended for three days for alleged coffee break abuses. One of the foremen, Arnold Knutson, claimed that his crew had to move its truck out of a customer's driveway at 4 PM. Because it was too late to set up again and get anything accomplished by quitting time, he decided to take the crew back to a substation for a coffee break before quitting at 4:30. He maintained that they had not taken a normal 15-minute break during the afternoon. The new rules specified that crews would return to the main dispatching area rather than stop at substations en route. Jack Simmons, the other foreman, did not comment on the specifics of his case, but did say that he wasn't even aware of any new rules covering suspensions, discharges, and other disciplinary measures. Other workers suggested that the new rules were adopted unilaterally by Municipal Light Superintendent Charles Newman without approval of the Civil Service Commission. Newman's comment was, "Municipal Light insists on being able to discipline employees when they fail to put in eight hours' work for eight hours' pay. There are standing work orders, dating back to 1970, explicitly requiring crews to return to headquarters at the close of their last job for the day. Loafing away from headquarters to round out the work day is not acceptable work procedure." He stated that citizens had complained that the two work crews involved were parking their trucks and loafing for 30 minutes or longer at the end of their work day.

The next day, about 700 workers of the electrical workers' union walked off the job, refusing to return until the suspensions were rescinded. By the second day, the strike had spread to over 1,000 of the 1,800 employees. An ad hoc committee representing the workers presented the following demands in the form of a memo to Superintendent Newman, the major of Hamilton, and the city council. The demands included:

1. Rescinding the suspensions of the two foremen
2. Resignation of Superintendent Newman
3. Suspension of the new work rules until they are approved by the employees, the union, and the Civil Service Commission
4. The development of an employees' bill of rights
5. The suspension of implementation of new programs that appeared to have exceeded the ability of the organization to absorb changes.

The superintendent responded by saying that he was willing to hold the suspensions in abeyance and meet with the ad hoc committee.

39

Atlantic Store Furniture

Atlantic Store Furniture (ASF) is a manufacturing operation in Moncton, New Brunswick. The company is located in the Industrial Park and employs about 20-25 people with annual sales of about $2 million. Modern shelving systems are the main products and these units are distributed throughout the Maritimes. Metal library shelving, display cases, acoustical screens, and work benches are a few of the products available at

ASF. The products are classified by two distinct manufacturing procedures that form separate sections of the plant, as illustrated in Exhibit 39-1.

THE METAL-WORKING OPERATION

In the metal-working part of the plant sheet metal is cut and formed into shelving for assembly. The procedure is quite simple and organized in an assembly-line method. Six or eight stations are used to cut the metal to the appropriate length, drill press, shape, spotweld, and paint the final ready-to-assemble product. The equipment used in the operation is both modern and costly, but the technology is quite simple.

The metal-working operation employs on average about eight or ten workers located along the line of assembly. The men range in age from 22 to 54 and are typically of French Canadian background. Most have high school education or have graduated from a technical program. The men as metalworkers are united by their common identity in the plant and have formed two or three subgroups

EXHIBIT 39-1 ORGANIZATIONAL CHART FOR ATLANTIC STORE FURNITURE

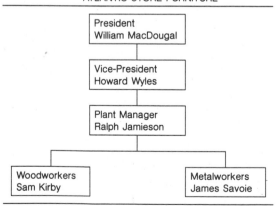

President
William MacDougal

Vice-President
Howard Wyles

Plant Manager
Ralph Jamieson

Woodworkers
Sam Kirby

Metalworkers
James Savoie

Reprinted with permission of Peter McGrady, Assistant Professor,
Lakehead University, Thunder Bay, Ontario.

based on common interests. One group, for example, comprising the foreman and three other workers has season tickets to the New Brunswick Hawks home games. Another group bowls together in the winter and attends horse races in the summer months.

The foreman's group is the most influential among the workers. The men in this group joined the company at the same time and James Savoie, the foreman, was once a worker with the three other men in the group. The group characteristically gets to the lunch counter first, sits together in the most comfortable chairs, and punches the time clock first on the way out of work. Conrad LeBlanc, another group member, has a brother who plays professional hockey in the NHL and he frequently describes the success of the team and the large home his brother lives in.

The metalworkers as a group operate on one side of the plant and work at a very steady pace. The demand for products in this section is high and the production is usually constant. The group adjusts well to changes in the order requests and the occasional overtime pressures. The salespeople on the road provide a constant flow of orders to the point where there is a small backlog of requisitions to be filled. The products vary in size and style but for the most part they are standardized items. A small amount of work is performed on a customized basis.

WOODWORKING OPERATIONS

The woodworking operation differs considerably from the metal-working operation. It is a new addition to the plant and has had some success. It is separated from the metal production unit by a sliding door.

The organizaton of the wood shop is haphazard. Some areas are organized to produce standard products like screening, but the majority of the woodworking section is organized around a particular project. Typically tools, equipment, and supplies are left in the area of the partially completed projects.

Custom cabinets and display cases are made for large department and retail stores. A small line of products is produced as a regular line while the rest of the products are custom designed. The flow of work is basically steady in the shop, but there are stages when the work orders become intermittent. Though the appearance of the woodworking shop is quite disorganized and messy, reflecting the nature of the work, the workers in this section of the plant see themselves as real craftsmen and take considerable pride in their work. Typically two or three projects are in progress simultaneously along with the normal run of standard products. The metal workers store some of their completed units in the woodworking area to the dislike of the woodworkers and to the disorganization of the section.

Unlike the metalworkers the woodworkers have a distinct hierarchy based on seniority and ability. The apprenticeship program within the company has produced a number of good carpenters. This section of the company, though still relatively young, has produced good work and has a reputation for quality craftsmanship.

The morning coffee break for the woodworkers follows that of the metalworkers. Lunch hour is staggered by 20 minutes as well. Only a minimal amount of interaction occurs between the woodworkers and metalworkers as there tends to be rivalry and competition between the two groups.

The supervisor who oversees the two sections of the plant (plant manager) is Ralph Jamieson, a production engineer from a local university. As plant manager he reports to the vice-president. He is responsible for the plant operation, which includes the metal and woodworking shops. At the time of his hiring ASF had not developed the woodworking section of the plant. Jamieson's work at the University became integrated into the production line when he discovered a method of galvanizing the product in final stages of production. He spends a good deal of his time in the metal-working operation, planning and discussing problems in production with the foreman, James Savoie. Laboratory research is another occupation assigned to Jamieson who enjoys experimentation with new methods and techniques in design and fabrication of metal products. Jamieson and Savoie are friends and they spend a good deal of time together both on and off the job. James Savoie is quite happy with the way his operation is running. He has good rapport with his men and absenteeism is minimal.

A recent personnel change within ASF is the addition of two new salesmen who are on the road in New Brunswick and Nova Scotia. Their contribution to the company is most notable in the metal work area. They have placed many orders for the company. The new sales incentive program has motivated these people to produce, and their efforts are being recognized.

Sam Kirby, the woodworking supervisor, blew up at the plant manager the other day after the metalworkers had pushed open the sliding door with an interest in storing more excess shelving units in the woodworking area. Sam is a hothead sometimes and has become quite annoyed recently with all the intergroup rivalry between the metalworkers and the woodworkers. Storage space has been a sore point between the groups for the last six months or so, ever since the metalworkers became very busy. Jamieson and Howard Wylie, the vice-president, were asked to settle the problem between the two shops. They decided that the metalworkers were to access the woodworking shop only if absolutely necessary and with consent of the foreman or supervisor.

This latest incident really upset the employees in the woodworking shop. The woodworkers feel intimidated by the metalworkers who are taking space and interrupting their work.

In a later conversation Kirby and Jamieson smoothed things over somewhat. It was explained to Kirby that it was the metalworkers who were really turning out the work and that they needed the space. The area that metalworkers want to use is not really needed by the woodworkers. It is simply an area around the perimeter of the room by the walls.

Kirby did not like Jamieson's response, knowing full well his commitment to the metal-working operations. With this decision the metalworkers proceeded to use the area in the woodworking shop and never missed an opportunity to insult or criticize the woodworkers. The effect of the situation on the respective groups became quite obvious. The metalworkers became increasingly more jocular and irritating in their interactions with the woodworkers.

The fighting continued and became of more concern to the president and vice-president. For example, the large sliding doors separating the shops were hastily closed one afternoon on a metalworker who was retreating from a practical joke he was playing on a woodworker. The resulting injury was not serious but it did interrupt a long series of accident-free days the company had been building up. This incident further divided the two groups. Meetings and threats by management were not enough to curtail the problems.

The woodworkers were now withdrawing all efforts to communicate. They ate lunch separately and took coffee breaks away from the regular room. Kirby became quite impatient to complete new products and to acquire new contracts. He urged management to hire personnel and to solicit new business. The climate changed considerably in the woodworking shop as the workers lost their satisfying work experience. Much of the friendly interaction that had gone on previously had ceased. Kirby's temper flared more frequently as small incidents seemed to upset him more than before. After work get-togethers at the tavern were no longer of much appeal to the men.

The metalworkers were feeling quite good about their jobs as the weeks passed. Their orders remained strong as demand continued to grow for their products. The metalworkers complained about the woodworkers and demanded more space for their inventory.

The metalworkers were becoming more cohesive and constantly ridiculed the woodworkers. Their concern for the job decreased somewhat as back orders filled up and talk of expansion developed for the metal-work operation.

Just as the metal shop became more confident there were more difficulties with the woodworking shop. The woodworkers were completing the final stages of an elaborate cabinet system when information came regarding a shipping delay. The new store for which the product was being built was experiencing problems, causing a two- or three-month delay before it could accept the new cabinet system. Kirby was very disturbed by this news as the woodworkers needed to see the completion of their project and the beginning of a new one.

The predicament was compounded somewhat by the attitude of the metalworkers who heard of the frustration of the woodworkers and added only more jeers and smart remarks. Morale at this stage was at an all-time low. The chief carpenter, and integral member of the woodworkers, was looking for a new job. One or two of the casual workers were drifting into new work or not showing up for work. Contracts and orders for new products were arriving but in fewer numbers, and casual workers had to be laid off. Defective work was beginning to increase, to the embarrassment of the company.

Management was upset with the conditions of the two operations and threatened the foreman and supervisors. Kirby was disturbed at the situation and was bitter about the deteriorating state of the woodworking plant. Despite many interviews he was unable to replace the head carpenter who had left the company, attracted by a new job prospect. Efforts to reduce the intergroup conflict were made but without success.

The president of ASF, William MacDougal, was alarmed with the situation. He recognized some of the problems with the different operations. One operation was more active and busy while the other section worked primarily on project work, i.e., building a custom display cabinet for a retail company. The organization was designed with the normal structure in mind. The men in the company, he thought to himself, were very much of the same background, and what little diversity there was should not have accounted for this animosity. As president, he had not developed a climate of competition or pressure in the company.

The disorganization and chaos in the woodworking plant was alarming, and there was very little that could be done about it. Kirby had been discussing the problem with the president trying to identify some of the alternatives. This had been the third meeting in as many days and each time the conversation drifted into a discussion about current developments in Jamieson's metal-working pursuits. James Savoie felt that there was too much worrying going on "over there"!!!

Plans for expanding the building at ASF were developing at a rapid pace. The president felt that more room might alleviate some of the problems, particularly with respect to inventory, warehousing, and storage.

Kirby became enthusiastic about the prospects of some relief for his side of the operation. He was very much aware of the fact that the performance of his operation was quite low. The president of the company felt satisfied that the woodworking concern was going to improve its performance. One or two new contracts with large department stores inspired the effort to improve the operation.

The men in the woodworking section became relaxed. A few positive interactions between the woodworkers and metalworkers became evident. One afternoon about two weeks after the disclosure by the president of the new plant development Kirby observed blueprints for the new expansion. The plans had been left on Jamieson's desk inadvertently and to Kirby's surprise revealed full details of the expansion for the new building.

Examining the details more carefully, Kirby recognized that the woodworking area was not to be included in the expansion plans. Kirby left the office in a rage, stormed into the president's office, and demanded an explanation.

Kirby shouted that he had changed things around in the woodworking shop on the promise of more room and the possibility of expansion. The president shook his head and apologized and explained he was going to be told but nothing could be done. The demand was simply just not that great for wood products. Kirby left the office and went straight for his car and drove off.

40

Space Support Systems, Incorporated

Space Support Systems, Incorporated (SSS) is a small but growing corporation located in Houston, Texas, adjacent to NASA's Manned Spacecraft Center. The corporation was founded four years ago with the objective of obtaining government contracts for research studies, for preliminary development in space suit technology, and for studies in other areas of environmental systems connected with space flight. At present, 25 people are associated with Space Support Systems.

The company was founded by its current president, Robert Samuelson, for the specific purpose of bidding on a study contract for an extravehicular hard suit (a special type of space suit) with lunar, and possibly Mars, capabilities. At the time of the company's inception, Samuelson, James R. Stone, and William Jennings comprised the entire Space Support Systems company.

Mr. Samuelson, the President, is 47 years old, holds a B.S.E.E. degree from a large southern state university, and prior to forming Space Support Systems, was a senior engineer with North American. He has worked for several large aircraft corporations since his graduation from college 25 years ago. The present venture, however, represented a technologically new slant for him.

James R. Stone, Vice-president and director of Technological Research, is 38 years old. He has a Ph.D. in physiology from a leading West Coast university and had, prior to the inception of Space Support Systems, taught for six years at a leading university. He also has degrees in the field of aeronautical engineering. He worked for two years in the aeronautics industry before returning to school to work toward his doctorate in aerospace applications. Dr. Stone's reputation among his colleagues in both the theoretical and creative aspects of aerospace environmental control is quite good.

William Jennings, Vice-president and Director of Technology Applications, is 42 years old. After graduating from high school, he attended college for three years before a shortage of funds forced him to quit school and seek employment in the then-lucrative

Chapter 13, "Space Support Systems, Incorporated" (pp. 59-67) from *Organizational Behavior: Cases and Situations* by B. J. Hodge, Herbert J. Johnson, and Raymond L. Read, copyright © 1974 by Harper & Row, Publishers, Inc.

aircraft industry. While in college, he majored in mechanical enginering. For three years prior to joining SSS, Mr. Jennings worked on an air force contract that involved the development of high-altitude flight suits. His particular specialty was in the development and construction of functional flight suits for initial testing, but he also showed considerable insight in new developments and changes in designs that were submitted to him prior to final construction. His reputation was such that Mr. Samuelson had been prompted to seek him out to join SSS four years ago.

The current organization chart for Space Support Systems is shown in Exhibit 40-1. There are two branches under Dr. Stone, the Environmental Studies Team and the Space Suit Studies Team. The Environmental Studies Team is primarily concerned with studies on environmental and physiological systems in spacecraft and modular structures for lunar (and other planetary) habitation. At present, there is no hardware output from the company along these lines. The team leader is Roger Swanson, and there are four men under him. Roger is 33 years old and has a master's degree in biology. He is highly respected by his peers and well thought of by Dr. Stone.

The Space Suit Studies Team works on

study contracts investigating either hard or soft space suits used primarily for extravehicular use. Its members have also worked on suits for wear within the spacecraft. Composed of bright men, the Team is led by Don Hammond, who is 28 years old and has a master's degree in physiology. He has had many opportunities to return to school to work on a Ph.D. but has elected to stay with the company each time. He is considered extremely bright and, while not as old as most of the men on his team, he is unanimously accepted as the leader. On occasion, Don and Dr. Stone have had differences of opinion and, while the two do not seem to like each other personally, they respect each other's professional abilities and qualifications.

Much of the actual management and leadership of both these teams comes from Dr. Stone. The team leaders serve as depositories for information and as spokesmen for their groups, rather than as centers of responsibility and authority. These teams are, for the most part, college-educated and well qualified technically. The average age of the 14 men under Dr. Stone is 31 years, and the average number of college degrees per man is 1.6.

Bill Jennings's area is responsible for actually developing and building suits for testing and presentation to NASA. This function is a logical extension of the work of the Space Suit Studies Team and requires a close coordination between the two groups. The five men under Jennings are all skilled technicians who are actually the craftsmen who build the technological systems. None of them has a college degree, although two of the men completed junior college. The average age of these men is 43 years. They work together well and have formed a close-knit work unit. Jennings may often be found in the middle of the group working on some aspect of building mockups of functional space suits. The group is quite autonomous and functions with little direction from Mr. Samuelson.

EXHIBIT 40-1   ORGANIZATION CHART OF SPACE SUPPORT SYSTEMS, INCORPORATED

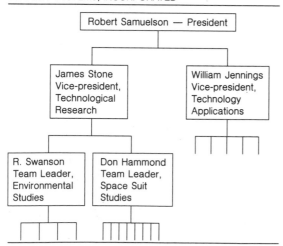

Mr. Samuelson had never had any managerial problems in SSS that he knew of. The work had always run along fairly smoothly and, being very project-oriented, the company's employees seemed to be constantly busy with one job or another. Mr. Samuelson had to be engaged in the work of obtaining contracts and serving as a liaison with the government once a contract was secured. As a result, he knew that he might not have as thorough knowledge as he should regarding the inner workings of the SSS organization. He particularly realized that he had little feedback from personnel in the firm, but since he had experienced no apparent difficulties, he felt that all must be going well.

One afternoon, Jennings came in to see Mr. Samuelson. Jennings seemed upset and it was apparent that something was on his mind.

Samuelson: What's on your mind, Bill?

Jennings: Bob, I have worked for you for four years and I have always enjoyed my work and, in particular, working under you. But I don't think I can continue to function much longer with Jim Stone's group hanging like an albatross around my neck.

Samuelson: I don't understand. What kind of problem are we talking about?

Jennings: Well, my group does its job, and does it well; now, we could do it much better if Don Hammond, in particular, would keep his nose out and let us work once a plan is submitted to us for building. I mean—that crew from Space Suit Studies think they are supposed to supervise our work. My men are proud of their jobs and of their work. But we are going to lose some of our best guys pretty soon if this meddling isn't stopped.

Samuelson: Have you discussed this with Stone?

Jennings: No. Jim's difficult to talk to. He looks down his nose at my group because we are not eggheads. One other thing—whenever I make a change that improves the suit, Hammond's crew gets upset, particularly when it is an obvious improvement.

Samuelson: We'll straighten this problem out, Bill, I promise. But what bothers me is that your group and Don's are supposed to work together.

Jennings: Yes, I know. But it has never worked out that way. They simply look over our shoulders and don't think we are competent to work with their precious designs— even when we can make them better—which is almost always.

The conversation was terminated when Samuelson told Bill that he would look into the problem thoroughly. Bill seemed relieved that Samuelson was taking action.

The first thing the next morning, Mr. Samuelson asked Dr. Stone if he would drop by for a chat. Upon Dr. Stone's arrival Mr. Samuelson asked him to be seated and opened the conversation.

Samuelson: Jim, how are things in your area? Any problems with the X-2B suit design?

Stone: No, we are working primarily on the breastplate design right now. I think we are ahead of our target schedule.

Samuelson: Bill mentioned some friction between his men and Don Hammond's group.

Stone: [*Thinking a moment*] Well—you know we have never gotten the support and cooperation from Bill's team that we need to do our job. Don's team has to have a significant amount of cooperation from Applications in order to do its job. We need to be able to work with Bill's group, to be there to make changes and alterations as needed. Their job is to build to our specifications and let them go from there. We have to provide continuing guidance, and Bill just won't accept it. On top of all this, Bill seems intent on putting his personal touch on each piece of hardware they build.

Samuelson: I don't understand.

Stone: He makes changes on his own, which alter the specs. His group often comes up with a different product from what we asked for. We can't do anything about it because he won't allow cooperation between our groups.

Samuelson: Are his changes worthwhile?

Stone: Oh, I suppose he has some good ideas. Yes, some of his changes were very imaginative and worthwhile. But the point is that his function is to build and ours is to create designs. His suggestions are sometimes worthwhile, but he should consult me before making any changes. That's why he is there and we are here. Otherwise, why don't we simply change the structure of the organization?

Samuelson: Are there any other problems that you have experienced?

Stone: No, otherwise things are fine. All in all, we don't really have any major problems. As long as everybody does his job and stays within bounds, everything functions fine. As I said before, only when someone usurps another's authority does a problem arise.

Samuelson: Well, thanks, Jim, you've been very helpful. Do you mind if I talk with Don about this problem?

Stone: No, go right ahead.

Mr. Samuelson immediately called in Don Hammond and opened the conversation.

Samuelson: Don, I'll get right to the point. How is the working relationship between your areas and Bill's?

Hammond: What relationship? Those guys won't do anything we say. We don't get along at all.

Samuelson: Why is this?

Hammond: I don't know. Maybe it's a defense mechanism.

Samuelson: Meaning what?

Hammond: Well, Mr. Samuelson, I think they resent us because we are educated. They want to do our jobs and don't seem to realize that they are not qualified. They want to do more than build suits, they seem to want to do our design function. They just aren't qualified. I really think they resent our superior knowledge. I have tried to get Dr. Stone to talk to them or you about this, but he seemed somewhat indifferent. I guess he finally did

something though. Anyway, something has got to be done. We can't do our jobs if we can't give them guidance in the building of our suits.

Samuelson: Are their changes ever worthwhile?

Hammond: No.

Samuelson: Never?

Hammond: Oh, I suppose so . . . sometimes. [*Hesitation.*] But that's not the point. It's not their job. They just aren't qualified to tinker with our designs. Don't they realize that is why we spent all those years getting our degrees? Did I waste my time? If a bunch of guys with no education can do my job, maybe I'd be better off uneducated.

Samuelson: Of course not, Don. You and your team are top notch. But you must, by the very nature of the work, have a working relationship with Bill's group. If they can suggest improvements, all the better.

Hammond: Yes, I guess so. But we can't seem to work together. They don't clear their changes through me or Dr. Stone.

Samuelson: Well, we've never made a definite statement about the arrangement for changes, as far as I can remember.

Hammond: Mr. Samuelson, I think all their recommendations should come through me. I can then study their merits and decide on which ones should be accepted. However, they just are not qualified to design this type of equipment. They should stick to their jobs of building.

Mr. Samuelson closed the conversation by thanking Don for his frankness and promising to take action when he had all the facts.

Left alone, Robert Samuelson pondered this new turn of events. He had thought everything was just fine. The work seemed to be getting done—and now this.

He realized that after four years of the successful operation of Space Support Systems, he was faced with the first real test of his managerial abilities.

41

The Old Stack Problem

The purpose of this exercise is to engage participants in the behavioral dynamics that occur within and between groups in competition. Each group is confronted with developing a solution to the problem described below. Solutions of the groups are to be evaluated for originality and feasibility. Each group should strive to develop the best solution.

STEP 1: *Group Problem-Solving (30 minutes)*

Divide into groups of from four to six persons each. Each group member should read "The Problem" below. The best procedure is for each person to develop a solution independently, and for the group to spend a period of time discussing these solutions without evaluating them. Then the solutions should be evaluated and the best solution adopted.

The problem may be assigned in advance of class in order to give students more time to develop solutions. However, the final discussion and selection process should be done as a group in the classroom.

STEP 2: *Select Judges and Spokespeople (5 minutes)*

Each group should select one member to serve on a panel of judges to select the best solution. A spokesperson must also be selected to present the solution to the panel of judges.

STEP 3: *Present Solutions (15 minutes)*

Spokespersons for each group will present their group solution to the judges and the remainder of the class. A chalkboard or flip chart should be used to illustrate the solution along with the spokesperson's explanation. The explanation should be brief and concise, and spokespeople may not criticize other solutions. The spokespeople should provide quality arguments in support of their solutions.

STEP 4: *Straw Vote (5 minutes)*

After all group solutions are presented, the judges may think about the solutions for one or two minutes, then judges will state in turn which solution they prefer. *Judges must*

The original source for this exercise could not be identified.

make their judgments independently, without discussion among themselves. Judges are asked simply to state the solution they prefer. They do not explain their reasons for voting. The instructor should record the number of votes given to each solution on the chalkboard or flip chart next to that solution.

STEP 5: *Modified Problem-Solving (10 minutes)*

Student groups re-form and discuss their approach. Judges and spokespersons return to their original groups. At this time, the groups may not change the basic strategy of their solution, but they may provide refinements. Groups are encouraged to compare their solution to other solutions at this point, and may instruct the spokesperson to present weaknesses in other solutions as well as strengths of their own. The group also has the freedom to nominate a new spokesperson or judge at this time.

STEP 6: *Restate Solutions (10 minutes)*

The group spokespeople briefly restate the solutions using the earlier illustration. Minor modifications can be made. Spokespersons are encouraged to point out the strengths of their group's solutions and to criticize other solutions. The goal of the spokespeople is to persuade the judges that their group's solution is best.

STEP 7: *Final Vote*

The judges are given one or two minutes to individually decide for which solution to vote. Judges may not discuss the solutions among themselves, and they must state their vote out loud. The instructor will indicate the number of votes next to each solution's illustration. The solution that receives the most votes is the winner.

STEP 8: *Discussion (15 minutes)*

The class as a whole should reflect back over their experience and discuss what happened.

Students are encouraged to be self-reflective about their feelings toward their own group's solution, toward the judges, and so on. Judges are encouraged to express their feelings about any pressures they felt from the group to vote in a certain way. The instructor or student may also wish to compare their observations to theories of intergroup behavior as illustrated in lectures or readings. The following questions may help guide that discussion.

1. Did any examples of scapegoating occur? Did losing groups express dissatisfaction or unfairness with the judges or the evaluation process?
2. Did any groups put pressure on the judges to act as a representative of their group rather than to vote in an unbiased fashion? Did judges feel pressure to represent their group even if pressure was not overtly expressed?
3. Did any groups develop a superiority complex, wherein they truly believed that their own group solution was best although from an objective perspective the solution may not have been best?
4. What was the reaction of winning versus losing groups? Did winners seem happy and satisfied, while losers seemed discontented with one another or with the exercise?
5. During the second round of presentations, were certain solutions singled out for more criticism? Were these solutions the ones that received the most votes in the straw ballot, as if people were trying to tear down the strongest contender?
6. How does this group exercise compare to functioning of groups in the real world? These groups existed temporarily, while groups in the real world engage in real competitions and have strong and lasting commitments. Would representatives of real-world groups tend to reflect group wishes or to reach unbiased decisions? How might intergroup difficulties be overcome in organizations?

THE PROBLEM

An explosion has ripped a hole in a brick smokestack. The stack appears to be perfectly safe but a portion of the access ladder has been ripped away and the remainder loosened. Your engineers need to inspect the damage immediately to determine whether the stack may collapse. How do you get one of your engineers up to inspect the hole safely and efficiently?

The smokestack is 140 feet high. The structure next to the smokestack is a water tower. In your solution you should use only those materials in the diagram that follows, including what you assume to be in the truck and sporting goods store.

220

EXHIBIT 41–1 THE PROBLEM

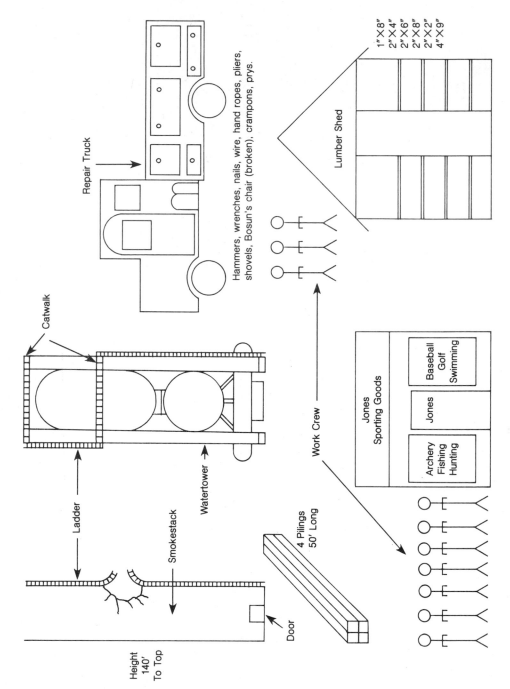

All fixed objects, with the exception of Jones's store, are spatially related as shown in this diagram.

42

Missouri Campus Bitterly Divided over How to 'Reallocate' Funds

On the campus of the University of Missouri here, the signs of spring came late and were decidedly makeshift: a white sheet bearing the spray-painted legend "SOCIAL WORK IS HERE TO STAY" draped from windows in Clark Hall; a crudely lettered placard taped to a glass door in Memorial Union defiantly announcing, "HELL NO, HOME EC WON'T GO!"

Hasty construction accounted for the homemade quality of the signs, for as the academic year drew quickly to a close, many students and faculty members were surprised to find themselves fighting for their academic lives—the survival of their programs.

In a year in which this campus has had to contend with a host of financial problems—some fabricated, critics allege—April was the cruelest month. It was on April 2 that proposals to "reallocate" nearly $12 million in operating funds over the next three years were announced. Among them were recommendations to eliminate two of the university's 14 colleges and to reduce substantially the offerings in five others.

The ensuing controversy divided the campus. "It has set department against department and colleague against colleague," says one dean. "It's civil war, with everyone trying to gore everyone else's bull."

In mid-April, the faculty voted to call for the resignation of Chancellor Barbara S. Uehling if she did not withdraw the proposals.

By the time graduating students were preparing for last week's commencement exercises, the subject of their conversations—whether or not they had jobs—also seemed to be a prime topic of talk among many members of the faculty and staff.

What led to this course of events was a decision last summer by President James C. Olson to take action "to preserve and even enhance the quality of the university in a time of severely limited resources."

"The university has coped with 10 years of inadequate funding by making cuts across the board," he says. "It became clear that a continuation of that policy was a prescription for mediocrity."

Mr. Olson announced last July that the university would attempt to save approximately

Written by Paul Desruisseaux. Reprinted with permission of *The Chronicle of Higher Education*, copyright © 1982.

$16 million over the next three years to finance pay raises as well as library, laboratory, and other improvements. He told the chancellors of the four Missouri campuses that their first priority was to be the development of an adequate compensation plan for the university staff. His plan was supported by the university's Board of Curators.

President Olson's goal is to bring salaries at the university up to the average of those at member institutions of the Big 8 and Big 10 athletic conferences—institutions that, he says, "are comparable to Missouri in mission." At the start of the 1981-82 academic year, Missouri had the lowest salary average in that comparison group, 8.9% below the midpoint.

Mr. Olson instructed the chancellors to find money for salary adjustments "by reducing the quantity of what you do rather than the quality."

That met with approval on the Columbia campus, where Chancellor Uehling has said "the concept of shared poverty is not viable for a competitive university," and where the faculty has been on the record for five years in opposition to across-the-board budget cuts.

The 24,000-student campus, biggest in the system, is scheduled for the largest reductions: as much as $12 million, or about 5% of its operating budget.

The curators adopted procedures for the "discontinuance" of program, and the university established four criteria for reviewing them: overall quality, contribution to the university's mission, need for the program, and financial considerations. Application of the criteria was left up the individual campuses.

"On two occasions I identified to the deans the ways in which we might go about this task," says Provost Ronald F. Bunn, who is faced with reducing the budget for academic programs by $7 million.

'A QUALITY MATRIX'

According to Mr. Bunn, most of the deans suggested that he take on the task. The Faculty Council recommended the same. "This was an administrative job," says David West, the council chairman and a professor of finance. "We wanted the administration to make its proposals, and then we'd take shots at it."

Mr. Bunn reviewed all of the campus's academic programs himself, rating them according to the four criteria established by the president. He compiled what he calls "a quality matrix," which resembles the box score of a baseball game. The programs that ranked lowest he proposed reducing.

Specifically, the provost recommended the elimination of the School of Library and Informational Science and the College of Public and Community Services (with the possible retention of its masters-in-social-work program). He also recommended major reductions in the College of Education, the College of Engineering, the School of Nursing, the College of Home Economics, and the School of Health Related Professions. In some cases the reductions would mean the elimination of one or more departments within those colleges.

All told, campus officials estimated that the cuts in academic programs would affect 2,500 students and as many as 200 faculty and staff members. Since tenure regulations require the university to give tenured faculty members 13 months' notice of plans to eliminate their jobs, the reduction proposals would have little effect on the 1982-83 budget.

When university administrators announced their plans on April 2, those in the academic programs predictably provoked the greatest response.

'IT INFURIATES ME'

An ad hoc committee of faculty members and students was charged with reviewing the provost's recommendations and conducting hearings.

Individuals in the targeted programs have been outspokenly critical of Provost Bunn's judgment.

"We are the only accredited library-science program in Missouri, and it infuriates me—as a citizen as much as anything—that this campus, unilaterally, has made the decision to eliminate programs that exist nowhere else in the state," says Edward P. Miller, dean of the library school. "I don't think the provost could have done a worse job of abrogating the criteria for review if he tried."

Bob G. Woods, dean of the College of Education, who supported the idea of programmatic cuts, says he was prepared to reduce his budget by as much as $500,000, but when he learned that reductions of $1.2 million were required, he changed his mind. "I want the process to be refuted as unnecessary at this time," he says.

Officials in the College of Home Economics charge that the recommendations to eliminate two departments there were based on outdated information. "The decision regarding my program was based on a three-year-old internal-review document," says Kitty G. Dickerson, chairman of the department of clothing and textiles, who is in her first year at Missouri. "I was brought here to strengthen this department. There were 35 recommendations in that internal review, and we have already addressed all but three. But there was never an opportunity to let it be known that we have made this enormous progress."

Martha Jo Martin, assistant dean of home economics, says that eliminating the two departments would cost the college its accreditation and half of its enrollment.

Opposition was not limited to those in programs proposed for reduction. Says Andrew Twaddle, a professor of sociology, "My main concern is not with the actual targeting of programs but the fact that the administration made these decisions with little input from the faculty, except for a select group of its supporters.

"I honestly don't know what the university's real fiscal situation is—there are so many conflicting figures flying around, and no one is backing them up very well," he

adds. "But according to the bylaws of this campus, the faculty is supposed to make academic policy, and when you're talking about what is or is not to be taught at the university, you're talking about policy."

Others are concerned about the impact of the proposals on women and minorities.

"We are assuming that the university is aware of its commitment to affirmative action," says W. L. Moore, an assistant professor of education and chairman of the Black Faculty and Staff Organization. "But we have not been kept informed, and we are very skeptical of all that is being done in this area."

Mr. Moore says his organization has determined that the proposed cuts would affect 63% of the black faculty members. The university's Office of Equal Opportunity says the figure is 33%. The discrepancy is due to the administration's inclusion of nonteaching blacks in its figures, says Mr. Moore. "But the precise number doesn't matter, because even 33% is too high a price to pay," he adds.

Of the campus's 620 black undergraduates, 255 are enrolled in targeted programs, says H. Richard Dozier, coordinator of minority-student services. "Blacks weren't admitted to this institution until 1950, and they make up only 3.7% of the student body," he says. "These cuts would be regressive."

Blacks on the campus have asked the administration for assurances that the university's five-year affirmative-action goals will be met.

There is also some feeling on the campus that faculty salary raises are being used as, in the words of one dean, "a smokescreen" for an attempt to change the institution from a multipurpose university to a research university. One reduction target, home economics, is, according to officials of that college, one of only two areas of study identified in federal farm-bill legislation as being part of the educational responsibility of a land-grant institution.

While some opponents of the proposals were testifying before the review committee, others were mustering support for them.

Students, faculty members, and alumni mounted massive letter-writing and phone-calling campaigns aimed at state legislators and the university's curators. Rallies were held, petitions circulated, press conferences staged. The Missouri State Teachers Association expressed outrage. The State Senate's Education Committee held a hearing.

On April 7, the Columbia campus's student senate passed a resolution denouncing the academic review.

On April 19, the faculty voted 237 to 70 to call for the resignations of the chancellor and the provost if the reduction proposals were not withdrawn. The vote, however, has been criticized—by, among others, Chancellor Uehling herself—for not being a true representation of the sentiments of the campus's 2,038-member faculty. Last November, when the faculty voted against midyear salary increases if they were to come at the expense of campus jobs, more than 800 members cast ballots.

THE 'POINT MAN'

The author of the resignation resolution, George V. Boyle, says he believes the vote was representative.

"We should not be cannibalizing ourselves in order to give people raises," says Mr. Boyle, director of labor education, a program not affected by the provost's proposal. "When you encounter heavy seas and the best plan the captain offers is to lighten the load by throwing crew members overboard, I think the crew has to try and come up with something better."

"Our approach to these reductions," says Provost Bunn, "required that I become the 'point man,' and the discussion stage has subsequently become an adversarial one: The source of the recommendations—me—has become as much a subject of debate as the recommendations themselves. It has also become a highly political one, and I think it's unfortunate that the debate has been brought to the legislature and the curators before we have completed the review process

on campus."

Chancellor Uehling also came in for some personal criticism when the campus learned that she was among the final candidates for the chancellorship of the 19-campus California State University system. She took herself out of the running for that job last week and announced that she was committed to working for policies that would enable the Columbia campus "not simply to survive but to carry into the future even greater strength than before."

The chancellor says she is not surprised by the demonstrations of hostility. "It's a very frightening and painful process," she says. "I can understand the anger on the part of some, but I still think our greater obligation is to the institution as a whole."

Ms. Uehling says that while she will not review or comment on the recommended proposals until they come to her in their final form, she supports the process and is convinced of its necessity.

"For the past five years, the State of Missouri has provided the university with budget increases that have amounted to only one-half the rate of inflation," she says. "When I came, the faculty was already on the record in opposition to across-the-board cuts to provide salary raises, and we must bring salaries up to attract and retain quality people. We *have* lost some good people.

"We have no hidden agenda. Our only agenda is our determination to take charge of our own fate. We are trying to anticipate the future so that we won't have to engage in crisis kind of planning. There are enough signs of an impending erosion of our quality to make us want to get ahead and start doing what we do smaller and better."

There have also been signs that the state can't afford to support the university to any greater extent. Missouri voters in 1980 passed an amendment prohibiting the legislature from increasing appropriations unless there were corresponding growth in the state economy. In 1981, Missouri ranked forty-sixth in state-tax-revenue growth, one of the reasons the governor, on two occasions, withheld portions of the university's budget totaling 13%.

Nevertheless, some critics charge that salary increases—if they are essential now—could be provided for next year without eliminating programs, since there has been a slight increase in the state appropriation from what was originally expected, and a 17% hike in student fees.

"If you take a short-term view, it's possible to conclude that we could have an acceptable level of salary adjustment for the coming year," says Mr. Bunn. "That isn't the case if you're looking ahead. Some on campus feel that it isn't important for us to strengthen our salary structure, but in my judgment that is a very narrow view of the aspirations this campus should have for itself."

To be sure, there is faculty support for the administration. "I think the faculty who approved of this strategy previously ought to be heard from again," says John Kuhlman, a professor of economics. "I don't think we can afford to sit back and watch a few departments create this big fight with the provost."

Adds Sam Brown, chairman of the psychology department, "It would be dfficult to find anyone to say they'd favor the cannibalization of their colleagues' jobs for the sake of a salary raise. But ignoring the source of funds, I can say as a department chairman that one of the major problems I face is insufficient salary increments for faculty."

OTHER IMPROVEMENTS SOUGHT

According to Provost Bunn, when salary raises are given out, they will not be distributed uniformly but will be based on individual merit and the salary market in the particular field.

While salaries will have the highest claim on the "reallocated" funds, the provost also hopes there will be enough money to strengthen equipment and expense budgets —"to bring them back to at least the real-dollar level of three years ago."

The provost said he would consider seriously the advice offered by the committee reviewing his proposals. What is not an option, in his view, is to back away from the $7 million in savings that his proposals would provide.

When it reported to the provost May 6, however, the review committee announced that it had voted to weaken the effect of all but one of the proposed reductions. Mr. Bunn is expected to submit his final recommendations to the chancellor by the end of this week.

The Board of Curators, at meetings on May 6 and 7, conducted lengthy discussions of the reallocation process underway at the Columbia campus. The result, William T. Doak, president of the board, told the press, was that the curators were so divided on the question that had a vote been taken on the proposals they would have been rejected.

"We are trying to plan for a very uncertain future," says President Olson, "and I'm not sure we've yet found the mechanism for doing that. We are seeking it."

Chancellor Uehling is expected to submit her reallocation proposals to President Olson sometime in June. The curators are scheduled to vote on the proposals in July.

"The board's resistance to any program eliminations has certainly given those who favor such a course of action cause for pause," says the Faculty Council's David West, who has supported the process from the outset. "There has been much more visible and vocal opposition to the process in the past four weeks than there had been support for it up to that time."

On the Columbia campus, faculty members were circulating petitions calling for votes of confidence and of no confidence in the administration. Mr. West says he is advising those faculty members not to call for campuswide votes at this time.

"There has already been too much confrontation, and faculty votes would just prolong it," he says. "I think everyone should try to gather additional information and rethink his position. And try to find some means by which all of this division can be mitigated."

43

The Air Force A-7D
Brake Problem

Mr. Vandivier: In the early part of 1967, the B. F. Goodrich Wheel & Brake Plant at Troy, Ohio, received an order from the Ling-Temco-Vought Co. of Dallas, Texas, to supply wheels and brakes for the A-7D aircraft, built by LTV for the Air Force.

The tests on the wheels and brakes were to be conducted in accordance with the requirements of military specification Mil-W-5013G as prepared and issued by the U.S. Air Force and to the requirements set forth by LTV Specification Document 204-16-37D.

The wheels were successfully tested to the specified requirements, but the brake, manufactured by Goodrich under BEG part No. 2-1162-3, was unable to meet the required tests.

The laboratory tests specified for the brake were divided into two categories: dynamic brake tests and static brake tests.

The dynamic brake tests basically consisted of 45 simulated normal energy stops, five overload energy stops, and one worn-brake maximum energy stop, sometimes called a rejected take-off, or RTO. These simulated stops were to be conducted on one

brake assembly with no change in brake lining to be allowed during the test. In addition, a maximum energy brake stop (or RTO) was to be conducted on a brake containing new linings, and still another series of tests called a turnaround capability test was to be performed.

The turnaround capability test consisted of a series of taxis, simulated takeoffs, flight periods, and landings, and time schedule for the turnaround test was supplied by LTV to coincide with conditions under which the A-7D brake might operate on a typical mission.

Generally speaking, the brake passed all the static brakes tests, but the brake could not and did not pass any of the dynamic tests I have just described, with the exception of the new brake maximum energy stop.

During the first few attempts to qualify the brake to the dynamic tests, the brake ran out of lining material after a few stops had been completed and the tests were terminated. Attempts were made to secure a lining material that would hold up during the grueling 51-stop test, but to no avail. Although I had

From the Hearing before the Subcommittee on Economy in Government of the Joint Economic Committee of the Congress of the United States, 91st Congress, August 13, 1969.

been aware for several months that great difficulty was being experienced with the A-7D brake, it was not until April 11, 1968, almost a full year after qualification testing had begun, that I became aware of how these tests were being conducted.

The thirteenth attempt at qualification was being conducted under B. F. Goodrich Internal Test No. T-1867.

On the morning of April 11, Richard Gloor, who was the test engineer assigned to the A-7D project, came to me and told me he had discovered that some time during the previous 24 hours, instrumentation used to record brake pressure had been miscalibrated *deliberately* so that while the instumentation showed that a pressure of 1,000 pounds per square inch had been used to conduct brake stop numbers 46 and 47 (two overload energy stops) 1,100 p.s.i. had actually been applied to the brakes. Maximum pressure available on the A-7D is 1,000 p.s.i.

Mr. Gloor further told me he had questioned instrumentation personnel about the miscalibration and had been told they were asked to do so by Searle Lawson, a design engineer on the A-7D.

Chairman Proxmire: Is this the gentleman who is with you now, Mr. Vandivier?

Mr. Vandivier: That is correct. I subsequently questioned Lawson who admitted he had ordered the instruments miscalibrated at the direction of a superior.

Upon examining the log sheets kept by laboratory personnel I found that other violations of the test specifications had occurred.

For example, after some of the overload stops, the brake had been disassembled and the three stators or stationary members of the brake had been taken to the plant toolroom for rework and, during an earlier part of the test, the position of elements within the brake had been reversed to distribute the lining wear more evenly.

Additionally, instead of braking the dynamometer to a complete stop as required by military specifications, pressure was released

when the wheel and brake speed had decelerated to 10 miles per hour.

The reason for this, I was later told, was that the brakes were experiencing severe vibrations near the end of the stops, causing excessive lining wear and general deterioration of the brake.

All these incidents were in clear violation of military specifications and general industry practice.

I reported these violations to the test lab supervisor, Mr. Ralph Gretzinger, who reprimanded instrumentation personnel and stated that under no circumstance would intentional miscalibration of instruments be tolerated.

As for the other discrepancies noted in test procedures, he said that he was aware that they were happening but that as far as he was concerned the tests could not, in view of the way they were being conducted, be classified as qualification tests.

Later that same day, the worn-brake, maximum energy stop was conducted on the brake. The brake was landed at a speed of 161 m.p.h. and the pressure was applied. The dynamometer rolled a distance 16,800 *feet* before coming to rest. The elapsed stopping time was 141 seconds. By computation, this stop time shows the aircraft would have traveled over 3 miles before stopping.

Within a few days, a typewritten copy of the test logs of test T-1867 was sent to LTV to assure LTV that a qualified brake was almost ready for delivery.

Virtually every entry in this so-called copy of the test logs was drastically altered. As an example, the stop time for the worn-brake maximum energy stop was changed from 141 seconds to a mere 46.8 seconds.

On May 2, 1968, the fourteenth attempt to qualify the brakes was begun, and Mr. Lawson told me that he had been informed by both Mr. Robert Sink, project manager at Goodrich —I am sorry, Mr. Sink is project manager— and Mr. Russell Van Horn, project manager at Goodrich, that "Regardless of what the brake does on test, we're going to qualify it."

Chairman Proxmire: What was that?

Mr. Vandivier: The statement was, "Regardless of what the brake does on test, we're going to qualify it."

He also said that the latest instructions he had received were to the effect that, if the data from this latest test turned out worse than did test T-1867, then we would write our report based on T-1867.

Chairman Proxmire: The statement was made by whom?

Mr. Vandivier: Mr. Lawson told me this statement was made to him by Mr. Robert Sink, project manager, and Mr. Russell Van Horn, project manager.

During this latest and final attempt to qualify the four-rotor brake, the same illegal procedures were used as had been used on attempt No. 13. Again after 30 stops had been completed, the positions of the friction members of the brake were reversed to distribute wear more evenly. After each stop, the wheel was removed from the brake and the accumulated dust was blown out. During each stop, pressure was released when the deceleration had reached 10 miles per hour.

By these and other irregular procedures the brake was nursed along until the 45 normal energy stops had been completed, but by this time the friction surfaces of the brakes were almost bare; that is, there was virtually no lining left on the brake. This lack of lining material introduced another problem.

The pistons that actuate the brake by forcing the friction surfaces together were almost at the end of their allowable travel, and it was feared that during the overload stops the pistons might actually pop out of their sockets within the brake, allowing brake fluid to spray the hot surfaces, resulting in fire.

Therefore, a metal spacer was inserted in the brake between the pressure plate and the piston housing.

This spacer served to make up for the lack of friction material and to keep the pistons in place. To provide room for the spacer, the adjuster assemblies were removed from the brake.

The five overload stops were conducted without the adjuster assemblies and with the spacer in place.

After stop number 48—the third overload stop—temperatures in the brake were so high that the fuse plug, a safety device that allows air to escape from the tire to prevent blowout, melted and allowed the tire to deflate.

The same thing happened after stop number 49—the fourth overload stop. Both these occurrences were highly irregular and in direct conflict with the performance criteria of the military requirements.

Chairman Proxmire: I understand you have a picture of this that might help us see it.

Mr. Vandivier: Yes.

Mr. Proxmire: Do you want to show that to us now?

Mr. Vandivier: I was going to show it here just a little bit later.

Chairman Proxmire: Go ahead.

Mr. Vandivier: For the worn-brake maximum energy stop, the adjusters were replaced in the brake and a different spacer was used between the pressure plate and the piston housing.

Now I have a copy, a picture of this brake just before it went on the maximum energy test, and here you may see at the top is the additional spacer that has been added to get sufficient braking action on the brake.

Chairman Proxmire: Who took that picture?

Mr. Vandivier: That was taken with a Polaroid camera. I am not sure———

Chairman Proxmire: I think it is only fair to the committee, Mr. Conable and the committee, to ask you about it later. You go ahead and we will ask questions.

Mr. Vandivier: All right.

In addition to these highly questionable practices, a turnaround capability test, or simulated mission test, was conducted incorrectly due to a human error. When the error was later discovered, no corrections were made.

While these tests were being conducted, I was asked by Mr. Lawson to begin writing a qualification report for the brake. I flatly refused and told Mr. Gretzinger, the lab supervisor, who was my superior, that I could not write such a report because the brake had not been qualified.

He agreed and he said that no one in the laboratory was going to issue such a report unless a brake was actually qualified in accordance with the specification and using standard operating procedures.

He said that he would speak to his own supervisor, the manager of the technical services section, Mr. Russell Line, and get the matter settled at once.

He consulted Mr. Line and assured me that both had concurred in the decision not to write a qualification report.

I explained to Lawson that I had been told not to write the report and that the only way such a report could be written was to falsify test data.

Mr. Lawson said that he was well aware of what was required but that he had been ordered to get a report written, regardless of how or what had to be done.

He stated that, if I would not write the report, he would have to, and he asked if I would help him gather the test data and draw up the various engineering curves and graphic displays that are normally included in a report.

I asked Mr. Gretzinger, my superior, if this was all right and he agreed. As long as I was only assisting in the preparation of the data, it would be permissible.

Both Lawson and I worked on the elaborate curves and logs in the report for nearly a month. During this time we both frankly discussed the moral aspects of what we were doing, and we agreed that our actions were unethical and probably illegal.

Several times during that month I discussed the A-7D testing with Mr. Line and asked him to consult his superiors in Akron to prevent a false qualification report from being issued. Mr. Line declined to do so and advised me that it would be wise to just do my work and keep quiet.

I told him of the extensive irregularities during testing and suggested that the brake was actually dangerous and, if allowed to be installed on an aircraft, might cause an accident.

Mr. Line said he thought I was worrying too much about things that did not really concern me and advised me to just "do what you're told."

About the first of June———

Chairman Proxmire: You skipped one line here.

Mr. Vandivier: Yes.

Chairman Proxmire: You said, "I asked him"———

Mr. Vandivier: Yes. I asked Mr. Line if his conscience would hurt him if such a thing caused the death of a pilot and this is when he replied that I was worrying about too many things that did not concern me and advised me to "do what you're told."

About the first of June 1968, Mr. Gretzinger asked if I was finished with the graphic data and said he had been advised by the chief engineer, Mr. H. C. Sunderman, that when the data were finished they were to be delivered to him—Sunderman—and he would instruct someone in the engineering department to actually write the report. Accordingly, when I had finished with the data, I gave it to Mr. Gretzinger who immediately took it from the room. Within a few minutes, he was back and was obviously angry.

He said that Mr. Sunderman had told him no one in the engineering department had time to write the report and that we would have to do it ourselves.

At this point, Mr. Line came into the room demanding to know "What the hell is going on." Mr. Gretzinger explained the situation again and said he would not allow such a report to be issued by the lab.

Mr. Line then turned to me and said he was "sick of hearing about this damned report. Write the———thing and shut up about it."

Chairman Proxmire: Let me ask you, you had this in quotes. Did you make a note of this at the time?

Mr. Vandivier: Yes.

Chairman Proxmire: Do you have your notes with you?

Mr. Vandivier: No. I have notes with me, yes. I am not sure if I have this note or not, but I have notes with me.

Chairman Proxmire: All right.

Mr. Vandivier: When he had left, Mr. Gretzinger and I discussed the position we were in, and Mr. Gretzinger said that we both should have resigned a long time ago. He added that there was little to do now except write the report.

Accordingly, I wrote the report, but in the conclusion, I stated that the brake had "not" met either the intent or the requirements of the specifications and was therefore "not" qualified.

When the final report was typewritten and ready for publication, the two "nots" in the conclusion had been eliminated, thereby changing the entire meaning of the conclusion.

I would like to point out at this time the various discrepancies between the military standards and procedures and the qualification tests actually conducted:

1. Brake pressure was cut on all stops at 10 miles per hour and the wheel allowed to coast to a stop.
2. The five overload stops were conducted with a spacer between the pressure plate and the piston housing.
3. The lining carriers used for the test were specially made with an additional 0.030 of an inch lining material. This was done to assure sufficient lining material on the carriers.
4. Stators in the brake were physically reversed after stop 30 and remained in these positions throughout the test.
5. The worn-brake RTO was conducted with an additional pressure plate between the

original pressure plate and piston housing. This was done because allowable piston travel had been exceeded and without the additional pressure plate the brakes could not have been applied.

Mr. Chairman, the next two sentences of my printed statement contain a typographical error, words have been omitted and I would like to insert those in at this time.

6. Prior to the worn-brake RTO [maximum energy stop], the inside diameter of the lining carriers was increased by 0.120 of an inch to alleviate the severe shrinkage of the lining carriers on the torque tube caused by overheating.
7. On stops 48 and 49 [overload stops 3 and 4], the fuse plug eutectic material—material designed to melt at a specified temperature—melted, allowing the tire to deflate.
8. The torque plate and keyway inserts for the wheel had their drive surfaces chromeplated because of extreme wear. This was not a production process on this brake.
9. Before the start of the tests and at teardowns the keyway inserts were sprayed with molybdenum disulfate (a lubricant).
10. After every stop the wheel and tire assembly were removed from the brake, the brake was blown out with high-velocity air, and the keyway inserts and heat shield were wiped clean.
11. After stops 10, 20, 30, 40, 45, and 50 the brake was disassembled and the expansion slots in the lining carriers were cleaned of excess lining material and opened. Excess materials removed from between the segments in the rotors and the lugs and links on the rotors were cleaned and radiused by machining processes. This in a sense is equivalent to a minor overhaul in the brake linings.

In addition there were at least four other major irregularities in the test procedure.

These, gentlemen, are only irregularities that occurred during the testing. As for the report itself, more than 80 false entries were made in the body of the report and in the logs.

Many, many of the elaborate engineering curves attached to the report were complete and total fabrications, based not on what had actually occurred, but on information that would fool both LTV and the Air Force.

I have mentioned already that the turn-around capability test that was supposed to determine what temperatures might be experienced by the brake during a typical flight mission had been misconducted through a human error on the part of the test lab operator.

Rather than rerun this very important test, which would have taken only some six hours to complete, it was decided to manufacture the data.

This we did, and the result was some very convincing graphic curves. These curves were supposed to demonstrate to LTV and the Air Force exactly what the temperatures in the brakes had been during each minute of the simulated mission.

They were completely false and based only on data that would be acceptable to the customers.

I could spend the entire day here discussing the various elaborate falsifications that went into this report but I feel that, by now, the picture is clear.

The report was finally issued on June 5, 1968, and almost immediately flight tests on the brake were begun at Edwards Air Force Base in California.

Mr. Lawson was sent by Goodrich to witness these tests, and when he returned, he described various mishaps that had occurred during the flight tests and he expressed the opinion to me that the brake was dangerous.

That same afternoon, I contacted my attorney and, after describing the situation to him, asked for his advice.

He advised me that, while I was technically not guilty of committing a fraud, I was certainly part of a conspiracy to defraud. He further suggested a meeting with U.S. Attorney Roger Makely in Dayton, Ohio.

I agreed to this and my attorney said that he would arrange an appointment with the federal attorney.

I discussed my attorney's appraisal of our situation with Mr. Lawson, but I did not, at this time, tell him of the forthcoming visit with Mr. Makely. Mr. Lawson said he would like to consult with my attorney and I agreed to arrange this.

Shortly thereafter, Mr. Lawson went to the Dallas offices of LTV, and, while he was gone, my attorney called and said that, upon advice of the U.S. attorney, he had arranged an interview with the Dayton office of the FBI.

I related the details of the A-7D qualification to Mr. Joseph Hathaway of the FBI.

He asked if I could get Mr. Lawson to confirm my story and I replied that I felt Mr. Lawson would surely do this.

Upon Mr. Lawson's return from Dallas, I asked him if he still wished to consult my attorney and he answered, "I most certainly do."

Mr. Lawson and I went to the attorney's office, and Mr. Lawson was persuaded to speak to the FBI.

I wish to emphasize that at no time prior to Mr. Lawson's decision to speak to the FBI was he aware that I had already done so. His decision and mine were both the result of our individual actions.

Mr. Lawson related his own story to Mr. Hathaway, who advised us to keep our jobs and to tell no one that we had been to see him. I might add here that he advised us that an investigation would be made.

About this time the Air Force demanded that Goodrich produce its raw data from the tests. This Goodrich refused to do, claiming that the raw data was proprietary information.

Goodrich management decided that, since pressure was being applied by the Air Force, a conference should be arranged with LTV management and engineering staff. A pre-conference meeting was set for Goodrich personnel to go over the questionable points in the report.

On Saturday, July 27, 1968, Mr. Robert Sink, Mr. Lawson, Mr. John Warren—A-7D project engineer—and I met and went over the discrepant items contained in the qualification report. Each point was discussed at great length and a list of approximately 40 separate discrepancies was compiled. These, we were told by Mr. Sink, would be revealed to LTV personnel the following week.

However, by the time of the meeting with LTV, only a few days later, the list of discrepancies had been cut by Mr. Sink from 43 items to a mere three.

Mr. Chairman, during this meeting Mr. Lawson took from the blackboard at the Goodrich conference room word for word listing of all these discrepancies. This contains the 43 items I have just mentioned. I would like to enter this into the record and also enter the subsequent list of three major discrepancies that later came out of this meeting.

Chairman Proxmire: Do you have copies of those documents?

Mr. Vandivier: Yes, I do have.

Mr. Vandivier: The following two-month period was one of a constant running battle with LTV and the Air Force, during which time the Air Force refused final approval of the qualification report and demanded a confrontation with Goodrich about supplying raw data.

On October 8, another meeting was held, again with Mr. Sink, Mr. Lawson, Mr. Warren, and myself present.

This was only one day prior to a meeting with Air Force personnel, and Mr. Sink said that he had called the meeting "so that we are all coordinated and tell the same story." Mr. Sink said that LTV personnel would be present at the meeting with the Air Force and our policy would be to "let LTV carry the ball." Mr. Sink appeared to be especially concerned because Mr. Bruce Tremblay, the Air Force engineer most intimate with A-7D brake, would be present at the meeting, and it was

felt at B. F. Goodrich that Mr. Tremblay was already suspicious.

Mr. Sink warned us that "Mr. Tremblay will probably be at his antagonistic best." He added that the Air Force had wanted to meet at the Goodrich plant, but that we—Goodrich—couldn't risk having them that close to the raw data. "We don't want those guys in the plant," Mr. Sink said.

What happened at the meeting with the Air Force, I do not know. I did not attend.

On October 18, I submitted my resignation to Goodrich effective November 1.

I would like to read that resignation. This is addressed to Russell Line, manager of technical services:

In May of this year I was directed to participate in the preparation of qualification report for the A7D, 26031. As you are aware this report contained numerous deliberate and willful misrepresentations, which according to legal counsel constitutes fraud and therefore exposes both myself and others to criminal charges of conspiracy to defraud. In view of this fact, I must terminate my employment with the B. F. Goodrich Company effective November 1, 1968. I regret that this decision must be made, but I am sure that you will agree that events of the past seven months have created an atmosphere of deceit and distrust in which it is impossible to work effectively and productively.

On October 25 I was told that my resignation was to be accepted immediately, and within 20 minutes I had left the Goodrich Co.

Gentlemen, I am well aware that the B. F. Goodrich Co. is a well-known and well-respected firm with an almost impeccable reputation. I am equally aware that the charges I have made are serious. However, everything I have said to you is completely true and I can prove my statements with documentary evidence.

The unfortunate part of a situation such as this is that, invariably, many innocent persons are made to suffer along with the guilty. Therefore, I should like to emphasize that three people whom I have mentioned here are, I feel, completely blameless and were implicated in this situation through no fault of their own.

Mr. Ralph Gretzinger from the very start fought this situation and tried very hard to use his influence to stop the issuance of the false report. Mr. Richard Gloor, in his own handwriting, listed the irregularities occurring during the test and was outspoken in his opposition to the report. This list was shown to B.F. Goodrich management.

Mr. Lawson, of course, was in a position similar to mine and the fact that he voluntarily disclosed the details of the A-7D test program to the FBI and GAO should stand upon its own merits. Thank you.

Chairman Proxmire: Thank you, Mr. Vandivier.

Mr. Lawson, you have heard the statement as read and I take it you have had a chance to see the full statement?

Mr. Lawson: No, I have not.

Chairman Proxmire: The statement you have just heard read by Mr. Vandivier, do you agree with it fully or in part or do you disagree and can you tell us your reaction to it?

Mr. Lawson: The factual data that Mr. Vandivier has presented is correct, to the best of my knowledge.

Chairman Proxmire: There is no statement that you heard him read with which you would disagree in any part?

Mr. Lawson: I really don't know. I haven't read the complete text.

Chairman Proxmire: Would you disagree with any part of what you heard him read right now in your presence?

Mr. Lawson: No, I don't believe there is.

Chairman Proxmire: Now I would like to ask you, Mr. Vandivier, you gave us a picture about which we may want to ask other witnesses, so I want to qualify that picture. As far as we know, it is a picture that you say was taken of the brake that was tested?

Mr.Vandivier: That is correct.

Chairman Proxmire: But we would like to make sure that we qualify that because it is going to be used later.

Now would you describe again, tell us how you came to have that, when the picture was taken and so forth?

Mr. Vandivier: Yes. This was taken just approximately an hour and a half or two hours before the worn-brake RTO was conducted. This was for the qualification test, and I asked the plant photographer if he would take a Polaroid picture of this for me. He did so, and I took the Polaroid shot and I had it enlarged. I have a certification on this. I had the original Polaroid negative. I have the negatives that the photographer used.

Chairman Proxmire: Will you give us the date, the time that was taken, if you have that?

Mr. Vandivier: If you will give me just a moment, I can.

Chairman Proxmire: Meanwhile, may I ask Mr. Lawson, while Mr. Vandivier is looking up that, if you can confirm that this is in fact the picture of the A-7D brake that was undergoing qualification?

Mr. Lawson: Yes, it appears to be.

Chairman Proxmire: It appears to be?

Mr. Lawson: I would say it is.

Chairman Proxmire: It is. All right. Well, you can supply that a little later for the record, Mr. Vandivier.

Mr. Vandivier: All right.

Chairman Proxmire: Let me ask you this. You say you worked for Goodrich for six years?

Mr. Vandivier: That is correct.

Chairman Proxmire: What was your previous employment before you were hired by Goodrich?

Mr. Vandivier: I worked for the Food Machinery and Chemical Corp. at their Newport, Ind., plant.

Chairman Proxmire: Technical writer is a professional position that requires considerable competence and ability. What experience did you have that would qualify you to be a technical writer?

Mr. Vandivier: I had none.

Chairman Proxmire: Did you immediately go into this or did they give you a training course?

Mr. Vandivier: No. I had no training course. I kind of worked into the job I guess. It was—

Chairman Proxmire: You were not hired to be a technical—

Mr. Vandivier: No, I was actually hired as an instrumentation technician, and Goodrich engaged in a mass changeover of instrumentation techniques, and they wanted degreed people for this kind of work so I was switched over to the technical writing section.

Chairman Proxmire: How long did you work as a technical writer?

Mr. Vandivier: Approximately three years.

Chairman Proxmire: Three years. How many reports did you prepare for B. F. Goodrich?

Mr. Vandivier: At least 100, possibly 150.

Chairman Proxmire: Were any of these reports questioned in any way?

Mr. Vandivier: No, they were not.

Chairman Proxmire: Were they accepted? Did you get any reaction at all favorable or unfavorable in these reports that you wrote?

Mr. Vandivier: Occasionally we would get a question from the manufacturer about a wording or a clarification, and these would be supplied.

Chairman Proxmire: Was there any question as to the accuracy or competence of the report?

Mr. Vandivier: No, none whatsoever.

Chairman Proxmire: Were you criticized at any time that the reports were not adequate?

Mr. Vandivier: No, I was not.

Chairman Proxmire: In your statement, you say, "Accordingly I wrote the report but in the conclusion I stated that the brake had not met either the intent or the requirement of the specification and therefore was 'not qualified.' Then you add "When the final report was typewritten and ready for publication the two 'nots' in the conclusion had been eliminated, thereby changing the entire meaning of the conclusion."

Now it seems to me that you have testified before this that you and Mr. Lawson constructed this report based on your instructions from your superiors, that this report was false in many ways that you knew, and that the report seemed to qualify the brakes, at least that was the impression I got, and yet you concluded, and I quote, "I stated the brake had not met either the intent or the requirement of the specifications and therefore was not qualified."

Doesn't it seem on the basis of your testimony that this is somewhat inconsistent? In other words, you had written a report that would qualify the brake and then you come in with a one-sentence conclusion in which you say it was not qualified? Do you see what I am getting at?

Mr. Vandivier: Yes. Mr. Chairman, this was probably one final gesture of defiance. I was so aggravated and sick at having to write this thing. I knew the words "not" would be taken out, but I put them in to show that, I do not know, they had bent me to their will but they had not broken me yet. It was a foolish thing perhaps to do, but it was showing that I still had a little spirit left. At least this is how I felt.

Chairman Proxmire: What did you think your superiors at B. F. Goodrich would do when they found the "not qualified" in your report, when you had been told to show the brake qualified?

Mr. Vandivier: I knew it would be changed probably without question. I was not worried if you are trying—I was not worried at being called on the carpet for this. I knew they would just merely change it.

Chairman Proxmire: Was this the only time in the three years you worked as a technical writer with Goodrich, the only time that you made false entries into a report of manufacture?

Mr. Vandivier: Yes, it was.

Chairman Proxmire: So far as you know B. F. Goodrich's record is clean in every other respect with your experience?

Mr. Vandivier: With me—

Chairman Proxmire: With this single incidence being an exception?

Mr. Vandivier: That is right; that is correct.

Chairman Proxmire: They had never before asked you to do this?

Mr. Vandivier: No.

Chairman Proxmire: Do you know of any other technical writers you worked with, in which Goodrich had instructed them to take this kind of action?

Mr. Vandivier: If they had done this, I would know nothing of it. I could not say.

Chairman Proxmire: This was the only incident?

Mr. Vandivier: Yes, as far as I know, the only incident in which I was asked to do this.

Chairman Proxmire: What was the normal procedure at Goodrich when a brake failed to meet all the requirements or when normal procedures were not followed?

Mr. Vandivier: If for some reason or other the normal procedure was not followed or the brake simply could not meet a particular requirement, the report was written and a deviation was requested from the manufacturer, which in other words is a request to allow him to accept the brake with these noted deviations from the procedure.

I might add that there are many times that a brake just could not meet a certain requirement specified by the manufacturer, and it was always the customary procedure to ask for a deviation, and many times it was granted or some sort of a compromise was reached between the manufacturer and Goodrich.

Chairman Proxmire: I cannot understand what was going through the minds of Goodrich's management the way you have told the story. I cannot see what they have to gain by passing on a brake that would not meet qualifications. Somewhere along the line this is going to be shown as an unqualified brake. As you pointed out, it might be under disastrous circumstances, but in any event Goodrich would suffer and suffer badly by passing on a brake to LTV or the Air Force that was not going to work. What is their motivation?

Mr. Vandivier: I cannot tell you what their motivation is. I can tell you what I feel was behind this.

Chairman Proxmire: All right.

Mr. Vandivier: I feel in the beginning stages of this program someone made a mistake and refused to admit that mistake, and to hide his stupidity or his ignorance, or his pride, or whatever it was, he simply covered up, you know, with more false statements, false information, and at the time it came time to deliver this brake, Goodrich was so far down the road that there was nothing else to do.

They had no time to start over; I think it was a matter not of company policy but of company politics. I think that probably three or four persons within the Goodrich organization at Troy were responsible for this. I do not believe for a moment that the corporate officials in Akron knew that this was going on.

44

The Plane The Pentagon Couldn't Stop

Strapped into a firm, narrow reclining seat, with a green radar screen about the size of a battery-powered portable television between his legs, a fighter jock becomes part of a more evolved organism. He can sit there like a man in a La-Z-Boy, his arms on the armrests, and with his left hand around a stubby black throttle mounted just below the rim of the cockpit, he can summon up 25,000 pounds of thrust; if he releases the brakes and pulls back the small control stick clutched in his right hand, in two minutes he can be traveling at twice the speed of sound eight miles above the earth. He can maneuver so sharply that his head weighs 135 pounds under a force nine times that of gravity while a computer constantly trims the tail and extends the flaps and keeps the plane within the borders of its aerodynamic limits, and he still won't need to move his g-force-imprisoned arms. With a flick of his left thumb on a dime-size gray plastic button on the throttle, he can electronically follow a target on the ground or in the air without ever looking down at the instrument panel just above his knees. With his right hand still on the stick, he can fire a 20mm rapid-fire cannon with his right forefinger, and by pressing a tiny red button with his right thumb, he can fire two heat-seeking missiles or unload five tons of conventional bombs. And if necessary, he can reach down to his right, flip a toggle switch indicated by a red label neatly inscribed "Nuclear Consent," pump the little red "pickle" button with his right thumb, and contribute two hydrogen fusion warheads to the unthinkable.

Thirty thousand people work inside the Pentagon, a walled city where standing armies of bureaucrats, enclaves of analysts, and isolated pockets of free-thinkers make up the Byzantine hierarchy of military decision-making. Routing new ideas through the Pentagon's bureaucratic meanders and ideological roadblocks is an intricate, seldom mastered craft, and John Boyd and Pierre Sprey, the first of the F-16's many architects, are two of the few to practice it with any claim of success.

Boyd and Sprey are an uncommon pair. Sprey is smooth, relaxed, with swept-back silver hair, and is given to blue blazers, starched

Written by Michael Ennis. Reprinted with permission from the June issue of *Texas Monthly*, copyright © 1981, by *Texas Monthly*.

shirts, and silk ascots. He drives a souped-up Fiat convertible and runs his own private environmental and military consulting firm. He has an undergraduate degree in aeronautical engineering from Yale and a master's degree in mathematical statistics from Cornell, and he worked for Grumman Aircraft Engineering Corporation before doing a stint as a full-time Pentagon analyst in the late 1960s. Today he is consulting on air and ground warfare for the Pentagon ("I've been interviewing German World War II armored commanders," he says clinically. "Brilliant men. Much smarter tactically than our own officers") and is proposing new tactics and radically new attack aircraft for the support of Army infantry and armored units.

John Boyd is a hulking ex-fighter pilot with a seamed, intense, craggy countenance; he wears down-at-the-heels desert boots and casual clothes that look like castoffs from Goodwill. His colorful ways have earned him a variety of nicknames, including Forty-Second Boyd, for the speed with which he dispatched opponents in aerial combat exercises; the Ghetto Colonel, because he lives on a retired colonel's pay with his wife and four children in one of Washington's less affluent neighborhoods; and Genghis John, for his warlike pursuit of the ultimate battle plan. Lately, though, people are starting to refer to him as "the next Clausewitz"; they think Boyd may just be the most significant military theoretician since the nineteenth-century Prussian genius.

Boyd, Sprey, and the group that is gravitating toward their views could be on the verge of stirring a national debate over what they see as a misplaced emphasis in American military spending. But both men, for all their energy and convictions, share a surprising cynicism. They are veterans of the Pentagon's internecine battles, and they know that victories are long in arriving and often short in duration. And should they forget that, they have only to look at their first victory and see what might have been, but isn't, the greatest fighter plane ever built, the plane that might

have changed the history of air power. They have only to look at the F-16.

Ever since World War I, when airplanes proved over considerable skepticism that they were indeed effective instruments of mayhem, military minds have debated the virtues of fighters versus bombers. In the early years of military aircraft, the argument went like this: Bombers have the potential to make war production, troop supply, and daily life very difficult for the enemy below; give a belligerent enough bombers, it is argued, and his enemy will soon have neither the will nor the capacity to fight. Fighters, on the other hand, while suitable for supporting ground troops in the thick of front-line action, cannot deliver those heavy strategic blows. But their speed and maneuverability do give them one significant advantage: they can shoot down lots of other airplanes, especially fat, slow-moving targets like bombers. With enough fighters, a combatant can swat the enemy from the skies, then proceed at leisure to the destruction of his cities and the harassment of his troops.

It was an argument over production as well as tactics. Bombers are airborne leviathans, with the huge wings, sturdy fuselages, and multiple engines necessary to lug heavy loads of bombs and fuel over long distances. Fighters have greater speed, maneuverability, and acceleration. But while a fighter might fly circles around a bomber, its performance could be severely degraded by even a moderate load of bombs. Trying to build one plane that could do both jobs would be somewhat like trying to train the same athlete to excel at both fencing and heavyweight power lifting. Since a plane had to be one of the other, proponents of bombers and proponents of fighters frequently battled over pieces of budgetary pie.

During World War II vast quantities of fighters and bombers were the key to Allied victory, but there was some dispute over which form of air power was most effective (current consensus favors the fighters). Bomber advocates pointed to the crippling effect of mass British and American raids on German war production. Fighter advocates cited the enormous attrition of bombers and their crews during such raids, as well as the failure of some bomber offensives (the Nazi blitz of England being a prime example) to break the will of an enemy. Fighters, they argued, performed the crucial role of sweeping the Luftwaffe from the skies and hammering German armor and infantry in order to usher the ultimately victorious Allied armored spearheads into Germany.

The TFX (Tactical Fighter Experimental), as the F-111 was known in its development days, ostensibly marked the beginning of a new era in American defense planning. President Kennedy and Secretary of Defense Robert McNamara wanted the military to develop a capacity for "flexible response" that would allow us to greet brushfire wars or limited Soviet aggression with something less than a nuclear holocaust. A plane like the TFX, with its hefty conventional payload and anticipated aerial combat abilities, conformed beautifully with this new doctrine, and its nuclear threat would assuage a considerable Air Force faction that still clung to the old philosophy of nuking everything in sight. And because of its varied abilities, it could accomplish one of Secretary McNamara's most important goals, reducing costly duplication in weapons systems. In late 1962 McNamara awarded a contract to General Dynamics for the development of a TFX that would theoretically supersede virtually every tactical warplane extant for both the Air Force and the Navy.

But the competing service branches couldn't come to terms on the plane. The Air Force had, as its major requirement for the TFX, stipulated a sea-level dash-to-the-target speed of Mach 1.2—that is, 1.2 times the speed of sound. However, because of the structurally complex swing wing and the stresses placed on the aircraft by penetrating the sound barrier in the thick air at low altitudes, the TFX required a reinforced airframe that was extremely heavy by fighter standards.

That made the aircraft too heavy for the Navy's carrier operations, and after strenuous effort the Navy finally succeeded in canceling its commitment to the F-111 in 1968. The Air Force was not so lucky; the tremendous weight of its version (90,000 pounds fully loaded) would ultimately make it the heaviest tactical plane in the Air Force inventory, which meant that the F-111 would be no match for anybody's air-to-air fighters. In trying to obtain a do-everything fighter-bomber, the Tactical Air Command (TAC) ended up with just what it had started with—an unmaneuverable, high-speed, low-level delivery system for nuclear bombs. So much for flexible response.

By the mid-60's, however, with TAC's fighter-bombers already in trouble against MiG-21s over North Viet Nam, it was apparent even to the Air Force that it needed a real fighter plane that could cleanse the skies of Soviet-built fighters. F-X, for Fighter Experimental, became the designation of a proposed new air-to-air dogfighting aircraft. The characteristics of the plane were initially specified by the Air Force's principal design group, the Aeronautical Systems Division at Wright-Patterson Air Force Base in Ohio. The designers envisioned a big, heavy aircraft (60,000 pounds) with swing wings that were very small in relation to the weight of the plane. They envisioned, remarkably, another F-111. But in late 1966, just before their heavy F-X design was to be approved, John Boyd was called to the Pentagon to look it over.

You have got to understand the mission. Then you have to decide which characteristics actually support the mission.
    —John Boyd.

Boyd had learned a great deal about fighter planes, both during the 1950s as a fighter tactics instructor at Nellis Air Force Base in Nevada and during the early 60s as an engineer at Georgia Tech, where he employed scientific methods to isolate the variables—weight, drag, thrust, and lift—that would contribute to the maneuverability of jet aircraft. Using computer analysis, Boyd tied all these variables into an "energy maneuverability concept" that could be applied to any new aircraft design. It was all quite technical, but the essence of Boyd's concept was what he called "making the trades," or making design tradeoffs between certain kinds of performance characteristics. At its simplest, his idea was that a design for a superior air-to-air fighter should be light and that it should trade off the ability to carry heavy bomb loads in order to maintain maneuverability; only by making the trades could high performance in any given role be maintained. It seemed like common sense, but the F-111 was a perfect instance of the designers' trying not to trade off a fighter's ability to be a bomber or vice versa.

By late 1966, Boyd and like-minded defense analysts had succeeded in scuttling the neo-F-111 F-X, and they were using Boyd's trade-off concept to whittle the F-X down to an outstanding air-to-air fighter configuration. They pared the plane down to 40,000 pounds and came up with a single-seat, fixed-wing, highly maneuverable aircraft. But the Air Force, frantic over the appearance in 1967 of the fearsome Soviet MiG-25 Foxbat—a Mach 3, high-flying interceptor that in the end turned out to be far less than it was cracked up to be—insisted on a high top speed for the new fighter, despite Boyd's warnings that high top speeds are rarely used in combat and, because of structural additions and complexities necessary to achieve them, actually impede performance in a dogfight. The Air Force also added a big load of sophisticated avionics, including a very powerful radar system. By the time the F-X was finally approved in 1968 and designated the F-15, it was in Boyd's opinion a bigger, more expensive aircraft than it needed to be.

Meanwhile, Pierre Sprey had come to the Pentagon in 1966 as one of Robert McNamara's "whiz kids." He was introduced to John Boyd and Boyd's design theories a year later. Sprey, already alarmed over the rapidly

increasing costs—and, consequently, steadily decreasing numbers—of American aircraft, realized that Boyd's design tradeoffs had everything to do with wider issues of military preparedness. To his mind, relatively inexpensive, lightweight fighters could be the key to an effective rearming of America, and he and Boyd joined forces in an extraordinary Pentagon conspiracy. That was the beginning of the notorious Fighter Mafia.

At first the Mafia was no match for the Air Force bureaucracy. Boyd and Sprey produced some proposals for a smaller, less costly, and higher-performance version of the F-15, and they set about briefing the Air Force brass, including General James Ferguson, the commander of the Air Force Systems Command, the agency responsible for all Air Force weapons procurement. The general was sympathetic, but he knew how difficult it was to defer the course of a weapon's development once the myriad of Air Force "add-on committees" had gotten their strangle-hold on it. "A lieutenant can add a tail hook to this airplane," Ferguson told Sprey, "but a four-star general can't take it off."

Persuaded that they could not halt the inexorable advance of the F-15, Boyd and Sprey started with an entirely new set of design and tradeoff requirements that would prove just how hot the F-15 really could have been. This concept, known as the F-XX, was an inexpensive (about one-half the cost of the F-15) 25,000-pound aircraft stripped down to perform one role—air-to-air combat—and to do it better than any other aircraft in the world. Those old TAC favorites, high top speed and the ability to drop bombs, were completely left out.

The F-XX became an underground sensation in aerospace circles and soon caught the attention of Colonel Everest "Rich" Riccioni, an Air Force test pilot and engineer assigned to the Pentagon to work on tactical fighter development. Riccioni was already convinced that the Air Force needed smaller, lighter fighters, but like many Air Force experts he felt that such a stripped-down aircraft would pay a price in lowered performance. After studying the Fighter Mafia's data, he changed his mind. By early 1970, Riccioni was an initiate.

Riccinio became more of an austerity zealot than even Sprey or Boyd. After consulting the tradeoff data, Riccioni set a goal of 17,000 pounds for a new "ultra-austere" fighter, a plane with simple radar and other avionics, relatively low top speed, exceptional maneuverability, and a fuel efficiency that would allow it to remain in energy-consuming dogfights for much longer periods than other fighters. But Riccioni wasn't foolish enough to run his ultra-austere fighter through the usual predatory Air Force channels. Instead, he innocently asked that funds be directed to two aerospace contractors for a "Study to Validate the Integration of Advanced Energy-Maneuverability Theory With Tradeoff Analysis." It was a move that was not likely to alarm anyone, since in the Pentagon studies are considered a harmless deflector of otherwise dangerous innovations. But the study was really just a well-placed smoke screen; Riccioni was in fact asking the contractors to come up with the preliminary designs for an ultra-austere fighter.

By the fall of 1970 Riccioni had received a commitment of $149,000 to pursue his study, which made him bold enough to advocate his ultra-austere philosophy at higher levels in the Department of Defense. That did not sit well with his superiors, who felt that he was stepping out of line. At a party in late 1970 Riccioni, after being questioned, made his reservations about the F-15 known to General J. C. Meyer, the Air Force vice chief of staff. Several weeks later, Riccioni was informed that he was being reassigned to Korea, where not many aircraft were being designed.

The F-15 has become a credo with the Air Force. The only way a second lieutenant can get promoted to a first lieutenant is to swear allegiance to the F-15.
—A defense analyst.

It was clear, then, that the F-XX, a plane whose whole reason for being was the notion

that the F-15 was seriously flawed, was not going to get any support from the Air Force brass. The brass was solidly behind the F-15. But the Fighter Mafia had an ace in the hole: an ally who outranked the brass. He was David Packard, Deputy Secretary of Defense under Richard Nixon, and he liked the F-XX because it gave him a chance to carry out a pet project of his—building a prototype.

Before the jet and computer age, a prototype of each proposed new military aircraft was considered a necessity. For one thing, planes were less complicated then, so a prototype was less expensive; for another, it was nearly impossible to anticipate a plane's cost, feasibility, and performance on paper. But as jet engines, supersonic speeds, and advanced electronics made aircraft much more complex, the cost—in both dollars and man-hours—of aircraft prototypes began to expand dramatically. Contractors now wanted firm commitments from the government before they would undertake the enormous expense of building a plane, and so the prototype went out of fashion. By the late 1950s, military aircraft were going into production without any proven assurance that they would work.

That bothered Robert McNamara enormously, and shortly after he came to the Pentagon in 1961 he put into effect a program called TPP, or Total Package Procurement, that was designed to take the risk out of prototype-free contracting. Henceforth, any new weapon would undergo exhaustive scrutiny on paper before the Department of Defense committed itself, and our dollars, to production. No only that, the costs of development and production were now to be fixed before a single plane was built, in order to discourage the cost overruns that were then endemic to most new high-technology aircraft. TPP was to be a real breakthrough.

But it didn't work. For one thing, it swelled design teams to the proportions of a good-sized town—4,000-6,000 for the F-111 and submerged the development process in a tidal wave of paperwork that came to tens of thousands of documents per month. It also meant that once a new weapon checked out on paper, it was gospel. The models used for test flights were built on the same machinery as production models; a plane would essentially be in midproduction at the same time it was making its first practice runs. When real-world problems arose, the production lines kept right on rolling. Two of the most important aircraft built under TPP were the infamous brittle-winged Lockheed C-5A Galaxy jumbo transport, which nearly bankrupted the contractor, and General Dynamics' F-111.

By the late 1960s TPP had left McNamara, Lockheed, and General Dynamics with bruised reputations, and a lot of people were anxious to reexamine the rituals of weapons procurement. One of those skeptics was David Packard. Packard realized that the programs going on under him, including the F-15, were operating under TPP procedures, and he began to cast about for a chance to try old-fashioned prototyping again. In 1971 he made an open commitment of $100 to $200 million for prototypes of any kind; he was bound and determined to have some prototypes going in the 1972 fiscal year, and he didn't care what they were.

The Fighter Mafia saw its opportunity and seized it. The Mafia was already enamored of the idea of prototyping; Sprey had advocated a competitive fly-off between two envisioned prototypes of the F-XX as far back as 1968. Boyd and Riccioni had visited several contractors, including General Dynamics, and sold them on the lightweight fighter idea, so there were some good preliminary designs already in the works. And the Air Force Prototype Study Group, which would review all the prototype proposals and select six projects for actual development, had been rigged by the Fighter Mafia. Colonel Lyle Cameron, a Korean War ace and a lightweight fighter convert, was head of the group, and John Boyd was his assistant.

Out of 200 prototype proposals, the Air Force Prototype Study Group in mid-1971 selected six for final review. Packard assigned priority to two of these programs—a transport designed to operate from short airstrips, and

the lightweight fighter. Later in the year Congress officially approved funding for the two projects, and five contractors submitted lightweight fighter designs. In the spring of 1972 two aircraft, the twin-engine Northrop YF-17 and the smaller, single-engine General Dynamics YF-16, were selected to be built as prototypes.

Less than two years later, the first planes were ready to fly, thanks to concise, unbureaucratic design teams that were producing a virtually undetectable, by military aerospace standards, 30 or 40 pages of documentation a month. Th YF-17 and YF-16 went through extensive comparative flight testing at Edwards Air Force Base in California, and in a unique display of Defense Department largess, Air Force pilots were actually allowed to fly them and make recommendations. By early 1975 the YF-16—the plane that had so far whipped the Defense Department and 200 competing proposals—had whipped the YF-17 and was selected for production.

But the Air Force was still resistant. It hurt, of course, that the new F-16 had not gone through the proper channels, but what was even worse about the new plane, from the point of view of the brass, was that it just didn't cost enough.

If that sounds like madness, there was considerable method behind it, given the defense budgeting process and the military force structure. Under the policies of the efficient Secretary McNamara, American military forces were fixed in size—in the case of the Air Force the ceiling was 21 aircraft "wings" —but no real limit was imposed on the cost of a particular weapon or, more important, on the percentage of the total defense budget that any one service arm could glom on to. This meant that the Air Force could have only so many planes, but that those planes could have on them everything money could buy to increase their theoretical effectiveness and killing power.

As a corollary, if the Air Force could pump up its share of the defense budget with the kinds of flashy new technology that would make its limited numbers more effective, it would also weaken the influence of the other service arms and assure a more receptive climate for further Air Force budget increases. But if the Air Force were stupid enough to come along with an inexpensive aircraft, it would just be giving away big slices of the defense budget to the Army and Navy without getting a single additional airplane in return for its naive generosity.

By the time the F-16 prototype was accepted for production, James Schlesinger was Secretary of Defense. Schlesinger had become receptive to the idea of lightweight fighters, but he met with considerable Air Force resistance to a plane that would cost about half as much as an F-15. So Schlesinger offered what was in effect a bribe: if the Air Force would take on the F-16, he would give the Air Force five more aircraft wings. This meant the brass could keep its F-15s; the new plane no longer directly threatened the old. The Air Force Systems Command snapped up the extra wings and got in line with the new fighter program.

It's like a fight between a guy with a long lance and a guy with a Roman short sword when they're both chained together at the wrist. If I've got that short sword, I know I'm going to stick him.
— Colonel Ralph S. Parr, USAF (Ret.), Korean War combat ace with service in World War II, Korea, and Viet Nam.

In 1975 the research and development arm of the Air Force Staff took over the prototype F-16 for "full development engineering," which effectively cut the bureaucracy in on the action that it had been missing since prototype development began. The Air Force development team grew from 25 to 300, and it went to work on modifications that would "missionize" the airplane, or add combat capabilities. This was curious, because the YF-16 was already equipped with the weapons it needed for its air-to-air mission—heatseeking Sidewinder missiles, a rapid-fire cannon, and a simple range-finding radar. The idea, after all, had been to eliminate complex

and perhaps marginally useful avionics and weapons systems and thereby to keep the weight and cost down.

But back in 1975, when the generals were working over the F-16, they were unaware of some of the F-15's weaknesses and convinced that the others were on their way to being solved. They saw no reason for another fighter plane. So they took the Fighter Mafia's F-16 and made it bigger, strengthened its airframe so that it could carry bombs, and equipped it to carry nuclear weapons.

Schlesinger, unable to repulse the bureaucratic onslaught of design changes, stood back while 4,000 pounds of avionics and structural changes were added to the airframe and $3 million was added to the cost. Caught between the outraged protests of the Fighter Mafia and the strong-arm tactics of the numerically superior Air Force team, he gave Sprey the final brush-off: "I don't want to hear any more from you lightweight fighter theologians." Schlesinger did, however, get a commitment from David Jones, then Air Force chief of staff (now the controversial chairman of the Joint Chiefs), not to wire the plane to handle nuclear weapons. A week after Schlesinger left office in 1975, Jones gave the go-ahead for nuclear wiring.

There were some problems in converting the F-16 to the delivery of bombs, the most notable being that during abrupt maneuvers, the aircraft tended to pitch out of control and crash when heavily loaded with bombs; the horizontal tail, which stabilizes the plane, wasn't designed for lugging big loads. This problem was recently redressed with some modifications that have further reduced the plane's maneuverability, but for the time being pilots were just told to cool it when the plane was heavily loaded. The Air Force had decided the F-16 would be a bomber, so a bomber it would be.

Now it was the contractor's turn to modify the F-16.

For an aerospace contractor, a successful airframe design is like a smash TV series; it can be very profitable to spin it off a time or two. For General Dynamics the first F-16 spin-off was the F-16/79, an export version powered by a General Electric J79 engine that is about 80% as powerful as the Pratt & Whitney F100. This intermediate version is considered suitable for the ravenous export market—a nice, roughly $10 million aircraft for American allies to whom it would be inappropriate to give the high-performance luxury model. Many of these countries, like Taiwan and Thailand, now fly the Northrop F-5 Freedom Fighter, which is currently America's number one export fighter. GD can also hope for extensive export sales to valued allies like Israel and Egypt—which have already ordered dozens—and to allies like South Korea that have recently been upgraded by the Reagan Administration to receive front-line American aircraft to replace their F-5s.

Exports, however, are not the only successful spin-off option. The contractor can also tempt the U.S. Air Force with more sophisticated and ambitious versions of its original design. This can be slightly risky, but a good concept can significantly extend the production run of an aircraft. Take the F-111, which never got produced in the expected quantities but still became the SAC FB-111 medium-range strategic bomber and which has a slim chance of being stretched into the SAC FB-111 long-range penetration bomber that would replace the senile B-52 fleet. It is this sort of hope on the part of the contractors that brings us to the story of the F-16, the Strike Eagle, and the SCAMP.

That story is rooted in the spirit of competition between the two St. Louis-headquartered aerospace titans, McDonnell Douglas (the F-15's manufacturer) and General Dynamics. By early 1977 Defense Department momentum had carried forward a commitment for 738 more F-16s, adding up to a total U.S. defense production run, extending far into the 1980s, of 1,388 of the fighters, now designated as "multirole." Score one for GD. At the same time, the McDonnell Douglas F-15 production run was stalled at 759

aircraft and could be expected to end by 1984. The F-15's cost and well-publicized technical problems did not make it an attractive item in a democratic system that in the late '70s was inclined to be penurious when it came to defense spending, and even the Air Force had to accept that.

But McDonnell Douglas would not give up. It led a campaign of sniping at the F-16's "limited capabilities," particularly its woeful lack of long-range radar and Sparrow missiles. In early 1980 McDonnell Douglas sent the Pentagon an "unsolicited" proposal suggesting that the Air Force scrap its plans for the 738 additional F-16s and replace them with F-15s. The rationale was that increased production and the resulting efficiencies could bring down the per-unit cost of the F-15 to within $2 million of the then-current F-16 cost of $10 million. McDonnell Douglas also suggested that the F-15 would do just fine in taking over the F-16's ground attack duties. The McDonnell Douglas offensive was aided by Dr. William Perry, the Pentagon Research and Development chief, who called the F-16 an "incomplete plane" in testimony before Congress. Dr. Perry, one of the principal architects of the very controversial and highly dubious M-X mobile missile plan, affirmed that the absence of long-range radar capability would make the F-16 quite vulnerable, particularly in the frequently cloudy skies over Europe.

General Dynamics fought back with a series of modifications, accepted by the Air Force in the summer of 1980, that it said would "enhance" the F-16. The plane was wired to enable it to fire the Sparrow, "hard points" under the wings were strengthened to allow an additional several thousand pounds of bombs to be bolted to them, and the troublesome horizontal tail was increased in surface area by 30%, which would help control the plane when it was lugging those extra bombs. But a big tail surface relative to the main wing impedes maneuverability, so the F-16 was further degraded as an air superiority fighter. GD also made wiring and structural changes to allow easy plug-in of new avionics and weapons systems whenever they became available. These add-ons would include LANTIRN (low-altitude navigation targeting infrared for night) a sort of super-BVR for ground attack missions; AMRAAM (advanced medium-range air-to-air missile), a sort of super-Sparrow; and assorted radar-jamming and communications systems.

In the summer of 1980 McDonnell Douglas unveiled a new plane called the Strike Eagle. It was a contractor-funded prototype designed to prove that the basic F-15 could be turned into the hottest nighttime/all-weather bomber since the F-111 without losing its fighter capability. According to McDonnell Douglas, the Strike Eagle can be expected by late this year to feature two brand-new avionics systems that will give it unprecedented capability for attacks on distant, unseen ground targets. Using SAR (synthetic aperture radar) signal processors in combination with FLIR (forward-looking infrared), the two-seater Strike Eagle (the guy in the back is operating all this stuff) will theoretically be capable of making a low-level approach, spotting a 10-foot target from 10 miles away (one problem: the Strike Eagle must ascend to 2,500 feet for 10 to 20 seconds in order to "see" the target), and then continuing to streak in under FLIR guidance until it releases a variety of ordnance at its unwitting (provided the enemy didn't happen to pick up any radar emissions or a brief pip at 2,000 feet on their radar) and still-distant target. It is the aircraft of the future, and McDonnell Douglas promotes it with a glossy brochure in the form of a secret report from a Russian intelligence agent to his comrades, warning them that Soviet hegemony will be a thing of the past if this weapon is ever deployed.

Not to be outdone, General Dynamics began briefing the Pentagon on its design for a bigger F-16. GD called it the F-16 SCAMP, or Supersonic Cruise and Maneuvering Proto-type. The SCAMP would have, theoretically, greater missile- and bomb-carrying capacity, longer range, and bigger wings than the F-16, albeit with less maneuverability. But clearly the SCAMP would have room for more bombs and all the hot-dog nighttime/all-weather avionics that McDonnell Douglas offers with the Strike Eagle.

The SCAMP, recently renamed the F-16XL, is now being put together at GD's Fort Worth plant in a sealed hangar next to the runway at the neighboring Carswell Air Force Base; GD is paying for the $40 million prototype out of its own corporate pocket. For the time being, the Strike Eagle concept is being resisted by some of the relatively pragmatic elements in the Air Force command. One major problem is price—an estimated $35 million for each Strike Eagle and $30 million for the F-16XL.

The F-16 is a damn fine compromise.
  —F-16 squadron commander.

The F-16 is, everyone agrees, a pretty decent compromise. The pilots think that it can perform both air superiority and ground attack missions—if they can train enough. Boyd and Sprey look at it as two big steps forward and one big step backward. The direction of that next step is what's important. For Pentagon Research and Development, which is pushing everything from the M-X to LANTIRN; for General Dynamics, which is building a plane to put all that stuff on; for the Air Force brass who are, now that money doesn't matter, exerting pressure to have F-16 procurement cut and to replace those numbers with the F-15; and for the congressmen and senators waiting to bring it all home, the direction of that next step is obvious. And maybe we should follow them. After all, they have the record to back it up. If you don't count Viet Nam, where we had one hand tied behind our back, those guys have never lost a war. Yet.

45

The Education of David Stockman

Three weeks before the inauguration, Stockman and his transition team of a dozen or so people were already established at the OMB office in the Old Executive Office Building. When his appointment as budget director first seemed likely, he had agreed to meet with me from time to time and relate, off the record, his private account of the great political struggle ahead. The particulars of these conversations were not to be reported until later, after the season's battles were over, but a cynic familiar with how Washington works would understand that the arrangement had obvious symbiotic value. As an assistant managing editor at the *Washington Post*, I benefited from an informed view of policy discussions of the new administration; Stockman, a student of history, was contributing to history's record and perhaps influencing its conclusions. For him, our meetings were another channel—among many he used—to the press. The older generation of orthodox Republicans distrusted the press; Stockman was one of the younger "new" conservatives who cultivated contacts with columnists and

reporters, who saw the news media as another useful tool in political combat. "We believe our ideas have intellectual respectability, and we think the press will recognize that," he said. "The traditional Republicans probably sensed, even if they didn't know it, that their ideas lacked intellectual respectability."

In early January, Stockman and his staff were assembling dozens of position papers on program reductions and studying the internal forecasts for the federal budget and the national economy. The initial figures were frightening—"absolutely shocking," he confided—yet he seemed oddly exhilarated by the bad news, and was bubbling with new plans for coping with these horrendous numbers. A government computer, programmed as a model of the nation's economic behavior, was instructed to estimate the impact of Reagan's program on the federal budget. It predicted that if the new President went ahead with his promised three-year tax reduction and his increase in defense spending, the Reagan Administration would be faced with a series of federal deficits without precedent in

From *The Education of David Stockman and Other Americans*,
by William Greider, © 1981, 1982 by William Greider. Reprinted by
permission of the publisher, E. T. Dutton, Inc.

peacetime—ranging from $82 billion in 1982 to $116 billion in 1984. Even Stockman blinked. If those were the numbers included in President Reagan's first budget message, the following month the financial markets that Stockman sought to reassure would instead be panicked. Interest rates, already high, would go higher; the expectation of long-term inflation would be confirmed.

Stockman saw opportunity in these shocking projections. "All the conventional estimates just wind up as mud," he said. "As absurdities. What they basically say, to boil it down, is that the world doesn't work."

Stockman set about doing two things. First, he changed the economic assumptions fed into the computer model. Assisted by like-minded supply-side economists, the new team discarded orthodox premises of how the economy would behave. Instead of a continuing double-digit inflation, they assumed a swift decline in prices and interest rates. Instead of the continuing pattern of slow economic growth, the new model was based on a dramatic surge in the nation's productivity. New investment, new jobs, and growing profits—and Stockman's historic bull market. "It's based on valid economic analysis," he said, "but it's the inverse of the last four years. When we go public, this going to set off a wide-open debate on how the economy works, a great battle over the conventional theories of economic performance."

The original apostles of supply side, particularly Representative Jack Kemp of New York and the economist Arthur B. Laffer, dismissed budget-cutting as inconsequential to the economic problems, but Stockman was trying to fuse new theory and old. "Laffer sold us a bill of goods," he said, then corrected his words: "Laffer wasn't wrong—he didn't go far enough."

The great debate never quite took hold in the dimensions that Stockman had anticipated, but the Reagan Administration's economic projections did become the source of continuing controversy. In defense of their counter-theories, Stockman and his associates would argue, correctly, that conventional forecasts, particularly by the Council of Economic Advisers in the preceding administration, had been consistently wrong in the past. His critics would contend that the supply-side premises were based upon wishful thinking, not sound economic analysis.

But, second, Stockman used the appalling deficit projections as a valuable talking point in the policy discussions that were underway with the President and his principal advisers. Nobody in that group was the least bit hesitant about cutting federal programs, but Reagan had campaigned on the vague and painless theme that eliminating "waste, fraud, and mismanagement" would be sufficient to balance the accounts. Now, as Stockman put it, "the idea is to try to get beyond the waste, fraud, and mismanagement modality and begin to confront the real dimensions of budget reduction." On the first Wednesday in January, Stockman had two hours on the President-elect's schedule to describe the "dire shape" of the federal budget; for starters, the new administration would have to go for a budget reduction in the neighborhood of $40 billion. "Do you have any idea what $40 billion means?" he said. "It means I've got to cut the highway program. It means I've got to cut milk-price supports. And Social Security student benefits. And education and student loans. And manpower training and housing. It means I've got to shut down the synfuels program and a lot of other programs. The idea is to show the magnitude of the budget deficit and some suggestion of the political problems."

How much pain was the new President willing to impose? How many sacred cows would he challenge at once? Stockman was still feeling out the commitment at the White House, aware that Reagan's philosophical commitment to shrinking the federal government would be weighed against political risks.

Stockman was impressed by the ease with which the President-elect accepted the broad objective: find $40 billion in cuts in a federal budget running well beyond $700 billion. But, despite the multitude of expenditures, the proliferation of programs and grants, Stockman knew the exercise was not as easy as it might sound.

Consider the budget in simple terms, as a federal dollar representing the entire $700 billion. The most important function of the federal government is mailing checks to citizens—Social Security checks to the elderly, pension checks to retired soldiers and civil servants, reimbursement checks for hospitals and doctors who provide medical care for the aged and the poor, welfare checks for the dependent, veterans checks to pensioners. Such disbursements consume 48¢ of the dollar.

Another 25¢ goes to the Pentagon for national defense. Stockman knew that this share would be rising in the next four years, not shrinking, perhaps becoming as high as 30¢. Another 10¢ was consumed by interest payments on the national debt, which was fast approaching a trillion dollars.

That left 17¢ for everything else that Washington does. The FBI and the national parks, the county agents and the Foreign Service and the Weather Bureau—all the traditional operations of government—consumed only 9¢ of the dollar. The remaining 8¢ provided all the grants to state and local governments, for aiding handicapped children or building highways or installing tennis courts next to Al Stockman's farm. One might denounce particular programs as wasteful, as unnecessary and ineffective, even crazy, but David Stockman knew that he could not escape these basic dimensions of federal spending.

As he and his staff went looking for the $40 billion, they found that most of it would have to be taken from the 17¢ that covered government operations and grants-in-aid. Defense was already off-limits. Next Ronald Reagan laid down another condition for the budget-cutting: the main benefit programs of Social Security, Medicare, veterans' checks, railroad retirement pensions, welfare for the disabled

—the so-called "social safety net" that Reagan had promised not to touch—were to be exempt from the budget cuts. In effect, he was declaring that Stockman could not tamper with three fourths of the 48¢ devoted to transfer payments.

No President had balanced the budget in the past 12 years. Still, Stockman thought it could be done by 1984 if the Reagan Administration adhered to the principle of equity, cutting weak claims, not merely weak clients, and if it shocked the system sufficiently to create a new political climate. He still believed that it was not a question of numbers. "It boils down to a political question, not of budget policy or economic policy, but whether we can change the habits of the political system."

The struggle began in private, with Ronald Reagan's Cabinet. By inaugural week, Stockman's staff had assembled 50 or 60 policy papers outlining major cuts and alterations, and, aiming at the target of $40 billion, Stockman was anxious to win fast approval for them before the new Cabinet officers were fully familiar with their departments and prepared to defend their bureaucracies. During that first week, the new Cabinet members had to sit through David Stockman's recital—one proposal after another outlining drastic reductions in their programs. Brief discussion was followed by presidential approval. "I have a little nervousness about the heavy-handedness with which I am being forced to act," Stockman conceded. "It's not that I wouldn't want to give the decision papers to the Cabinet members ahead of time so they could look at them, it's just that we're getting them done at eight o'clock in the morning and rushing them to the Cabinet room...It doesn't work when you have to face these Cabinet officers in front of the President with severe reductions in their agencies, because then they're in the position of having to argue against the group line. And the group line is cut, cut, cut. So that's a very awkward position for them, and you make them resentful very fast."

Stockman proposed to White House counselor Edwin Meese an alternative approach—a budget working group, in which each Cabinet secretary could review the proposed cuts and argue against them. As the group evolved, however, with Meese, chief of staff James Baker, Treasury Secretary Donald Regan, and policy director Martin Anderson, among others, it was stacked in Stockman's favor. "Each meeting will involve only the relevant Cabinet member and his aides with four or five strong keepers of the central agenda," Stockman explained at one point. "So on Monday, when we go into the decision on synfuels programs, it will be [Energy Secretary James B.] Edwards defending them against six guys saying that, by God, we've got to cut these back or we're not going to have a savings program that will add up."

In general, the system worked. Stockman's agency did in a few weeks what normally consumes months; the process was made easier because the normal opposition forces had no time to marshal either their arguments or their constituents and because the President was fully in tune with Stockman. After the budget working group reached a decision, it would be taken to Reagan in the form of a memorandum, on which he could register his approval by checking a little box. "Once he checks it," Stockman said, "I put that in my safe and I go ahead and I don't let it come back up again."

The check marks were given to changes in 12 major budget entitlements and scores of smaller ones. Eliminate Social Security minimum benefits. Cap the runaway costs of Medicaid. Tighten eligibility for food stamps. Merge the trade adjustment assistance for unemployed industrial workers with standard unemployment compensation and shrink it. Cut education aid by a quarter. Cut grants for the arts and humanities in half. "Zero out" CETA and the Community Services Administration and National Consumer Cooperative Bank. And so forth. "Zero out" became a favorite phrase of Stockman's; it meant closing down a program "cold turkey" in one

budget year. Stockman believed that any compromise on a program that ought to be eliminated—funding that would phase it out over several years—was merely a political ruse to keep it alive, so it might still be in existence a few years hence, when a new political climate could allow its restoration to full funding.

"I just wish that there were more hours in the day or that we didn't have to do this so fast. I have these stacks of briefing books and I've got to make decisions about specific options...I don't have time, trying to put this whole package together in three weeks, so you just start making snap judgments."

In the private deliberations, Stockman began to encounter more resistance from Cabinet members. He was proposing to cut $752 million from the Export-Import Bank, which provides subsidized financing for international trade—a cut of crucial symbolic importance because of Stockman's desire for equity. Two thirds of the Ex-Im's direct loans benefit some of America's major manufacturers—Boeing, Lockheed, General Electric, Westinghouse, McDonnell Douglas, Western Electric, Combustion Engineering—and, not surprisingly, the program had a strong Republican constituency on Capitol Hill. Stockman thought the trade subsidies offended the free-market principles that all conservatives espouse—in particular, President Reagan's objective of withdrawing Washington from business decision-making. Supporters of the subsidies made a practical argument: the U.S. companies, big as they were, needed the financial subsidies to stay even against government-subsidized competition from Europe and Japan.

The counter-offensive against the cut was led by Commerce Secretary Malcolm Baldrige and U.S. Trade Representative William Brock, who argued eloquently before the budget working group for a partial restoration of Ex-Im funds. By Stockman's account, the two "fought, argued, pounded the table," and the meeting seemed headed for deadlock. "I sort of innocently asked, well, isn't there a terrible political spin on this? It's my impression that most of the money goes to a handful of big corporations, and if we are ever caught not cutting this while we're biting deeply into the social programs, we're going to have big problems." Stockman asked if anyone at the table had any relevant data. Deputy Secretary of the Treasury Tim McNamar thereupon produced a list of Ex-Im's major beneficiaries (a list that Stockman had given him before the meeting). "So then I went into this demagogic tirade about how in the world can I cut food stamps and social services and CETA jobs and EDA jobs and you're going to tell me you can't give up one penny for Boeing?"

Stockman won that argument, for the moment. But, as with all the other issues in the budget debate, the argument was only beginning. "I've got to take something out of Boeing's hide to make this look right. . . You can measure me on this, because I'll probably lose but I'll give it a helluva fight."

Stockman also began what was to become a continuing struggle, occasionally nasty, with the new secretary of energy. Edwards, a dentist from South Carolina, was ostensibly appointed to dismantle the Department of Energy, as Reagan had promised, but when Stockman proposed cutting the department in half, virtually eliminating the vast synthetic-fuels program launched by the Carter Administration, Edwards argued in defense. In the midst of the battle, Stockman said contemptuously, "I went over to DOE the other day and here's a whole roomful of the same old bureaucrats I've been kicking around for the last five years—advising Edwards on why we couldn't do certain things on oil decontrol that I wanted to do." The relationship did not improve as the two men got to know each other better.

But Stockman felt only sympathy for Secretary of Agriculture John Block, an Illinois farmer. The budget cuts were hitting some of Agriculture's principal subsidy programs. A billion dollars would be cut from dairy-price supports. The Farmers Home Administration loans and grants were to be sharply curtailed. The low-interest financing for rural electric cooperatives and the Tennessee Valley Authority would be modified. In the early weeks of the new administration, the peanut growers and their congressional lobby had campaigned, as they did every year, to have the new secretary of agriculture raise the price-support level for peanuts. Stockman told Block he would have to refuse—for Stockman wanted to abolish the program. "I sympathize with Jack Block," Stockman said. "I forced him into a position that makes his life miserable over there. He's on the central team, he's not a departmental player, but the parochial politics of that department are fierce." Victories over farm lobbies could be won, Stockman believed, if he kept the issues separate—attacking each commodity program in turn, and undermining urban support by cutting the food and nutrition programs. "My strategy is to come in with a farm bill that's unacceptable to the farm guys so that the whole thing begins to splinter." An early test vote on milk-price supports seemed to confirm the strategy—the dairy farmers lobbied and lost.

The only Cabinet officer Stockman did not challenge was, of course, the secretary of defense. In the frantic preparation of the Reagan budget message, delivered in broad outline to Congress on February 18, the OMB review officers did not give even their usual scrutiny to the new budget projections from Defense. Reagan had promised to increase military spending by 7% a year, adjusted for inflation, and this pledge translated into the biggest peacetime arms buildup in the history of the republic—$1.6 trillion over the next five years, which would more than double the Pentagon's annual budget while domestic spending was shrinking. Stockman acknowledged that OMB had taken only a cursory glance at the new defense budget, but he was confident that later on, when things settled down a bit, he could go back and analyze it more carefully.

In late February, months before the

defense budget became a subject of Cabinet debate, Stockman privately predicted that Defense Secretary Caspar Weinberger, himself a budget director during the Nixon years, would be an ally when he got around to cutting back military spending. "As soon as we get past this first phase in the process, I'm really going to go after the Pentagon. The whole question is blatant inefficiency, poor deployment of manpower, contracting idiocy, and, hell, I think that Cap's going to be a pretty good mark over there. He's not a tool of the military-industrial complex. I mean, he hasn't been steeped in its excuses and rationalizations and ideology for 20 years, and I think that he'll back off on a lot of this stuff, but you just can't challenge him head-on without your facts in line. And we're going to get our case in line and just force it through the presses."

Stockman shared the general view of the Reagan Administration that the United States needed a major buildup of its armed forces. But he also recognized that the Pentagon, as sole customer for weapons systems, subsidized the arms manufacturers in many direct ways and violated many free-market principles. "The defense budgets in the out-years won't be nearly as high as we are showing now, in my judgment. Hell, I think there's a kind of swamp of $10 to $20 to $30 billion worth of waste that can be ferreted out if you really push hard."

Long before President Reagan's speech to Congress, most of the painful details of the $41.4 billion in proposed reductions were already known to Capitol Hill and the public. In early February, preparing the political ground, Stockman started delivering his "black book" to Republican leaders and committee chairmen. He knew that once the information was circulating on the Hill, it would soon be available to the news media, and he was not at all upset by the daily storm of headlines revealing the dimensions of what lay ahead. The news conveyed, in its drama and quantity of detail, the appropriate political message: President Reagan would not be proposing business as usual. The President had in mind what Stockman saw as "fiscal revolution."

But it was not generally understood that the new budget director had already lost a major component of his revolution—another set of proposals, which he called "Chapter II," that was not sent to Capitol Hill because the President had vetoed its most controversial elements.

Stockman had thought "Chapter II" would help him on two fronts: it would provide substantially increased revenues and thus help reduce the huge deficits of the next three years; but it would also mollify liberal critics complaining about the cuts in social welfare, because it was aimed primarily at tax expenditures (popularly known as "loopholes") benefiting oil and other business interests. "We have a gap which we couldn't fill even with all these budget cuts too big a deficit," Stockman explained. "Chapter II comes out totally on the opposite of the equity question. That was part of my strategy to force acquiescence at the last minute into a lot of things you'd never see a Republican administration propose. I had a meeting this morning at the White House. The President wasn't involved, but all the other key senior people were. We brought a program of additional tax savings that don't touch any social programs. But they touch tax expenditures." Stockman hesitated to discuss details, for the package was politically sensitive, but it included elimination of the oil-depletion allowance; an attack on tax-exempt industrial-development bonds; user fees for owners of private airplanes and barges; a potential ceiling on home-mortgage deductions (which Stockman called a "mansion cap," since it would affect only the wealthy); some defense reductions; and other items, 10 in all. Total additional savings: somewhere in the neighborhood of $20 billion. Stockman was proud of "Chapter II" and also very nervous about it, because, while liberal Democrats might applaud the closing of "loopholes" that they had attacked for years, powerful lobbies—in Congress and business—would mobilize against it.

Did President Reagan approve? "If there's a consensus on it, he's not going to buck it, probably."

Two weeks later, Stockman cheerfully explained that the President had rejected his "tax-expenditures" savings. The "Chapter II" issues had seemed crucial to Stockman when he was preparing them, but he dismissed them as inconsequential now that he had lost. "Those were more like ornaments I was thinking of on the tax side," he insisted. "I call them equity ornaments. They're not really too good. They're not essential to the economics of the thing."

The President was willing to propose user fees for aircraft, private boats, and barges, but turned down the proposal to eliminate the oil-depletion allowance. "The President has a very clear philosophy," Stockman explained. "A lot of people criticize him for being short on the details, but he knows when something's wrong. He just jumped all over my tax proposals."

Stockman dropped other proposals. Nevertheless, he was buoyant. The reactions from Capitol Hill were clamorous, as expected, but the budget director was more impressed by the silences, the stutter and hesitation of the myriad interest groups. Stockman was becoming a favorite caricature for newspaper cartoonists—the grim reaper of the Reagan Administration, the Republican Robespierre —but in his many sessions on the Hill he sensed confusion and caution on the other side.

"There are more and more guys coming around to our side," he reported. "What's happening is that the plan is so sweeping and it covers all the bases sufficiently, so that it's like a magnifying glass that reveals everybody's pores . . . In the past, people could easily get votes for their projects or their interests by saying, well, if they would cut food stamps and CETA jobs and two or three other things, then maybe we would go along with it, but they are just picking on my program. But, now, everybody perceives that everybody's sacred cows are being cut. If that's what it takes, so be it. The parochial player will not be the norm, I think. For a while."

46

Political Processes in Organizations

The purpose of this exercise is to analyze and predict when political behavior is used in organizational decision-making and to compare participants' ratings of politically-based decisions with ratings of practicing managers.

Politics is the use of influence to make decisions and obtain preferred outcomes in organizations. Surveys of managers show that political behavior is a fact of life in virtually all organizations. Every organization will confront situations characterized by uncertainty and disagreement, hence standard rules and rational decision models can't necessarily be used. Political behavior and rational decision processes act as substitutes for one another, depending upon the degree of uncertainty and disagreement that exists among managers about specific issues. Political behavior is used and is revealed in informal discussions and unscheduled meetings among managers, arguments, attempts at persuasion, and eventual agreement and acceptance of the organizational choice.

In the following exercise, you are asked to evaluate the extent to which politics will play a part in 11 types of decisions that are made in organizations. The complete exercise takes about one hour.

STEP 1: *Individual Ranking (5 minutes)*

Rank the 11 organizational decisions listed on the scoring sheet below according to the extent you think politics plays a part. The most political decision would be ranked 1, the least political decision would be ranked 11. Enter your ranking on the first column of the scoring sheet.

STEP 2: *Team Ranking (20 minutes)*

Divide into teams of from three to seven people. As a group, rank the 11 items according to your group's consensus on the amount of politics used in each decision. Use good group decision-making techniques to arrive at a consensus. Listen to each person's ideas

Thanks to Don Hellreigel for suggesting the idea for this exercise. The scoring sheet is based on Jeffrey Gandz and Victor V. Murray, "The Experience of Workplace Politics," *Academy of Management Journal* 1980, 23, 237-251.

and rationale fully before reaching a decision. Do not vote. Discuss items until agreement is reached. Base your decisions on the underlying logic provided by group members rather than on personal preference. After your team has reached a consensus, record the team rankings in the second column on the scoring sheet.

STEP 3: *Correct Ranking* (5 minutes)

After all teams have finished ranking the 11 decisions, your instructor will read the correct ranking based on a survey of managers. This survey indicates the frequency with which politics played a part in each type of decision. As the instructor reads each item's ranking, enter it in the "correct ranking" column on the scoring sheet.

STEP 4: *Individual Score* (5 minutes)

Your individual score is computed by taking the difference between your individual ranking and the correct ranking for each item. Be sure to use the *absolute* difference between your ranking and the correct ranking for each item (ignore pluses and minuses). Enter the difference in column 4 labeled "Individual Score." Add the numbers in column 4 and insert the total at the bottom of the column. This score indicates how accurate you were in assessing the extent to which politics plays a part in organizational decisions.

STEP 5: *Team Score (5 minutes)*

Compute the difference between your group's ranking and the correct ranking. Again, use the *absolute* difference for each

SCORING SHEET

Decisions	1. Individual Ranking	2. Team Ranking	3. Correct Ranking	4. Individual Score	5. Team Score
1. Management promotions and transfers					
2. Entry level hiring					
3. Amount of pay					
4. Annual budgets					
5. Allocation of facilities, equipment, offices					
6. Delegation of authority among managers					
7. Interdepartmental coordination					
8. Specification of personnel policies					
9. Penalties for disciplinary infractions					
10. Performance appraisals					
11. Grievances and complaints					

	Team Number						
	1	2	3	4	5	6	7
Team Scores:							
Lowest individual score on each team:							

item. Enter the difference in the column 5 labeled "Team Score." Add the numbers in column 5 and insert the total at the bottom of the column. The total is your team score.

STEP 6: *Compare Teams (5 minutes)*

When all individual and team scores have been calculated, the instructor will record the data from each group for class discussion. One member of your group should be prepared to provide both the team score and the lowest individual score on your team. The instructor may wish to display these data so that team and individual scores can be easily compared as illustrated on the bottom of the scoring sheet. All participants may wish to record these data for further reference.

STEP 7: *Discussion (15 minutes)*

Discuss this exercise as a total group with the instructor. Use your experience and the data to try to arrive at some conclusions about the role of politics in real-world organizational decision-making. The following questions may facilitate the total group discussion.

1. Why did some individuals and groups solve the ranking more accurately than others? Did they have more experience with organizational decision-making? Did they interpret the amount of uncertainty and disagreement associated with decisions more accurately?

2. If the 11 decisions were ranked according to the importance of rational decision processes, how would that ranking compare to the one you've completed above? To what extent does this mean both rational and political models of decision-making should be used in organizations?

3. What would happen if managers apply political processes to logical, well understood issues? What would happen if they applied rational or quantitative techniques to uncertain issues about which considerable disagreement existed?

4. Many managers believe that political behavior is greater at higher levels in the organization hierarchy. Is there any evidence from this exercise that would explain why more politics would appear at higher rather than lower levels in organizations?

5. What advice would you give to managers who feel politics is bad for the organization and should be avoided at all costs?

V

View from the Top

47

The Man Who Killed Braniff

It was a gray June morning in 1979. Under the taupe concrete spars and crossbars of the Braniff International terminal at the Dallas-Fort Worth Regional Airport (DFW), hundreds of people had gathered on the apron of the runway. It was a bizarre corporate festivity, a combination diplomatic ceremony and high school halftime. A band played. Twenty ticket agents in designer uniforms had been pressed into service as flag bearers. They carried 12-foot poles with foreign flags and marched in choreographed patterns. Their faces wore a variety of expressions, from amusement to lock-jawed company loyalty to irritation at being forced to participate in the spectacle.

The occasion was the inauguration of Braniff air service from DFW to the European continent. After speeches by local dignitaries, the stars of the show, three Boeing 747 jets, were introduced. They flew over the field a few hundred feet off the ground, circling back over the crowd again and again. A rented film crew recorded the pageantry, and all retired to the terminal.

In a VIP lounge, champagne flowed and strudel was served. An accordion player mingled with the crowd. Harding Lawrence, the Braniff chief executive, moved serenely among the guests, nodding here, touching an elbow there. It was his special day. His planes would now fly not only to London but also to Frankfurt, Paris, Brussels, and Amsterdam. So calm was Lawrence that, uncharacteristically, he was talking to the press. He even admitted that there was a cloud on Braniff's horizon. "The problem we have, of course, is the price of petroleum products," he said to a television reporter. "Jet fuel is about 55¢ a gallon, and that's awfully expensive." The reporter was accustomed to the airline industry's cries of concern over fuel prices. What he wasn't used to came at the end of the interview, when Lawrence nodded benignly and said, "God bless you."

It takes a man with a special kind of self-image to bestow a blessing on a reporter after an interview. But Lawrence had always been extraordinary—he stood out as a showman even in a business where executives were

Written by Byron Harris. Reprinted with permission from the July issue of *Texas Monthly*, copyright © 1982 by *Texas Monthly*.

known for their flamboyance. He was the spitting image of a captain of industry: gray hair, bushy salt-and-pepper eyebrows, a gravelly voice that exuded self-confidence. Lawrence *was* his airline, and vice versa. When he took it over in 1965, Braniff was an obscure regional carrier that had barely entered the jet age. Lawrence immediately expanded the jet fleet. He bought routes to South America from Pan American Grace Airways. He painted his planes in exotic colors, dressed his stewardesses in uniforms designed by Pucci, and then had them actually take off parts of those outfits after the planes were airborne, in what was promoted as the "air strip." Lawrence's Braniff was flashy and au courant, and it made money. In 1974, the airline earned an 18.2% return on equity, the best in the industry. By 1978, it had become the nation's seventh-largest carrier, with a 19.6% return on equity, double the industry average.

But just as the airline's fortunes had risen on the wings of Lawrence's vision, so they fell. By the end of 1980, when Lawrence was forced out, Braniff was losing nearly $6 million a week, consumed by the very flair that had propelled it to greatness. Less than 16 months later the airline went out of business, bankrupted by monstrous debt and a skittish public. Texas was obsessed with the drama of those last months—the acrimonious fare wars, the desperate selling off of routes, the celebrity ad campaigns, all the financial gymnastics that sustained the illusion that the company was still salvageable. For a while, the day-to-day headlines even obscured the truth: that Braniff's demise was a certainty long before Harding Lawrence left it, as much a certainty as that his genius was the seed of its success and his ego the seed of its destruction.

A ONE-MAN AIR SHOW

The identification of an airline with one man was not unique to Braniff and Harding Lawrence, although they may have been its most extreme embodiment. It was a historical part of the airline industry. TWA, originally Transcontinental Air Transport, hired Charles Lindbergh to survey its early routes and called itself the Lindbergh Line. Juan Trippe started Pan Am as a mail carrier after failing to establish a passenger line on Long Island with nine used Navy biplanes. The airline grew in a large part because of Trippe's extraordinary skill at securing foreign routes. Eastern carved its identity under the tutelage of Eddie Rickenbacker, the top U.S. flying ace in World War I, who was referred to by Eastern's employees simply as "the captain." Continental was founded by a young pilot named Robert Six in 1934. He borrowed $90,000 from his father-in-law and converted a small Western mailcarrier into a passenger airline. Six, who is 6' 4" tall, built his airline on the strength of his personality and his physical presence. He was the only one of the early pioneers still in the business when he retired this spring. His chief assistant until 1965 was Harding Lawrence.

Both Lawrence's genius and his ego were honed in the adolescence of the airline industry. He was born in 1920 in Perkins, Oklahoma. During World War II, he helped run an Army Air Force pilot training school in Terrell, east of Dallas. He hired on with Pioneer Airlines after the war, working at Houston's Hobby Field in the hanger next to that of another rising star: Lamar Muse of Trans-Texas Airways. Muse, who went on to pilot Southwest Airlines and Muse Air, remembers Lawrence vividly. "He was convinced he was a brillant man," says Muse. "He was very smart and very astute." Lawrence stayed with Pioneer after it merged with Continental, ascending rapidly through the ranks to the number two spot under Robert Six. When Braniff, which had toddled along on the fringes of the industry for 37 years, went looking for a president in 1965, it looked to Continental.

From the day of Lawrence's arrival, Braniff was a one-man show. He was a master salesman, a persuader, above all a consummate actor who, according to staff members, often appeared to be rendering his own thespian interpretation of what an executive ought to be. Sometimes he would test his persuasive powers just to see how far he could go with them; at the height of his form he could talk people into believing things they knew to be untrue. Dave Stamey, a former Braniff vice-president, tells a story similar to those told by others who worked for Lawrence. "He could sit here in this chair, look out the window, and convince you it was raining, even though the sun was shining," Stamey says. "He'd say it was climatic aberration, or that it was a seasonal variation, or that the angle of the sun was refracting the light, making the rain invisible. Even though all your experience told you it wasn't raining, when you went outside you'd put your raincoat on."

Sometimes, say the executives who worked closely with him over the years, Lawrence didn't seem to know where the actor stopped and the real person began. But the real person had acumen as well as charm. Revenue passenger miles, available seat miles, break-even load factors, all these data were in his brain, evolving into a matrix of facts and figures that reflected the airline's health from day to day. In addtion to being an "operations guy," he was a big thinker, a maestro of creative marketing. He was a brilliant man, his executives say, a brillant man whose skills were rewarded. After three years as president, he became chairman of Braniff Airways in 1968 and chairman and chief executive officer of its parent company, Braniff International, in 1973.

That noteworthy year was marred only by Lawrence's pleading guilty to making illegal contributions to Richard Nixon's reelection campaign, a $40,000 indiscretion made in Braniff's name for which he was fined $1,000. The $40,000 was a fraction of a slush fund that Braniff used principally to pay kickbacks to travel agents in South America. The Civil Aeronautics Board, which investigated and even made noises about taking away some of Braniff's routes, decribed the fund as holding more than $641,000; Lawrence described it as

less than $1 million. Whatever the amount, the CAB backed down in 1976, letting Braniff off with a $300,000 fine. In those days it seemed that nothing could keep Lawrence from leaving the airline in triumph at retirement age. No one foresaw the economic turns that would prove Braniff's mortal enemies. But the airline's biggest enemy had been there all along. It was Harding Lawrence himself.

THE TERROR OF FLIGHT 6

Lawrence the enemy won notoriety on Braniff's Flight 6, an early-evening run from DFW to La Guardia. Lawrence's wife, Mary Wells, lived in New York City, where she ran her advertising agency, Wells, Rich, Greene, so he spent his workdays in Dallas and commuted to New York for weekends. Flight 6 was a Boeing 727. Lawrence always sat in seat 6B of first class. He demanded it. If another passenger had somehow been assigned to 6B, that passenger would have to be coaxed out of his seat by the ticket agent—and God help the agent for making the oversight in the first place.

Hell hath no fury like the wrath Lawrence could unleash on an employee who did not meet his standards. After all, he *was* the airline. A slip in the airline's service was a personal insult to him. His tantrums on Flight 6 are legend. On one flight a stewardess served him an entire selection of condiments with his meal instead of asking him which ones he preferred. He slammed his fist into the plate, splattering food on the surrounding seats of the first-class cabin. "Don't you *ever* assume what I want!" he screamed.

Another time he arrived at the plane in what the flight attendant describes as a state of inebriation. Shortly after takeoff he began yelling orders and shouting profanity, she says. As the flight progressed he became more intoxicated, continued to swear, and threatened the whole crew with dismissal. He broke a wine glass over his dinner tray. He charged that the attendants had used the wrong plates for dessert. Gradually, other passengers began leaving the cabin for the quieter coach section. The tirade continued: he complained repeatedly that the attendants were mixing his drink wrong. He was drinking Scotch on the rocks.

"On several occasions flight attendants came to me in tears, fearful of losing their jobs," says Ed Clements, former director of flight attendant services at Braniff. "I was sickened by what he was doing to the employees." Clements says few of the incidents were reported in writing because the women were afraid they'd suffer reprisals. And he says Lawrence abused his flight privileges as well as the cabin crews. On transatlantic flights, Clements says, Lawrence would commonly block the first two rows on one side of the coach section in addition to taking his two complimentary seats in first class. This was so he and his wife could lie down and sleep on their way to London. The practice often left six paying passengers in Dallas, for the planes to London regularly flew full.

The transatlantic flights were not without incident either. On one flight Lawrence dumped a trayful of food onto a stewardess's lap because it had gotten cold while he was away from his seat. On another he overturned a champagne bucket that was being used to store fruit. On a third he threw a dinner roll at a flight attendant. Stories about these displays spread rapidly through the employee ranks. By the late 1970s Lawrence's appearance on an aircraft was likely to arouse two emotions in the crew: fear and hatred. Workers went to great lengths to prevent a tantrum. Row six in first class would be made spotless before Lawrence's arrival: even the windows on his aisle would be washed. Flight attendants would study their service manuals before takeoff. The rest of the plane might be a mess, coach service might suffer, but Lawrence's service would be up to par.

Inevitably, perhaps, dissatisfied employees meant dissatisfied customers. Marketing surveys showed that Braniff was not popular with many of the people who flew on it. While an ostentatious, entrepreneurial customer was attracted to the airline's first-class

service, many of the passengers who flew in coach chose Braniff because there was no other airline that flew at the time of day they had to travel. Although Braniff was Dallas's hometown airline, it did not enjoy great goodwill there. Says Hal Salfen, a Braniff vice-president from 1971 to 1973, "People hated Braniff. That's absolutely true. The employees had the attitude that they were doing you a favor to get you on the plane."

THURSDAY, BLOODY THURSDAY

If Lawrence was a terror in the air, he cut just as wide a swath through his executives on the ground. Thursdays were dreaded by vice presidents, for on Thursday the big boss held his top-level staff meeting. The executives grouped around a large table, Lawrence at the head. The focus of attention would shift from man to man (no more than two women were ever listed among the corporate officers) as each gave a report on his department. The process would go smoothly for the first few reports, then a snag would develop. A computer was down, say, or traffic had been lower than expected over the previous weekend. Suddenly the bearer of bad tidings would find himself stopped in midsentence.

"Why is the computer down?" Lawrence would ask. Then, "Why didn't you fix it?" Then, "When will it be fixed?" or "Why didn't you tell me this sooner?" Then, "How will this affect projected revenue?" The volume would rise as the questions went on, until the unlucky executive found Lawrence standing beside him, yelling, "I pay you a good salary and I expect you to do your job! Why don't you do it?" Leaning forward, Lawrence would stop with his bushy eyebrows just inches from the malefactor's face, his eyes, which sometimes appeared to be solid brown, devoid of pupils, boring in. And finally would come the growled question "Why don't you get *on the team*?"

When the meeting ended, recalls one staff member, the victim would have to be "shoveled into his seat and wheeled down the hall." In some cases the sufferer would have invited the explosion by falling down on his job. But often the outbursts were simply a chance for the chief to flex his muscles— Lawrence had to have his sacrificial lamb every Thursday. For the top-level staff, the lesson of these episodes had little to do with Braniff's computer problems, traffic projections, or other facets of running the company. Smart executives simply learned not to give Lawrence bad news.

Thursdays evolved their own ritual, in which details such as where one sat became urgent matters of self-preservation. No one wanted to be "downwind" of an executive who was to be sacrificed: some of the invective might splatter. Early on a Thursday, the phone lines at Braniff headquarters would begin to buzz as executives asked each other the question: who is going to give Harding bad news today? Shortly before the meeting was to begin, a decorous scramble for chairs ensued—after the lamb had selected his seat.

A few stubborn souls would brave the machine-gun fire and persist in the delivery of a report even if its contents were unfavorable. One of these was Ed Acker, president of the airline under Lawrence from 1970 to 1975 and now chairman of Pan Am, who was widely known for his ability to handle the big boss. "Nobody gave Harding bad news," he says, "because nobody *wanted* to give him bad news." The point recurs in other descriptions of the Lawrence regime. Many of his executives were weak, untrained as managers, selected haphazardly from the airline's ranks by Lawrence himself. Appointed to their positions through his magnanimity, they were reluctant to displease him. In addition, they were often unsure of their own abilities. Their insecurity, combined with Lawrence's natural tendency toward management by intimidation, created a climate that was at best paralytic.

"They started out as strong customers," says Neal Robinson, a veteran of the Lawrence years, now executive vice-president of U.S. Telephone. "They were very serious about themselves and their jobs. But the constant pounding from Harding over the years sapped them of the will to fight."

The result was a group that could carry out decisions once they were made but generally deferred to Lawrence on policymaking, no matter how flawed the policies he made might be. By the late 1970s the company's managerial structure resembled a pyramid with an illusory base, the chief executive floating above an ineffectual management corps. Braniff lacked what management analysts call infrastructure, the network of people who transmit information and make decisions, giving the company internal direction. The big boss didn't get all the information he needed, and his ego often prevented him from trusting what his subordinates did tell him. He flew the airline by the seat of his pants. For a while, though, it was quite an air show. The 1978 balance sheet showed a profit of $45.2 million, the company's largest ever.

Much of Braniff's success, however, was as attributable to good fortune as to shrewdness. Between 1973 and 1975, for example, many airlines were laboring to pay for widebodied jets—DC-10s, L-1011s and 747s—that were flying nearly empty or were mothballed because passenger traffic had not grown as fast as they had expected. (There are still more than 100 747s and DC-10s for sale on the world market.) Braniff was widely congratulated in the press for having sagaciously decided not to buy the big jets, for taking the conservative road when others took chances. But the truth is that when other airlines were ordering those planes in 1969 and 1970, Braniff didn't have the money to buy them. "It was sheer-ass luck," says one former vice-president. And by the end of 1978, record profits notwithstanding, that luck was running out.

FLYING TOO HIGH

That year was a watershed for the entire industry. On October 24, the Airline Deregulation Act became law. Over a short period of time, it started phasing out regulation of routes and fares, the two elements that had shaped the industry since its beginning. Airlines had been rigidly regulated by the Civil Aeronautics Board since 1938. Until deregulation, the CAB decided where individual airlines would be allowed to fly by awarding route authorities. These pearls were parceled out after hearings and deliberations that often took years. Airlines vying for routes had to present detailed arguments as to why they, and not their competitors, should be allowed to fly from one city to another. This protracted process conditioned executives like Lawrence to think of routes as commodities of immense value. In a world where routes were scarce, they must be procured and protected at any cost.

The CAB's first move in implementing deregulation was to open dormant routes—those for which authority had been granted but which were not being flown—on a first-come, first-served basis. The airlines dispatched representatiaves to the CAB in Washington to snap up these windfalls. Press accounts of the event describe lawyers in pin-stipped suits queued up all day, briefcases in hand, outside the CAB office. At night they would turn over their places to paid stand-ins who bedded down in sleeping bags on the sidewalks.

The frenzy was prompted partly by the airlines' uncertainty as to how far deregulation would go. Braniff, which had decided to seize every route it could get its hands on, applied for more than 300 of them in one day. The airline had nowhere near the resources to fly all those routes; the strategy was to take the most suitable ones and incorporate them into the existing system, to establish Braniff's presence in new markets before the CAB changed its mind and went back to parceling out routes the old way. The flaw in the strategy was fundamental. The reason the routes were dormant was that other carriers had found them unprofitable. That didn't dissuade Lawrence, however. He insisted that routes that had failed for other carriers would

work for Braniff if properly integrated into the system.

To Lawrence, the decision transcended considerations of short-term profit and loss; it was a matter of survival. He foresaw the deregulated industry as one with a few large airlines and several small ones, but few middle-sized competitors. And in this he may have been right. For Braniff, Lawrence believed, it was grow or be eaten, so he made the airline bigger. On December 15, 1978, Braniff began service on 32 routes to 16 new cities. It was now making runs such as Memphis to Orlando, Kansas City to Philadelphia —flights that other airlines had found they couldn't make money on. Meanwhile, most carriers were either expanding cautiously or waiting to see how deregulation developed. "Lawrence was off on a trip that boggled the minds of most people in this business," says Morten Beyer, president of Avmark, a Washington-based aviaton consulting firm. "From a business standpoint he was off his rocker. You should dominate the markets you're in, but the Braniff expansion was helter-skelter. They did not support their DFW operations. If they had done that, they might have succeeded."

Lawrence's empire building was approved by a board of directors that had for years been a rubber stamp for his proposals. Company records indicate that the board members may have regarded their positions as honors rather than duties. In 1978 six of the eleven outside directors of the company—those who were not Braniff officers—attended less than 75% of the board's meetings and committee meetings. But if the board seemed to lack diligence in reviewing Lawrence's plans, it was not acting any differently from most airline boards of the day. Moreover, Lawrence's past success was a convincing reason to let him have his way.

His way took money. New stations had to be opened, personnel to be moved to new cities, new employees to be hired. A new Boeing 727 cost $12 million, a 747 more than $45 million. According to the 1978 annual report, Braniff planned to spend $925.2 million on 41 new aircraft through 1981. Some experts say that to service the new routes properly, the company would have had to spend even more than that on planes, well over $1 billion. Airline analysts stress that a route is in essence a business in itself. Although part of a larger system, it must be conceived, executed, staffed, advertised and sold as a trip between two cities. By the end of 1978 Braniff was on the verge of adding four cities in Europe and four in the Pacific on top of the 16 new cities in the U.S. It was starting 24 new businesses in less than 12 months.

That the board acquiesced in this decision is no less surprising than that the company was able to borrow money to do it. Even though Braniff had earned $45.2 million in 1978, it still had long-term debt and lease obligations of $423 million, and its current liabilities exceeded its assets by $14 million. In the short term, Braniff was $14 million in the hole. The proposed spending spree meant that the company's debt-to-equity ratio would climb astronomically. Still, in 1978 Lawrence was able to secure credit from Boeing and $100 million in insurance company and bank loans.

How did he do it? It was the Lawrence charm, the acting skill, and the ability to persuade, aided considerably by the past record of success. "He had them mesmerized," says one insider, "and he had himself convinced he could do it too." At age 58, he wanted to establish Braniff as a worldwide airline before he retired. The plans were going forward: applications were filed to fly to a dozen additional destinations in Latin America and to Bahrain in the Middle East, Peking, Shanghai, Canton, Bangkok, Djakarta, and New Delhi. With just a few more links, Braniff would girdle the globe!

FORT LAWRENCE

Meanwhile, back in Dallas, another of Lawrence's dreams was consuming more than $70 million. Lawrence conceived Braniff Place, on the outskirts of DFW, as the gemstone of the airline. Not only would it house the company's world headquarters—its executive offices and training facilities—but when completed in 1978 it would also be a 113-room hotel for Braniff employees. It would include an employee recreation center with a nine-hole, par-three golf course, a swimming pool, saunas, and tennis and hand-ball courts.

The complex was as unconventional as Lawrence himself. The design was Mediterranean: four brilliant white terraced buildings, flanked by raised earthern shoulders, set beside a man-made lake. A sunken parking lot was rimmed with blue tile and centered around a fountain. The buildings made a glittering monument to Lawrence, but they looked better than they functioned. Lawrence had selected a California firm as the architect and a Texas company as the interior designer. He insisted on overseeing the minutest construction details himself. Communication between the three was cumbersome; hundreds of change orders were necessary. The complex was funded in 1976 with $35 million in DFW Airport bonds, but in 1978 Braniff had to go back for more bonds totaling $36 million to cover cost overruns and equipment.

Executive offices were to have gardens on the terraces outside their windows, so French doors were installed to open onto the gardens, but then the garden plan was scrapped. The doors leaked air, creating drafts strong enough to blow papers off desks. Some of them eventually had to be welded shut. Many of the desks, which were custom designed, had to be repaired shortly after installation. The office and hotel wings each had courtyards with imported Italian marble benches and olive trees flown in from California. Two of the trees were so big they had to be lifted in with cranes. The landscapers had neglected to note, however, that North Texas winters are too cold for olive trees. The trees died.

Every office had stark white walls enlivened only by a work from Braniff's collection of 54 paintings by Alexander Calder (whom Lawrence also commissioned to decorate two of the airline's jets). No personal artifacts or mementos were allowed. Each desk held two phones, one a normal telephone, the other an intercom that allowed any executive, including Lawrence, to speak directly into any office, even if the phone was not taken off the hook. Frequently, a vice-president would be in the middle of a meeting in his office when Lawrence's voice would interrupt. The executive could shut the device off, but only at the risk of enraging Lawrence. Some referred to the instruments as Gestapo phones and to the office complex as Fort Lawrence.

The back secton of the top floor in the executive wing was Harding Lawrence's apartment, which he rented from the company for $1,775 a month. Furnished and decorated at airline expense, it was a sumptuous exercise in white and off-white. Paintings from Lawrence's private collection hung on the walls. In the living room, a neon sculpture adorned a glass coffee table, a large antique birdcage occupied one corner, a polar bear rug lay in front of the fireplace. All these objects belonged to the airline. With a restaurant-size kitchen, the living room, a sitting room, two bedrooms, two and a half baths done in Italian marble, and a small swimming pool on the terrace out back, the apartment was well worth what the big boss paid for it.

Lawrence lived in his suite alone. He had a full-time personal valet and a housekeeper. They were provided at company expense, and most employees knew it. They saw the valet pick up Lawrence's rawhide luggage when he flew on the airline. (A special handler made sure his luggage was always last on and first off the plane and was carried to him directly at the baggage claim, which tended to draw the interest of the other passengers.)

There were other fringe benefits that the employees knew less about: a three-story house in London and a villa in Mexico. The latter was maintained at a cost, according to Braniff's 1978 proxy statement, of $92,000 a year. (That would rise to $172,000 a year in 1980.) Like top executives of many corporations, Lawrence also had a stock option plan. It gave him thousands of shares of company stock at a fixed value, which he could sell back to the company at the market price. If the market price increased, he could make a lot of money. In 1977 Lawrence exercised options on more than 78,000 shares, netting $236,000. In 1978 he sold another 200,000 shares, netting $1.4 million. He also received $871,794 in "salaries, fees, directors' fees, commissions, bonuses, and incentive compensation" during those two years.

THE STORM GATHERS

Even in those flush days, however, there was serious trouble in paradise. In December 1978 a high-ranking financial officer told Lawrence privately that Braniff's prospects for survival were nil. The airline was at the height of its expansion, and Lawrence was ginning out copious projections on the profits the coming months would bring. But he had already committed himself to spend so much on new planes and new routes that Braniff wasn't going to be able to bring in enough money to pay its bills. When the executive spoke to him, however, Lawrence insisted that eveything would work out just as he predicted, that the executive "just didn't know about airlines." As the months passed and profits evaporated, the big boss talked to the man less and less.

Fuel costs, which represented about one fourth of the carrier's operating expenses, were fast becoming a critical drain on profits. They rose from 40¢ a gallon in 1978 to 62¢ in 1979, making the delicate economics of expansion more delicate still. Many of Braniff's new domestic routes were "add-ons" to old ones. Service to Milwaukee, for example, could be added because the airline had a plane in Chicago late in the evening. A 727 could be flown from there to Milwaukee less than half full without losing money. If more than half the seats could be filled, the flight would turn a profit. But as the price of fuel rose, the break-even load factor, the number of passengers needed to make the flight pay for itself, also rose. Soon the flight might have to be two-thirds full to be profitable, and who wants to go from Chicago to Milwaukee in the late evening? Not that many people, the airline found.

On international flights, where the operating costs were multiplied over vast distances, the stage was set for huge losses. Some of the bolder executives advised Lawrence to delay inaugurating Braniff's new foreign routes, but the expansion moved on. In June 1979 came the four European cities. A month later, four destinations in the Pacific—Seoul, Hong Kong, Singapore, and Guam—were added over the protests of those who warned Lawrence that price cutting among nationally owned airlines in the Pacific is vicious and the volume of travelers small. Who wants to go to Seoul, South Korea, regardless of the time of day? Not that many people, the airline found.

At the same time all this was happening, the CAB was unexpectedly speeding up deregulation instead of slowing it. Route access was loosened even further. The franchise to fly from one city to another, that valuable commodity that in the past had been so difficult to acquire, had almost no value at all. The analysis of each route's cost and yield potential, which previously had been performed as part of the CAB route certification process, was no longer routine. The agency that had acted as a restraint to over-zealous airlines was no longer a barrier to them. Decisions had to be based on economics, not chauvinism.

Airlines that made their decisions on the basis of economics have little sympathy with the course Braniff took. At the March 1982 stockholders' meeting of Continental Airlines in Los Angeles, Frank Lorenzo, president of Continental's parent company, Texas

Air, which also owns Texas International Airlines, took pains to distinguish Continental from Braniff. "It's important to note that Continental took a fundamentally different approach to deregulation than the management of Braniff took," Lorenzo said. "The management of Braniff had a basic belief that deregulation was an opportunity to become more aggressive; Continental looked upon deregulation as a time of extreme caution. Time will tell who was right."

GOING DOWN

In fact, time had already told. In late 1979 Lawrence began receiving news that might have shaken the confidence of another executive. His new routes, particularly those in the Pacific, were losing millions a month. The company's total operating expenses were 92% higher than they had been two years earlier. Braniff lost $9.8 million in the third quarter. But chauvinism won out over economics: the jumbo jets kept flying.

As costs rose, fares were falling. On June 1, 1979, the very same day that Braniff was serving strudel to the Dallas-Fort Worth city fathers, Texas International trotted out a brass band in its DFW terminal to inaugurate service to New Orleans. It was selling round-trip tickets for 35¢ that day, as a promotion, and would soon be selling one-way "peanuts fare" tickets for $35. A ticket to New Orleans on Braniff cost twice as much. Price was now a selling point in a business where it never had been before. To compete on price, airlines would have to trim profits, and Braniff's profits were already nonexistent.

By the end of 1979 the company had lost $44.3 million. In the first quarter of 1980 its losses exceeded $21 million. Lawrence's tirades at staff meetings continued. The big boss seemed unable to fully admit to himself the severity of Braniff's illness. He dispatched two executives to Los Angeles to inquire about the possibility of purchasing Continental—which at that time was an independent company. They returned with the answer that no, it was Continental that wanted to buy Braniff.

The big boss lived at Braniff Place, needing only to step through a door in his living room to be in the Braniff boardroom, and yet another door to be in his office. Employees called Lawrence's sanctuary the Howard Hughes suite because they rarely saw him outside of it. He was occassionally spied padding about the halls of the headquarters building late at night in his stocking feet, but he was cut off from the outside world. He never had to leave Fort Lawrence even to go to the 7-Eleven to buy a quart of milk or a newspaper. His valet did that.

His insularity was only compounded by his dealings with upper managment. Occasionally an executive working late in the evening would be summoned to Lawrence's flat to thrash out one problem or another with the big boss. But Lawrence usually did most of the talking, sometimes until the early hours of the morning, pacing back and forth, drink in hand, in the all-white living room. One did not speak unless spoken to or voice an opinion unless asked; it was so much easier to find ways of agreeing with Lawrence than to tell him the truth.

As 1980 progressed, however, the truth became inescapable. The red ink was a hemorrhage—second-quarter losses were more than $48 million. The Pacific routes were consuming millions every month. Fuel prices were still headed upward. The economy edged into a recession, eroding the base of potential customers. And inflation continued to bloat expenses. Eventually, even Lawrence was compelled to acknowledge the need to cut costs. A labor relations expert was hired to help negotiate pay concessions with employee groups. Braniff was forced to do something it had never done much of: talk to its employees. On two occasions Lawrence was persuaded to attend the meetings to stress the urgency of Braniff's predicament. The very prospect sent ripples through the

rank and file. Here was the man who threw food at his workers asking them to do him a favor. At the first gathering with the flight attendants, the big boss had the temerity to arrive in his chauffeur-driven Mercedes. "There was," says an executive who attended, "a broad-based feeling of contempt for Harding."

THE FINAL DAYS

With his airline in a nose dive, Lawrence became even more unpredictable. He singled out certain executives for early-morning phone calls. Awakened at 3 A.M., they would have to endure harangues about their "mistakes." The big boss was frustrated: at himself, at events, at the staff of incompetents who had let him down. Still, most employees stayed loyal; they felt a need to help the firm through its bad times. Moreover, after years of being told they were incompetent, many had come to believe it. "He had them believing they were so dumb they couldn't get a job anywhere else," says one who lived through this period. Two executives regularly sat in their offices and wept. Another concocted a series of business trips that kept him away from headquarters continuously; by staying away, he avoided the misery of the disintegration.

Lawrence sequestered himself in his apartment, which became known as the bunker. "He was out of touch with reality," says one vice-president. "He said we were gonna line up this loan and that loan, but he was dreaming. The numbers he talked about were much different from what was really happening. The airline was falling apart, but people were still running around trying to figure out how to deal with Harding. He had us moving armies we didn't have."

The employees who dealt with the public evey day only heard rumors of this disintegration. But they had been whipsawed by the airline's growth and contraction. They had seen their ranks swell from 11,500 in 1977 to

15,200 in 1979 and then shrink back to 11,500 the very next year as the airline finally pared its unsuccessful routes. Never among the best-trained personnel in the industry, they tended to take their long-festering frustration with management out on the ticket buyers. At the same time, the company was in the midst of a "We Better Be Better" advertising campaign that in the eyes of Sam Coats, who later became senior vice-president for marketing, conveyed a sense of arrogance. It was as if all the company's difficulties—its financial problems, its managmenet style, its public image—were converging at once to seal its destruction.

Lawrence met with financial reporters in August, during Braniff's last profitable quarter, to convince them of the airline's good health. "Braniff is a financially sound company." he said. "Braniff is not a company that is in financial trouble." But even he seemed to know the end was near. "My board, my stockholders, and all those peopole, I have a responsibility to them." he said. "I will be here as long as they require my services." He gave his home phone number to reporters, urging them to call him at any time with their questions. Indeed, it was not unusual for reporters to receive calls from Lawrence during this period—calls accusing them of biased reporting.

In the last quarter of 1980 the airline lost $77 million. In December the board of directors, at the mandate of the lenders, had no choice but to call for Lawrence's resignation. With a pension of $306,969 guaranteed for each year of the rest of his life, the big boss resigned without putting up a fight. (Now that Braniff is bankrupt, he may get less.) Quietly, on the night of December 30, 1980, Lawrence climbed the outside stairs of a Braniff gate at DFW, avoiding reporters waiting for him inside the terminal. He was boarding a jet for Mexico, for what he has since described as retirement. He keeps an office at his wife's advertising agency in New York, but there employees say he is traveling and unavailable for interviews.

AMONG THE RUINS

John Casey, vice-chairman under Lawrence, was promoted to fill the big boss's shoes. He succeeded in lessening the flow of red ink somewhat in 1981, but to reverse the airline's fortunes, he decided, new talent was needed. In September, Casey hired Howard Putnam as president and Philip Guthrie as executive vice-president for finance. Both men were lured away from Southwest Airlines, which had been the wunderkind of the industry in the '70s, compiling the highest profit margin of any U.S. airline. Even with their impressive credentials, Putnam and Guthrie would need a huge chunk of luck to succeed at Braniff: the airline had a demoralized work force, a degenerating public image, debts totaling well over $700 million, and creditors growling at the door. But Putnam was known for being tough, unpretentious, and unorthodox, and Guthrie had a reputation for financial expertise.

So it was with some optimism that the two of them drove out to the Braniff offices in Putnam's Oldsmobile last fall. Neither had ever seen Braniff Place before, and as they drove across the treeless grassland north of the airport, it loomed up in all its sparkling white glory. It was entirely different from Southwest's spartan offices in a converted airline terminal at Love Field. As they drew closer, they could see 28 flagpoles, which had been placed at the entrance to the complex at Harding Lawrence's direction. Originally there had been only two, but Lawrence had ordered the number increased as the airline expanded, so that the flag of every Braniff nation would fly above his office. Now, with the routes dropped to save money, the poles were empty. "My God," said Putnam, gazing at them, "they look just like the masts of a sunken ship."

48

Palace Products Company

You are J. C. Kramer, Executive Vice-President of Palace Products Company. John Maguire, President of Palace Products, hired you from another company and you began work only one week ago. You were to train under Walter Hopkins, who was Executive Vice-President for one year until his retirement. You have 22 years of experience working in manufacturing companies, with 10 years at middle and upper management levels. You have a Bachelor of Science Degree in Engineering.

Walter Hopkins is critically ill, and will not be returning to work. You have not been with the company long enough to learn very much about the management system. You have just had time to learn the names of other managers. John Maguire wants you to assume full responsibility as Executive Vice-President because you are an experienced manufacturing executive. He told you that you are in complete control of internal operations. He does not want to interfere in your decisions because his role is to work with people in the environment and with International Controls Company, the company that purchased Palace Products two years ago.

HISTORY

Palace Products was started in 1948 by John Maguire and two other World War II veterans. They invented a flow control device and pooled their resources to develop and manufacture it. Palace Products grew rapidly, and now produces control valves to regulate almost anything that flows through pipe. Palace originally established a niche as an innovative new product leader in the field of control valves and flow control instruments. Over the last 10 years, however, innovation has been less frequent. The products are rather standard. Other companies are gaining a new-product edge, and Palace has gradually experienced a decreasing market share. Palace Products was taken over two years ago by

This case is adapted from several sources, including James B. Lau, "Crofts Products Company," *Behavior in Organization: An Experiential Approach* (Homewood, IL: Richard D. Irwin, 1975), 269-277; Harry R. Knudson, Robert T. Woodworth, and Cecil H. Bell, "Electronics, Incorporated," *Management: An Experiential Approach* (New York: McGraw-Hill, 1979), 128-138; E. Paul Smith, "You Are Bob Waters, Assistant Administrator at Unity Hospital," distributed by the Intercollegiate Case Clearing House, Soldiers Field, Boston, MA 02163; and the authors' own management experiences.

International Controls Co. in a friendly merger. To date, Palace has kept substantial autonomy from International.

THE SITUATION

Palace Products is located in central Ohio. It has a capital investment in excess of $30,000,000, and produces seven major products for civilian (82%) and government markets (18%). Four products represent distinct types of control valves, and three products are instruments for flow control regulation. A control valve and instrument are typically combined to fit a specific flow control application. Palace also produces many valves on a custom order basis to meet unusual applications.

A fifth major product, called the 830 Butterfly Valve, is under development.

Flow control products have a variety of applications in refineries, pipelines, and utilities. Industrial applications represent 70% of Palace's business. Small control valves are used in virtually every home and building, and account for about 30% of total sales.

Palace's employees now include 64 engineers and 38 technicians. There are approximately 1,200 production employees who work two shifts. The manager in charge of production is Keith Malone. He has been in his current job for less than a year, but has been with the company about 21 years. His previous job included manager of quality control and manager of the machine shop. The marketing manager is Ray Thomas, who has been in his job four years. He was promoted from field sales manager into his present position. He is now responsible for the field sales manager (Mike McKay) and for the advertising and research manager (Bruce Parker). Marketing functions include promotion, merchandising, market research, market development, and direct sales to customers. Sixty-five employees work in the marketing department.

Pete Tucker is the manager in charge of research and development. Tucker has a Master's Degree in Electrical Engineering. Prior to his promotion 30 months ago, he was the manager in charge of electrical engineering. The Research and Development Department includes 19 engineers and several technicians. Pete Tucker refuses to appoint anyone to supervisor roles because he believes his people should work as a team. Because of John Maguire's strong interest in research and development, nearly 8% of Palace's profits are allocated to this function.

The Engineering Department is managed by Bill Urban. Engineering typically implements the products created in Research and Development. Several engineering specialties are represented within the department, including electrical, mechanical, product, and systems engineering. The contracting specialist handles technical details involved in contracts with clients.

Al Wagner is in charge of employment and administrative services. His responsibility also includes community relations. This department has a staff of 19 people. Wagner transferred from the corporate personnel department over 18 months ago.

The finance manager is Ed Brock. He has been in his job about two years. Brock has an M.B.A. and is a specialist in management information systems. He is responsible for general and cost accounting, payroll, the computer unit, and accounts receivable and payable. Finance has a staff of about 20 people.

The demand for control valves has traditionally fluctuated with general business activity, especially construction. When construction and business activity is high, the control valve business booms. For the last two years, industry output has been stable, and the number of units shipped by Palace has declined slightly. Palace is not yet in financial trouble, but money is tight. High interest rates on short-term loans is drawing off cash.

Control valve innovation follows developments in electronics, metallurgy, and flow control theory. Developments in these fields are used by manufacturers to increase the

EXHIBIT 48–1 ORGANIZATION CHART FOR PALACE PRODUCTS CO.

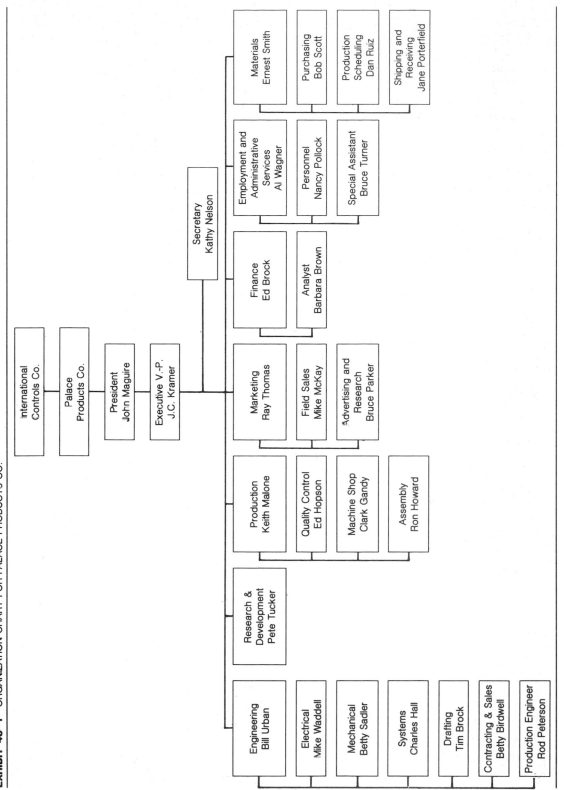

sensitivity and efficiency of valves and instruments. Recent developments in electronics have led to new control valve applications based upon miniaturization and automatic controls. Palace has been working for three years on a new control valve design called the Butterfly. This design has the potential to regulate the flow of liquids at 75% of the cost of traditional designs.

Palace has a reputation for product quality and reliability. Engineering, research, and production have traditionally been important departments in the company.

In the single conversation you had with Walter Hopkins before he became ill, he confided to you that Palace should retrench for the next two years or so until economic conditions improved. He insisted that Palace's reputation for product quality would hold the customer base if the marketing department concentrated on servicing established customers rather than on finding new customers. Hopkins said that Maguire always wanted more money budgeted to R & D for new developments, but he disagreed. New products have been an enormous hassle, and Hopkins could not see their contribution to profit. He believed new products were more trouble than they were worth. Hopkins planned to concentrate on improving internal efficiencies. "Cutbacks now will leave us lean and strong for the economic upturn ahead." He also said, "One dollar saved in production is worth $3 in sales."

Hopkins also confided to you that a staff member from International Controls Company headquarters suggested to President Maguire that a project or matrix form of structure be adopted at Palace. Maguire isn't sure whether that is a good idea, but most managers, including Hopkins, don't see any need to change organization structure. They are more concerned with human resources—finding and keeping good people.

SATURDAY, MARCH 7

You were appointed Executive Vice-President on Thursday, March 5. On Friday morning you got word to all those reporting to you (see Exhibit 48-1) asking them to write you a memorandum if they had any issues to be discussed with you. By Friday night, your in-basket contained the memoranda below. You take these memoranda home for evaluation so you can plan your next week's activities.

YOUR ASSIGNMENT

Study the memoranda and answer the following questions:

1. What are the four most important problems facing you? Specify and rank the problems in priority order of importance. What are the two least important problems facing you?
2. What techniques will you use to work on the problems during the coming week? Be specific. State exactly how you plan to approach and solve the problems listed in response to question 1.
3. What overall strategy should Palace Products adopt? Should the company cut back, retrench, and stress efficiency? Should it invest heavily in research and development in order to be innovative and reestablish itself as a product leader?
4. Based upon the information available to you, is a change in organization structure warranted? What would you recommend to Maguire?

PALACE PRODUCTS COMPANY

OFFICE MEMORANDUM   DATE: March 6, 1983

TO: J. C. Kramer
FROM: Kathy
SUBJECT: Your Meetings and Correspondence

Here are the memos that came in today. Mr. Maguire's memo is on top. Your luncheon appointments for the week are as follows:

Tuesday, March 10	11:30 AM - 1:30 PM	Award lunch
Wednesday, March 11	12:00 AM - 1:30 PM	Peter O'Reilly of O'Reilly Construction Co.
Thursday, March 12	10:00 AM - 1:00 PM	Corporation meeting
Friday, March 13	12:30 PM - 2:00 PM	Mrs. Rogers of the United Way

The following meetings were already scheduled by Mr. Hopkins.

| Tuesday, March 10 | 8:00 AM - 9:00 AM | Weekly staff meeting. This will include a discussion of new policies and procedures by Al Wagner and expanding opportunities for women by Nancy Pollock. A program for using less energy will be proposed by Bruce Turner. |
| Wednesday, March 11 | 9:00 AM - 10:00 AM | Meet Chamber of Commerce representative. |

See you on Monday.

PALACE PRODUCTS COMPANY

OFFICE MEMORANDUM   DATE: March 6, 1983

TO: J. C. Kramer
FROM: John Maguire, President
SUBJECT: New Products and Corporate Meetings

J.C., let me welcome you aboard once again. I'm looking forward to working with you. I will be out of town for the next two weeks but will get together with you immediately upon my return.

I am quite concerned that Palace continues developing new control valve products and adding to our line. New developments have not been progressing very well, and decisions will have to be made in the near future for allocating funds and people to this endeavor. Could you get together right away with Pete Tucker and find out what new developments they would like to work on? We need to have these ideas consolidated and to select promising projects in the near future.

By the way, would you also check into the progress of our new model 830 butterfly valve? I've heard grumblings from two customers, but told them I didn't believe there was any problem. Where is the monthly report? It should have been on my desk by March 1st. Would you please have that completed and bring it to my office?

One other thing. I'm scheduled to attend the International Controls Company meeting on Thursday at 10:00 AM Since I will be out of town, could you attend for me? We do not have to make a presentation and the corporation will send me a copy of the minutes. The executives from the other companies within International Controls will be there, and you can meet them.

I look forward to seeing you when I return.

PALACE PRODUCTS COMPANY

OFFICE MEMORANDUM   DATE: March 6, 1983

TO: J. C. Kramer, Executive Vice-President
FROM: Ray Thomas, Marketing Department
SUBJECT: Model 830 Butterfly Valve

I understand that the new model 830 butterfly valve will not begin production for another two months. We have had repeated delays introducing this new system. It was originally scheduled to begin production last August, then January 1 of this year. Now the earliest date appears to be May 1. This is creating a serious problem for us, because we've been telling our customers about it and they want to have an opportunity to experiment with it. I anticipate a 30-60 day lag from the beginning of production before we will have products ready for delivery to customers. One of the salesmen heard from a customer that a small control valve company in Texas was about to introduce a new butterfly valve.

Another urgent matter is the model 820 retrofit. This should go on the market immediately. It also needs to be priced low or it could affect sales. Our retrofit is a small item, but it is badly needed because it will provide the precision control our competitor's products already have. Mr. Hopkins agreed with me that every effort should be made to have this product in the field immediately. We have promised our customers that the retrofit would be ready for delivery on April 1.

The sales forecasts for this year were based on the expectation that new products would go into production and sales as planned. Further delays in the introduction of the model 820 retrofit and the model 830 butterfly valve could seriously reduce sales forecasts for the year.

PALACE PRODUCTS COMPANY

OFFICE MEMORANDUM   DATE: March 6, 1983

TO: J. C. Kramer, Executive V.-P.
FROM: Ernest Smith, Materials Manager
SUBJECT: Material Costs and Inventory Needs

I have been concerned for a long time about our steadily increasing materials costs. Due to the nature of our business almost 30% of our direct costs are materials-related. Walter Hopkins agreed with me that we should do everything possible to increase efficiency at Palace Products. Reducing materials costs was a top priority for him. My people work hard to reduce costs and establish decent manufacturing schedules, but we can't do it alone. We always have to revise production schedules because of manufacturing problems, especially with the new models. My purchasing people don't get word on what to buy until the last minute, and then their materials need to be rush ordered and expedited. This increases costs at least 10%. By the time we get the materials, another design change may be underway, so the parts we rush-ordered may not be appropriate. Because of the way Engineering, Research, and Production work, our material costs are almost out of control.

Another important matter is the inventory problem. During the spring and summer we receive many small orders for one or two items. Setting up and manufacturing a special order is expensive. Sometimes after we complete the order the customer will decide they want one or two more of the same item. This means two setups for the same product and customer. For approximately $275,000 we could keep these small orders in inventory and fill orders much more efficiently. Ed Brock in Finance tells me he doesn't have $275,000 for inventory. Walter Hopkins agreed with me that this was another priority in our efforts to increase efficiency. An investment in inventory would be the best thing for this company right now.

The final problem are the designs for the model 830 butterfly valve. We need to get these designs finalized so we can establish decent manufacturing and purchasing schedules. The model 830 is supposed to go into manufacturing shortly, but as yet we have not been able to get a parts list that we can rely on. How can we go into production without acquiring parts? I wish the people in Engineering and Research would be more cooperative on this.

PALACE PRODUCTS COMPANY

OFFICE MEMORANDUM   DATE: March 6, 1983
TO: J. C. Kramer
FROM: Barbara Brown
SUBJECT: Request for Appointment

Since you have an open door policy, I must see you. I am about to resign from the company and want to discuss it with you before I make the final decision. I have been here for six months. The assignments I am receiving from Mr. Brock simply are not challenging. I am not having any impact upon Palace Products Company. The projects I have been assigned are small and do not utilize the theoretical and analytical abilities I acquired during my M.B.A. training.

My mid-year progress report was excellent, which frustrates me even more. I would rather be rewarded for making a major contribution to this company than for doing small projects. I have tried to explain the problem to Mr. Brock, but he hardly has time to discuss it. He says he understands, but still hasn't assigned me to do anything really important. It is becoming clear to me that the Finance department does not control anything here at Palace Products Company.

PALACE PRODUCTS COMPANY

OFFICE MEMORANDUM   DATE: March 6, 1983
TO: J. C. Kramer, Executive Vice-President
FROM: Al Wagner, E. & A.S.
SUBJECT: Employment of the Disadvantaged

I received important information at a personnel meeting last night. The word is out that federal equal opportunity agencies will be looking at industrial plants in this area during the next six months. Currently, we have a very low ratio of disadvantaged employees. We may be in serious trouble.

I believe we should begin a crash program to employ 50 non-whites in all areas of the company. In order to save time, we should not use our normal testing procedures for these employees. Besides, our regular aptitude and intelligence tests may open us to charges of discrimination. Of course we can continue to use these tests for our normal employment of whites.

A crash program may involve some increased training and labor costs. Increased costs are better than losing government contracts. Besides, employing the disadvantaged is the right thing for Palace Products to do.

PALACE PRODUCTS COMPANY

OFFICE MEMORANDUM   DATE: March 6, 1983
TO: J. C. Kramer, Executive V.-P.
FROM: Bill Urban, Manager, Engineering
SUBJECT: Engineering Activities

There is really not too much to report from here. Things are in good shape. I would like to give you a complete briefing on our activities and plans whenever your schedule will allow it. For now, I would like to call four things to your attention.

1. I heard a rumor that International Controls was planning to centralize many of the contracting and engineering activities to the corporate level. This would mean a transfer of people to corporate headquarters, and many of our activities would be done away with at this plant. I think this is a terrible idea because centralized engineers wouldn't know the details of what we're doing here. The International people seem to think it would save money by consolidating engineers into a central facility and allow them to use up-to-date equipment. That would be a poor tradeoff in my opinion.

2. We continue to be short-handed by two engineers. Betty Sadler and Charles Hall both told me that some of their people have job offers from other companies. We may have to make counter-offers in the next few weeks.

3. A related item is the need to send five people to the American Engineering Society meeting in Las Vegas. Some of the engineering and research people want to report in a scientific paper some of the theoretical work behind the 830 butterfly valve. They will conduct a full-day session. This would be a great reward for them, but it will cost $7,500. We will need your approval because this will be well in excess of the travel budget.

4. The model 820 and model 830 developments seem to be coming along quite well. There is no urgency, but we do not have the most recent data and the final report from R & D. R & D claims we already have the data, but I think they are too busy to write the final report. We can't make the final decisions about production designs until we know the exact figures. I discussed this with Walter Hopkins last week, and he was going to see Pete Tucker about it.

PALACE PRODUCTS COMPANY

OFFICE MEMORANDUM   DATE: March 6, 1983
TO: J. C. Kramer, Executive Vice-President
FROM: Nancy Pollock, Personnel
SUBJECT: Award Lunch

Don Jameson, a machinist, has been with the company 35 years and is being given an award as the most senior employee. He has been with the company since its founding, and a luncheon has been scheduled for him on Tuesday, March 10, from 11:30 to 1:30. It will be held in the luncheon room at the Townshire Hotel.

Walter Hopkins was going to present a company pin and give a brief talk. He always believed it was good human relations to emphasize the company's interest in those working here. Several of the senior production employees will attend the luncheon. Keith Malone agreed to substitute for Walter, but I'm sure you will also want to attend Don's luncheon.

PALACE PRODUCTS COMPANY

OFFICE MEMORANDUM   DATE: March 6, 1983
TO: J. C. Kramer, Executive V.-P.
FROM: Al Wagner, E. & A.S.
SUBJECT: Reporting on the Model 820 and Model 830

I have attached a note from Bruce Turner, a bright young employee with the company. It reflects the problems he is having and I have not been able to do much about it. The memo illustrates the lack of cooperation when we try to coordinate new product developments.

Dear Mr. Wagner:

One of my most important jobs is coordinating the monthly report for the Model 830 butterfly valve. In the initial meeting with you and Ed Brock from Finance, we worked out a monthly reporting plan for the 830 project.

The plan was designed to record budget expenditures, and to keep upper management informed on the progress of each aspect of the development. We have tried to use a similar procedure for the Model 820 retrofit.

I'm getting no cooperation whatsoever. As it turns out, I am nothing but a pencil-pusher. I am having no influence at all on running and coordinating the 830 program. The departments are not taking this project seriously, no matter how many memos I write. R & D wants to do its own thing. Pete Tucker tells me that I give too much emphasis to reporting procedures and that I can expect the final report in a month or so. He says he is busy with important new developments, and the 830 is now old stuff. Keith Malone in Production says that they are having problems, and have not yet started production, but I don't know why. Marketing is pressing me to get the report moving, but they don't provide any useful information either. None of the departments bother to meet my deadline for a monthly report. As an administrative coordinator, I can't enforce compliance. What should I do?

Bruce Turner

PALACE PRODUCTS COMPANY
OFFICE MEMORANDUM   DATE: March 6, 1983
TO: J. C. Kramer, Executive Vice-President
FROM: Edward Brock, Finance
SUBJECT: Integrated Management Information System

After a long struggle, we finally completed our computer-based integrated management information system last month. It cost $110,000, but will be well worth it. The new system will provide daily, weekly, or monthly information about sales, production scheduling, the status of customer orders, vendor deliveries, and the like. The system will also provide me with more detailed cost accounting data.

Unfortunately, although we debugged the computer software, the system is not working very well. One problem is that the managers are not providing the correct information and they are not using it. They are maintaining their own reports. They don't seem to want me to have the detailed figures I need for the cost-accounting reports. This system is important to the efficient operation of this company. Another problem is that we aren't using the most recent technical developments for data processing. I've set aside $60,000 for acquiring updated equipment. We will have the best MIS in the industry.

Walter Hopkins gave me his full backing to install the MIS. Would you talk to the other managers about adhering to the rules and procedures necessary to make the system work? Any assistance you can give me will be greatly appreciated. My staff and I have spent almost full time on this project for several weeks.

PALACE PRODUCTS COMPANY
OFFICE MEMORANDUM   DATE: March 6, 1983
TO: J. C. Kramer
FROM: Keith Malone
SUBJECT: Model 820 Retrofit

I can't possibly make the production schedule for the Model 820 retrofit if I also have to be concerned about beginning production of the new Model 830 butterfly valve. The research, engineering, and marketing people are driving us crazy. Engineering keeps making design changes, and marketing people keep coming out to the shop to see when they can get their hands on the finished products. My people are working overtime to make production changes to meet design changes so the 820 won't be delayed any further. I strongly recommend that we stop all production activities on both the 820 and the 830 until all design issues are resolved once and for all.

I see that I made a mistake in accepting the 820 for production. The engineering people convinced me that there would be no more changes but they did not have the final figures ready for me. It turns out they weren't clear about the final design. I won't make that mistake again.

By the way, can you get the finance people off my back? They have installed a computer system and want to have us run everything into that computer. It creates a lot of extra work for us at a time when we don't need extra work. The computer has not been debugged, so my people still have to keep their own reports.

PALACE PRODUCTS COMPANY
OFFICE MEMORANDUM   DATE: March 6, 1983
TO: J. C. Kramer, Executive V.-P.
FROM: Pete Tucker, Manager, Research and Development
SUBJECT: New Products

Our most pressing need is to get budgets approved for new developments. John Maguire has always supported new-product development in this company. Our people in R & D have a number of original ideas, and they are ready to start working on them. We will need a budget allocation of about $325,000 beginning April 1. We will have the people to allocate full time to the projects then. Would you contact Ed Brock about assigning the needed budget to us? He hasn't even responded to my memos. And please don't ask for a lot of formal plans and approvals. My people are very creative, which is their strength, and paperwork inhibits them. Palace Products has been a success because of new-product developments, and we need to maintain our momentum.

I also want to call your attention to problems in Production and in Engineering. The Model 820 retrofit has turned into a joke. We gave those people a perfect retrofit design, and somehow things have been screwed up so that it is not yet in production. It may be the people in production engineering or a lack of cooperation in the machine shop. Somebody was not able to follow through on an excellent design.

I have also heard that Engineering and Production are having problems with the new Model 830 butterfly valve. I want to assure you that everything is under control. We have completed the design work and the final report will be written as soon as we have some free time. Engineering has all the figures they need. I admit there were some slippages in the development of the 830. One hangup was due to the failure of the system to pass the high pressure flow control tests, but we anticipate no further difficulty. I don't see any reason why Engineering and Production should not be able to meet their schedules. By far the most important thing for us is to get the $325,000 so we can commit ourselves full time to new developments.

49

Panalba

The purpose of this exercise is to analyze the decision-making actions of an organization faced with conflicting responsibilities to its constituents and to society. This exercise may be conducted as a role-play, with members representing various constituents, or as an "unaffiliated" group decision process.

Strategic actions/planning in an organization may take into consideration constituents internal and external to its operations. Stockholders, employees, the board of directors, competitors, and government are a few of those to be considered. In the following exercise you will be challenged to determine the course of action to be taken by a major pharmaceutical manufacturer in the face of various demands.

STEP 1: *Group Assignment (5 min.)*

The class will be divided into groups of seven people. Each group will read the problem description below; the instructor will assign either the "Financial Accounting" or the "Social or Interest Group Accounting" to each group.

STEP 2: *Group Decision (20 min.)*

After reading the problem description each group will discuss and propose a course of action to be followed for the U.S. market. Select from the possible solutions A, B, C, D, or E.

STEP 3: *Group Decision (5-10 min.)*

Repeat step 2 for the foreign markets, again selecting from solutions A, B, C, D, and E.

STEP 4: *Class Discussion (20 min.)*

Each group will briefly present its proposal and justification. The class will then discuss the relevant issues in relation to the theories and models that may have been presented earlier in classroom lectures and discussions. The following questions are provided to stimulate the discussion.

DISCUSSION QUESTIONS

1. Which constituents and environmental factors must the company consider? Which are most important?

Abstracted from "Social Irresponsibility in Management," J. Scott Armstrong,
Journal of Business Research, 5 (Sept. 1977), 185-213.

2. What role should the constituents play in the decision-making process? Should the company involve each in making a decision?

3. How would you describe the strategy of the Upjohn Corporation before the Panalba incident? What strategic shift, if any, would your course of action require?

4. What do you think are the internal cultural values of the Upjohn Corporation? How would these support the strategic goals of the company?

5. Can you cite other instances when an organization's cultural values conflicted with society's? How was this resolved?

6. Can organization theory teach managers to act ethically?

BACKGROUND INFORMATION FOR PANALBA

Assume that it is August, 1969, and that Upjohn Corporation has called a Special Board Meeting to discuss what should be done with the product known as "Panalba."

Panalba is a fixed-ratio antibiotic sold by prescription, that is, it contains a combination of drugs. It has been on the market for over 13 years and has been highly successful. It now accounts for about $18 million per year, which is 12% of Upjohn Company's gross income in the U.S. (and a greater percentage of net profits). Profits from foreign markets, where Panalba is marketed under a different name, are roughly comparable to those in the U.S.

Over the past 20 years there have been numerous medical scientists (e.g., the AMA's Council on Drugs) objecting to the sale of most fixed-ratio drugs. The argument has been that (1) there is no evidence that these fixed-ratio drugs have improved benefits over single drugs and (2) the possibility of detrimental side effects, including death, is *at least* doubled. For example, these scientists have estimated that Panalba is causing about 14 to 22 unnecessary deaths per year, i.e.,

deaths that could be prevented if the patients had used a substitute made by a competitor of Upjohn. Despite these recommendations to remove fixed-ratio drugs from the market, doctors have continued to use them. They offer a shotgun approach for the doctor who is unsure of his diagnosis.

Recently a National Academy of Science—National Research Council panel, a group of impartial scientists, carried out extensive research studies and recommended unanimously that the Food and Drug Administration (FDA) ban the sale of Panalba. One of the members of the panel, Dr. Eichewald of the University of Texas, was quoted by the press as saying, "There are few instances in medicine when so many experts have agreed unanimously and without reservation" (about banning Panalba). This view was typical of comments made by other members of the panel. In fact, it was typical of comments that had been made about fixed-ratio drugs over the past 20 years. These impartial experts believed that while all drugs have some possibility of side effects, the costs associated with Panalba far exceed the possible benefits.

The Special Board Meeting has arisen out of an emergency situation. The FDA has told Upjohn that it plans to ban Panalba in the U.S. and wants to give Upjohn time for a final appeal to them. Should the ban become effective, Upjohn would have to stop all sales of Panalba and attempt to remove inventories from the market. Upjohn has no close substitute for Panalba, so consumers will be switched to close substitutes that are easily available from other firms. Some of these substitutes offer benefits that are equivalent to those from Panalba, yet they have no serious side effects. The selling price of the substitutes is approximately the same as the price for Panalba.

It is extremely unlikely that bad publicity from this case would have any significant effect upon the long-term profits of other products made by Upjohn.

The following possible solutions were

considered by the Board:

A. Recall Panalba immediately and destroy.

B. Stop production of Panalba immediately but allow what's been made to be sold.

C. Stop all advertising and promotion of Panalba but provide it for those doctors who request it.

D. Continue efforts to most effectively market Panalba until sale is actually banned.

E. Continue efforts to most effectively market Panalba and take legal, political, and other necessary actions to prevent the authorities from banning Panalba.

You, as a member of the Board, must help reach a decision at today's meeting. The Chairman of the Board, Ed Upjohn, has provided this background information to each of the board members. He is especially concerned about selecting the most appropriate alternative for the U.S. market. (You must decide which of the possible alternatives is *closest* to your preferred solution.)

A similar decision must also be made for the foreign market *under the assumption that the sale of Panalba was banned in the U.S.* This decision will be used as a contingency plan.

FINANCIAL ACCOUNTING

To assist with this decision, the Chairman had asked the Controller's Office to make some quick estimates of what would happen as a result of each course of action. These estimates are summarized in the memo from the Controller.

MEMO: To E. G. Upjohn, Chairman of the Board
FROM: Samuel Hardy, Controller
(copies to Board of Directors)

The following estimates were prepared on very short notice by the Controller at Upjohn. As a result, these figures should be regarded as crude estimates as to what will happen. After-tax profits at Upjohn *prior* to this crisis have been predicted to be $39 million for 1969. The figures below are estimated losses from this prediction under each alternative. The figures represent only the financial losses to Upjohn stockholders.

Alternative	Estimated LOSSES* (In millions of dollars)
A. "Recall Immediately"	20.0
B. "Stop Production"	13.0
C. "Stop Promotion"	12.0
D. "Continue Until Banned"	11.0
E. "Take Actions to Prevent Ban"	4.0

*This estimate represents present value loss to Upjohn and covers all items (e.g., lawsuits, legal fees, expenses involved with recall). The losses would be spread out over a number of years.

SOCIAL OR INTEREST GROUP ACCOUNTING

To assist with this decision, the Chairman had asked the Controller's Office to make some quick estimates of what would happen as a result of each course of action. These estimates are summarized in the memo from the Controller.

MEMO: To E. G. Upjohn, Chairman of the Board
FROM: Samuel Hardy, Controller
(copies to Board of Directors)

The following estimates were prepared on short notice by the Controller of Upjohn. As a result, these figures should be regarded as crude estimates as to what will happen. After-tax profit at Upjohn *prior* to this crisis had been predicted to be $39 million for 1969. The figures below are estimated losses from this prediction under each alternative for each group. All other important effects from this decision have also been estimated.

Alternative	Estimated LOSSES* (in millions of dollars)			
	(1) Stock-holders	(2) Customers	(3) Employees	(1)+(2)+(3) Total Losses
A. "Recall Immediately"	20.0	0.0	2.0	22.0
B. "Stop Production"	13.0	13.6	1.8	28.4
C. "Stop Promotion"	12.0	16.8	1.2	30.0
D. "Continue Until Banned"	11.0	19.6	1.0	31.6
E. "Take Actions to Prevent Ban"	4.0	33.8	0.2	38.0

*These estimates represent present value losses to each group that is affected by this decision. The losses to customers represent deaths and illnesses caused by Panalba for which no compensation is received; losses to employees represent lost wages and moving expenses beyond those covered by severance pay and unemployment benefits.

50

Recreation Products, Inc.

By early 1969 Leroy Harden and James Nicklus were indeed satisfied with the rapid growth in Recreation Products, Inc. They were aware, however, that this very growth could produce organizational strains; they were concerned that any such tendencies not be overlooked but be dealt with. They realized that the rapid growth in RPI had moved them further from operational control and might lead to problems in coordination among the functional units. They were also determined that one key current organizational relationship, selling several product groups through a single force, continue to operate as they continued to pursue their strategies of acquisition and rapid growth.

HISTORY

In 1964 Nicklus and Harden left McKinsey to look for a company to purchase and manage. After a five-month search, they purchased Gorman Manufacturing Company, an established but unimaginative maker of lawn sprinklers. Gorman had what Nicklus and Harden were looking for: a consumer product with an established reputation for quality but a feeble marketing effort. The two men felt that their M.B.A. education and consulting experience plus an infusion of younger, more aggressive management talent could markedly improve Gorman's profitability and growth.

Recreation Products, Inc. (RPI) developed as the founders expanded their original ambitions into the larger concept of a leisure-time recreation company. In early 1969 the firm was an agglomeration of eight youth, recreation, lawn, and sports equipment companies, all acquired in a carefully developed strategy that would eventually take RPI into most areas normally defined as "leisure time" or "recreation." Between 1965 and 1967, RPI grew at about 15%. RPI acquired four firms and grew from sales of $1,291,000 to $9,631,000, and its net income after taxes rose from $81,000 to $536,000. Exhibit 50-1 presents key financial data for the period 1965-68.

The first acquisition was Rich Spray Gun Company, picked up in 1965 and merged into Gorman. Since the two product lines were similar, this marriage was relatively easy to effect organizationally. Next came Tom Carver, Inc., the world's largest manufacturer of archery equipment. Nicklus and Harden were attracted to this company because of potential for savings in operating costs and the possibility of increasing sales by streamlining the organization and providing increased marketing punch.

They felt certain they could accomplish this by substituting RPI management procedures for those of the founder, Tom Carver, a professional archer. Leroy Harden described the situation as it developed:

Tom Carver is still on the payroll. Only now he is doing what he likes to do best. This includes promoting Carver products by traveling the United States staging archery tournaments and attracting attention to his entourage, a stuffed animal caravan. Tom Carver is to Carver's product line what Colonel Sanders is to Kentucky Fried Chicken.

In 1967 RPI acquired Nile Sled Company, makers of Snowbird sleds since 1889. Once again the pattern was consistent with the general strategy: a branded consumer product with accepted quality but moribund marketing ideas. James Nicklus commented on the marketing inputs RPI had to inject to rebuild Snowbird sales:

This Snowbird situation really took an effort. This company virtually dominated the sled market during the 1920s. By 1967, they were lucky to have 15%, and I'll bet part of that was a gift. This company probably survived because nostalgic fathers insisted their children have the same sled they once used. The products were generally overpriced and unwanted by dealers. We had to redesign the sleds to make them competitive, cut prices to chain stores, and really promote them at retail. We also had to win back dealers with special promotional offers as well as the lowered prices.

In 1968, RPI accelerated acquisition growth by absorbing four more companies. First came Brockman Sprinkler. This purchase was designed to widen the product line in lawn and garden equipment. In March 1968, RPI picked up Green Thumb Company, manufacturers and marketers of indoor plant care products. In June the group moved into still another new field by acquiring Quality Arms Company. Quality Arms manufactured quality lines of firearms, both handguns and shoulder guns. This "top of the line" product

EXHIBIT 50-1   KEY FINANCIAL DATA FOR PERIOD OF 1965-68

	1968		1967		1966		1965	
Sales	$17,662,000		$ 9,631,000		$ 7,324,000		$ 1,291,000	
Gross margin	5,839,000	33%	3,584,000	41%	2,296,000	31%	506,000	39%
Income before taxes	1,922,000	11%	1,004,000	10.4%	432,000	6%	138,000	10.4%
Net income	962,000		536,000		235,000		81,000	
Earnings per share	$ 1.08		$ 0.76		$ 0.40		$ 0.23	
Working capital	5,673,000		2,547,000		2,176,000		141,000	
Net plant and equipment	7,095,000		2,686,000		2,360,000		671,000	
Shareholders' equity	8,177,000		1,380,000		676,000		121,000	
Number of plants	7		4		3		2	
Number of employees	1,700		700		530		120	

Stock Price Movement
(bid-asked prices)

Insured 4/68	5/1/68	6/1/68	7/1/68	8/1/68	9/1/68	10/1/68
13	33-35	41-44	43-45	45-48	48-51	58-62
Insured 11/1/68	12/1/68	1/1/69	2/1/69	3/1/69	4/1/69	
61-65	68-72	63-67	68-72	55-59	59-63	

Capitalization, 1,039,000 shares 20 percent held by top officers

Source: Annual reports.

group included Tournament Caliber firearms for competition accuracy as well as a complete array of hunting rifles and shotguns. Finally, in October 1968, RPI added to its line of winter products by acquiring Alpine Industries, a Canadian maker of toboggans and other winter sporting equipment. Alpine was also intended to provide an entrée into Canadian markets. Thus, by February 1969, Recreation Products, Inc. consisted of the broad product groups shown in Exhibit 50-2.

STRATEGY

The key elements of RPI strategy were formulated explicitly by Harden and Nicklus during 1966 as a reaction to factors in the environment. They saw two significant trends that strongly affected the growth possibilities of the companies managed at that time. One trend was the rapid *growth* in demand for leisure-time products and services. The factors contributing to this demand are generally known: (1) gradual shortening of workweeks, from today's 38-39 hours to estimates of 20 hours by the year 2000; (2) changing population mix, such that the number of young families, ages 25-34, will increase by 46% in the next decade alone; (3) rising disposable income per capita, projected to increase by 45% by 1975; and (4) increased education and better communication, which serve to "socialize" Americans to use their free time actively.

The second trend, equally important in RPI's competitive environment, was the changing nature of distribution methods for leisure products: *the emergence of the high-volume mass merchandiser*. This evolution brings significant changes in the way goods are moved: self-service, point-of-sale displays, increased importance of packaging, and more sophisticated promotion techniques. It also brings centralized buying of chains and cooperative groups of independents.

The result of these two trends is the cornerstone of RPI strategy: to market various leisure-time products through a single sales force. Mr. Nicklus commented to the case writer:

This choice is more significant than might seem to be the case at first glance. The most obvious result is, of course, the economies of the selling effort spread over several products. Because the products are not highly technical, one salesman can handle the various lines. Equally significant, however, is an ability to provide the buyers at larger distributors with facts and data quickly and concisely. What we are working toward is a two-tiered salesforce: (1) a small number of expert salesmen who can provide these buyers the benefits of our centralized information on several product groups and (2) a larger number of "retail detail" men who stock shelves, handle promotional material, etc., at the various retail outlets. The result is that we are able to overpower most of our competitors in dealing with buyers; these competitors are still organized as though they were selling to a network of small retailers. In fact, over 50% of the sales of products such as ours are sold through mass merchandisers.

Mr. Harden, commenting on questions of strategy, added:

EXHIBIT 50-2   PRODUCT GROUPS AND PRODUCTS

Archery	Firearms	Lawn and Garden Equipment	Winter Products	Commercial and Industrial Products
Tom Carver	Quality arms	Gorman Manufacturing Company	Snowbird	Farm equipment
		Rich Spray Gun Company	Alpine Industries	Private brands
		Green Thumb Company		Government sales

In terms of where we hope to take RPI, we are really still in Phase I. Our present lines can easily be handled by one salesforce. The questions I grapple with are what happens when sales of our present groups (and acquisitions to be made in these existing lines) reach $100 million or more and we move into fields such as travel, education, or entertainment. We might have to leave Recreation Products, Inc. at that time as a separate organization and start almost from scratch with the added services. You know, we can go a long way under the umbrella "leisure time" and "recreation."

To provide even more direction to these strategic goals, RPI has translated them into specific financial objectives. The first page of the 1968 RPI annual report sets forth these objectives and invites stockholders to evaluate the efforts of the management team in its pursuit of their accomplishment:

Since formation of the company in November 1964, our objective has been to build a major business enterprise engaged in the manufacture and marketing of leisure-time products. At that time we established financial and operating goals as follows: (1) 15% annual sales increase through internal growth; (2) 50% annual sales increase through acquisition; (3) net income equal to 6% of sales and a minimum annual increase in earnings per share of 25%.

ORGANIZATIONAL STRUCTURE

In 1969, Recreation Products, Inc. was organized functionally into three major units: marketing, operations (production), and product development. A fourth unit, the controller, provided centralized accounting, finance, and customer relation activities for the group at the corporate level. While no formal organization chart existed, Exhibit 50-3 portrays the case writer's impressions of how it might have looked. Approximate ages are presented in this exhibit, and those men with M.B.A. degrees are noted.

MARKETING

The marketing unit performed essentially two types of functions: sales management and product management. Since marketing was critical at RPI, product managers occupied key roles in the operations of the firm. Mr. Nicklus indicated the scope of their responsibilities:

I'm sure the concept of the product manager is a familiar one. Most of the large consumer products companies, General Foods, Procter & Gamble, Kellogg, etc., are built on product managers. Around here, though, the term connotes a much broader span of responsibilities than I think exists in most firms. Our PMs are responsible for product strategies, market evaluation, merchandising and advertising tools, just as are their counterparts at General Foods. However, a more appropriate term at Recreation Products, Inc. would be product general *manager. We hold these guys responsible for the product planning and for monitoring the ongoing situation to see that plans are fulfilled [in reference to the rough organization charts constructed by the case writer]. We don't really believe in these lines and boxes. If problems at a plant are holding back a product's sales, we expect the product manager to be on the phone immediately talking to the plant manager to iron out the problems. You know if I see a forecast not being met, I'll expect that PM to know why this exists, and what he plans to do about it. Similarly, if a PM expects to be under or over forecast in any particular quarter, it is his job to work with the plant manager to adjust production to avoid stocking out or excessive inventories. This information doesn't move up to Ralph Spiegel [director of marketing] and then down. It moves by the shortest route.*

Product managers were each responsible for a particular product line: archery, winter products, lawn and garden equipment, firearms. In some instances, a line included more than one type of product; for instance, the PM for lawn and garden equipment handled sprinklers (acquired with Gorman Manufacturing Company), spray guns (once made by Rich), and the indoor plant care products of Green Thumb. The various products in a line might be manufactured at different plants, as is in fact the case in the above example. Thus, the product manager had to

EXHIBIT 50-3   ORGANIZATION CHART

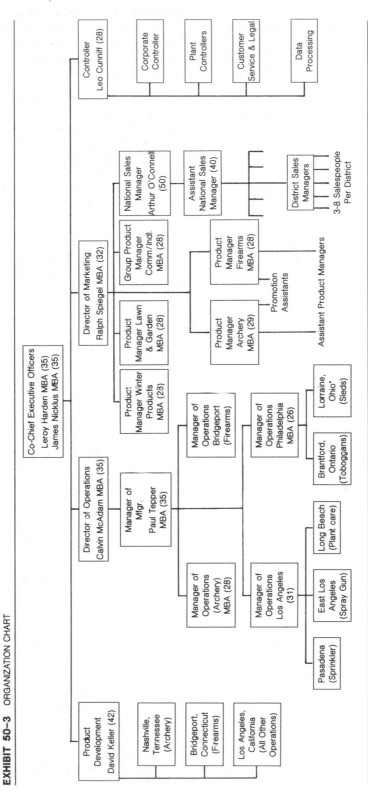

*Under construction.

maintain contact with various plant people—the manager of operations and workers at each specific plant—as well as the salesforce and the director of marketing, to do his job.

Bob Vroom, product manager for lawn and garden equipment, described the facets of his job to the case writer:

I'll tell you the one thing I could use most around here, a 30-hour day! But we really relish the work and the responsibility that goes with being a product manager. I spend a good portion of my time at daily "firefighting" chores like attending to a problem raised by a customer or something popping up at the plant. And over the course of a month I am usually engaged in a few specific projects, such as planning a new product or altering packaging on an existing one. Of course, I spend quite a bit of time preparing the budgets and forecasts for next fiscal year. And I guess the remainder of my time is spent monitoring the current performance of my product line and keeping everyone aware of its status.

Jacob Sanford, product manager for archery, added:

I have to do most of my planning around and between "firefighting" on daily operations. You'll usually find the lights on around here until 9:00, often much later. But I think most PMs do it because of their stake in RPI and their large measure of responsibility for their product line. This stake in the company motivates me to go across functional areas when necessary.

The salesforce was divided geographically, with each person responsible for sales of all product lines within a geographic area. In 1969 the national sales area was divided into seven districts, each headed by a district manager. The district managers reported to Arthur O'Connell, the national sales manager. As of 1969 these district managers (DSMs) were dividing their time between selling and administrative duties. The DSM usually handled the larger accounts: centralized buying offices of chain stores and the larger independents. He would sometimes be accompanied by various product managers in calls to these large chains, usually at the beginning of the selling season for a particular product. The purpose of this joint effort would be to provide the intensive information and data mentioned earlier as a critical element of the marketing strategy.

The field salespeople usually called on smaller accounts and handled shelving, promotional material, and similar needs at individual outlets of the chain retailer. Mr. O'Connell commented on the current situation in the sales force.

RPI is really in a state of transition, a state of rapid growth. We began in 1968 with 15 salesmen; by December we had 50. What we are doing is moving toward our eventual target of a two-tiered sales organization. But if you're looking for an established formal organization, I doubt if you'll find it. As the force expands we must be constantly thinking of the future personnel demands. We have men in the field selling who will some day be district or area managers. Some of the men are obviously more talented than others; some possess far greater potential to grow with us. So at the present, our fieldmen have varying assignments. Some perform primarily the "detailing" functions at specific retail outlets. Others do the selling to larger buyers, or at least participate in this effort.

This marketing unit was headed by Ralph Spiegel, a 32-year-old M.B.A. Mr. Spiegel, a former product manager, had been made director of marketing in early 1969. Since the previous director had left RPI in June 1968, the position had remained unfilled while Messrs. Harden and Nicklus waited for a replacement to develop. In the interim Mr. Nicklus became more deeply involved with coordinating the efforts of the marketing organization.

OPERATIONS

Calvin McAdam, 35-year-old M.B.A., headed the operations organization. Reporting to Mr. McAdam were four managers of operations, each responsible for plants producing a particular product line. In early 1969, Paul Tepper, also an M.B.A., joined the group as the manager of manufacturing under Mr. McAdam and assumed responsibility for monitoring the day-to-day operations of the various plants. This new position was intended to reduce the extraordinary work load carried by Mr. McAdam.

I'm really glad to have Paul around here. Shifting part of my responsibility to him should permit me to spend some time on areas that I just haven't been able to get around to yet. We really haven't yet fully defined his job, as he has been here only a month. Right now I expect him to be on top of all current operations, that is, assuring the plants are meeting their production plans, meeting their cost reduction goals, and watching inventories.

As you know, I'm usually involved in our acquisitions in the early stages, because we usually have to make a number of significant changes in the production system of these firms. We are committed to our stockholders and the financial markets for making our profit estimates, and that often means getting these acquisitions turned around pronto! I also hope to devote more time now to specific projects, for instance, developing proposals for new plants or additions and developing a uniform labor policy for all plants.

The managers of operations were given full responsibility for the plant or plants under their supervision. They were responsible for translating marketing forecasts into production quotas and for monitoring ongoing operations to assure it met these goals. Allan Temple commented to the case writer on what this responsibility meant:

You know, we're shrewd enough to realize that even though we spend a great effort planning around here, we have to retain the flexibility to react to the inevitable changes. That obviously makes the smooth operation of a product line highly dependent on the personal relationship between guys like me and their product manager. I'm on the phone to Bob Vroom (product manager for lawn and garden products) several times a week. When he sees a likely deviation from the marketing plan, he'll alert me to watch the inventory. If this confirms his thoughts, we will discuss the changes

necessary in my production plan. Of course he'll have to justify these changes to Ralph Spiegel [director of marketing], but it will be his decision. I don't see how we'd effectively handle the situation without this continuous personal contact.

PRODUCT DEVELOPMENT

Most product-development activities were centralized in Los Angeles, with only the groups at Nashville, Tennessee (archery), and Bridgeport, Connecticut (firearms), remaining at those particular plants.

David Keller, director of product development, commented to the case writer:

Like the rest of RPI, the product-development unit is constantly in a state of transition. We are working toward centralizing everything here at Los Angeles. At the present, the plants at Nashville and Bridgeport are still in need of work on production processes, so there are engineers at these plants.

The typical sequence of a particular project usually began with a suggestion from a product manager for a new or modified product, from a manager of operations for a process change, or from a designer or engineer in the product development group. A preliminary feasibility analysis was done, with time and dollar commitments estimated. Mr. Keller discussed the more frequent contacts he maintained during a project.

During the early phases of a project, I'm in pretty close contact with the particular PM or manager of operations who suggested the project. We gradually develop a cost-benefit analysis to see if the project warrants further work. Gradually, the director of marketing will be brought in, and sometimes the director of operations. And, of course, a "go/no-go" decision on all but very small projects will usually involve the top guys, James Nicklus and Leroy Harden.

CONTROLLER

In early 1969 the controller's office had recently been expanded as more and more functions were centralized under the responsibility of Mr. Leo Cunniff, the controller. Typical corporate accounting functions were directed to L.A. even before the group had data-processing facilities. Because the A/R and A/P data were there, it was a logical step to establish a central office for handling customer service: orders, complaints, and reports requested by customers. The data-processing unit provided data for use by both marketing and operations managers. Mr. Cunniff talked about the current problem areas with the case writer:

At present we have two chief areas of concern. Our present crisis stems from the fact that we are now doing our own data processing in-house, rather than having it done by a service bureau. We're still in the "debugging" stage, so our output isn't getting to product managers or operations people as fast as it should. But this is temporary I'm sure, and we'll get it working.

Secondly, we're now thrashing around the idea of having plant controllers report to their respective plant managers, rather than to me. The intent would be to provide these MOs with more responsive information on their respective operations. The change is now being considered both by myself and by people in operations, particularly Paul Tepper [manager of manufacturing].

THE ANNUAL PLANNING PROCESS

Board Chairman Leroy Harden explained why there was an emphasis on planning at Recreation Products, Inc.:

Given our backgrounds, it's not hard to understand why we are so thorough in our planning efforts around here. James and I were consultants, exposed to a broad range of situations where we could observe a number of different planning systems. Most of our marketing organization comes from companies like General Foods, Procter & Gamble, and Xerox—so we have the benefit of knowing how these rather sophisticated firms went about it. And most of us are MBAs, so I'm sure we're all still recovering from the pounding of "planning is a way of life."

He continued:

Detailed emphasis on planning fits integrally with the style of James and myself here at RPI. We both believe it is possible to make certain types of decisions once, and then disseminate procedures for how these recurring problems should be handled. We have seen so many examples of rather simple decisions being made over and over, each time with a new analysis. In this vein, we are convinced that a strong emphasis on planning forces our people to think in strategic terms. With well-thought plans, the everyday events can be interpreted in the context of the larger plan. Planning also contributes to setting goals and specific action routes to accomplishing these goals.

Because RPI was essentially a marketing organization, planning began with the individual product managers. In late spring product managers began their planning effort for the following fiscal year (beginning November 1). These men were responsible for the preparation of five formal documents, covering in general the industry and market and potential new products, and specifically sales forecasts and budgets for various marketing expenses. The "bottom line" figure for product managers was one that measured sales dollars minus all marketing expenses controllable by PMs, such as advertising and promotion. As mentioned earlier, PMs were held entirely responsible for the performance of their product line. Thus, their completed product plans also specified the efforts they expected to make to increase market share or sales dollars: efforts such as special promotions, new product introductions, intensive advertising campaigns, etc.

As these product plans were the basis for forecasting efforts by other units, substantial pressure existed for these men to produce accurate plans. Ralph Spiegel, director of marketing, explained this to the case writer:

I'm sure it is obvious we use our planning system as a mechanism to coordinate efforts of the various units of the company. As such, it is imperative that we get accurate plans from our product managers. While it is sometimes difficult to do, I try to be just as upset when a

PM has underforecast as when he falls short of his goals. Of course, each PM has to project at least a 15% annual gain in sales; as a matter of corporate strategy, these are our overall goals. But I want these guys to formulate a marketing strategy they think will be effective, and then give me forecasts based on what they really expect to happen, not just tack 15% onto last year's sales figures. We're a long way from being perfect at it, but we are getting closer. And since these PMs have total responsibility for a product line, I believe there is strong motivation to give me good data, rather than leave themselves a "cushion" in their forecasts.

Based on the individual plans of the product managers, the sales organization made its annual forecasts and established targets. The sum of all PM forecasts was reviewed by the national sales manager (NSM) and the director of marketing to determine whether the total load could be handled by the salesforce. The figures were broken down by the NSM to specific sales quotas for each district by product line and by quarter. District managers then further divided the district among the various salesmen, again by product line by quarter. Once these quotas had been established, the sales managers have them as a basis for evaluation, unless they receive a formal correction by a PM of his forecast.

On the operations side, the planning effort once again began at the bottom and moved upward. A PM's forecast for his line was given to the manager of operations (MO) responsible for plants producing those products. As the sales forecasts were estimated by quarter, the MOs would then translate this data into volumes by quarter. From this information, production rates, standard cost data, and inventory levels were established; these then became the standards against which these MOs were evaluated.

These MOs were also responsible for initiating requests for capital expenditures. As a part of the annual budgets, managers of operations were expected to submit capital expenditure proposals that met RPI's corporate criteria for ROI and payback period. The director of operations, Mr. McAdam, would review these requests and consult Messrs. Harden and Nicklus if it were necessary to place priorities because of limited available funds.

Once the MOs had established operating forecasts and submitted them to Mr. McAdam, these figures became the basis for measuring performance. Weekly and monthly reports showing key ratios, operating costs, and inventory were reviewed by Mr. McAdam. MOs were also responsible for initiating a cost-reduction program as a part of each annual forecast. They were then measured on meeting these cost-reduction targets.

FUNCTIONAL INTERFACES

Many of the managers were concerned, in some way or other, with the interfaces between functional areas. While often not stated in precise terms, these men were aware of the potential for problems at these boundaries. The case writer posed this possibility to various managers; the comments below reflect their concern. The problems of multiple products/single salesforce will be discussed later and are not specifically mentioned below. Chairman Leroy Harden commented:

I can think of a few ways in which we have tried to "manage these interfaces" as you put it. Clearly the most general fact is our informal communication and the access everyone has to everyone else. Being M.B.A.s James and I expect these men to have an orientation broad enough to fit their job into the more general picture. We also expect them to be problem oriented: to go where they have to and speak to whomever they need, to solve their particular problem.

Secondly, our detailed emphasis on planning and review allows each unit to operate without being totally dependent on other functional units. Once our annual plans are established, the PMs and MOs practically live with each other, going across the functional boundaries. And since PMs have responsibility for meeting sales forecasts, they have what I believe to be a very strong incentive to keep in touch with everyone necessary to do so, everyone being other managers in RPI, the salesforce, customers, suppliers.

Last, James and I have mentioned our belief that a lot of decisions in any firm can be procedurized. We hope to have made the process easier for our people by disseminating procedures and criteria. This provides a framework within which our managers can work.

Mr. Temple, manager of operations for lawn and garden equipment, added:

The procedures around here are what I call "methodology procedures," that is, general guidelines. I used to be with a large, rather prosaic metals organization, and there I considered the procedures stifling. Here, they are really the formalized thoughts of Leroy and James. These men really serve as the ultimate resource around here. Whenever there are arguments that can't be resolved they enter the discussion. Leroy usually handles operations and control, while James oversees the marketing side. And believe me, when it gets kicked upstairs, it gets solved.

Calvin McAdam, director of operations, added his thoughts on the topic:

I believe the most critical mechanism for operating across the functions is keeping communications channels open. We have a couple of ways of keeping these channels forced open. First, the mass of written data that flows at RPI serves to provide communication. We get weekly reports and monthly reports on plants; equally precise data is provided on how products are being moved by salesmen. Second, I believe there is a pressure downward to keep information flowing upward. For example, there are plenty of instances where one of my MOs will have indications that some costs are rising, etc., but this would not appear in a report for two or three weeks. I have made it clear that I want such information as soon as they get these first indications. Obviously, this cuts down our reaction time to such contingencies. When I get information on inventories or quality control, for example, the product manager and I can go over it and discuss a possible course of action immediately.

There are, however, a couple of things I'm concerned about as we grow as an organization. I see first signs that we're nearing the size where informal mechanisms become more rigid. I know this has happened personally in at least one instance. In the past, I would react to a PM's first thought that he was over or under forecast by reworking the production plans for the plant involved. Recently, though, I find myself less willing to accept his first indications. There have been times when my quick reaction meant changing a production flow, only to have to reestablish the old volume as the product line got back on forecast. As a result, I generally won't have MOs rework their operating forecasts until the product manager is certain enough of the change to formally commit himself by changing his forecasts in writing.

More significantly, the interface I am most concerned about is that between operations and product development. As I see it no one in PD is responsible for coordinating the efforts of product-development people and the operations people on a particular project. I don't believe David Keller [director of production development] can do this; he has to manage so many different projects. As a result, my MOs are really assuming this responsibility by default. This is tough on them, since they already have plenty to do. The solution that comes to my mind is to have one of the product development engineers assume formal leadership of the project group. Then when the project is ready for production it would be handled by the MO.

Walter Grace, manager of operations for winter products, also commented on handling the interdependencies:

I really believe we have just overwhelmed the potential problems by the type of people we have at RPI. We have MBAs with experience in well-run companies or consulting organizations—a collection of good, honest, greedy, capable people. Everyone has that problem-solving orientation imbedded at the business school. When [Ralph] Spiegel was the product manager for archery, they couldn't keep him out of the Nashville plant; he was always snooping around, figuring a way to do something better.

I am not convinced, however, that this alone will permit us to function effectively as we grow. There are a few things I believe we have to try to do. The relationship between PMs and MOs during the planning cycle has to be maintained. I have sensed the tendency for PMs to make their forecasts assuming the best of all possible worlds. Once I even saw a PM complete his unit forecast unaware that his plant could not possibly crank out the predicted volume. I think we have to try and keep a slight bit of manufacturing orientation a part of the PM's perspective.

It also seems likely to me we might end up decentralizing the product development units. Two of them operate out of particular plants already, in Bridgeport and Nashville. And the operations people are already integrally involved in the process. I think the centralized PD group may lose its flexibility across product lines. Perhaps the solution would be "decentralized" product (and process) development at the plants with a headquarters staff providing specific expertise in packaging, materials, design, etc.

MULTIPLE PRODUCT—SINGLE SALESFORCE

Another topic of general concern was that of the single salesforce. Mr. Nicklus commented:

We are always thinking about the implications of selling a group of products through a single salesforce. While this concept seems to work well for some very large marketing firms, we want to make certain that as we grow in size, we make any modifications necessary to keep this system working here at RPI.

Mr. Nicklus continued his comments in this regard:

What we have really done is encourage a "tunnel vision" perspective on the part of the product managers by giving them full responsibility and rewarding them for performance of their time. To compensate for this, I look to the director of marketing and national sales manager to resolve any frictions which arise. And, of course, I am usually pretty involved in things, especially if a conflict can't be settled.

The national sales manager and director of marketing did have several mechanisms to translate the product managers' forecasts into salesmen's quotas and to monitor their efforts in meeting these quotas. The primary tools have been mentioned previously: the planning process itself and the review to assure that the salesforce could handle the total job as determined by the various PMs. In addition, most of the product lines were seasonal in nature, so it was possible to schedule intensive sales efforts for the various products so that they did not occur simultaneously. Thus, the salesmen's yearly routine normally included a sequence of peak efforts plus a continuing selling job of much less intensive nature.

Arthur O'Connell, national sales manager, commented further:

I feel we have good data with which to insure that the salesmen concentrate where it will be most effective. District managers get weekly reports showing sales calls, orders booked, and dollar volume for each man, for each product line. There is also a "super" bonus for the salesman who achieves this target sales goal in each product group.

District Sales Manager Jim Grabowski also spoke on this topic:

Our salesman routes himself through his territory, subject to the review of myself and Mr. O'Connell. The frequency with which each customer is called upon is also determined by the individual men, based on our expectation of the importance of the account. Again, his choices are subject to review. By watching the reports for call frequencies and sales by product line, I can usually spot a situation where quotas might not be met. This might be symptomatic of a man feeling low, since he is so distant from us and his home, or it could be just a poor salesman. The super bonus at RPI also depends on every man in the district meeting his overall dollar quotas. Obviously, I'm very interested in finding out about potential trouble spots quickly, for the sake of my bonus as well as those of my men.

There are a couple of other areas I think we have to work harder on. First, we aren't getting good communication between the salesmen and product managers. These men in the field can supply valuable information on the market and competitors; we haven't yet brought the two groups together. I think it would also be valuable for the salesmen to provide estimates on potential sales of various lines by customer. This might help the PMs in their forecasts. Secondly, we are still establishing individual quotas from the top down. I've read many places that since we are paying these guys based on their accomplishing these quotas they ought to bear some responsibility for establishing them.

INCORPORATING ACQUISITIONS

Leroy Harden described the acquisition process:

We've had enough experience at making acquisitions to have distilled a few generalizations. The process can be visualized in four stages.

First, James and I evaluate the opportunity in the context of our established strategy. Does this situation fit? Can it take us where we want to go? Next we enter a period of negotiating with the present owners as to the value of the firm. Being human, these owners generally want more than a firm is worth; sometimes they seem to expect us to pay them for value we intend to introduce by making changes.

The third stage is probably the most critical: to arrange for integrating an acquisition into Recreation Products, Inc. We take a task force into the new firm, usually someone from marketing, operations, and control. Each of these men analyzes the situation he finds and is responsible for developing an "action plan." This plan should tell us, in specific language, what has to be done to turn this company into a contributor to the company. We spend quite a bit of time as a task unit, preparing changes we believe necessary.

The action plans indicated what types of inputs RPI expected to inject into an acquisition, both in the immediate future and over the longer term. In most cases to date the immediate emphasis was on reducing general overhead expenses and instituting cost control measures in the plants. More significant were the sophisticated marketing ideas and techniques that RPI brought to bear: products were added and others discontinued to strengthen the line, some products were altered and improved to be more attuned to changes in the markets, and more emphasis was placed on providing retail outlets with data helpful in making their decisions as to product mix and space allocations.

Potential acquisitions could reach Messrs. Harden and Nicklus through a variety of sources. Product managers might suggest a firm for its addition of products to the existing line. Salesmen could pass back information on possible candidates. Outside sources, such as business brokers, etc., might supply leads. And Mr. Harden and Mr. Nicklus spent much of their time keeping up on possible acquisition sources.

Walter Grace contributed some thoughts on possible dysfunctions in the acquisition process:

I think we might be failing to gear up for longer term development of an acquisition. There is tremendous pressure to turn a problem situation around as quickly as possible because we can't afford the losses that could be incurred. We are committed to earnings growth, and we can't have our existing operations support a losing situation for long. As a result, we tend to cut it apart if necessary to accomplish our transition quickly.

While a change in ownership and operating procedures was bound to have an impact on existing personnel, the severity of the changes varied and could be considerably less disruptive than is implied above. In a typical company before acquisitions, much of the administrative work was usually handled by the owner and one or two assistants. On several occasions these people, who were often involved in negotiating the role, had elected not to remain with the company. Plant personnel were usually retained, although the force might have been reduced by some amount. Engineers and most plant supervisors remained with the firm. In most cases, the original companies relied on man-ufacturers' representatives for their sales effort. Therefore, no large salesforce had to be disbanded.

RPI had not yet faced the difficulties of acquiring a larger company with a highly technical product line. They had not yet faced the situation of having to rely on existing managers for detailed market infor-mation, or on engineers for highly technical product and process characteristics. Mr. Grace commented on this subject:

As we grow and take larger firms, we will probably face the possibility of having to keep existing management. As we get further from where we are, we might in fact need them for their expertise to compensate for our not knowing the specifics of the business.

IMPLICATIONS OF GROWTH

Many of the managers realized that a continu-ation of the rapid growth at RPI could mean changes in its structure or procedures. Thus, many had comments relevant to a discussion of the implications of this potential growth. Mr. Harden commented:

I devote quite a bit of time thinking about this. "Growth" for RPI means something distinct from what it has for most other firms, and even conglomerates. In addition to extrapolation of trends in existing products or markets, growth often means to us completely new markets. This usually means subsuming an existing firm, with its own ways of doing things, into our present organization. Whereas conglomerates normally operate new acquisitions as semiautonomous units, we incorporate them into our present structure. As we move further from our existing lines into leisure services, for instance, we will have to learn new tasks, develop new expertise. I think you'll agree, it's exciting and certainly very challenging.

I see growth forcing us to gradually replace our

informal access to one another with more formal mechanisms. Not that we want to but I think size and distance will force us to. James and I will always want as much personal involvement as possible, but I believe size, and in time diversity, will force us to spend more of our time working with acquisitions and less working with the existing lines. In fact, hiring Paul Tepper is a step in the direction of providing for someone to monitor our established operations. Calvin McAdam will now spend more time working on acquisitions and special projects.

Our growth potential poses a unique pressure on James and myself, that is, providing the opportunities for our existing management team to develop and grow. We have been able to attract such talent by giving them responsibility and challenging tasks today, but also by promising them opportunities for more of both tomorrow. I personally feel a greater pressure to provide these opportunities than I do to perform for the "auction judges" of the financial markets.

The potential growth of the salesforce at RPI was well planned, and in rather specific detail. The broad intention was for the size of territory covered by each man to gradually contract as he (1) penetrated more of the potential customers in his area, (2) carried more products and possible new product lines, and (3) convinced each customer to take more products from the lines offered. Indices had been developed to anticipate when new men were needed and where each new man would go. This planning for the force's expansion extended five years into the future and was closely watched for accuracy and relevance to the next time interval. Plans were also developed to add to the administra-tive capabilities of the salesforce by adding additional levels of zones, regions, etc. Ralph Spiegel, director of marketing, made addi-tional comments on the subject:

The potential always exists here for competition among the product managers for the resources of RPI, in several aspects. Already, I can see the competition for the efforts of the salesforce. Arthur and I try to control this by translating the individual forecasts into a total forecast and insuring it can be met. The plans for expansion of the salesforce are also designed to reduce this potential bottleneck.

A second potential bottleneck could develop, I feel, in competition among PMs for product development or capital expenditure dollars. Right now product development effort is allocated on a "first-come-first-served" basis. If a PM wants a new product, process change, etc., he will request a product from David Keller. David will accept projects that meet our established ROI criteria until his budget is exhausted. Thus, the only way we can determine priorities among products is to bring in James Nicklus. And yet we might want a disproportionate share of product development going into a product with greater growth potential, for example.

A final possibility is that the nature of our selling task will change as we grow, and as our salesforce matures. Right now the effort is primarily on building the sales of a narrow line to a customer who bought it from the firm that we took over. A secondary emphasis is on developing new customers. As we mature, I think greater emphasis will be placed on getting a particular customer to carry all our lines. We will also find a way to get better information back from the field. And I think we might gradually increase our efforts in providing customer service. While we are prepared to provide such service now, many of our customers don't know yet how much help we can provide.

Another existing mechanism for providing for growth in the sales force was the unit bonus system for rewarding districts. Jim Grabowski, a district sales manager, discussed this:

We know that one thing that can seriously damage a salesman's morale is to have part of his territory taken away after he has cultivated it. We have tried to cope with this by placing a heavy reliance on the total effort of a district as the basis for determining bonuses. Then, as we contract these territories, we hope the transition will be smoother. This team effort feeling also helps keep my men from feeling they are alone in the field. I think it brings them one step closer to RPI.

Walter Grace, manager of operations for winter products, also commented on the ramifications of growth at RPI:

I don't think we are really geared up to provide for product introduction in the long run. I think this is because of our strategy of acquiring new lines by acquisition. However, we must continue to innovate with new products to remain competitive. Many of these innovations must come from within the present organization rather than by acquisition.

Calvin McAdam, director of operations, added his thoughts on the implications of growth:

I think we have to do two things with our people as we expand. First, James and Leroy will of necessity be less involved in ongoing operations. We have to compensate for their not being the final arbiter around here. More important, we still must attract capable people to the organization. This, I think will be more difficult than it has been in the past. We'll have less to offer in terms of growing with the firm, as most of us are the benefactors of getting in on the ground floor. Someday we'll have to attract people on the same criteria as does General Foods.

†